Community Informatics in China and the US: Theory and Research

社群信息学：理论与研究

Edited by Kate Williams, Han Shenglong （韩圣龙）
Yan Hui （闫慧） and Abdul Alkalimat

国家图书馆出版社

图书在版编目（CIP）数据

社群信息学：理论与研究 / Kate Williams，韩圣龙 等编. —北京：国家图书馆出版社, 2012.7

ISBN 978-7-5013-4804-6

Ⅰ.①中… Ⅱ.①Kate Williams… ②韩… Ⅲ.①信息化进程—中国—文集②信息化进程—美国—文集 Ⅳ.①G203-53

中国版本图书馆CIP数据核字（2012）第124187号

书名 社群信息学：理论与研究

著者 Kate Williams，韩圣龙
闫慧，Abdul Alkalimat 编

出版 国家图书馆出版社 （100034 北京西城区文津街7号）

发行 010－66139745 66151313 66175620 66126153
66174391（传真） 66126156（门市部）

E-mail btsfxb@nlc.gov.cn（邮购）

Website www.nlcpress.com

经销 新华书店

印刷 北京佳顺印务有限公司

开本 710×1000毫米 1/16

印张 28

版次 2012年7月第1版 2012年7月第1次印刷

字数 750千字

书号 ISBN 978-7-5013-4804-6

定价 90.00元

Permissions

The editors and publishers are grateful to the authors, editors and publishers of sections of the book that are reprinted from other sources, including the following copyright holders:

Sage Publications Inc. for chapter 1, which originally appeared in the March 1979 issue of *Urban Affairs Quarterly* (Volume 14, number 3).

International Network for Social Network Analysis for chapter 2, which originally appeared in the January 1999 issue of *Connections* (Volume 22, number 1).

The MIT Press for chapter 3, which originally appeared as "The Informational City is a Dual City", pp. 25–42, in *High Technology and Low-Income Communities: Prospects for the Positive Use of Advanced Information Technology*, edited by Donald A. Schön, Bish Sanyal, and William J. Mitchell. © 1998 Massachusetts Institute of Technology, by permission of The MIT Press.

Bellwether Publishing, Ltd.for chapter 4, which originally appeared in the May 1999 issue of Urban Geography (Volume 20, number 4).

Editions La Decouverte and Perseus Books for chapter 5, which originally appeared in English in the 1997 book by Pierre Lévy, *Collective Intelligence*.

For chapter 8: Copyright © 2009 From *The Encyclopedia of Library and Information Science, Third Edition* edited by Marcia Bates and Mary Niles Maack. Reproduced by permission of Taylor and Francis Group, LLC, a division of Informa plc.

Taylor & Francis Books (UK) for chapter 9, which originally appeared in 2001 in *Community Informatics: Shaping Computer Mediated Social Relations*, edited by Leigh Keeble and Brian Loader and published by Routledge.

Taylor & Francis Books (UK) for chapter 10, which originally appeared in 2004 in *Community Practice in the Network Society: Local Action, Global Interaction*, pp. 120–136, edited by Peter Day and Douglas Schuler and published by Routledge.

The MIT Press for for chapter 11, which originally appeared as "A Census of Public Computing in Toledo, Ohio," pages 85–110 in *Shaping the Network Society: The*

Table of Contents

序

赖茂生　（北京大学信息管理系）

本书是中美两国信息界专家合作的产物。它得益于2011年夏天北京大学首届“社群信息学”暑期学校的成功举办和推动。本书的编者请我为本书作序，我既感到十分荣幸，又觉得责任很重。

“Community Informatics”是一个新的领域，在国外已经有十多年的研究历史。据查，Jones Steven 1995年就主编出版了论文集“ Cybersociety: Computer-mediated Communication and Community ”（Thousand Oaks. SAGE Publications）。Brian D. Loader 和 Leigh Keeble 2004年发表的一篇文献综述“A literature review of community informatics initiatives”就收录了49项相关研究工作的成果。文中还提到早期阶段产生的相关文献数量要超过1600种。

在中国内地，与“Community Informatics”相对应的词是“社群信息学”或“社区信息学”。利用维普资讯数据库检索，发现“社群信息学”0篇，“社区信息学”1篇（2011年发表）；而利用“社区信息化”及相关术语进行检索，却可以查出很多文章，其中，“社区信息化”198篇（最早的一篇是报道，1998年发表），“数字社区”232篇（最早的一篇也是报道,2000年发表），“网络化社区”2篇（说明：实际情况可能并不完全是这样，因为存在着数据库收录范围和分类标引方面的误差）。从中不难发现国内外此领域的研究工作不仅存在着时间上的差距，使用的术语也有很大差异。

术语上的差异可能反映出国内外的文化和认知上的差异。“信息化”和“数字化”这样的概念，在中国学界和公众的文化和认知上可以说很流行和深入人心，而国外却不是如此。相应地，对于“Community Informatics”这样一个在国际上比较流行的术语，如果翻译为“社群信息学”或者“社区信息学”，在中国就显得非常“阳春白雪”，和者盖寡。这就给中国的研究者提出了一个严重的挑战：如何使我们的话语和思想既要被国人理解和接受又要与国际接轨？

据本人的考察和体验，在西方，“Informatics”这个词的实践色彩很强，“Community Informatics”这个术语的实践性更强（在本书中也有充分体现，如行动研究、案例调查以及二者的结合）。联想到美国文献中不难看到“Law Informatics”、“Museum Informatics”、“Medical Informatics”、“History Informatics”等术语，可以认为，“Community Informatics”与“社区信息化”或“数字社区”在含义上是很接近的。因此，在国内的交流中，我们需要灵活理解、翻译和使用“Community Informatics”这个术语。中国的社区信息化和数字社区的实践和研究工作不仅很有自己的特色，而且内容上也很丰富，涉及面和应用面比较广泛，并有一定深度。这些成果和信息对国外的同行有参考价值，需要我们很好地传播。

当然，我们也要努力地吸收和借鉴国外同行的研究成果，包括他们的研究视野、思路、模式、方法等。本书收录的文章中有相当一部分出自外国专家之手。他（她）们分别贡献了有关社区研究的网络分析法、社会资本、社会资本与“网络力量”（Cyberpower）、信息城市、与地理空间对应的“流空间”（space of flows）、集体智能（collective intelligence）、社群信息学（Community Informatics）、非裔美国人社区的社会“网络力量”和社会资本、公共计算设施（网站）的人口调查、“信息学时刻”（Informatics Moments）等方面的研究成果。其中许多成果在研究视角、研究方法和结论上都很有特色或创新。例如，以“社会资本”为切入点就很有新颖性，社会资本（包括集体智能）确实是建设数字化社区和解决数字鸿沟问题时需要充分重视的一种资源。又如，有关“Social Cyberpower”的研究，阿布杜（Abdul Alkalimat）教授和凯特（Kate Williams）教授认为存在三种“网络力量”：个人的、社会的和意识形态上的，他们把学校、图书馆、社区技术中心等“公共计算”设施视为社会化的“网络力量”，认为把这些力量组织起来，去应对当今社会的数字鸿沟等问题的挑战，是一个新涌现的研究和教学领域。凯特教授提出的“信息学时刻”概念，认为“信息学时刻”就是某个人在使用新的数字技术时寻求帮助的时刻，就是他克服数字鸿沟的时刻。社会资本也与许多这种信息时刻相关联：从那些拥有技术的人和家庭成员寻求帮助，并和其他人在他们的网络上一起这样做。理解这种信息学时刻就可能加快人（和社会）所渴望的转变，即过渡到包容性的数字时代。

还有 Manuel Castells 先生的文章中提出的“The Informational City is a Dual City”的观点也很有趣。他所说的“信息城市”是信息技术革命催生的一种新的“双城记”，不同于狄更斯笔下的“双城记”，实际上是由新的信息技术和社会重构运动结合所造就的一种“复式城市”。Castells 先生认为“信息城市”是技术、经济、战略、社会利益、文化价值观和权力斗争等多种要素交互作用过程的产物，是城市的多层面转型，需要通过密集利用 ICT 才能管理好这样的城市。然而，这种新的城市系统会产生或者加强两极分化现象，即一方是高价值社群，另一方则是贬值社群。这种极化现象导致城市系统的社会和空间核心功能的日益集聚，同时分裂出贬值的空间和社群，并使后者面临被边缘化的危险。使信息化与社会空间排斥现象相关联的原因不是新的信息技术，而是自 20 世纪 80 年代以来流行的资本重组政策，信息技术只不过是加剧和加深这一趋势。作者想探讨利用信息技术来使城市更仁慈、更智能和更公正的可能性。

本书还收录了中国作者撰写的文章，分别探讨了数字公平、老少边穷地区的社区信息化、数字鸿沟、中美两国社群的数字不平等现象、城市中的网吧、中国互联网的历史、作为公共计算设施的商业网站等方面的问题，在一定程度上可以代表中国内地的“社群信息学”研究水平和主要研究兴趣。另外，还有中美两国学者合作撰写的 2 篇文章，题目分别是：“Toward Building the Information Society with Chinese Characteristics”（创建有中国特色的信息社会）和“Toward Global Measurement of the Information Society: A US—China Comparison of National Government Surveys”（全球信息社会测度：美中两国政府调查比较），主题和内容都很有意义，使中美两国学者在此领域的合作研究有了一个良好的开端。

最后，特别值得一提的是，在本书的策划、组稿、审稿、出版和举办“社群信息学”暑期学校方面，阿布杜教授、凯特教授、韩圣龙副教授和闫慧博士都做出了宝贵的贡献。他们的奉献精神、良好的合作风范和认真负责的工作态度都令我敬佩值得我学习。衷心希望这样的合作和这一有意义的事业能永续和不断发展壮大。

2012 年 3 月于燕园

Preface

Lai Maosheng

This book is a product of collaboration between Chinese and American information professionals. It benefits from and is promoted by the first community informatics summer school held at Peking University in 2011, which proved a success. It is my great honor to be invited by the editors to write the preface. And it is also a great responsibility for me to accomplish it.

Community Informatics is a new field, but it has been studied for more than 10 years outside of China. Steven Jones edited the book *Cybersociety：Computer-mediated Communication and Community* (Thousand Oaks. SAGE Publications) in 1995. A literature review of community informatics initiatives by Brian D. Loader and Leigh Keeble published in 2004 includes 49 related studies, and mentions 1600 relevant publications from the early years.

In mainland China, one translation for "Community Informatics" is "She Qun Xin Xi Xue" (社群信息学) and another is "She Qu Xin Xi Xue" (社区信息学). When these terms are searched in the WeiPu database, the results are none for "She Qun Xin Xi Xue" and one paper published in 2011 for "She Qu Xin Xi Xue".But many articles can be retrieved using the search term "community informationization" and related terms. There are 198 articles on "community informationization" (the earliest is a news report published in 1998), 232 articles on "digital community" (the earliest is also a news report published in 2000), and two articles on "networked community" .The actual publications may not be exactly as retrieved, because there are database errors in terms of range, classification and indexing. But there is clearly a gap in this field between research in China and elsewhere, not only in the dates of publications, but also in the terms used.

Differences in terms may reflect cultural and cognitive differences between China and elsewhere. The terms informationization and digitalization are very popular and deeply rooted in the Chinese academy and among the public as aspects of culture and cognition, but that is not the case outside of China. Correspondingly, the overseas term community informatics, if translated as "She Qun Xin

Xi Xue" or "She Qu Xin Xi Xue", would scarcely meet the same welcome in China. So it is a serious challenge to Chinese scholars: how can our academic discourse and ideas be understood by the Chinese public, and how can we be on the same page as the global academy?

Through my own investigation and experience, I think the word informatics is closely related to practice in western countries, while the term community informatics is even more so as incarnated in this book, for example action research, case study or a combination of both. In American literature, terms such as law informatics, museum informatics, medical informatics and history informatics are commonly used, so the meaning of community informatics can be regarded as close to community informationization and digital community. Therefore, in communications within China, it is necessary to understand, translate and use the term community Informatics flexibly. Practice and research in community informationization and digital community in China has its own special features and is rich, broad and deep. Our existing research and information is valuable to our global peers, and need to be widely disseminated.

Of course, we need to learn from and refer to research from our global peers, including their research perspectives, frameworks, models and methods. Ten of the 19 articles in this book come from foreign professionals. They have contributed research including network analysis methods, social capital, social capital and cyberpower, informational city, space of flows, collective intelligence, community informatics, cyberpower and social capital in African American communities, census of public computing facilities (sites), informatics moments, and so on. This research is innovative as to perspectives, methods and conclusions. For example, the perspective of social capital is novel, as social capital (including collective intelligence) is indeed a resource we must pay fully attention to when building digital community and solving problems of digital divide. Another example is the research on social cyberpower. Abdul Alkalimat and Kate Williams propose three types of cyberpower: individual, social and ideological cyberpower. They consider public computing sites such as schools, libraries, and community technology centers as enabling social cyberpower. They think that organizing cyberpower from those institutions to meet the challenge of the digital divide and related issues in current society is an emerging research and teaching field. Kate Williams has proposed the notion of informatics moments, which represent the moment when someone asks for help in using new digital technology, or in other words the moment when someone overcomes the digital divide. Social capital has a relationship with these informatics moments. People do not only seek help from those who have knowledge of technology and family members, but also share their experience together with others through their network. Understanding the informatics moment may help accelerate the changes desired by individuals (and society) which means the transition to the inclusive digital age.

Manuel Castells advances an interesting idea in his article "The Informational City is a Dual City". His notion is that the informational city represents a new kind of *A Tale of Two Cities* impelled by the information technology revolution, which is different from Charles Dickens' *A Tale of Two Cities*. This dual city is constructed by means of new information technology and social reconstruction movements. Castells takes the informational city as a product of interactive processes of various factors such as technology, economy, strategy, social benefit, cultural value and power struggle. The informational city is a multi-level city transformation. Managing an informational city requires intensive use of ICT. However, such a new city system may lead to or exacerbate social disparity, which means there are high valued communities on one side and devalued communities on the other side. Social disparity will cause increasingly aggregation of the core functions of society and space in the city system, from which devalued space and community diverges, facing the danger of being marginalized. It is not new information technology but prevalent capital restructuring policy since 1980s that associates informationalization with social space exclusion. Information technology has just intensified and deepened that trend. Castells tried to explore the possibility of a better, more intelligent and fair city with information technology.

This book also includes seven chapters by Chinese scholars, which discuss the issues of digital equity, community informationization in old and poor cities as well as minority and border areas, digital divide, digital inequality in Chinese and US communities, the history of Internet in China, commercial sites as public computing sites, and digital and information inequality. Those articles to some extent represent the development and main interests of community informatics research in Mainland China. Additionally, there are two articles based on the collaboration between Chinese and US scholars: "Toward Building the Information Society with Chinese Characteristics" and "Toward Global Measurement of the Information Society: A US—China Comparison of National Government Surveys". Their subjects and contents are very meaningful and make a good start at collaboration between Chinese and US scholars in this field.

Finally, it must be mentioned that professors Abdul Alkalimat, Kate Williams, Han Shenglong and Yan Hui have made valuable contributions in planning, compiling, reviewing, and publishing this book as well as organizing the community informatics summer school. Their dedication, good collaboration, responsible attitude deserve admiration and study. I sincerely hope that the collaboration and this significant enterprise will be sustainable and become even stronger.

March 2012, Peking University

Introduction

Kate Williams, Han Shenglong, Yan Hui, and Abdul Alkalimat

This book is the result of research collaboration between US and Chinese scholars. Our mission is to advance the field of community informatics by coordinating a research program in China and the US. This program includes an annual summer school, a conference, coordinated research and publications that contain the emerging scholarship. This volume is the foundational volume in this research program as it contains chapters on theory as well as empirical chapters that demonstrate research methods and findings. Chapters are from North America, that is to say, Canada and the US, and China. Most were used in the 2011 Peking University Community Informatics Summer School. They are assembled to serve as a text for introductory courses in community informatics in both China and the US.

The four of us represent the University of Illinois at Urbana-Champaign, Peking University and Nankai University. Encouraged by Chen Jianlong, Yan Hui came to Illinois as a visiting doctoral student during 2008–2009 and we began a productive partnership. Supervised by Lai Maosheng, Yan Hui completed what we think of as the first community informatics dissertation in China. (although, please, we want to hear of any earlier one!) Once on the faculty at Nankai, he invited us to bring a group of researchers to China where Peking University faculty led by Lai Maosheng organized a community informatics conference and other leading information management departments also welcomed us. Han Shenglong at Peking University, familiar with the United States and informatics from his 2008–2009 year in Champaign-Urbana, and with informatization from his own experiences and teaching, stepped forward to organize a summer school. Our research collaboration continues as Yan Hui and a fifth partner, Wang Sufang of Zhejiang University, carry out research closely linked with ours in rural and urban China, respectively.

What is community informatics?

A number of reflection pieces and review essays, most cited in this volume, have attempted to explain what is community informatics. For us, this question is best answered by careful theoretical framing. Technology is created by society and in turn impacts the nature of society and social change. Critical technological innovations have made a great impact, such as the railroad, the automobile, jet air planes, telephone, radio, and TV. Community informatics focuses on how communities interact with digital technology, both how they create technology and how using it impacts their social and individual lives.

In the grand sweep of world history, after the hunter gatherer communities, there have been three kinds of socioeconomic communities combining social organization and class with technologies (tools and techniques): agricultural, industrial, and informational. Agricultural communities were relatively small, relying on the domestication of plants and animals to develop economies and culture. The power driving this system was human and animal effort, the power of organic muscle. People did not travel far, and most politics were feudal with hereditary systems of rule.

The industrial period of history led to a total transformation of society. The farm was joined by the factory as the center of material production. Animal power was replaced by machine generated power being fueled by water, wood, and coal. This new environment meant that new forms of socialization and education were needed because change was happening too fast for the apprenticeship system to keep up with what was needed.

The US was the first anti-colonial war of independence in the 18th century, breaking free from the feudal rule of England and its King. However the US economy was held captive by the slave system so it took about 90 years later and a civil war to end the backward system of slavery and unleash the full industrialization of the US economy. The industrial system meant rapidly changing civil society and raising standards on education and vocational skills. China, in the words of Mao Tse-tung, faced the three mountains of feudalism, bureaucratic capitalism, and imperialism. So it was the revolutionary victory in 1949 that unleashed the industrial revolution in China. There have been these two roads to industrialization, the US and the capitalist road and China and the socialist road.

Now there is another systemic change taking place that has shaken the foundation of industrialization in all political forms, the information revolution. The early adopters of the digital technologies, especially computers and the Internet, have been the military and government, the corporations, and education especially higher education. This has spread to the masses of people all over the world in the form of digital telephones (cell phones) that are smart meaning Internet enabled. Our focus is not on the individual but on the community. And we translate community in community informatics as She Qun (社群), not She Qu (社区) as some others have done.

People live in social groups and it is these groups that make up the historical form of social life, how we eat, sleep, work, play and practice our culture. Out of the agricultural and industrial period we have a narrative of spatial (physical location) , organic (family and bonding social capital), and historical (trans-generational) experience. People lived in social groups that interacted daily on a face to face basis, shared trust and common culture, and linked their fate to the quality of life of the group/community. All of this is now in turmoil.

In any basic social transformation there is both destruction and construction, the old gets replaced while the new emerges. This relationship between construction and destruction is a central feature of the sustainability of social progress, especially whether they are in sync and continue to provide the necessary environment for socialization and education for everyone. While this applies to all aspects of society, the distinguishing feature of the information society is the inequality referred to as the digital divide, differential access and use of digital technology. Community informatics defines the digital divide not in terms of individuals but in terms of social groups and the community in general. The CI questions focus on social groups and institutions that impact the collective experience in a community.

The three universal institutions in most societies that provide good empirical focus for community informatics are the family, the school, and the library.

The model

Social studies of computing, what some call the field of social informatics, contributes a fundamental concept that people and organizations adopt and use computer technology when and how it suits them. This concept of *agency* means that the community, not the technology, is our starting point. We are studying transformation, so community (at a later point in time) is also our end point. Our full model can be described as a circle or spiral whereby a community C exists, adopts and uses technology T, and that leads to a measurably changed community, or C', that is,

$$C \rightarrow T \rightarrow C'$$

The earliest time-sharing machines, for instance PLATO (1961) afforded a space for communication as well as for running programs. William Gibson 1984 novel Necromancer popularized a name for this space—cyberspace. Howard Rheingold explored and explained it in his 1993 book *The Virtual Community: Homesteading on the Electronic Frontier*. This gives us a more generalized model,

$$\text{Actuality} \rightarrow \text{Virtuality} \rightarrow \text{Actuality}'$$

which we express as A-V-A prime and which has been the focus of social informatics, internet researchers as well as community informatics.

The model needs one additional component, because all virtuality is accessed through the tools which comprise a digital information infrastructure that exists in the real world. Moreover, as several of the chapters here explain, access to and use of this infrastructure is uneven across and within our societies. It is helpful to conceptualize the digital information infrastructure in three aspects: the content, the code, and the conduit. Content is the data. Code is the software. These are virtual. But conduit is the devices, the infrastructure, and the human IT help that enables people to we manipulate the content and the code. Those exist in the physical world. In chapter 11 we conceptualize this "conduit" as personal (at home), private (at work), and public (shared in other locations). While all these are important, in light of the digital divide and scarce resources for most of the world's population, community informatics emphasizes the public. So our complete framework for community informatics research is in figure 1 below:

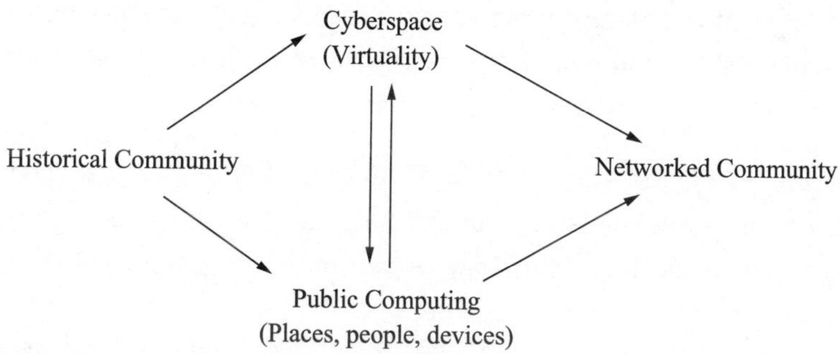

Figure 1 Research framework for community informatics

The model finishes with the community, but at a later time. What has changed? Compared to the community at an earlier time, is there an observable difference?

Community informatics in the US

Because chapter 8 of this volume provides a detailed US history of the research field known as community informatics, it is worth reviewing here the practical activity that the research studied. The earliest evidence of community informatics, in fact, was not scholarship but practice, variously known as community networking, community computing, and community technology. But before any of these names came PLATO (1961), the first time-sharing computer system used for formal and informal education at all levels, including terminals in schools, universities, libraries and elsewhere. Teachers as well as the interested public got free accounts, used curriculum, development curriculum, and began to communicate and even play online games. PLATO was funded at least in part by the Office of Naval Research in the US Department of Defense, and invented by researchers at the University of Illinois.

In 1973 Berkeley Community Memory began as a timesharing system with terminals in two local shops and the public library where anyone could post or read messages. An early book theorizing about computers in people's everyday life was Ted Nelson's *Computer Lib: You Can and Must Understand Computers Now* (1974). By the 1980s, community networks (online resources, some providing public computing resources) and community technology centers (public computing sites) were flourishing. Libraries were involved since the so-called "card catalog" was becoming a database and public librarians moved their local information files onto the computer.

As these experiments multiplied, university researchers became involved, often as practical partners since large grants were typically not given to small organizations. Campus-community conferences fostered discussion and then publication of case studies that explained "what we did and what happened."

In the 1990s the Clinton Administration popularized the term digital divide, began to measure this divide via large household surveys, and launched a $230 million funding stream called the Technology Opportunities Program (TOP) through the Federal Department of Commerce. The "dot-coms" and the telecommunications companies brought corporate funding to this movement. The community technology movement, as it was called, was in full swing. The National Science Foundation granted $2 million to a leading community technology center, Playing to Win in New York City, to build a national network of such centers and carry out surveys on what was happening in them. Community Technology Center Network, or CTCNet, informed and galvanized community organizations and city agencies across the US. Along with CTCNet numerous state and local associations of community technology organizations formed during this time. The dot-com bust and certainly the Bush administration that entered the White House in 2001 signaled the end of some funding and ridiculed the digital divide as a Mercedes divide ("I don't have one, but I want one," said one official). But so much had been accomplished that many institutions had already crossed a line. The informationization of US communities, imperfect of course, was well underway.

Skipping over many more historical events, we direct people to two long-running surveys: Charles McClure and John Carlo Bertot's studies of the take up of computers and internet by US public libraries, and the US government's computer and internet use population surveys. The latter compares to the work of CNNIC and is discussed in the chapter by Yan and Williams. We also point to a second important federal funding program, the Broadband Technology Opportunities Program, which is an echo of the original TOP funding (1994–2005), but larger and focused on expanding broadband construction and use in under-served areas of the US (2009–2012).

Community informatics in China

In China, there was no discourse regarding community informatics by that name, for instance, as a keyword for research papers, until Yan Hui's "Community Informatics: an emerging field" (社群信息学：一个值得关注的新兴领域) was published in 2010 in issue 4 of *Library and Information Services* (《图书情报工作》). However, from the 1990s, a large number of research or work papers on community informatization, which refers to the processes of applying information and communication technologies to the official issues in community neighborhood committees (the basic-level government agencies) and local residents' daily lives, was published in journals or proceedings. CI research in China relies heavily on policy background and practice advances.

In 1954, two famous scientists, Hua Luogen and Qian Xuesen proposed to Chairman Mao Tse-Tung to develop electronic computer technology. Soon after, in 1956, computing technologies was listed as one of the badly-needed technologies in "Science and Technology Development Strategy in Future Twelve Years" (《十二年科学技术发展规划》). The first college students majoring in computer science in China graduated from Tsinghua University in July 1957. At the same time, Peking University started its first computing mathematics and software training classes. In 1979, the State Council founded the State Administration of Computer (SAC) under the Fourth Ministry of Machinery Industry, which is the first government agency related with computing technologies.

ICT application practices in China's communities started as early as the beginning of the informatization movement after the implementation of Reforming and Opening Up in 1978. In 1992, the State Council announced an official document on spreading decision support systems in governments and this moment is always regarded the starting point of informatization. In 1996, The State Council's Working Group on Informatization was established and originally chaired by Zou Jiahua, Vice Premier of the time.

The first time that community informatization appears in a national policy document was in "National Informatization Development Strategy in 2006–2020". The strategy declares that community Informatization should include:

- integrating different kinds of community information systems and resources
- developing uniform community information platforms
- strengthening the management of local residents and floating population using ICT, and improving community services.

Although there was an opportunity for China's Ministry of Civil Affairs to enact "A National Guide to Promote Community Informatization" (《关于推进社区信息化工作的指导意见（征求意见稿)》) in 2007, no such document has been signed to date except the draft calling for citizens' comments. Some large cities and provincial governments such as Jiangsu, Fujian, Tianjin, Qingdao, and others have implemented local community informatization strategies.

As the administrative agency for domain name registration and DNS root server operations in China, CNNIC (China Internet Network Information Center) began to publish its *Internet Development Report* (IDR) in 1997. The latest of these is the 29th Chinese Internet Development Report issued on January 16, 2012 and included here as Chapter STET. As Yan and Williams discuss in Chapter STET, IDR reports include many important aspects of ICT in China, for instance uses, connecting, places, attitudes, devices, frequency, identity, and discourse.

The discourse concerning community (she qu, 社区) in Chinese policy documents and community informatization practice is characterized by its geographical, administrative, bureaucratic meanings. The scope of community in the Western academic community informatics discourse is much wider, with research objects not limited to the local administrative community but focusing on what we call the local, historical, organic community and the virtual communities, disadvantaged social groups and the like in relation to that. Local, historical, organic communities sometimes align with administrative communities, and sometimes not. That's why we decide to translate "community" as she qun (社群)。

Guide to this volume

The content of the book is selected and organized as an introduction to community informatics theory and research in both the US and China. Chapters 1 through 8 provide foundational concepts and frameworks for the field of community informatics. More are from the West than we would like, but as Lai Maosheng suggests in his preface, if we all look more carefully in the Chinese literature using better search terms, Chinese-born theory will surface. This section, then, is an opening move for community informatics theory in China, and we look forward to China's return move.

In chapter 1, Barry Wellman and Barry Leighton reflect on an earlier search for community in the industrial age. Community and its persistence in the face of overarching social change was the original and driving concern of urban sociology. Wellman and Leighton lay out a framework for thinking about whether and how community can survive and transform in the digital age. This is the question of community informatics, expressed at its most abstract. It is well complemented by Chen Jianlong's 'informatics of happiness' formulation in chapter 13.

In chapter 2, Nan Lin explains social capital. This concept became very popular correction to the theory that a person acts rationally and in their own narrow self-interest at all times, offering a way to explain the conditions under which people make choices. Perhaps because of its popularity, social capital requires rigorous definition and use. Lin provides intellectual anchors for the concept of social capital, first in Marx's capital and other usages that emerged later, and then in the social networks that exist in all societies. He also proposes a research agenda that intersects with community informatics.

In Chapter 3, Manuel Castells challenges us to find and learn about solutions to the social polarization that has accompanied informatization. He explains this polarization using key concepts from his work on the technopoles, of the world and proposes where to look for solutions. Chapter 4, also by Castells, is an answer to the questions he poses in chapter 3. He reviews the ways in which people are actually using information and communications technology to respond to and even overcome social polarization. Network society, informational city/dual city, space of flows/space of place, and grassrooting are powerful and accessible concepts for scholars and the public alike, as are the other concepts in this section of the book.

In Chapter 5, Pierre Lévy offers and explains his widely adopted concept collective intelligence. While humans have always shared (and not shared) knowledge, his definition highlights what is new about the sharing in the information society. To pass from *cogito* (Latin for I think) to Levy's digitally enabled *cogitamus* (we think) where no one knows everything, everyone knows something, we have to transcend our dual city gaps. As he puts it, "If you are tempted to judge someone as ignorant, look for the context in which his knowledge can be turned into gold". We see collective intelligence exactly as he has defined it as one of three core values of the information age, alongside cyberdemocracy (everyone can access the technology) and information freedom (no cost or other barrier to the information).

In chapter 6, Lai Maosheng explores the origin and development of the digital equity movement, introduces methods and indicators for measuring social equity and digital equity, analyzes the measurement data and research results regarding the condition of digital equity, and then reviews the major obstacles, principles and possible approaches towards realizing digital equity.

Chapter 7, by the editors of this book, is our first joint effort to explain the reasons and the possibilities for community informatics in China. It recapitulates key ideas and proposes a research program. Lai Maosheng was very helpful in posing the four questions to us and our intended audience was the Chinese academy, especially information management scholars and students.

The second part of the book has two parts: five chapters with our most relevant empirical work from the US and eight chapters about China which each constitute a first step in the direction that we propose in chapter 5. We hope that the US work included here provides a standard that Chinese scholars can grasp and then go beyond.

First, in chapter 8 Kate Williams and Joan Durrance provide a definition of community informatics and a brief history, especially in relation to libraries, librarians, and library scholars. Like the theory section of this book above, this chapter is Eurocentric and US-centric, and invites a Chinese answer, from inside the

Chinese field of information management but also from beyond that field to others in China.

Chapter 9 is the first community informatics study done by Abdul Alkalimat and Kate Williams. This chapter emerged from practical work that they did for close to a decade. This work linked the university to an existing community technology center. A case study where the research is invested in the community's own success is a tremendous learning opportunity quite unlike "learning to grow crops on the blackboard". Scientific method keeps the researcher honest and the memories continue to inform and inspire. This study presents a model whereby social capital, from outside the community but more importantly from within a community, is invested in a public computing site, generating cyberpower, that is, the ability to effect change using computers and the internet.

In chapter 10, Abdul Alkalimat explains five projects which emerged out of the work analyzed in chapter 9. These were all experiments at virtualizing community and generating cyberpower, and can be reinterpreted today, with all our communities so much more connected to the internet.

Chapter 11, by Kate Williams and Abdul Alkalimat, is a survey of public computing sites in the same cities as the studies in chapters 9 and 10. This research method follows naturally from a case study, because when you have learned a lot about one instance of a phenomenon, you can post questions to many and collect data that can show trends. The typology of public computing (government, commercial, higher education, and community or non-profit) suggests that different outcomes result from each type and that effective digital divide policy takes all four into consideration.

In Chapter 12, Kate Williams applies community informatics theory and methods to the public library and identifies a new phenomenon, the informatics moment. Unlike the digital divide, or digital literacy, which are each states of being, informatics moment is a process. It is a process that is repeated across society and (as long as new technologies emerge) in each of our lives as we set out to do something new. Her finding that social capital, especially bonding social capital, matters here, even in a bureaucratic organization such as an urban public library, is also a policy proposal: Digital literacy programs will succeed if they allow for and encourage the contribution of bonding social capital.

The remaining chapters shift the focus to China.

In Chapter 13, Chen Jianlong summarizes field work in the economic, social, technological and information strengths and weaknesses of the Lao Shao Bian Qiong areas—the old revolutionary areas, ethnic minority areas, remote border areas, and underdeveloped areas—of China. His conclusion: community informatics is the informatics of happiness. That means that for information management researchers, it is a high ethical and moral priority.

In chapter 14 Yan Hui and Kate Williams look from a great distance at the national population surveys of both the Chinese and US internet agencies. "A great distance" because at the time, from the US, we could not get in touch with CNNIC itself, so we backwards-engineered their reports to estimate what questions they asked, and this combined with the actual US survey questions suggested a set of standard questions that all national surveys should ask. We were gratified to later meet CNNIC researchers and find them on the same path towards international standards.

As a result of that meeting, we are able to include chapter 15, the most recent translated report of the actual statistics from The China Internet Network Information Center (CNNIC). No work in this area can go forward without using and grappling with the national census data their researchers collect, analyze and publish every six months.

In chapter 16, Han Shenglong and Yang Xueling walk us through the development of the internet in China, especially national status quo of internet, wireless internet, network devices and products, electronic government movement, electronic commerce, internet governance, etc. They provide a whole picture of China's internet since the 1980s.

Chapter 17 from Yan Hui offers the voices of leaders of what he calls "non-profit information organizations". His method is exactly in line with the theory of emphasizing bonding social capital: to understand community informationization, you must listen to local people with the social capital to effect change.

In chapter 18, Wang Sufang, helped by others in the 2011 Community Informatics Summer School, provides us with a solid critique of a commercial public computing site, the world-famous Starbucks café. This is the type of case study produced in the first summer school and we hope it will inspire readers to carry out more such case studies.

Helping us conclude this volume, Yu Liangzhi in chapter 19 lines up theory from China and abroad on information inequality and digital inequality. She finds theoretical unity between these two research threads and her findings, not to mention her approach, can only help us go forward faster in the US, Chine and elsewhere.

We are grateful to our publisher, the National Library of China Publishing House; Brian Zelip for editorial assistance; Zhao Kang for her graceful translation of the preface; each author in this volume for his or her contribution; and to our four families. We hope they forgive us for our absences as we carried out the work in this volume, and we deeply appreciate their support for the values and goals expressed here.

March 2012, Champaign, Beijing, and Tianjin

Part I
THEORY

1

Networks, Neighborhoods and Communities: Approaches to the Study of the Community Question① (1979)

Barry Wellman Barry Leighton

Abstract

We propose a network analytic approach to the community question in order to separate the study of communities from the study of neighborhoods. Three arguments about the community question—that "community" has been "lost," "saved," or "liberated"—are reviewed for their development, network depictions, imagery, policy implications, and current status. The lost argument contends that communal ties have become attenuated in industrial bureaucratic societies; the saved argument contends that neighborhood communities remain as important sources of sociability, support and mediation with formal institutions; the liberated argument maintains that while communal ties still flourish, they have dispersed beyond the neighborhood and are no longer clustered in solidary communities. Our review finds that both the saved and liberated arguments proposed viable network patterns under appropriate conditions, for social systems as well as individuals.

---

① Preparation of this paper was supported by the Canada Ministry of Manpower and Immigration (YoungCanada Works Program), the Centre for Urban and Community Studies, University of Toronto (Urban Housing Markets Program), and the Social Sciences and Humanities Research Council of Canada.

Neighborhood or community?

Urban sociology has tended to be *neighborhood sociology*. This has meant that analyses of large-scale urban phenomena (such as the fiscal crisis of the state) have been neglected in favor of small-scale studies of communities. It has also meant that the study of such communities has been firmly rooted in the study of neighborhoods, be they the "symbiotic" communities of Park (1936) or the "street corners" of Liebow (1967). It is to the sorting out of this second tendency, the merger of "neighborhood" with "community" that we address this paper.

There are a number of reasons why the concept of "neighborhood" has come to be substituted for that of "community":

First, urban researchers have to start somewhere. The neighborhood is an easily identifiable research site, while the street corner is an obvious and visible place for mapping small-scale interaction.

Second, many scholars have interpreted the neighborhood as the microcosm of the city and the city as an aggregate of neighborhoods. They have emphasized the local rather than the cosmopolitan in a building block approach to analysis which has given scant attention to large-scale urban structure.

Third, administrative officials have imposed their own definitions of neighborhood boundaries upon urban maps in attempts to create bureaucratic units. Spatial areas, labeled and treated as coherent neighborhoods, have come to be regarded as natural phenomena.

Fourth, urban sociology's particular concern with spatial distributions has tended to be translated into local area concerns. Territory has come to be seen as the inherently most important organizing factor in urban social relations rather than just one potentially important factor.

Fifth, and most importantly, many analysts have been preoccupied with the conditions under which solidary sentiments can be maintained. Their preoccupation reflects a persistent overarching sociological concern with normative integration and consensus. The neighborhood has been studied as an apparently obvious container of normative solidarity.

For these reasons at least, the concentration on the neighborhood has had a strong impact on definitions of, research on, and theorizing about community.

Neighborhood studies have produced hundreds of finely wrought depictions of urban life, and they have given us powerful ideas about how small-scale social systems operate in a variety of social contexts. But does the concept of "neighborhood" equal the concept of "community"? Are the two really one and the same?

Definitions of community tend to include three ingredients: *networks of interpersonal ties* (outside of the household) which *provide sociability and support* to members, residence in a *common locality*, and *solidarity sentiments and activities* (see Hillery 1955). It is principally the emphasis on common locality, and to a lesser extent the emphasis on solidarity, which has encouraged the identification of "community" with "neighborhood."

Yet the paramount concern of sociologists is social structure, and concerns about the spatial location of social structures and their normative integration must necessarily occupy secondary positions. To sociologists, unlike geographers, spatial distributions are not inherently important variables, but assume importance only as they affect such social structural questions as the formation of interpersonal networks and the flow of resources through such networks.

The community question

With its manifest concerns for the activities of populations in territories (Tilly 1974), urban sociology has often seemed to stand apart from broader theoretical concerns. Yet its concentration on the study of the neighborhood-as-community is very much a part of a fundamental sociological issue. This fundamental issue, which has occupied much sociological thinking, is the *community question*: the study of how large-scale divisions of labor in social systems affect the organization and content of interpersonal ties.

Sociologists have been particularly concerned with that form of the community question which investigates the impact the massive industrial bureaucratic transformations of North America and Europe during the past two hundred years have had on a variety of primary ties: in the home, the neighborhood, the workplace, with kin and friends, and among interest groups. Have such ties attenuated or flourished in contemporary societies? In what sort of networks are they organized? Have the contents of such ties remained as holistic as alleged to be in preindustrial societies or have they become narrowly specialized and instrumental?

The community question thus forms a crucial nexus between macroscopic and microscopic analysis. It directly addresses the structural integration of a social system and the interpersonal means by which its members can gain access to scarce resources. We urge, therefore, that the study of the community question be freed from its identification with the study of neighborhoods.

Neighborhood ≠ community

The entangling of the study of community ties with the study of the neighborhood has created a number of problems for the analysis of the community question.

First, the identification of a neighborhood as a container for communal ties assumes the a priori organizing power of space. This is spatial determinism. Even if we grant that space-time costs encourage some relationships to be local, it does not necessarily follow that all communal ties are organized into solidary neighborhood communities. These neighborhood ties may exist because of the attraction of ready accessibility to a few people and not because of a tangible neighborhood social organization.

Second, even the presence of many local relationships does not necessarily create discrete neighborhoods. There may well be overlapping sets of local ties, the range of these ties being affected by the needs and physical mobility of the participants.

Third, the identification of neighborhood studies with community studies can omit major spheres of interaction. There are important ties outside of the neighborhood even in the most "institutionally complete community"; (Breton 1964). Perhaps work relationships are the most serious and prevalent omission from community studies: residents tend to disappear from view in the morning and mysteriously reappear at dusk.

Fourth, the focus on the neighborhood may give undue importance to spatial characteristics as causal variables. Are cities just concrete and concentrated manifestations of larger structural forces? For instance, Castells (1976) argues that most Western urban sociology can be explained by studying capitalist modes of production.

Fifth, many analyses of neighborhoods have been preoccupied with the conditions under which solitary sentiments can be maintained. Consequently, when there has been an observed lack of locally organized behavior and sentiments, the assumption has easily been made that community has decayed. When not found in the neighborhood, community is assumed not to exist.

The network perspective

We suggest that the *network analytic perspective* is a more appropriate response to the community question in urban studies than the traditional focus on the neighborhood.② A network analysis of community takes as its starting point the search for social linkages and flows of resources. Only then does it enquire into the spatial distribution and solidary sentiments associated with the observed linkages. Such an approach largely frees the study of community from spatial and normative bases. It makes possible the discovery of network-based communities which are neither linked to a particular neighborhood nor to a set of solidary sentiments.

However, the network perspective is not inherently antineighborhood. By leaving the matter of spatial distributions initially open, this perspective makes it equally as possible to discover an "urban village" (Gans 1962) as it is to discover a "community without propinquity" (Webber 1963). A network analysis might also tell us that strong ties remain abundant and important, but that they are rarely located in the neighborhood. With this approach we are then better able to assess the position of neighborhood ties within the context of overall structures of social relationships.

The community question has been extensively debated by urban scholars. In this paper, we evaluate three competing scholarly arguments about the community question from a network perspective. The first two arguments to be discussed both focus on the neighborhood: the *community lost*, asserting the absence of local solidarities, and the *community saved* argument, asserting their persistence. The *community liberated* argument, in contrast, denies any neighborhood basis

② Network analysis is essentially a perspective which focuses on structured relationships between individuals and collectivities. As yet there is no commonly agreed definition. We believe that network analysis's salient characteristics are that it gives attention to: (a) structured patterns of relationships and not the aggregated characteristics of individual units, analyzed without reference to their interrelationships; (b) complex network structures and not just dyadic ties; (c) the allocation of scarce resources through concrete systems of power, dependency, and coordination; (d) questions of network boundaries, clusters and cross-linkages; (e) structures of reciprocal relationships and not just simple hierarchies. For summaries of the network perspective, see White (1965); Mitchell (1969, 1974); Barnes (1972); White, Boorman and Breiger (1976). See also the bibliographies of Wellman and Whitaker (1974); Freeman (1976); Klovdahl (1977).

to community. General tendencies in each argument are summarized, although not every article making each argument neatly fits into the analytic categories we have imposed on them. We review each argument's development, portrayal of urban networks, underlying normative imagery, policy implications, and current scholarly status. We conclude the paper by suggesting different circumstances in which saved and liberated network structures might be more prevalent and more useful.

Community lost

Development

The community lost argument contends that the transformation of Western societies to centralized, industrial bureaucratic structures has gravely weakened primary ties and communities, making the individual more dependent on formal organizational resources for sustenance (see the reviews in Stein 1960; Nisbet 1962; Gusfield 1975; Castells 1976; Mellor 1977). The first attempts to deal with the community question (e.g., Tönnies 1887) were, at the turn of the century, closely associated with broader sociological concerns about the impact of the Industrial Revolution on communal ties and normative integration (e.g., Durkheim 1893; Simmel 1908).

Scholars working in the lost tradition have initiated the analysis of the impact of large-scale social changes upon community structures. A number of such significant changes have been suggested, although not all analysts proposing them would necessarily agree that the loss of community was the ultimate outcome:

a) an increase in the scale of the nation-state's activities, with a concomitant decrease in local community autonomy and solidarity;
b) the development of bureaucratic institutions for production and reproduction, which have taken over many family, neighborhood, and friendship activities;
c) the large size of cities, which provides a basis for the population and organizational potential for more, and diverse, interest groups;
d) the high social density of interactions among segments of the population (even where spatial density is decreasing), with the ensuing complexities of ecological sorting and social arrangements;
e) the diversity of people with whom city dwellers can come into contact under conditions of heightened physical mobility;

f) the proliferation of cheap, efficient, and widespread transportation and communication facilities, increasing the ease with which contact can be made and enabling urbanites to be less tied to the neighborhood. The increased velocity of transactions fosters interactional density, and links to multiple social circles are even more readily maintained.

The lost argument has had continuing academic attention. It underlay much of the 1920s–1930s theoretical writing of the dominant "Chicago school" of urban studies (although the Chicago scholars found much evidence of communal organization in their empirical work). Robert Park's early programmatic statement asserted that "the growth of cities has been accomplished by the substitution of indirect 'secondary' for direct, face-to-face 'primary relations' " (Park 1925a, p. 23). Over a decade later, Louis Wirth (1938) summarized the lost argument well in his now classic statement of "urbanism as a way of life." Primary ties are recognized as still existing, but in a weaker, more narrowly instrumental fashion than those which had flourished in traditional solidary communities. More recent statements making the lost argument have not been as closely associated with empirical research but have been primarily concerned with normative theorizing and moralizing (e.g., Kornhauser 1959; Nisbet 1962; Banfield 1968; Slater 1970).

Lost scholars have seen modern urbanites as alienated isolates who bear the brunt of the transformed society on their own. Many research procedures have reinforced this perspective by using survey techniques which lump together individuals *qua* individuals in analytically imposed categories which do not take into consideration their structural connectedness (i.e., the statistical assumption of independence elevated to a world view). Such individual-as-unit oriented research techniques have been particularly suited to social psychologistic explanations which see internalized attitudes as determining social activity; they have not been nearly as well-suited towards the direct study of social-structural effects.

Lost networks

The community lost argument makes a number of specific assertions about the kinds of primary ties, social networks, and community structures that will tend to be present under its assumptions. By casting the lost argument in network analytic terms, we shall be better able to evaluate it in comparison with the community saved and community liberated arguments:

a) Rather than being a full member of a solidary community, urbanites are now *limited members* (in terms of amount, intensity, and commitment of interaction) of *several social networks.*
b) Primary ties are *narrowly defined*; there are *fewer strands* in the relationship.
c) The narrowly defined ties tend to be *weak in intensity.*
d) Ties tend to be *fragmented* into isolated *two-person* relationships rather than being parts of extensive networks.
e) Those networks that do exist tend to be *sparsely knit* (a low proportion of all potential links between members actually exists) rather than being densely knit (a high proportion of potential links exists).
f) The networks are *loosely bounded*; there are few discrete clusters or primary groups.
g) Sparse density, loose boundaries and narrowly defined ties provide *little* structural basis for *solidary activities or sentiments.*
h) The narrowly defined ties dispersed among a number of networks create *difficulties in mobilizing assistance* from network members.

Imagery

Community lost imagery has had a good deal of scholarly impact, appealing to radical (e.g., Engels 1845; Castells 1976), liberal (e.g., Kornhauser 1959; Stein 1960; Slater 1970), and conservative (e.g., Nisbet 1962; Banfield 1968; Grant 1969) concerns. Lost scholars of all political persuasions have been concerned about the upheavals caused by the large-scale transformation of industrial bureaucratic societies and the social disorganization and depravity allegedly let loose by the weakening of traditional communal bonds. Running through many lost analyses has been the implicit assumption that human beings are fundamentally evil (or easily capable of being driven to evil by industrialism, bureaucraticism, or capitalism), and that where restraining communal structures have been destroyed by the Industrial Revolution, riot, robbery, and rape have swept the city.

The social disorganization theme has remained a popular one in North American thought (for reviews, see White and White 1962; Marx 1964; Bender 1978). Nostalgia for "the myth of the lost paradise" (Gusfield 1975) has mingled with the identification of the contemporary city as the home of rootless masses in a continuing tradition from Jeffersonian pastoralism through Progressive reformism (e.g., Woodsworth 1911) to such recent urban panic movies as "Death Wish" (1974).

Affluent suburbs (see the review in Popenoe 1977) as well as poor inner cities are despaired of as privatized, isolated, and alienated.

Policy implications

The community lost argument has significantly affected urban policy in North America and Western Europe. There have been extensive "community development" programs designed to end alienation and to grow urban roots, such as the putative War on Poverty. The desired community ideal in such programs has been the regeneration of the densely knit, tightly bounded, solidary neighborhood community. When, despite the programs, a return to the pastoral ideal has not seemed achievable, then despair about social disorganization has led to elaborate social control policies, designed to keep in check the supposedly alienated, irrational, violence-prone masses. When even the achievement of social control has not seemed feasible, policies of neglect—benign or otherwise—have developed. Administrators have removed services from inner-city neighborhoods, asserting their inability to cope with socially disorganized behavior and leaving the remaining inhabitants to fend for themselves. The residents of such inner-city American areas as Pruitt-Igoe and the South Bronx have come to be regarded as unredeemably "sinful" as they suffer the supposed war of all against all.

Current status

The principal scholarly value of the community lost argument has been the attention it has focused on some important theoretical issues. First, it has sharpened perceptions of the ways in which industrial bureaucratic social systems can affect the nature of traditional communities. Second, it has raised the problem of the impact of residential and social mobility on the maintenance of community ties. Because it has seen community as only existing in neighborhoods, the lost argument has interpreted such mobility as a loss of community. However, if community becomes redefined in nonspatial terms, then the lost argument has served as an important precursor of the more recent community liberated argument (see below).

Despite its tenacity, the lost argument has received little empirical confirmation. Indeed, much of the impetus behind the saved and liberated arguments since World War II has been to disprove the loss of community contention (see the reviews in Craven and Wellman 1973; Feagin 1973; Hunter 1975; Fischer 1976). A modified version of the lost argument has recently emerged, taking into account the extensive documentation of primary ties that has been performed by saved and liberated scholars (see below). This modified lost version acknowledges the persistence of primary ties but contends that they are now markedly narrower in scope: the former wide range of content in kinship, neighborhood, and friendship ties has been reduced to sociability and emotional support, with formal institutions and the nuclear family now taking over much of the former content of such relationships (e.g., Sennett 1970; Lasch 1977). While this new version of the lost argument offers its scholars an opportunity to move from normative ideologizing to systematic investigations, extensive empirical confirmation of its contentions has not yet appeared.

Community saved

Development

The community saved argument maintains that neighborhood communities have persisted in industrial bureaucratic social systems as important sources of support and sociability. It argues that the very formal, centralizing tendencies of bureaucratic institutions have paradoxically encouraged the maintenance of primary ties as more flexible sources of sociability and support. The saved argument contends that urbanites continue to organize safe communal havens, with neighborhood, kinship, and work solidarities mediating and coping with bureaucratic institutions.

The saved argument shares with the lost argument the identification of "community" with "neighborhood". However, saved scholars have reacted against the tendency of some lost scholars to write secondary analyses *about* the neighborhood community rather than primary analyses *of* neighborhood communities.

In marked contrast to the lost argument scholar's proclivity for armchair theorizing, much of the saved argument's case has rested on the sheer empirical demonstration of the continued vitality of those urban primary ties which had been pronounced lost. Since World War II, hordes of scholars have presented carefully documented community studies, using systematic survey and field-work techniques, to make the saved argument. These studies have concentrated on delineating the social structure of neighborhood communities and have not just presented urbanites as aggregates of unconnected individuals. They have shown that urbanites still neighbor, still have a sense of local community, and still use neighborhood ties for sociability and support (see the reviews in Keller 1968; Wellman and Whitaker 1974; Warren and Warren 1976; Fischer 1976; Warren 1978).

Saved networks

The saved argument, cast into network analytic terms, is quite different from the lost argument:

a) Urbanites tend to be *heavily involved members of a single neighborhood community*, although they may combine this with membership in other social networks.
b) There are *multiple strands* of relationships between the members of these neighborhood communities.
c) While network ties vary in intensity, many of them are *strong*.
d) Neighborhood ties tend to be organized into *extensive networks*.
e) Networks tend to be *densely knit*.
f) Neighborhood networks are *tightly bounded*, with few external linkages. Ties tend to loop back into the same cluster of network members.
g) High density, tight boundaries, and multistranded ties provide a structural basis for a good deal of *solidary activities and sentiments*.
h) The multistranded strong ties clustered in densely knit networks *facilitate* the *mobilization* of assistance for dealing with routine and emergency matters.

Imagery

Saved scholars have tended to regard human beings as fundamentally good and inherently gregarious. They are viewed as apt to organize self-regulating communities under all circumstances, even extreme conditions of poverty, oppression, or catastrophe.

Hence the saved argument has shared the neighborhood community ideal with the lost argument, but it has seen this ideal as attainable and often already existing. Neighborhood communities are valued precisely because they can provide small scale loci of interaction and can effectively mediate urbanites' dealings with large-scale institutions. Densely knit, tightly bounded communities are valued as structures particularly suited to the tenacious conservation of its internal resources, the maintenance of local autonomy, and the social control of members (and intruders) in the face of powerful impinging external forces (e.g., Jacobs 1961;

Newman 1972).

Policy implications

Public acceptance of the saved argument has greatly increased during the past two decades. Active neighborhood communities are now valued as antidotes to industrial bureaucratic societies' alleged impersonality, specialized relationships, and loss of comprehensible scale. "Streetcorner society" (Whyte 1955), "the urban village" (Gans 1962), and "Tally's Corner" (Liebow 1967) have become exemplars of saved communities.

The neighborhood unit has been the twentieth-century planning ideal for new housing. Saved ideologues have also argued the necessity for preserving existing neighborhoods against the predations of ignorant and rapacious institutions. The saved argument has been the ideological foundation of the neighborhood movement which seeks to stop expressways, demolish developers, and renovate old areas (e.g., Powell 1972). Some neighborhoods have been successfully rescued from "urban renewal", although Gans' West End in Boston (1962) and Clairmont and Magill's Africville in Halifax (1974) have been lost.

In political analyses, rioters, far from being socially disorganized, are now seen to be rooted, well-connected community members (see Feagin and Hahn 1973; Tilly 1973, 1978). Their motivations tend to be in defense of existing communal interests or claims to new ones, rather than the irrational, individualistic, psychologistic responses claimed by the lost argument. Indeed, the means by which urbanites get involved in a riot are very much associated with the competitions, coalitions, and solidary ties of their social networks.

Many saved social pathologists have encouraged the nurturance of densely knit, bounded communities as a structural salve for the stresses of poverty, ethnic segregation, and physical and mental diseases (see the review in Caplan and Killilea 1976; Ratcliffe 1978). Getting help informally through neighborhood communities is alleged to be more sensitive to peculiar local needs and protective of the individual against bureaucratic claims. Furthermore, such programs have been welcomed by administrators as more cost-effective (or, as some critics allege, merely cheaper to operate) than the formal institutional intervention implied by the lost argument.[3]

---

③ One mental health technique, questionably labeled "network therapy",has as a principal goal the "retribalization" of those with whom the patient is in close contact (see Speck and Attneave 1973).

Current status

In the early nineteen-sixties the saved argument became the new orthodoxy in community studies with the publication of such works as Gans' *The Urban Villagers* (1962), Greer's (1962) synthesis of postwar survey research, and Jacob's (1961) assertion of the vitality of dense, diverse central cities. Such case studies as Young and Willmott's (1957) study of a working-class London neighborhood, Gans's (1967) account of middle-class, new suburban networks, and Liebow's (1967) portrayal of inner-city blacks' heavy reliance on network ties helped clinch the case.

The rebuttal of the lost argument's assertion of urban social disorganization has therefore been accomplished, theoretically and empirically, by studies emphasizing the persistence of neighborhood communities. In the process, though, the lost argument's useful starting point may have come to be neglected: that the industrial bureaucratic division of labor has strongly affected the structure primary ties. Saved scholars have tended to look only for—and at—the persistence of functioning neighborhood communities. [④] Consequently we now know that neighborhood communities persist and often flourish, but we do not know the position of neighborhood-based ties within overall social networks.

Many recent saved analyses have recognized this difficulty by introducing the "community of limited liability" concept, which treats the neighborhood as just one of a series of communities among which urbanites divide their membership (see Janowitz 1952; Greer 1962; Suttles 1972; Kasarda and Janowitz 1974; Hunter 1975; Warren 1978). Hunter and Suttles (1972: 61), for example, portray such communities as a set of concentric zones radiating out from the block to "entire sectors of the city". However, while such analyses recognize the possibilities for urbanites to be members of diverse networks with limited involvement in each network, the "limited liability community" formulation is still predicated on the neighborhood concept, seeing urban ties as radiating out from a local, spatially defined base.

Community liberated

Development

The third response to the community question, the liberated argument, agrees

④ Perhaps only Banfield (1958) and Vidich and Bensman (1958) have set forth in search of solidary communities and not found them.

with the lost argument's contention that the industrial bureaucratic nature of social systems has caused the weakening of neighborhood communities. But the liberated argument also agrees with the saved argument's contention that primary ties have remained viable, useful, and important. It shares the saved argument's contention that communities still flourish in the city, but it maintains that such communities are rarely organized within neighborhoods.

The liberated argument contends that a variety of structural and technological developments have liberated communities from the confines of neighborhoods and dispersed network ties from all-embracing solidary communities to more narrowly based ones: (a) cheap, effective transportation and communication facilities; (b) the separation of workplace and kinship ties into nonlocal, nonsolidary networks; (c) high rates of social and residential mobility (e.g., Crump 1977).

The liberated argument, like the other two arguments, begins with the concept of space. Yet where the other arguments see communities as resident in neighborhoods, the liberated argument confronts spatial restrictions only in order to transcend them. Although harkening back to some of the more optimistic writings of Simmel about the liberating effect of urban life (e.g., 1902–1903: last portion; 1908, p. 121) and Park (e.g., 1925b, p. 65), the argument has become prominent only in the past two decades following the proliferation of personal automotive and airplane travel and telecommunications in the Western world. It contends that there is now the possibility of "community without propinquity" (Webber 1964) in which distance and travel time are minimal constraints (e.g., Hiltz and Turoff forthcoming).

Liberated networks

With its emphasis on aspatial communities, the liberated argument has been methodologically associated with network analytic techniques (e.g., Kadushin 1966; Walker 1977; Wellman 1979). However, it must be emphasized that network analysis does not necessarily share the liberated argument's ideological bias and can be used to evaluate the existence of *all three* community patterns: lost, saved, and liberated.

In network terms, the liberated argument contends that:

a) Urbanites now tend to be *limited members of several social networks*, possibly including one located in their neighborhood.
b) There is *variation in the breadth of the strands* of relationships between

network members; there are multistranded ties with some, single-stranded ties with many others, and relationships of intermediate breadth with the rest.

c) The ties range in intensity: *some* of them are *strong*, while others are weak but nonetheless useful.

d) An individual's ties tend to be organized into a *series of networks with few connections* between them.

e) Networks tend to be *sparsely knit* although certain portions of the networks, such as those based on kinship, may be more densely knit.

f) The networks are *loosely bounded, ramifying* structures, branching out extensively to form linkages to additional people and resources.

g) Sparse density, loose boundaries, and narrowly defined ties provide *little structural basis for solidary activities and sentiments* in the overall networks of urbanites, although some solidary clusters of ties are often present.

h) Some network ties can be mobilized for general-purpose or specific assistance in dealing with routine or emergency matters. The likelihood of mobilization depends more on the quality of the two-person tie than on the nature of the larger network structure.

Imagery

The liberated argument is fundamentally optimistic about urban life. It is appreciative of urban diversity; imputations of social disorganization and pathology find little place within it. The argument's view of human behavior emphasizes its entrepreneurial and manipulative aspects. People are seen as having a propensity to form primary ties, not out of inherent good or evil, but in order to accomplish specific, utilitarian ends.

The liberated argument, as does the lost argument, minimizes the importance of neighborhood communities. But where the lost argument sees this as throwing the urbanite upon the resources of formal organizations, the liberated argument contends that sufficient primary ties are available in nonneighborhood networks to provide crucial social support and sociability. Furthermore, it argues that the diverse links between these networks organize the city as a "network of networks" (Craven and Wellman 1973) to provide a flexible coordinating structure not possible through a lost formal, bureaucratic hierarchy or a saved agglomeration of neighborhoods.

The liberated argument recoils from the lost and saved arguments' village-like community norm. The argument celebrates the structural autonomy of being able to move among various social networks (e.g., Cox 1966; Burt 1976). It perceives solidary communities as fostering stifling social control and of causing isolation from outside contact and resources. Multiple social networks are valued because the cross-cutting commitments and alternative escape routes limit the claims that any one community can make upon its members.

Policy implications

Liberated analysts have called for the reinforcement of other social networks in addition to the traditional ones of the neighborhood and the family. Whereas industrial power considerations have worked against the development of solidary networks in the workplace, much attention has been paid recently to fostering "helping networks" that would prevent or heal the stress of physical and mental diseases (e.g., Caplan and Killilea 1976; Hirsch 1977; Ratcliffe 1978). No longer is the neighborhood community seen as the safe, supportive haven; no longer are formal institutions to be relied on for all healing attempts. Instead, networks are to be mobilized, and where they do not exist they can be constructed so that urbanites may find supportive places. However, the efficacy of such deliberately constructed "natural support systems" (to use current jargon) has not yet been adequately demonstrated.

The liberated argument has had an important impact on thinking about political phenomena, especially that related to collective disorders. Research by Charles Tilly (e.g., 1975, 1978) and associates, in particular, has shown such collective disorders to be integral parts of broader contentions for power by competing interest groups. In addition to the internal solidarity emphasized by the saved argument, a contending group's chances for success have been shown to be strongly associated with the capacity for making linkages in external coalitions that crosscutting ties between networks can provide (e.g., Gans 1974a, 1974b; Granovetter 1974b).

Recent British New Town planning (e.g., Milton Keynes) has been predicated on the high rates of personal automotive mobility foreseen by the liberated argument. However, the argument's contention that there are minimal costs to spatial separation has come up against the increase in the monetary costs of such separation associated with the significant rise in the price of oil within the last decade. One response has been to advocate increased reliance on telecommunications to maintain community ties over large distances.

New developments in computer technology foreshadow major increases in telecommunications capabilities, such as "electronic mail" and "computer conferencing" (see Hiltz and Turoff forthcoming). Yet the strength of the liberated argument does not necessarily depend on technological innovations. Recent research in preindustrial social systems has indicated that long-distance ties can be maintained without benefit of telephone or private automobiles, as long as such ties are structurally embedded in kinships systems or common local origins (e.g., Belshaw 1965; Cohen 1969; Laslett 1971; Jacobson 1973; Howard 1974; Mayer and Mayer 1974; Ross and Weisner 1977; Bender 1978).

Current status

Contemporary studies making the liberated argument have proliferated in the past decade. They have examined the nature of membership in multiple social networks (e.g., Kadushin 1966; Laumann 1973; Boissevain 1974; Breiger 1976; Bell and Newby 1976; Shulman, 1976), the use of network ties to obtain needed resources (e.g., Cohen 1969; Lee 1969; Granovetter 1974a; Jacobson 1975), and the ways in which links between social networks can structure social systems (e.g., Granovetter 1973; Wireman 1978; Laumann, Galaskiewicz, and Marsden forthcoming).

The strength of the liberated argument is that it can account for, and at the same time propose, socially close communities which stretch over large distances. "Community" need no longer necessarily be tied to "neighborhood". However, in propounding the virtues of nonlocal communities the liberated argument may have unduly neglected the usefulness of quick local accessibility and the advantages of the solidary behavior that can come with densely knit, tightly bounded, multistranded ties. To assert that one should not set out initially to search for solidarities, as the network perspective does, may be quite a different matter than the liberated argument's assertion of the nonexistence of such solidarities.

Communities: Lost, saved or liberated?

Are communities lost, saved, or liberated? Too often, the three arguments have been presented as (a) competing alternative depictions of the "true" nature of Western industrial bureaucratic social systems, or (b) evolutionary successors, with preindustrial saved communities giving way to industrial lost, only to be superseded by postindustrial liberated.

In contrast, we believe that all three arguments have validity when stripped of their ideological paraphernalia down to basic network structures. [⑤] Indeed their structural character might be highlighted by thinking of them as sparse, dense, and ramified network patterns. Different network patterns tend to have different consequences for the acquisition and control of resources (see the discussion of kinship systems in Wolf, 1966). We might then expect to find the prevalence of lost, saved, and liberated communities to vary according to the kinds of societal circumstances in which they are located.

Saved communities/dense networks

In saved networks, densely knit ties and tight boundaries tend to occur together. This may be because network members have a finite lump of sociability, so that if they devote most of their energies to within-network ties, they do not have much scope for maintaining external linkages. Conversely, tight boundaries may also foster the creation of new ties within the community, as internal links become the individual's principal hope of gaining access to resources.

Such dense, bounded saved networks, be they neighborhood, kinship, or otherwise based, are apt to be solidary in sentiments and activities. They are well-structured for maintaining informal social control over members and intruders. The dense ties and communal solidarity should facilitate the ready mobilization of the community's resources for the aid of members in good standing. But because solidarity does not necessarily mean egalitarianism, not all of the community's resources may be gathered or distributed equally.

Community studies have shown the saved pattern to be quite prevalent in situations in which community members do not have many individual personal resources and where there are unfavorable conditions for forming external ties. Certain ethnic minority and working-class neighborhoods clearly follow this pattern (e.g., Liebow 1967). In such situations, concerns about conserving, controlling and

---

⑤ Our review of the saved literature has already indicated the abundant evidence for the presence of densely knit, tightly bounded communities in contemporary Western social systems (e.g., Whyte, 1955; Young and Willmott 1957; Gans 1962; Liebow 1967). While only Bender (1978) has explicitly attempted to argue the prevalence of liberated patterns in preindustrial social systems, historians have begun reporting nonsolidary aspects of preindustrial Western Europe (e.g., Laslett 1971; Scott and Tilly 1975; Shorter 1975; Tilly 1975). We can look to studies of peer groups, interest groups, travel out of the local area, and complex households (masters, servants, laborers; multiple generations, with nonlocal marriages) having a variety of external ties as providing some basis for the existence of liberated patterns. The prevalence of long-distance, liberated ties in contemporary non-Western social systems has been more extensively documented (see review of the liberated literature).

efficiently pooling those resources the beleaguered community possesses also resonate with its members' inability to acquire additional resources elsewhere. A heavy load consequently is placed on ties within the saved community.

Liberated communities/ramified networks

If saved network patterns are particularly suited to conditions of resource scarcity and conservation, liberated network patterns are particularly suited to conditions of resource abundance and acquisition. Such sparsely knit, loosely bounded networks are not structurally well-equipped for internal social control. Implicit assurance in the security of one's home base is necessary before one can reach out into new areas.

Loose boundaries and sparse density foster networks that extensively branch out to link up with new members. These ramifying liberated networks are well-structured for acquiring additional resources through a larger number of direct and indirect external connections. Their structure is apt to connect liberated network members with a more diverse array of resources than saved networks are apt to encounter, although the relative lack of solidarity in such liberated networks may well mean that a lower proportion of resources will be available to other network members.

It may well be that the liberated pattern is peculiarly suited to affluent sectors of contemporary Western societies. It places a premium on a base of individual security, entrepreneurial skills in moving between networks, and the ability to function without the security of membership in a solidary community. However, its appearance in other social contexts indicates that it reflects a more fundamental alternative to the saved community pattern.

Both the saved or liberated community patterns can appear as desirable alternatives to those enmeshed in the other pattern. To those unsatisfied with the uncertain multiplicities of liberated networks, holistic, solidary saved communities can appear as a welcome retreat. To those who feel trapped in all-embracing saved networks, the availability of alternative liberated primary networks may offer a welcome escape route. Much migration from rural areas may follow this tendency.

Lost communities/sparse networks

What of circumstances where no alternative network sources of escape or retreat are possible? It is in such situations that the lost pattern of direct affiliation with formal institutions can become attractive: the army, the church, the firm, and the university (see Shorter 1973). However, the lost pattern may always be unstable for individuals and communities as formal institutional ties devolve into complex primary network webs. Therefore, as primary ties develop between the within organizations, we may expect to find networks taking on the patterns of saved or liberated communities.

Personal communities

When studying neighborhoods and communities, we are likely to find diversity rather than a universal pattern to either local or personal networks. We have proposed that dense saved network patterns are better suited for internal control of resources while ramified liberated patterns are better suited for obtaining access to external resources. Although we have suggested that each of these patterns should be more prevalent in one sort of a society than another, it is quite likely that the total network of a community will comprise a mixture of these two patterns in varying proportions. That is, some of the ties within a network will be densely knit and tightly bounded, while others will be sparsely knit and ramified. The different patterns are useful or different things. As Merton (1957) early pointed out, most communities have some network members for exchanging resources with the outside world ("cosmopolitans") and some for allocating them internally ("locals").

Our own research in the Borough of East York, Toronto, has revealed that individuals, too, may be simultaneous members of both saved and liberated pattern networks.[6] Some of an urbanite's ties tend to be clustered into densely knit, tightly bounded networks, their solidarity often reinforced by either kinship structures or residential or work-place propinquity. Such saved networks are better able to mobilize help in emergencies through efficient communication and structurally enforced norms. Their density and boundedness tend to give these clusters more of a tangible collective image, so that network members have a sense of solidary attachment.

---

⑥ The data collected in 1968 random-sample, closed-ended survey of 845 adult East Yorkers, directed by Donald B. Coates, with Barry Wellman as coordinator. East York (1971 population = 104,646) is an upper working-class, lower middle-class, predominantly British-Canadian inner-city suburb of Toronto. It has the reputation of being one of the most solidary areas of the city. Respondents were asked about "persons outside your home who you feel closest to" up to a maximum of six. See Wayne (1971), Shulman (1972, 1976), Crump (1977), Wellman (1979), and Wellman, Shulman, Wayne, and Crump (forthcoming) for the findings.

Yet we have found (Wellman 1979) that such clusters are likely to comprise only a minority of one's important network ties. The other ties tend to be much less densely connected. Instead of looping back into one another within boundaries, they tend to be ramified, branching out to encounter new members to whom the original network members are not directly connected. These sparsely knit, loosely bounded liberated networks are structurally not as efficient in mobilizing collective assistance for their members, but their branching character allows additional resources to be reached. Furthermore, the liberated ties, while not as conducive to internal solidarity as the saved clusters, better facilitate coalition building between networks.

Neighborhood and community

Almost all of the people we studied have many strong ties and they are able to obtain assistance through a number of close relationships. Yet only a small proportion of these "intimate" ties are located in the same neighborhood (Wellman 1979). While neighboring ties are still prevalent and important in East York, they rarely achieve the intensity of intimacy (see Gates, Stevens, and Wellman 1973).

Neighborhood relationships persist but only as specialized components of the overall primary networks. The variety of ties in which an urbanite can be involved—with distant parents, intimate friends, less intimate friends, coworkers, and so on—and the variety of networks in which these are organized can provide flexible structural bases for dealing with routine and emergency matters.

In sum, we must be concerned with neighborhood *and* community rather, than neighborhood *or* community. We have suggested that the two are separate concepts which may or may not be closely associated. In some situations we can observe the saved pattern of community as solidary neighborhood. In many other situations, if we go out and look for neighborhood-based networks, we are apt to find them. They can be heavily used for the advantages of quick accessibility. But if we broaden our field of view to include other primary relations, then the apparent neighborhood solidarities may now be seen as clusters in the rather sparse, loosely bounded structures of urbanites' total networks.

2

Building a Network Theory of Social Capital (1999)[①]

Nan Lin (林南)

Introduction

In the past two decades, social capital in its various forms and contexts has emerged as one of the most salient concepts in social sciences. While much excitement has been generated, divergent views, perspectives, and expectations have also raised the serious question: is it a fad or does it have enduring qualities that will herald a new intellectual enterprise? This presentation's purpose is to review social capital as discussed in the literature, identify controversies and debates, consider some critical issues, and propose conceptual and research strategies in building a theory. I will argue that such a theory and the research enterprise must be based on the fundamental understanding that social capital is captured from embedded resources in social networks. Deviations from this understanding in conceptualization and measurement lead to confusion in analyzing causal mechanisms in the macro-and microprocesses. It is precisely these mechanisms and processes, essential for an interactive theory about structure and action, to which social capital promises to make contributions.

The paper will begin by exploring the nature of capital and various theories of capital, so that social capital can be properly perceived and located. It will then identify certain controversies which, unless clarified or resolved, will hinder the

① An earlier version of this paper was presented as the Keynote Address at the XIX International Sunbelt Social Network Conference, Charleston, South Carolina, February 18—21, 1999. Contact the author at nanlin@duke.edu.

development of a theory and the research enterprise. By considering social capital as assets in networks, the paper will discuss some issues in conceptualizations, measurements, and causal mechanisms (the factors leading to inequality of social capital and the returns following investments in social capital). A proposed model will follow. The paper will conclude by calling attention to the rise of a new form of social capital, cybernetworks, and briefly suggesting how research on this topic promises to make important contributions to the research enterprise.

What is capital?

The notion of capital can be traced to Marx (1933/1849; 1995/1867, 1885, 1894; Brewer, 1984). In his conceptualization, capital is part of the surplus value captured by capitalists or the bourgeoisie, who control production means, in the circulations of commodities and monies between the production and consumption processes. In these circulations, laborers are paid for their labor (commodity) with a wage allowing them to purchase commodities (such as food, shelter, and clothing) to sustain their lives (exchange value). But the commodity processed and produced by the capitalists can be circulated to and sold in the consumption market at a higher price (user value). In this scheme of the capitalist society, capital represents two related but distinct elements. On the one hand, it is part of the *surplus value* generated and pocketed by the capitalists (and their "misers," presumably the traders and sellers). On the other hand, it represents an *investment* (in the production and circulation of commodities) on the part of the capitalists, with expected returns in a marketplace. Capital, as part of the surplus value, is a product of a process; whereas capital is also an investment process in which the surplus value is produced and captured. It is also understood that the investment and its produced surplus value are in reference to a return/reproduction of the process of investment and of more surplus values. It is the dominant class that makes the investment and captures the surplus value. Thus, it is a theory based on the exploitative social relations between two classes. I call Marx's theory of capital the *classical theory of capital*.

Subsequent theoretical modifications and refinements have retained the basic elements of capital in the classical theory, as represented in Table 1.

Fundamentally, capital remains a surplus value and represents an investment with expected returns. Human capital theory (Johnson 1960; Schultz 1961; Becker 1964/1993), for example, also conceives capital as investment (e.g., in education) with certain expected returns (earnings). Individual workers invest in technical skills and knowledge so that they can negotiate with those in control of the production process (firms and their agents) for payment of their labor-skill. This payment has value that may be more than what the purchase of subsisting commodities would require and, thus, contain surplus values which in part can be spent for leisure and lifestyle needs and in part turned into capital. Likewise, cultural capital, as described by Bourdieu (Bourdieu 1990; Bourdieu & Passeron 1977), represents investments on the part of the dominant class in reproducing a set of symbols and meanings, which are misrecognized and internalized by the dominated class as their own. The investment, in this theory, is in the pedagogic actions of the reproduction process, such as education, the purpose of which is to indoctrinate the masses to internalize the values of these symbols and meanings. Cultural capital theory also acknowledges that the masses (the dominated class) can invest and acquire these symbols and meanings, even if they misrecognize them as their own. The inference is that while cultural capital is mostly captured by the dominant class through inter-generation transmissions, even the masses (or at least some of them) may generate returns from such investment and acquisition.

However, these theories break significantly from the classical theory. That is, because the laborers, workers or masses can now invest, and thus acquire certain capital of their own (be they skills and knowledge in the case of human capital, or "misrecognized" but nevertheless internalized symbols and meanings), they (or some of them) can now generate surplus values in trading their labor or work in the production and consumption markets. The social relations between classes (capitalists and non-capitalists) become blurred. The image of the social structure is modified from one of dichotomized antagonistic struggle to one of layered or: stratified negotiating discourses. I call these the *neo-capitalist theories*. The distinctive feature of these theories resides in the potential investment and capture of surplus value by the laborers or masses. Social capital, I argue, is another form of

	The Classical Theory	The Neo-Capital Theories			
		Human Capital	Cultural Capital	Social Capital	
eorist	Marx	Schultz, Becker	Bourdieu	Lin, Burt, Marsden, Flap, Coleman	Bourdieu, Coleman, Putnam
planation	Social relations: Exploration by the capitalists (bourgeoisie) of the proletariat	Accumulation of surplus value by laborer	Reproduction of dominant symbols and meanings (values)	Access to and use of resources embedded in social networks	Solidarity and reproduction of group
pital	A. Part of surplus value between the use value (in consumption mark -et) and the exchange value (in production labor market) of the commodity. B. Investment in the production and circulation of commodities	Investment in technical skills and knowledge	Internalization or misrecognition of dominant values	Investment in social networks	Investment in mutual recognition and acknowledgme
vel of alysis	Structural (classes)	Individual	Individual/class	Individual	Group/individu

Table 1. Theories of capital

the neo-capital theories. ②

② There is some ambiguity in Bourdieu's writings as to whether cultural capital should be seen as a structural theory or a theory which allows choice actions. He (Bourdieu 1990; Bourdieu & Passeron 1977) defines culture as a system of symbolism and meaning (Jenkins 1992, p. 104). The dominant class in the society imposes its culture by engaging in pedagogic action (e.g., education), which internalizes the dominant symbols and meanings in the next generation, thus reproducing the salience of the dominant culture. The result is an internalized and durable training, *habitus*, in the reproduction of the culture. The mass is not cognitively aware of the imposition and takes on the imposed culture as their own—misrecognition. This rendition of capital can trace its lineage to Marx. The social relations described by Marx are also assumed; there is a class, capitalists, who control the means of production—the process of pedagogic action or the educational institutions (in the homes, in schools, etc.). In the production (schooling) process, laborers (students or children) invest in the educational process and internalize the dominant class culture. Acquisition of this culture permits or licenses the laborers to enter the labor market, earn payments and sustain expenditures for their lives. The capitalists, or the dominant class, gain cultural capital which supplement their economic capital and accumulate capital of both types in the circulation of the commodities (educated mass) and the domination of the means of production (the educational institutions). However, there is a break from Marx and an important one. Bourdieu does not assume perfect correspondence between the accumulation of economic capital and cultural capital. Some economic capitalists do not possess cultural capital and some cultural capitalists are not economically endowed. This less than perfect correspondence would seem to open the possible path for some of the laborers, using their cultural habitus, to gain a foothold in the dominant class. It is conceivable that they become part of the educational institutions and gain returns in the labor market, due to their cultural capital. Bourdieu did not carry his analysis this far, but seems to leave open the process of social mobility and the possibility of agency.

Why does social capital work?

The premise behind the notion of social capital is rather simple and straightforward: *investment in social relations with expected returns*. This general definition is consistent with various renditions by all scholars who have contributed to the discussion (Bourdieu 1983/1986; Bourdieu 1980; Burt 1992; Coleman 1988; Coleman 1990; Erickson 1995; Erickson 1996; Flap 1994; Flap 1991; Lin 1982; Lin 1995; Portes 1998; Putnam 1993; Putnam 1995a). Individuals engage in interactions and networking in order to produce profits. Generally, three explanations can be offered as to why embedded resources in social networks will enhance the outcomes of actions. For one, it facilitates the flow of *information*. In the usual imperfect market situations, social ties located in certain strategic locations and/or hierarchical positions (and thus better informed on market needs and demands) can provide an individual with useful information about opportunities and choices otherwise not available. Likewise, these ties (or their ties) may alert an organization (be it in the production or consumption market) and its agents, or even a community, about the availability and interest of an otherwise unrecognized individual. Such information would reduce the transaction cost for the organization to recruit "better" (be it skill, or technical or cultural knowledge) individuals and for individuals to find "better" organizations which can use their capital and provide appropriate rewards. Second, these social ties may exert *influence* on the agents (e.g., recruiters or supervisors of the organizations) who play a critical role in decisions (e.g., hiring or promotion) involving the actor. Some social ties, due to their strategic locations (e.g., structural holes) and positions (e.g., authority or supervisory capacities), also carry more valued resources and exercise greater power (e.g., greater asymmetry in dependence by these agents), in organizational agents' decision making. Thus, "putting in a word" carries a certain weight in the decision-making process regarding an individual. Third, social tie resources, and their acknowledged relationships to the individual, may be conceived by the organization or its agents as certifications of the individual's *social credentials*, some of which reflect the individual's accessibility to resources through social networks and relations—his/her social capital. "Standing behind" the individual by these ties reassures the organization (and its agents) that the individual can provide "added" resources beyond the individual's personal capital, some of which may be useful to the organization. Finally, social relations are expected to reinforce identity and recognition. Being assured and recognized of one's worthiness as an individual and a member of a social group sharing similar interests and resources not only provides emotional support but also public acknowledgment of one's claim to certain resources. These *reinforcements* are essential for the maintenance of mental health and the entitlement to resources. These four elements—*information, influence, social credentials and reinforcement*—may explain why social capital works in instrumental and expressive actions not accounted for by forms of personal capital such as economic capital or human capital.[③]

Perspectives and controversies in social capital

However, two perspectives can be identified relative to the level at which return or profit is conceived—whether the profit is accrued for the group or for the individuals. In one perspective, the focus is on the use of social capital by individuals—how individuals access and use resources embedded in social networks to gain returns in instrumental actions (e.g., finding better jobs) or preserve gains in expressive actions. Thus, at this relational level, social capital can be seen as similar to human capital in that it is assumed that such investments can be made by individuals with expected return, some benefit or profit, to the individual. Aggregation of individual returns also benefits the collective. Nonetheless, the focal points for analysis in this perspective are (I) how individuals invest in social relations, and (2) how individuals capture the embedded resources in the relations to generate a return. Representative works (see review in Lin 1999) can be found in Lin (Lin & Bian 1991; Lin & Durnin 1986; Lin, Ensel & Vaughn 1981), Burt (1992; 1998; 1997), Marsden (Marsden & Hurlbert 1988; Campbell, Marsden & Hurlbert 1986), Flap (Boxman, DeGraaf & Flap 1991; DeGraaf & Flap 1988; Flap & De Graaf 1988; Flap 1991; Sprengers, Tazelaar & Flap 1988; Volker & Flap 1996), and Portes (Portes & Sensenbrenner 1993) as well as in discussions of social capital by Coleman and Bourdieu.

Another perspective has its focus on social capital at the group level, with discussions dwelling on (1) how certain groups develop and maintain more or less social capital as a collective asset, and (2) how such a collective asset enhances group members' life chances. Bourdieu (1983/1986; 1980) and Coleman (1988; 1990) have discussed this perspective extensively and Putnam's empirical work (1993; 1995a) is exemplary. While acknowledging the essentiality of individuals

---

③ Another element, control, has also been mentioned for the usefulness of social capital. I consider control reflecting both the network location and the hierarchical position, central to the definition of social capital itself. Thus, information, influence, social credential, and reinforcement are all reasons why social capital works or controls.

interacting and networking in developing payoffs of social capital, the central interest of this perspective is to explore the elements and processes in the production and maintenance of the collective asset. For example, dense or closed networks are seen as the means by which collective capital can be maintained and reproduction of the group can be achieved. Another major interest is how norms and trust, as well as other properties (e.g., sanctions, authority) of a group, are essential in the production and maintenance of the collective asset.

Whether social capital is seen from the societal-group level or the relational level, all scholars remain committed to the view that it is the interacting members who make the maintenance and reproduction of this social asset possible. This consensual view puts social capital firmly in the neo-capital theory camp.[④]

However, the divergence in analyzing social capital at different levels has created some theoretical and measurement confusions. Further confusion arises from the fact that some discussions have flowed freely between levels. For example, Bourdieu provides a structural view in pointing to the dominant class and nobility groups' reproduction as the principal explanation of social capital, which is represented by aggregating (1) the size of the group or network and (2) the volume of capital possessed by members (Bourdieu 1986, p. 248). This representation makes sense only when it is assumed that all members maintain strong and reciprocal relations (a completely dense or institutionalized network), so that strength of relations does not enter into the calculus. Yet, Bourdieu also describes how individuals interact and reinforce mutual recognition and acknowledgment

---

④ Two major and different theoretical positions distinguish scholars in the collective asset camp. For Bourdieu, social capital represents a process by which individuals in the dominating class, by mutual recognition and acknowledgment, reinforce and reproduce a privileged group which holds various capital (economic, cultural and symbolic). Nobility and titles characterize such groups and their members. Thus, social capital is another way of maintaining and reproducing the dominant class. I would characterize this theoretical position as one that views social capital as class (privilege) goods. The other position on social capital as collective asset is represented by the works of Coleman and Putnam. Coleman, while defining social capital as consisting of any social-structural features or resources that are useful to individuals for specific actions, stresses social capital as public good. These collective assets and features are available to all members of the group, be it a social group or community and regardless of which members actually promote, sustain or contribute to such resources. Because social capital is public good, it depends on the good will of the individual members to make such efforts and not to be free riders. Thus, norms, trust, sanctions, authority and other structural "features" become important in sustaining social capital. If one were forced to trace the theoretical lineage of these two explanatory schemes, one could argue that the privileged good view is principally an extension and elaboration of the social relations in the Marxian capital theory and that the public good view is primarily an extension and elaboration of the integrative or Durkheimian view of social relations.

as members of a network or group. Coleman (1990, ch. 12), while emphasizing how individuals can use socio-structural resources in obtaining better outcomes in their (individual) actions, devotes much discussion to the collective nature of social capital in stressing trust, norms, sanctions, authority, and closure as part or forms of social capital. It is important to identify and sort through these confusions and reach some understandings before we can proceed to build a coherent theory of social capital. I identify some of these issues in Table 2.

Issue	Contention	Problem
Collective or individual asset (Coleman, Putnam)	Social capital as collective asset	Confounding with norms, trust
Closure or open networks (Bourdieu, Coleman, Putnam)	Group should be closed or dense	Vision of class society and absence or mobility
Functional (Coleman)	Social capital is indicated by its effect in particular action	Tautology (cause is determined by effect)
Measurement (Coleman)	Not quantifiable	Heuristic, not falsifiable

Table 2. Controversies in social capital

One major controversy generated from macro–versus relational-level perspectives is whether social capital is collective goods or individual goods (see Portes' critique, 1998). Most scholars agree that it is both collective and individual goods; that is, institutionalized social relations with embedded resources are expected to be beneficial to both the collective and the individuals in the collective. At the group level, social capital represents some aggregation of valued resources (such as economic, political, cultural, or social, as in social connections) of members interactive as a network or networks. The difficulty arises when social capital is discussed as collective or even public goods, along with trust, norms, and other "collective" or public goods. What has resulted in the literature is that the terms have become alternative or substitutable terms or measurements. Divorced from its roots in individual interactions and networking, social capital becomes merely another trendy term to employ or deploy in the broad context of improving or building social integration and solidarity. In the following, I will argue that social capital, as a relational asset, must be distinguished from collective assets and goods such as culture, norms, trust, etc. Causal propositions may be formulated (e.g., that collective assets, such as trust, promote the relations and networks and enhances the utility of embedded resources, or vice versa), but it should not be assumed that they are all alternative forms of social capital or are defined by one another (e.g., trust is capital).

Another controversy, related to the focus on the collective aspect of social capital, is the assumed or expected requirement that there is closure or density in social relations and social networks (Bourdieu 1986; Coleman 1990; Putnam 1993, 1995). Bourdieu, from his class perspective, sees social capital as the investment of the members in the dominant class (as a group or network) engaging in mutual recognition and acknowledgment so as to maintain and reproduce group solidarity and preserve the group's dominant position. Membership in the group is based on a clear demarcation (e.g., nobility, title, family) excluding outsiders. Closure of the group and density within the group are required. Coleman, of course, does not assume such a class vision of society. Yet, he also sees network closure as a distinctive advantage of social capital, because it is closure that maintains and enhances trust, norms, authority, sanctions, etc. These solidifying forces may ensure that it is possible to mobilize network resources.

I believe that the requirement for network density or closure for the utility of social capital is not necessary or realistic. Research in social networks has stressed the importance of bridges in networks (Granovetter 1973; Burt 1992) in facilitating information and influence flows. To argue that closure or density is a requirement for social capital is to deny the significance of bridges, structural holes, or weaker ties. The root of preferring a dense or closed network lies, rather, in certain outcomes of interest (Lin 1992a; Lin 1986; Lin 1990). For *preserving or maintaining resources* (i.e., expressive actions), denser networks may have a relative advantage. Thus, for the privileged class, it would be better to have a closed network so that the resources can be preserved and reproduced (e.g., Bourdieu 1986); or for a mother to move to a cohesive community so that her children's security and safety can be assured (Coleman 1990). On the other hand, for *searching and obtaining resources* not presently possessed (i.e., instrumental actions), such as looking for a job or better job (e.g., Lin; Marsden; Flap; Burt), accessing and extending bridges in the network should be more useful. Rather than making the assertion that closed or open networks are required, it would be theoretically more viable to (I) conceptualize for what outcomes and under what conditions a denser or more sparse network might generate a better return, and (2) postulate deduced hypotheses (e.g., a denser network would be more likely to promote the sharing of resources which, in turn, maintain group or individual resources; or, an open network would be more likely to access advantaged positions and resources, which in turn enhance the opportunity to obtain additional resources) for empirical examination.

A third controversy that requires clarification is Coleman's statement that social capital is any "social-structural resource" that generates returns for an individual in a specific action. He remarks that "social capital is defined by its function" and "it is not a single entity, but a variety of different entities having two characteristics: They all consist of some aspect of a social structure, and they facilitate certain actions of individuals who are within the structure" (1990, p. 302). This "functional" view may implicate a tautology: social capital is identified when and if it works; the potential causal explanation of social capital can only be captured by its effect, or whether it is an investment depends on the return for a specific individual in a specific action. Thus, the cause factor is defined by the effect factor. Clearly, it would be impossible to build a theory where causal and effectual factors are folded into a singular function. This is not to deny that a functional relationship may be hypothesized (e.g., resources embedded in social networks enhance obtaining better jobs). But the two concepts must be treated as separate entities with independent measurements (e.g., social capital is the investment in social relations and better jobs are represented by occupational status or supervisory position). It would be incorrect to allow the outcome variables to dictate the specification of the causal variable (e.g., for actor X, kin ties are social capital because these ties channel X to get a better job, and for actor Y, kin ties are not social capital because these ties do not channel Y to get a better job). The hypothesized causal relationship may be conditioned by other factors (e.g., family characteristics may affect differential opportunities for building human and social capital) which need be specified in a more elaborate theory. A theory would lose parsimony quickly if the conditional factors become part of the definitions of the primary concepts. In fact, one would question whether it remains a theory if it is required to make a good prediction for every individual case and individual situation.

Perhaps related to this view of social capital as indistinguishable from its outcome—and perhaps given his view that social capital, as collective good, can also be seen in many different forms such as trust, norms, sanctions, authority, etc.—Coleman questions "whether social capital will come to be as useful a quantitative concept in social science as are the concepts of financial capital, physical capital, and human capital remains to be seen; its current value lies primarily in its usefulness for qualitative analyses of social systems and for those quantitative analyses that employ qualitative indicators" (1990, pp. 304—305).

Again, the confusion can be seen as resulting from extending the notion of social capital beyond its theoretical roots in social relations and social networks and the unattainable theoretical position that prediction holds for every individual case. Once these issues are resolved, social capital should and must be measurable.

Conceptualizing and measuring social capital

These debates and clarifications lead to the suggestion that social capital, as a concept, is rooted in social networks and social relations, and must be measured relative to its root. Therefore, social capital can be defined as *resources embedded in a social structure which are accessed and/or mobilized in purposive actions*. By this definition, the notion of social capital contains three ingredients: resources embedded in a social structure; accessibility to such social resources by individuals; and use or mobilization of such social resources by individuals in purposive actions. Thus conceived, social capital contains three elements intersecting structure and action: the structural (embeddedness), opportunity (accessibility) and action-oriented (use) aspects.

These elements have been mentioned by most scholars working on social capital. The social resources theory (Lin 1982) has specifically proposed that access to and use of social resources (resources embedded in social networks) can lead to better socioeconomic statuses. Further, the theory proposes that access to and use of social resources are in part determined by positions in the hierarchical structure (the strength of position proposition) and by the use of weaker ties (the strength of tie proposition). Bourdieu defines the volume of social capital as a function of the size of the network and the volume of capital (economic, cultural and symbolic) possessed by networked individuals. Burt (1992) postulates that certain network positions (structural holes and structural constraints) have effects on individuals getting better positions or rewards in organizations. Flap (1995) defines social capital as a combination of network size, the relationship strength, and the resources possessed by those in the network. Portes (1998) also advocates focusing on social relations and networks in the analysis of social capital.

Embedded resources and network locations

Given the significance of resources and relations in social capital, it is not surprising that scholarly research has shown differential focus on one of the two elements. Some have chosen to focus on the locations of individuals in a network as the key to social capital. Burt's work (1990) typifies this approach. By identifying the locations of individual nodes, it is possible to assess how close or how far the node is from a strategic location, such as a bridge, where the occupant has the competitive advantage in possible access to more, diverse, and valued information. Strength of ties (Granovetter 1973, 1974) is also a well-known conceptually argued network location measurement of a bridge's usefulness. Other location measures are readily available in the literature, such as density, size, closeness, betweenness, and eigenvector (see review of such location measures in Borgatti, Jones and Everett (1998). Implicit or explicit in this approach is the argument that network location is the key element of identifying social capital.

Another approach focuses on the embedded resources. In social resource theory, valued resources in most societies are represented by wealth, power and status (Lin 1982). Thus, social capital is analyzed by the amount or variety of such characteristics of others with whom an individual has direct or indirect ties. Measurement of social resources can be further specified as network resources and contact resources. Network resources refer to resources embedded in one's ego-networks, whereas contact resources refer to resources embedded in contacts used as helpers in an instrumental action, such as job searches. Thus, network resources represent accessible resources and contact resources represent mobilized resources in instrumental actions. For contact resources, the measurement is straightforward—the contact's wealth, power and/or status characteristics, typically reflected in the contact's occupation, authority position, industrial sector, or income.

There is little dispute that embedded resources are valid measures for social capital. There is some debate as to whether network locations are measures of social capital or precursors to social capital. My own view is that if it is assumed that social capital attempts to capture valued resources in social relations, network locations should facilitate, but not necessarily determine, access to better embedded resources. What types of network locations evoke resources in order to generate returns depend on the type of returns one expects. In the Modeling Section below, I will argue that two types of outcomes are possible as returns to social capital: instrumental and expressive. In instrumental actions, the return is the gaining of added resources, resources not presently possessed by ego—whereas in expressive actions, the return is the maintaining of possessed resources. For example, if we assume that bridges link to different information, the utility of that information depends on whether it concerns resources valued by the individual but not yet attained. If it does not, then the bridge serves little utility. If it does, the bridge is very useful. That is, not all bridges (or network locations) lead to better information, influence, social credentials or reinforcement. A bridge linking an individual looking for a job in a corporation to people occupying influential positions in large corporations will likely be of significantly more utility to that individual than from a bridge that leads to others who are members of a health club. On the other hand, a mother with young children would prefer to live in a dense, cohesive community rather than one with a mobile population and open access to the external world. Likewise, a person facing personal stresses such as divorce might benefit from access to and interaction with others who have had similar stress and understand its psychological effects, rather than someone who is happily married. These are expressive actions and we should expect the benefit of a dense network and homogenous partners.

These considerations would suggest that network locations should be treated as exogenous variables rather than endogenous variables of social capital itself. I will return to this topic in the Modeling section. Suffice it to conclude here that social capital is more than mere social relations and networks; it evokes the resources embedded and accessed. Nevertheless, such embedded resources cannot possibly be captured without identifying network characteristics and relations. Network locations are necessary conditions of embedded resources. In a given study, it is advisable to incorporate measures for both network locations and embedded resources.

Measuring social capital as assets in networks

Paralleling these two conceptual elements of social capital have been two principal approaches in measuring social capital as assets captured by individuals in social networks, as depicted in Table 3.

Focus	Measurements	Indicators
Embedded resources	Network resources	Range of resources, best resources, variety of resourses, composition (average resources), contact resources
	Contact statuses	Contacts' occupation, authority, sector
Network locations	Bridge to access to bridge	Structural hole, structural constraint
	Strength of tie	Network bridge, or intimacy, intensity, interaction & reciprocity

Table 3. Social capital as assets in networks

The first approach is to measure embedded resources. In this approach, resources embedded in the social networks are seen as social capital's core element. Thus, measurements focus on the valued resources (e.g., wealth, power, and status) of others accessed by individuals in their networks and ties. Such measurements can be made relative to two frameworks: (1) network resources and (2) contact resources. Network resources tap resources represented in the network an individual has access to. Typically, they include (1) the range of resources among ties (or the "distance" between the highest and lowest valued resources), (2) the best possible resources in the networks or among ties (or upper "reachability" in the resource hierarchy), (3) variety or heterogeneity of resources in the networks, and (4) composition of resources (average or typical resources). Research evidence is that these measures are highly correlated and tend to form a single factor, with the highest loading usually on the range of upper-reachability measures. Contact resources indicate the valued resources represented by contacts or helpers in specific actions. These measures, usually the valued resources (wealth, power, and status) of the contact(s), are applied in the context of specific actions, such as job searches. There is consistent and strong evidence that both network resources and contact resources positively affect the outcome of instrumental actions, such as job search and job advances (Lin 1999).

Another prevailing measurement strategy focuses on network locations as measurements of social capital. A major perspective is the argument that bridges or access to bridges facilitates returns in actions. Granovetter's notion of bridges as expressed in the strength of weak ties (1973) was a preview of this argument, which is elaborated and formalized by Burt in his notions of structural holes and constraints (1992). Other measures of bridges (e.g., betweenness) would also be candidates for social capital, even though they are used less in the social capital context.

There are many other measures such as size, density, cohesion, and closeness of social networks which are candidates as measures for social capital. However, research evidence is much less clear as to their viability in a social capital theory. Unless clear theoretical arguments are presented along with the use of any specific measures, as both measures of social resources and network locations have been, it would be ill-advised to simply use any network measure as an indicator of social capital.

Sampling techniques

Three sampling techniques have been employed to construct measures of social capital, as can be seen in Table 4. The saturation sampling technique is useful when it is possible to map a definable social network. In such networks, data from all nodes are gathered and their relationships identified, and measurements of network locations can be developed. The advantage of this technique is that it allows detailed and complete analyses of each and every network location as well as embedded resources in each node. Because of the requirement that the network has a defined and manageable boundary, it is a technique most useful for studies of social capital within an organization or a small network among organizations.

Technique	Advantages	Disadvantages
Saturation survey	Complete mapping of network	Limited to small networks
Name generator	Customized content areas Ego-centered network mapping	Lack of sampling frame Biased toward strong ties
Position generator	Content-free Sampling of hierarchical positions Multiple "resources" mapped Direct and indirect accesses	Lack of specificity of relations

Table 4. Measurement techniques

For larger and less definable networks, ego-network sampling techniques are used. Typically, the name-generator technique (Laumann 1966; Wellman 1979; McCallister & Fischer 1978; Burt 1984; Marsden 1987) is employed. This measurement technique elicits a list of ties from ego, and the relationships between them as well as among them are identified. From these data, locations of ego as well as these ties, relative to one another, can be computed. Network resources can also be obtained from the name-generator technique. Measures such as composition (typical resource characteristics), heterogeneity (diversity of resources), and upper reachability (best possible resources) can be computed. The advantages of this approach include (1) the identification of specific content areas, relative to actions under investigations, as naming items, and (2) the mapping of ego-network locations and characteristics as well as social resources embedded in the ego-network. The disadvantages include: (1) the lack of frames for sampling naming items, and (2) bias toward the inclusion of stronger ties.

The position-generator technique, a more recently developed technique (Lin and Durnin 1986), samples positions in a given hierarchy representative of resources valued in the collective (e.g., occupational status or prestige, authority positions, sectors, etc.). In this technique, a sample of positions with identified valued resources (occupational statuses, authority positions, industrial sectors, etc.) is used and the respondent is asked to indicate if she/he knows anyone having that job or position. From the responses, it then becomes possible to construct network resource indexes such as composition, heterogeneity, and upper reachability.

This technique has several advantages: (1) it can be based on a representative sample of positions meaningful in a given society, (2) it can directly or indirectly identify linkages to such resource positions, and (3) it can be based on multiple resource criteria (e.g., occupation, authority, and industry). Studies in North America (Erickson 1996), as well as Europe (e.g., Flap and Boxman in the Netherlands; Boxman, DeGraaf & Flap 1991; Volker and Flap in East Germany; Volker and Flap 1996; Argelusz and Tardos in Hungary; Angelusz & Tardos 1991; Tardos 1996) and Asia (e.g., Lin, Hsung and Fu in Taiwan; Lin, Fu & Hsung 1998) have proven the utility of this theoretically derived methodology in the context of social capital and instrumental action. It seems particularly useful if the valued resources are considered the core element of social capital. A sample of the position-generator instrument is presented in Table 5.

Here is a list of jobs (show card). Would you please tell me if you happen to know someone (on a first-name basis) having each job?								
Job	1. Do you know anyone having this job?*	2. How long have you known this person? (# of years)	3. What is your relationship with this person?	4. How close are you with this person?	5. His/ her gender.	6. His/ her job.	7. Dou you think you may find such a person through someone you know (Person M)	8. Repeat #2-6 for Person M
Job A								
Job B								
Job C								
etc.								

*If you know more than one person, think of the one person whom you have known the longest (or the person who comes to mind first)

Table 5. Position generator for measuring accessed social capital: An example

Modeling social capital

To explicitly operationalize the critical elements, we may sharpen the definition of social capital as *investment in social relations by individuals through which they gain access to embedded resources to enhance expected returns of instrumental or expressive actions*. From this, three processes can be identified for modeling: (1) investment in social capital, (2) access to and mobilization of social capital, and (3) returns of social capital. While the above discussion clarifies social capital's definition, elements, and measurements, it is necessary to discuss briefly the types of outcomes which can be considered as expected returns. I propose two major types of outcomes: (1) returns to instrumental action, and (2) return to expressive action (Lin 1992a; Lin 1986; Lin 1990). Instrumental action is taken to obtain resources not possessed by the actor, whereas expressive action is taken to maintain resources already possessed by the actor.

For instrumental action, we may identify three possible returns: economic return, political return, and social return. Each return can be seen as added capital. Economic return is straightforward. Political return is similarly straightforward, represented by hierarchical positions in a collective. Social gain needs some clarification. I have argued that reputation is an indication of social gain. Reputation can be defined as favorable/unfavorable opinions about an individual in a social network. A critical issue in social exchange where social capital is transacted is that the transaction may be asymmetric: a favor is given by the alter to ego. The ego's action is facilitated, but what is the gain for the alter, the giver of the favor? Unlike economic exchange, where reciprocal and symmetric transactions are expected in the short or long term, social exchange may not entail such expectation. What is expected is that the ego and the alter both acknowledge the asymmetric transactions which create the former's social debt to the latter, who accrued social credit. Social debt must be publicly acknowledged in public for the ego to maintain his/her relationship with the alter. Public recognition in the network spreads the reputation of the alter. The greater the debt, the larger the network, and the stronger the need for the ego and the alter to maintain the relationship, the greater the propensity to spread the word in the network and, thus, the greater the reputation gained by the alter. In this process, the alter is gratified by the reputation, which, along with material resources (such as wealth) and hierarchical positions (such as power) constitutes one of the three returns fundamental in instrumental actions. I have discussed this issue elsewhere (Lin, 1998).

For expressive action, social capital is a means to consolidate resources and to defend against possible resource losses (Lin 1986; Lin 1990). The principle is to access and mobilize others who share interest and control of similar resources so that embedded resources can be pooled and shared in order to preserve and protect existing resources. In this process, alters are willing to share their resources with ego because the preservation of the ego and its resources enhances and reinforces the legitimacy of alters' claim to like resources. Three types of return may be specified: physical health, mental health, and life satisfaction. Physical health involves maintenance of physical functional competence and freedom from diseases and injuries. Mental health reflects capability to withstand stresses and maintenance of cognitive and emotional balance. Life satisfaction indicates optimism and satisfaction with various life domains such as family, marriage, work, and community and neighborhood environments.

Oftentimes, returns to instrumental actions and expressive actions reinforce each other. Physical health offers the capacity to handle the enduring work load and responsibility needed to attain economic, political, and social statuses. Likewise, economic, political or social statuses often offer resources to maintain physical health (exercises, diet, and health maintenance). Mental health and life satisfaction are likewise expected to have reciprocal effects with economic, political and social gains. However, factors leading to the instrumental and expressive returns are expected to show differential patterns. As mentioned earlier, it may well be that open networks and relations are more likely to enable access to and use of bridges to reach to resources lacking in one's social circle and to enhance one's chances of gaining resources/instrumental returns. On the other hand, a denser network with more intimate and reciprocal relations among members may increase the likelihood of mobilizing others with shared interests and resources to defend and protect existing resources/expressive returns. Further, exogenous factors such as community and institutional arrangements and prescriptive versus competitive incentives may differentially contribute to the density and openness of networks and relations and the success of instrumental or expressive actions.

Having discussed the core elements of social capital, clarified some of the measurement and sampling issues, identified the types of returns, and briefly postulated differential patterns of causal effects, I would like to propose a model as an initial step of theorizing social capital. As can be seen in Figure 1, the model contains three blocks of variables in causal sequences (see bottom of figure). One block represents pre-conditions and precursors of social capital: the factors in the social structure and each individual's position in the social structure which facilitate or constrain the investment of social capital. Another block represents social capital elements, and a third block represents possible returns for social capital.

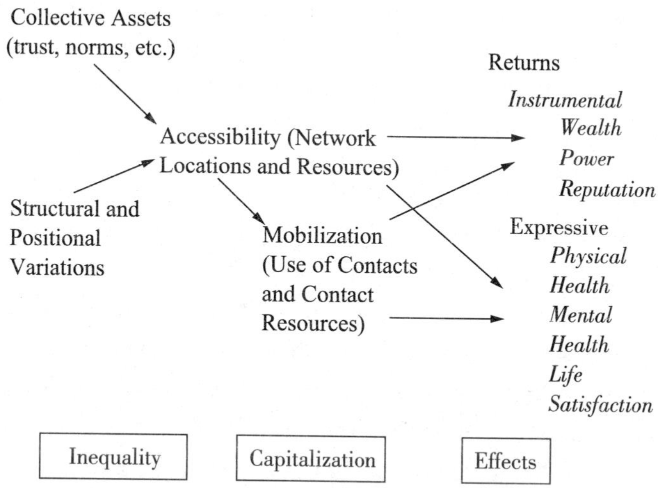

Figure 1. Modeling a theory of social capital

The process leading from the first block to the second block describes the formation of inequality of social capital: what structural elements and positional elements in the structure affect opportunities to construct and maintain social capital. It delineates patterns of differential distributions for social resources that are embedded, accessed, or mobilized. It should further demonstrate that there are social forces that determine such differential distributions. Thus, it is incumbent on a theory of social capital to delineate the patterns and determinants of the three ingredients of social capital or the *inequality of social capital* as collective assets, accessible social resources, and mobilized social resources. Two types of causation forces are of special interest to scholars in the analysis of inequality of social capital: structural and positional variations. A structure may be characterized in many variations, such as diversity in culture and ideology, level of industrialization and technology, level of education, extent of physical and natural resources, economic productivity, etc. Within a structure, individuals may be described as occupying different positions in social, cultural, political, and economic strata. These variations may be hypothesized to affect the richness or poorness of various social ingredients.

Within the second block, there is a process linking two elements of social capital:

access to social capital and use of social capital. The process linking the two elements represents the process of social capital mobilization. That is: given the unequal distributions of social capital how would an individual be enabled or disabled to mobilize such capital for specific actions? This is where the model, while recognizing structural contributions to social capital, as captured in the inequality process, also emphasizes possible choice action in mobilization.

Third, the theory needs to demonstrate that the three ingredients are inter-connected. Thus, it needs to propose a causal sequence in which embedded resources constrain and enable individual choices and actions. The general expectation is that the better the accessible embedded resources, the better embedded resources can and will be mobilized in purposive actions by an individual. The more intriguing question is why given the same level of accessible embedded resources, some individuals mobilize better resources than others in actions. One contingency may be the network location. One could hypothesize that being a bridge or being closer to a bridge might make a difference: those at or near these locations are better able to mobilize embedded resources. Also, the cognitive recognition that there is a structural advantage of using better embedded resources may make a difference.

Finally, the process linking the second block (social capital) and the third block (outcomes) represents the process where social capital produces returns or yields. Here, the theory should demonstrate how social capital is capital, or how it generates return or gain. That is, it should propose how one or more of the elements of social capital directly or indirectly impact an individual's economic, political and social capital (resources) or her/his physical, mental and life well-beings.

These conceptualizations, as individual components and processes, are not new. Research on the social resources theory (Lin 1999) has verified the proposition that social resources or social capital enhances an individual's attained statuses such as occupational status, authority, and placement in certain industries. Through these attained positions, social capital enhances economic earnings as well. These relationships hold up after family background and education are taken into account. Burt (1997, 1998) and others (Podolny & Baron 1997) have shown that advances and economic rewards are also enhanced in organizations for individuals at strategic locations in the informal networks. For those closer to structural holes or bridges, and, thus, less structural constraints, they seem to gain better returns, presumably because such locations give these individuals better opportunities to access certain capital in the organization. Research is progressing on how organizations use social capital in recruiting and retaining individuals. Fernandez and associates (Fernandez & Weinberg 1997) have shown that referrals increase applications, recruit better qualified candidates, and reduce costs in the screening process.

In Putnam's studies (1993; 1995a; 1995b), this is indicated by participation in civic associations (e.g., churches, PTAs, Red Cross) and social groups (bowling leagues). Coleman (1990) provides examples of diffusion of information and mobilization through social circles among radical Korean students (i.e., network as capital), a mother moving from Detroit to Jerusalem in order to have her child walk to playground or school safely (norm as capital); and diamond traders in New York making trades through informal ties and informal agreements (network and trust as capital). Partes (1998) also specified "consummatory" and instrumental consequences of social capital (see Partes and Sensenbrenner 1993 for the consummatory consequences—solidarity and reciprocal support—of social capital for immigrant groups). The primary focus here is on the development, maintenance, or decline of collective assets.

At the meso-network level, the focus is shifted to how individuals have differential access to resources embedded in the collective. The question posed is, in a given collective, why certain individuals have better access to embedded resources than others. The nature of social networks and social ties becomes the focus of analysis. Granovetter (1973; 1974; 1982; 1985; 1995) proposes that bridges, as usually reflected in weaker ties, provide better access to information. Burt (1992; 1997; 1998) sees that strategic locations in the networks, structural holes or structural constraints, imply better or worse access to information, influence, or control. Lin (1982; 1990; 1994a; 1995; 1999) has suggested that hierarchical positions as well as network locations facilitate or hinder access to embedded resources. Embedded resources are indicated by the wealth, status, and power of social ties.

At the micro-action level, social capital is reflected in the actual linkage between the use of embedded resources in instrumental actions. For example, there is substantial literature on how informal sources and their resources (contact resources) are mobilized in job searches and their effects on attained socioeconomic statuses (Lin, Ensel & Vaughn 1981; DeGraaf & Flap 1988; Marsden & Hurlbert 1988).

Research has also been extensive in the area of expressive actions' returns. Much is known about the indirect effects of networks on mental health and life satisfaction (Lin 1986; House, et al 1988; Berkman & Syme 1979; Berkman 1984; Hall & Wellman 1985; Wellman 1981; Kadushin 1983). That is, network locations enhance the likelihood of accessing social support which, in turn, improves one's physical or mental well-being.

Cybernetworks: The rise of social capital

The final section will be devoted to a discussion of the phenomenon I call cybernetworks, defined as social networks in cyberspace. In 1997, US consumers bought more computers than automobiles, according to Steven Landefeld, director of the Bureau of Economic Analysis (*USA Today*, March 17, 1999). Worldwide PC sales will overtake television sales in 2000, according to Paul Otellini of the Intel Architecture Business Group (Intel Developer Forum, February 25, 1999). In fact, PC sales already outnumbered sales of TV sets in 1998 in Australia, Canada, Denmark, and Korea. In 1999, 50 percent of US households will have computers and 33 percent will be online (Bob Metcalfe, *Info World*, January 18, 1999, p. 90, quoting International Data Corp.)

E-commerce has become big business. In 1998 online shopping registered at $13 billion (with an average order amount of $55) and it is projected to reach $30 to $40 billion in 1999 (the Boston Consulting Group, as quoted in *PC Magazine* March 9, 1999, p. 9). Greatest growth is expected in travel (88% in 1999 over 1998), PC hardware (46%), books (75%), groceries (137%), music (108%), and videos (109%) (Jupiter Communication, as quoted in *PC Magazine*, March 9, 1999, p. 10). It has been estimated that 24 million US adults plan to buy gifts online in 1999, or almost quadruple the 7.8 million who said they bought gifts online in 1998; online holiday shopping alone in 1999 could exceed $13 billion (International Communications Research, as quoted in *PC Week*, March 1, 1999, p. 6). During 1999, Internet commerce, which is growing 30 times faster than most world economies, will reach $68 billion (Bob Metcalfe, *Info World*, January 18, 1999, p. 90, quoting International Data Corp.). By year 2002, the projection is that online shopping will account for $32 billion for convenience items such as books and flowers, $56 billion for researched purchases like travel and computers, and $19 billion for replenishment goods such as groceries (Forrester Research Inc., as quoted in *PC Week*, January 4, 1999, p. 25). Another projection suggests that 40 percent of Web users will be online buyers by 2002, resulting in $400 billion of e-commerce transactions (International Data

Corporation, as quoted in *ZDNet Radar*, Jesse Berst, "Technology of Tomorrow", January 6, 1999). In the first half of 1998, one out of every five retail stock trades occurred online. There are now an estimated 4.3 million people shopping for stocks and funds online, and online trading is expected to reach 31 percent of the total US investment market by 2003 (Piper Jaffray, March 1999 *PC Computing*, p. 14).

On March 16, 1999, the US Commerce Department scrapped a 60-year-old industry classification system which had little relevance to an information-based economy (*USA Today*, March 17, 1999). For example, computers were not even an industry category; they were grouped with adding machines. Thus, a new system was installed which better reflected categories brought about by the information revolution. The system is also designed to be similar to those in Mexico and Canada as trade with those countries continues to grow (*USA Today*, March 17, 1999). Further, the US Commerce Department will begin publishing figures that show the impact of online shopping on retail activity, a key indicator of the nation's economic health. Until now the Department has lumped online shopping figures together with catalogue sales in its overall retail sales numbers. New figures that break out Internet sales as a separate entity will be available by the middle of 2000 for 1998 and 1999 (*Info World*, February 15, 1999, p. 71).

The growth of the Internet in the past few years has been nothing short of phenomenal. In 1995, 14.1 million of 32 million US households had modems and in January 1999, 37.7 million of 50 million US households had modems (*USA Today*, March 17, 1999, p. 9D). Worldwide, there were 68.7 million web users in 1997, 97.3 million in 1998, and the projection is that the number of web users will grow at a compound annual growth rate of26 percent, reaching 227 million by 2001 (IDC, as quoted in *PC Magazine*, February 9, 1999, p. 10). During 1999, the number of Internet users will surge by 28 percent to 147 million. Two-thirds of the people who will be online by 2002 are not online in early 1999 (Bob Metcalfe, *Info World*, January 18, 1999, p. 90, quoting International Data Corp.). At the end of 1997, only about 4,000 hotel rooms around the world offered Internet access, but the prediction is that by 2002 about four million hotel rooms in the United States alone will be online (Jupiter Communications, quoted in *PC Computing*, February, 1999, p. 14). Currently, over 90 percent of hotel Internet users used the accesses for e-mail, 60 percent for Web surfing, 50 percent for directions and maps, and close to 40 percent for faxing. Although business travelers are most likely to take advantage of this service, about 32 percent of these hotel guests surf the Web for entertainment purposes.

More than 45 million PC's in the US accessed the Internet regularly in early 1998, a 43 percent increase in the first quarter of 1998 versus the first quarter of 1997. Nearly 49 percent of all US households had at least one personal computer (ZD Market Intelligence, January, 1999). This year, for the first time, most users—51 percent—will live outside the United States (Bob Metcalfe, *Info World*, January 18, 1999, p. 90, quoting International Data Corp.) The number of Internet users in China surged to 1.5 million in 1998, from 600,000 in 1997 (Xinhua News Agency, January 15, 1999). US Internet guru Nicholas Negroponte predicted in January 1999 that the number of Internet users in China will balloon to 10 million by the year 2000 (Reuters, January 15, 1999).

Female participation on the net has increased dramatically. In January 1996, only 18 percent of net users aged 18+ were females; by January 1999, fully 50 percent of the users were females (*USA Today*, March 17, 1999, p. 9D). By the end of the year, it is expected that women will become the majority of users on the Internet (Bob Metcalfe, *Info World*, January 18, 1999, p.90, quoting International Data Corp.). In 1997, more e-mail was sent than letters via the post office for the first time.

Personal computer experts have announced, without surprise to anyone, that the Internet is changing everything. Michael J.Miller, Editor-in-chief of *PC Magazine* wrote in February 1999 (*PC Magazine*, February 2, 1999, p. 4) that the Internet changes "the ways we communicate, get information, entertain ourselves, and run our businesses." In January 1999, Paul Somerson stated the same in *PC Computing*. It is practically impossible to get a credible estimate of how many discussion groups, forums, and clubs of multitude types have been formed and are continually being formed. What is the implication of cyberspace and cyber-network growth for the studies of social networks and social capital? The short answer is: incredible.

Take two important theoretical debates: the decline of social capital and the class-domination of globalization. The decline of social capital, a thesis based on enormous empirical work conducted by Putnam and others (Putnam, 1995a; Putnam, 1995b) is that social capital has been in the decline in the United States for the past three to four decades. As mentioned earlier, Putnam defined social capital, at least in the context of democratic societies, as civic engagements, or social relations that sustain and promote voluntary associations and groups. By examining many time-series data sets to trace the patterns of participation in relationally based associations and groups such as bowling leagues and PTAs, he concluded that for the past thirty to forty years, social capital has been on the decline in the United States.

There are a number of conceptual (tautological) and measurement (what associations are relational) flaws one can find in this research program. In view of the dramatic growth of cybernetworks, a fundamental question can be raised: do cyber-networks carry social capital? If so, there is strong evidence that the declining thesis is false. I suggest that indeed we are witnessing a revolutionary rise of social capital, as represented by cyber-networks. In fact, we are witnessing a new era where social capital will soon supersede personal capital in significance and effect.

Just as pertinent is the debate on whether globalization represents a reproduction of the world system where the core states continue to dominate and indeed "colonize" peripheral states by the incorporation of the latter into global economic systems dominated by the former (Sassen & Appiah 1998; Browne & Fishwick 1998; Brecher & Costello 1998). This argument is supported by evidence that international organizations, international corporations, and international economic forms, such as commodity chains, are dominated by the values, culture, and authority of dominant states' corporations or these states themselves. Yet, cyber-networks suggest the possibility of a bottom-up globalization process where entrepreneurships and group formations become viable without the dominance of any class of actors (Wellman 1998). Do cyber-networks suggest a neo-globalization process? I argue that, while not denying that the dominant states and actors remain actively interested in controlling the development of cyberspace, cyber-networks represent a new era of democratic and entrepreneur networks and relations where resources flow and are shared by a large number of participants with new rules and practices, many of which are devoid of colonial intent or capability.

With the increasing availability of inexpensive computers and ever-increasing web capabilities which transcend space and time, we are facing a new era of social networks in the form of global villages. Globalization is no longer necessarily a reproduction of the core-peripheral world system where the core states establish links and networks to the peripheral states for their continuing domination of information, resources, and surplus values. Instead, information is freer and more available to more individuals than ever before in human history. While access to computers and Internet remains distributed unequally and under varying dictatorial control, it is nevertheless clear that such constraints and control are waning fast as inexpensive computers and access to the Internet become available and at minimal cost, and technology leapfrogs the traditional authoritarian control of access to information and resources. There is strong evidence that an increasing number of individuals are engaged in this new form of social networks and social relations, and there is little doubt that a significant part of the activities involve the creation and use of social capital. Access to free sources of information, data, and other individuals create social capital at unprecedented pace and ever-extending networks. Networks are expansive and yet at the same time "intimate." Networking transcends time (connecting whenever one can and wants to) and space (accessing to sites around the globe directly or indirectly if direct access is denied). Rules and practices are being formulated as such networks are being built and constructed. Institutions—borrowed from past practices, deliberately deviating from past practices, or consensually arrived at by participants—are being created as such networks (e.g., villages) are being built.

There is little doubt that the hypothesis that social capital is declining can be refuted if one goes beyond the traditional interpersonal networks and analyzes the cyber-networks as they have emerged in the 1990s. Indeed, we are witnessing the beginning of a new era where social capital far outpaces personal capital in significance and effect. We need to compile basic data and information on the extent to which individuals are spending time and effort engaging others over cyber-networks, as compared to the use of time and effort for interpersonal communications, other leisure activities (TV watching, travel, eating out, movie- and theater-going), attending civic and local meetings, etc. We need to estimate the amount of useful information gathered through cyber-networks as compared to traditional media.

What kind of research agenda should we consider in view of the emerging cyber-networks in the coming millennium? I propose the following topics:

1. Emergence and development of cyber-networks and villages: the formation and development of social groups and social organizations (the villages). We need data on cyber-networks as global villages—how each village is being constructed and rules and practices routinized, especially (a) how each group and territory is defined or undefined (closure versus openness), (b). how membership is claimed, defined, or acknowledged (ie., residents and citizens); (c). how the members are composed (e.g., demographics: individuals, households, and clusters; age, gender, ethnicity, linguistics, socioeconomic assets); and (d) how resources are distributed

within a village and across villages: class and inequality among villages.

2. Organizations and patterns of networking: the development and implementation of networking and network locations. For example, it would be useful to study: (a) patterns of interactions and exchanges, (b) size, density, and heterogeneity of participants, and (c) network locations of various actors and their resources (see next topic).

3. Socio-economic characteristics of participants: the potential social capital. It would be necessary to explore what resources the various actors bring to bear. These resources, including social relations and networks, would possibly account for (a) unequal opportunities to network locations, and (b) unequal access to embedded resources in each village.

4. Globalization and localization: the formation and development of linkages across villages as social capital is extended beyond each group-village. These linkages further explore whether classes of villages are being formed. These structural and dynamic elements of networks further expand differential access to social capital. Important issues also include whether and how villages can develop and maintain domination-subordination relations and exchanges and what mechanisms would account for the functioning or not functioning of such relations (e.g., gender, age, ethnicity, and linguistic imperialism, technical skills and requirement, etc.), and the consequences of these relations on relative accessibility to social capital.

5. War and peace in the global village—or competition and coordination among villages. Inevitably there will be tensions, conflicts, violence, competition, and coordination issues among villages. How do villages claim "self-defense" or "self-interest" and invade other villages for resources? How do villages become imperial or colonial powers? How do villages defend themselves and form coalitions? Would a "united nations" emerge and under what rules and practices? Would such a global body be dominated by the core villages? Thus, cybernetworks serve as vehicles to examine society as it emerges in real time. They are also analyzed as counter-evidence to the proclaimed demise or decline of the global village and social capital.

6. Technology, commerce, and the global village. With the increasing

development of technology and the ever-presence of commercial interests, cyber-networks fuse socio-economic-technological elements in social relations and social capital. This new feature of mixed economic and social capital poses new questions regarding the access and use of social capital. As technology has already made it possible to actualize the "virtual" reality (e.g., audio-visual, 3-D, touch-sensitive) and to transcend time and space (wireless and inexpensive equipment, for example) such that love, passion, as well as hatred and murder are being "real-ized" and personalized—for example, Internet romances and murders have occurred (*Washington Post*, March 6, 1999, p. A2); decency and free speech are clashing (*Time*, February 15, 1999, p. 52); personal data and history are becoming increasingly public (*USA Today*, January 18, 1999, p.3B); Yugoslav sites used e-mails to engage "cyberwar" during the Kosovo conflict (*Wall Street Journal*, April 8, 1999). Is it possible that cyber-networks might break the dominance of elite classes and differential utility in social capital? Yet, technology requires resources and skills. While the globalization process is underway, there might be a trend for cyber-networks to exclude many under-developed societies and disadvantaged members of many societies. Thus, would these developments further unequalize the distribution of social capital? And under what conditions? Would these developments further segregate the world into the haves and the have-nots? Analyses must evaluate these questions relative to the different aspects of social capital (information, influence, social credentials, and reinforcement) and different outcomes (instrumental and expressive).

I suspect that the entire spectrum of the development and utility of all forms of capital can be examined on cyber-networks, which fundamentally is relations and embedded resources—a form of social capital. In short, then, much work is urgently needed to understand how cybernetworks build and segment social capital. The above-mentioned topics will provide some of the data for scholars to understand new institutions and cultures as they emerge and the interactions between human and social capital. Most importantly, I suggest that they will provide clues as to whether and how social capital may be outpacing personal capital in significance and effect, and civil society, instead of dying, may be becoming expansive and global.

Concluding remarks

Social networks scholarship has much to say and to do about the development and future of social capital. Without anchoring the concept in social networks and embedded resources, chances are that social capital would fade away as an intellectual enterprise for the ever-broadening and -confounding definitions and almost utopian expectations of its practical applications. With ever sharpening definitions and measurements, social network scholarship may have much to contribute to the sustained development of social capital as an intellectual enterprise. As cyber-networks emerge as a major source of social capital, a new era is dawning and providing opportunities as well as challenges for theoretical development and practical analysis—an era exciting and yet daunting for social networks scholars everywhere.

3

The Informational City is a Dual City: Can It Be Reversed? (1999)

Manuel Castells

Introduction

We are living through one of the most fundamental technological and social changes in history. The revolution in information technologies that took shape in the early 1970s, and diffused throughout the economy, society, and culture in the last quarter of the twentieth century, has profoundly transformed the way we live, work, produce, consume, communicate, travel, think, enjoy, make war and peace, give birth, and die. It has also transformed, as have all major technological revolutions, the material foundations of human life, time, and space (Castells 1996). Consequently, the combination of new information technologies and socioeconomic restructuring is reshaping cities and regions, ushering in new urban forms and processes that I identified as the "informational city" (Castells 1989). This multidimensional transformation is not technologically determined. Rather, it is the outcome of an interactive process between technology, economic strategies, social interests, cultural values, and power struggles. Thus, in principle, new social and spatial structures resulting from this multilayered process of change can be modified by social action, private strategies, and public policies. Prevailing trends, however, cloud what could be an exhilarating moment for humankind, opening up extraordinary possibilities for material prosperity and spiritual fulfillment, with the inducement of social exclusion in parallel to social development, deepening existing patterns of sociospatial segregation. These trends are rooted in powerful processes of economic globalization and capitalist restructuring that use to their advantage the potential of new information technologies, conditioning the social trajectory of technological change.

Thus, the emerging, informational city is by and large a dual city. By informational city, I understand an urban system with sociospatial structure and dynamics determined by a reliance of wealth, power, and culture, on knowledge and information processing in global networks, managed and organized through intensive use of information/communication technologies. By dual city, I understand an urban system socially and spatially polarized between high value-making groups and functions on the one hand and devalued social groups and downgraded spaces on the other hand. This polarization induces increasing integration of the social and spatial core of the urban system, at the same time that it fragments devalued spaces and groups, and threatens them with social irrelevance (Mollenkopf and Castells 1991; Castells 1992). I argue that the two processes, informationalization and dualization, are intertwined under the current social, political, and economic conditions in most of the world, certainly including American cities. New information technologies are not the cause of this association between informationalization and sociospatial exclusion. The roots of social exclusion are in the politics of capitalist restructuring that have prevailed in most societies since the 1980s. The power of new information technologies, however, enhances and deepens features present in the social structure and in power relationships. This is why we are at the crossroads of a new urban age. A real possibility exists of evolving toward systemic urban schizophrenia, that is, toward the dissolution of urban civilization in an undifferentiated exurban sprawl through telecommunicated/freeway-connected, discontinuous spaces, leaving behind "black holes" of poverty, dereliction, and ignorance, abandoned to their fate. Yet it does not have to be that way. The promise of information technology may lead to a different, more humane city, in the framework of a new, more intelligent, and more just society. This chapter examines both possibilities on the basis of available evidence and exploratory thinking.

Information technology and the space of flows

In various quarters of futurology, the diffusion of advanced information and communication technologies has prompted prophetic statements about the end of cities. In fact, a review of empirical evidence on the relationship between telecommunications and urban forms (Graham and Marvin 1996) shows a simultaneous process of concentration and decentralization of activities and population to be the prevailing pattern. Throughout the world, directional centers continue to be concentrated in a few selected nodes of major metropolitan areas precisely because telecommunications and information systems allow directional activities to reach out to the entire country, or to the entire world, from their concentrated locations, be it in the old cores or in the new peripheries of metropolitan areas. Research by Moss (1987), Daniels (1993), and Sassen (1991), among others, shows empirical evidence on the pattern of persistent concentration, and presents arguments for the spatial clustering of corporate centers and their ancillary networks of advanced services: the historical development of a supply base of firms, services, and labor, clustered around corporate centers; the symbolic marking of prestigious space; the face-to-face, secretive interaction required by decision makers at the top; the value of assets invested in prime real estate, precluding a collective flight from business centers that would collapse property values for everybody. Thus, in spite of functional congestion and social problems, most old metropolitan centers continue to thrive, starting with downtown New York, London, and Tokyo; and when new centers are constituted, for example in northern Atlanta or Irvine, they arise in clusters, not along scattered locations on the urban edge.

The geography of innovation, the decisive activity of the informational economy, also shows its spatial clustering in what Peter Hall and I have identified as "milieux of innovation" around the world (Castells and Hall 1994). Innovation may be spurred by synergistic interaction facilitated by territorial complexes of research, design, and production, such as Silicon Valley, Route 128, or Austin in the case of high technology. In Hollywood and San Francisco's South of Market, milieux and innovation arise in the fields of multimedia and computer graphics; on Wall Street in financial products; or in Manhattan or West Los Angeles in fashion design. From these milieux of innovation, telecommunicated information systems ensure the hierarchical diffusion of production, management, and distribution of new products and processes throughout the interconnected nodes of the global system.

The new industrial space reflects this kind of technological/spatial division of labor among centers of innovation, advanced manufacturing, assembly manufacturing, and customized production near the final markets in an asymmetrical set of functional interdependencies. Different locations are selected according to specific characteristics of labor and production inputs, required for each step of the manufacturing process. This changing *spatial* division of labor was first identified in the case of electronics manufacturing and it has been increasingly seen to characterize most industries, as information technology becomes prevalent in all lines of manufacturing, gradually eliminating the old distinction between high-tech and low-tech industries.

Ancillary business activities, such as banking, insurance, and professional services, also follow this "double pattern," concentrating back offices in new suburban centers while diffusing customer-oriented services, some of them automated, throughout the residential sprawl. Social services also concentrate and diffuse simultaneously. For instance, medical services are clustered around major hospitals, while primary care centers are neighborhood based. The higher the specialization, the higher the concentration in a few locations in the metropolitan area and, to the highest level, in the nation (e.g., the Mayo Clinic complex in Rochester, Minnesota). Residential location is increasingly dispersed in suburbs and exurban edges; yet social segregation by income, education, and race still clusters communities, forming a discontinuous space of internally homogeneous social units, both in the city and in the suburbs.

Thus, in all dimensions of the urban/suburban fabric, we observe the emergence of a new form of space: the space of flows, characterized by simultaneous concentration and decentralization of people and activities. Under the new technological conditions the key feature is the linkage of different spatial locations into a new spatial process that reintegrates the functional unity of different elements in distant locations through information technology. This new spatial logic is present in the location of advanced services centers, in the geography of innovation, in the territorial distribution of services, in the emergence of a new industrial space, and in the variable geometry of residential patterns in the megacities that will characterize third-millennium urbanization (Borja and Castells 1997).

The impact of the space of flows on a highly segregated urban structure deepens segregation and accentuates inequality as a result of several converging processes: (1) traditional manufacturing, based on low-skilled labor, declines in American cities, as it is either automated or relocated to cheaper production sites around the world; (2) large employers of middle- and low-skilled service workers move to the suburbs as back-office complexes escape real estate prices, environmental congestion, and social problems of the central city, following manufacturing's relocation to the suburbs forty years ago; (3) personal and social services also follow the residential sprawl of their users and consumers. Thus most central cities lose their functions and economic base, accelerating the urban decline that took place in the 1960s. But something else is happening. The few nodal functions still located in central cities, around Central Business Districts (CBDs) and high-quality urban spaces, can be bridged to their regional, national, and global hinterlands via telecommunications, fast transportation, and information systems, without needing to renovate their surrounding urban areas. Thus the central city's islands of prosperity and innovation can further isolate themselves from the city, while integrating into the archipelago of the space of flows and delinking themselves from their social and territorial environments. So the space of flows links up *valued* spaces at the same time that it separates and isolates *devalued* spaces in the inner city, and sometimes in the suburbs, where low-income communities, a significant proportion of ethnic minorities, rundown schools, dilapidated housing, the institutions of the urban welfare state, and the shop floors of the criminal economy remain trapped. Given that these spaces, these populations, and these institutions have a decreasing relevance for functions valuable to the central city's islands of prosperity and innovations, from the point of view of the system logic, there is a self-reinforcing process of spatial marginalization, social exclusion, and functional devaluation in these neglected places, which the information highways of the space of flows have bypassed. Under such conditions traditional patterns of urban segregation are deepened. Informationalization induces dualization and reinforces it in the structure and dynamics of space.

The transformation of work and employment

Along with the transformation of space, a major transformation of social structure is also under way, fundamentally rooted in the transformation of work and working arrangements. As in all periods of rapid technological change, the population-at-large has expressed considerable anxiety concerning prospects for employment. Formidable changes are under way, but not in the form of widespread unemployment as a result of the substitution of machines for labor (Carnoy and Castells 1996; Carnoy, Castells, and Benner 1996). Against the prophecies of uninformed doomsayers, America is not experiencing a job shortage. Between 1979 and 1994, 27 million new jobs were created, 60 percent of which were in the technical and professional occupations, thus significantly upgrading the skill profile of the overall occupational structure. From 1992 to 1996, over 10 million new jobs have been created, so that unemployment remains at about 5.5 percent, a low level by historical standards, in spite of the massive incorporation of women into the labor force in the last three decades. Most regular jobs, however, now require some higher level of education, and college education is becoming a requirement for any decently paying job. So, the mismatch between an embattled educational system and the skill requirements of the expanding sectors of the labor market is growing.

People's heightened anxiety concerning new patterns of employment has a different origin, however. On the one hand, it reflects the decline in real wages for full-time male workers, and more recently stagnant wages for women, in spite of the higher skills content of their jobs. On the other hand, it stems from increasing job insecurity and unpredictability, as the traditional model of a stable, full-time job in a large organization with a predictable career pattern fades away. Both aspects are linked: because jobs are no longer secure, and because labor contracts are increasingly individually negotiated, it follows that a downward spiral of wages and working conditions would result in spite of a higher average level of skills and steady job creation. Job instability and lowering of real wages are linked to major structural changes made possible by information technology: globalization of the economy and decentralization of manufacturing and services and transformation of firms' operations through networking and subcontracting. Under such conditions management has a number of options vis-a-vis labor: automate, relocate production, outsource part of the production, downsize, and network. Usually, a combination of all these strategies is pursued: a highly flexible system which is tantamount to the individualization of labor conditions and to the foreseeable end of collective bargaining, except in public services. Our studies on the United States (with Martin Carnoy and Chris Benner) provide evidence of the growing role of different forms of nonstandard, full-time labor: temporary workers, part-time, self-employment, subcontracting, consulting, networking. This desocialization of labor is happening at all levels of skills, not just at the low end. But unskilled workers are the most vulnerable under such new patterns of management/labor relations, and thus they are forced to accept lower wages, job insecurity, and fewer or no benefits. Ethnic minorities and youth are most frequently subject to the devaluation of their labor conditions. The use of information technologies, although not the cause of such labor practices, allows for its diffusion. On the one hand, this is because low- and medium-skilled labor can be automated if it becomes too expensive or too rigid for the requirements imposed by relentless, global competition. On the other hand, it is because the use of information technologies makes it possible to keep the coherence of the production process through a network of interaction among spatially distant units. As a result, a major polarization occurs between a core labor force, with high skills, and a mass of disposable labor that can be used or replaced or employed under different statuses, depending on the needs and requirements of the market. Each discontinuity in the work's trajectory could send into oblivion some workers who, by falling in one of the "black holes" of the new socioeconomic structure, will find it difficult to reinstate themselves in the pool of the fully employable. Thus, even though mass unemployment does not exist, there are growing segments of semi-employed, in and out of the labor market, creating a potential danger for some individuals, particularly among minority youth, to join the ranks of the criminal economy. Decreasing cultural skills forbid entry into the informational labor market that increasingly requires the ability of "symbol processing", in Reich's expression.

To these structural factors of the new labor markets, induced by the combination of informationalization and economic restructuring, we must add the crisis of the patriarchal family, and the weakening of the urban welfare state, currently under the assault of neoconservativism. Thus we observe the formation of a growing segment of urban poor that includes fallen workers, marginal youth, and impoverished families, usually headed by females. These social segments continue to concentrate in the devalued spaces constituted by the process of urban dualism. Given that the school system is spatially segregated, public schools in devalued spaces become mechanisms of reproduction of social devaluation, unable to provide the necessary skills for the informational labor market, and becoming instead training grounds for survival in a world of social irrelevance. Then, the criminal economy takes over these devalued spaces, providing the only alternative for many youths. The justice system (including prisons) links up these devalued spaces, providing the social networks and cultural glue, to develop an alternative form of survival, however precarious. Under such conditions, no telecommunications infrastructure or training programs can save people trapped in these "black holes" of the informational city, as Blakely, et al (1995) have argued in their pioneering study of "the information city and the ghetto" in Los Angeles. Is this self-reproducing process of sociospatial exclusion inevitable and irreversible? Are we creating an Athenian democracy of informational, creative elites while ignoring a derelict mass of slaves and barbarians?

Can the new urban informational dualism be reversed? Information technology with a human face

At first sight, the prospect of using the promise of information technology to improve the fate of low-income communities, thus reversing the current trend, appears rather bleak. This is because the informational economy does not have much use for an unskilled, uninformed population, and because the institutional fabric of low-income communities provides scarce opportunity to overcome the vicious cycle of poverty, functional illiteracy, occasional work, social/racial discrimination, and criminalization of misery (Susser 1997)· In addition, fashionable neoconservative thinking seems to be ready to give up on inner cities, dooming their dwellers with the dwellings. As George Gilder put it: "The problem with cities today is that they are parasites, and they will have to go off the dole" (1995).

Yet, as Lisa Servon and John Horrigan (1996) argue in their study on urban poverty and information technology in Austin, local governments in several American cities have recorded some successes in enhancing access of low-income communities to information technologies, and putting this access to the benefit of education, job training, and broadening of opportunities to break out of the ghetto, particularly for minority youth. A courageous policy of linking up technological change and social reform is not only possible, albeit difficult, but necessary, not only for moral reasons, but for pragmatic reasons as well. It cannot be seriously argued that a democratic society can live peacefully on the basis of the systemic exclusion of one-quarter to one-third of its people, even confining them spatially in implicit apartheid style. In what follows, I propose some strategic elements of the possible content of a policy using information technology as an additional tool for revitalizing poor communities. These proposals are simply illustrations that should be taken as only hints of what a more detailed, empirically grounded study/design could propose. The basic assumption is that the diffusion of technology is necessary but not at all sufficient to reverse informational inequality. Thus only 10 percent of African American households have personal computers, in contrast to 50 percent of white households. The real issue, however, is how and what to use these computers for.

In terms of strategic goals, in the new sociotechnological structure, the *key* to fighting self-reproducing marginality *is access both to jobs and to income generation*. For this, *education* is a must: general education, not narrow job training. It is increasingly unlikely that investment in the deprived communities will change their fate. Rather, it is the transformation of the residents of these communities, by finding jobs and earning income outside the community, that will change their character. It is important, however, that individual improvement does not translate into immediate residential mobility to the suburbs, leaving trapped behind the less fortunate. Poor communities must find ways to keep their best residents long enough so that the ripple effects of nonmarginal households will enhance the community by their very presence, bringing up the ladder the borderline households. For this, at the roots of *community improvement*, they have to get rid of the criminal economy, which thrives precisely on the deterioration of the community. Innovative urban design (defensible spaces, street life-oriented design, nonpastiche beautification of the neighborhood, etc.) and an active media policy by the community to fight negative images and project the real life of real people to the city at large can also enhance the community. These *efforts, geared toward jobs, education, and community*, require mobilization of social and political resources. At present, *local governments are the key actors in the process*, but they must rely both on citizen participation via community organizations and on the contribution from socially responsible corporate businesses, through *urban partnerships between business, citizens, and local/state governmental agencies*.

All this, however, is not new. It has been tried in many cities over the last three decades, and the positive outcome has been rather meager. Nonetheless, we must try again, this time using experience and knowledge to correct past mistakes (such as excessive reliance on a bureaucratic, urban welfare state), and perhaps marshaling the power of information technology to help innovative programs that, with the support of corporate business, could contribute to breaking the dualizing logic of the informational city. Six developmental policy initiatives could help cement the proposed interaction between information technology and urban social reform as we approach the twenty-first century.

The first initiative concerns the necessary spurring of *entrepreneurialism and small business* among low-income communities' residents as the most likely way to break through the structural discrimination of the labor market. Indeed, entrepreneurial immigrants are quickly becoming the driving economic force in many poor communities in New York and Los Angeles, thus following the classic, historical pattern of American cities. Online selling, advertising, and contacting over the Net could ease the difficulty of locating these start-up businesses in the invisible, dangerous areas of the city.

The second initiative refers to the expansion of telework not from home but from *community telecenters* set up jointly by governments and corporations, where workers could be employed on a flexible basis without having to commute, thus reducing costs and saving time. Furthermore, these community-based telecenters would keep jobs in the community, while not requiring physical investment by employers in communities that, at least for some time, might constitute hazardous locations.

Naturally, entrepreneurialism and teleworking require a substantial enhancement in the educational potential of residents in low-income communities, which requires reversing the declining quality of public schools and finding additional sources of learning specific to the characteristics of these residents. Thus the third initiative should be a focus of the corporate-public urban partnerships on revamping the quality of the public school system. With the cooperation of Parent-Teacher Associations, schools should be converted in the evening into community centers, open to the society at large, making them less vulnerable to gangs and more in touch with the community's real problems. Experimental programs of tele-education should be geared toward adult education, starting with computer literacy campaigns, followed (not preceded) by rental/donations of computer equipment. Youth could be recruited, and paid, to educate their families in using computers. University extension programs should go online, with subsidize fees for targeted areas, as part of the universities' contribution to the communities. Furthermore, information technology should be called to the rescue of children's education. It is well known that one of the key handicaps for poor children in their education is that their parents do not support them in doing their homework, not because of lack of interest, but because their parents lack education and cultural skills. It is in this way that cultural/social inequality reproduces itself. In some California schools teachers supervise and help their students with their homework online. This practice is often limited to predominantly middle-class schools; its real need, however, is among children of poor families. The building of these programs could start reversing the vicious cycle linking poor families and poor education that would continue in spite of improvement in the schools because of the unsupportive family environment for children's learning.

A fourth initiative can also be used to emphasize the potential of information technology for improving the educational chances of poor populations. It is well known that a significant proportion of poor males, particularly among ethnic minorities, spend considerable amounts of time in prison and in the justice system early in their lives. Indeed, to a large extent, prisons appear to be an extension of the community in many ghetto areas. They are often schools of specific criminal trades. To cut another vicious circle between poverty, racism, discrimination, an jails, *information technology could be used to educate and train the prison population,* to provide opportunities for teleworking and to interact with prospective employers while in prison, so that the link with education and jobs is not lost and, as so often happens, replaced by the link of the criminal economy. This strategy would involve the cooperation of the justice system, the educational system, and corporate sponsorship of experimental programs that could be generalized if successful. We must acknowledge the problem of mass imprisonment of the poor in the United States, and introduce mechanisms to reduce it gradually, starting with the nonreproduction of the criminal system through the institutions of punishment. Telecommunications offer the possibility of keeping the minds linked with, and open to, society, even while the bodies suffer incarceration.

Fifth, if we want to reform, not abandon, cities, community enhancement has to proceed in parallel to educational development and individual job opportunities. Two policy areas could be improved. The first area is *community-based media,* particularly cable television and local radio, that could induce social cohesiveness in the community while projecting its images to broader audiences. The advent of multimedia may help this symbolic interaction, as community-based media could become part of an interactive, electronic hypertext that would broaden the sources of information and images, as well as help citizens to value their own input in the media system. The second area is *urban design in and for poor communities*. The restoration of meaning and culture in communities that have been written off as public spaces for the city implies the search for a new monumentality, for the creation of urban art (e.g., the murals in Latino communities), and for the residents' self-recognition of their public space by being involved in environmental beautification projects. Here information technology is no more than a tool, but an important one, as computer design may considerably help facilitate citizens' participation in the design and redesign of their newly valued space.

None of these policies stands a chance of implementation without the sixth initiative, *revitalizing local governments*. As demonstrated in the 1996 Habitat II United Nations Conference, local governments worldwide are being decisive in improving urban living conditions. Paradoxical as it may seem, in a world dominated by global flows of wealth, information, and power, local governments are as limited in their power as national governments are nowadays, but much more flexible, adaptive, and representative of their constituencies (Castells 1997). When linking up with citizen groups and business partnerships, local governments, under the right political conditions, may become key public entrepreneurs, altering the conditions under which poor communities sink into oblivion. For this, however, they need information and connectivity to compensate for their lower political capacity and financial resources. Information technology provides the tools for local governments to manage in real time the complex interaction between citizens, decentralized public agencies, and business decisions, substituting initiative for bureaucracy through strategic planning and real-time management of multiple initiatives. Furthermore, local governments may network among themselves via shared data banks and online consultations, as is already the case of intermunicipal networks in Europe (Graham 1995). Flexible information systems provide the tools for informed bargaining with corporations and national governments in a resurrection of the vitality of the city-state that characterized the previous period of formation of a world economy in Renaissance Europe. Local governments aim at anchoring spaceless flows in specific places, reversing the structural logic of uncontrolled globalization, and negotiating on behalf of their citizens the conditions under which flows of information and wealth are distributed in local societies. Thus the current powerlessness of localities vis-a-vis the variable geometry of corporations may be reversed, as networks of local communities gradually take up the role of declining national governments in reestablishing social control over the conditions of economic development.

Conclusion: The politics of dreams

As in most prospective elaborations aimed at fighting the harsh realities stemming from structural trends, these initiatives may seem like dreams. I would not dispute this characterization, except to emphasize the extremely general, indicative character of my suggestions as I try to propose a style of policymaking rather than present a finished blueprint. I also want to remind the reader that many of these initiatives are being practiced in cities around the world. Yet the fundamental point to be made, following Gilder's cynical statement, is that to accept the current state of affairs is to give up cities. Thus either we accept the ruin of urban civilization, entrapping its last, unfortunate dwellers, and escape into a telecommunicated exurban sprawl, or we take up our courage, invent, calculate, think, fight, and work to turn the extraordinary opportunity of information technology into the promise of a more humane society, based not on social exclusion but on shared creativity. Yet, to do so, dreams have not just to be blueprinted but fought over, because the information age has not changed the reality that the power of technology still depends on the technology of power.

Note

Throughout this chapter, I refer often to my own publications. I do this to avoid repeating data and sources on the whole range of topics presented here that are covered in detail in these publications. Thus each reference to Castells must be considered as a generic reference to the bibliography and evidence provided in each of the books cited. Similarly, Graham and Marvin (1996), Blakely, et al (1995), Servon and Horrigan (1996), and Susser (1996) are useful bibliographic sources to the vast body of information that should be consulted when analyzing in depth the issues explored in this chapter.

4

Grassrooting the Space of Flows (1999)

Manuel Castells

Abstract

The "space of flows", the concept I advocated a decade ago, represents the material arrangements that allow for simultaneity of social practices without territorial contiguity. In this article, I refer to a series of dimensions of autonomous expression of social meaning in the space of flows, with emphasis on electronic spaces, but in interaction with the space of places. I argue that a new dynamics is operating, a dynamics of interpenetration of uniformity and autonomy, of domination and resistance, and of instrumentality and experience, within the space of flows. The geography of the new history will not be made of the separation between places and flows, but out of the interface between places and flows and between cultures and social interests, both in the space of flows and in the space of places.

Our historic time is defined fundamentally by the transformation of our geographic space. This is a key dimension of the multilayered social and technological transformation that ushers in the so-called "Information Age." Ten years ago. I proposed the concept of space of flows in order to understand such a spatial transformation. At that time, the aim was to acknowledge the reality and the significance of the transformation without yielding to the simplistic notions of futurologists announcing the death of distance and the end of cities.

Empirical evidence continues to show that new information and communication technologies fit into the pattern of flexible production and network organization—

permitting the simultaneous centralization and decentralization or activities and population settlements—because different locations can be reunited in their functioning and interaction by means or the new technological system. This system is created from telecommunications, computers, and fast reliable transportation systems, as well as dispatching centers, nodes, and hubs. Therefore, new communication technologies allow for the centralization or corporate activities in a given space, precisely because the can reach the whole world from the City of London and from Manhattan without losing the dense network or localized, ancillary firms as well as the opportunities for face-to-face interaction created by territorial agglomeration.

At the same time, back offices can decentralize into the suburbs, in newly developed metropolitan areas, or in some other country and be part of the same system·. New business centers can be created around the country and around the world that always follow the logic or clustering and decentralizing at the same type and of concentrating and networking, thus creating a selective world wide web of business services. The new industrial space is characterized also by its similar pattern of spatial dispersion of activities, concentration of innovation, and strategic decision-making—around what Peter Hall and I propose to label as "milieux of innovation", following the evidence gathered by a series of studies undertaken in the 1980s at Berkley by the Institute of Urban and Regional Development. The new media also have become built around the double process of globalization of capital and customization/networking of information and images that respond to the localization of markets and segmentation of audiences. In territorial terms, the age of information is not just the age of spatial dispersal, it is the age of generalized urbanization. In the next decade, it is likely that most people of the world will be living in the cities for the first time. Yet cities are, and will be, of very different kinds depending on cultures, institutions, histories, and economies, but they will continue to share a spatial logic that is specific to the Information Age. This logic is characterized by the combination of territorial sprawl and locational concentration. Thus, intrametropolitan, interregional and international networks connect with global networks in a structure of variable geometry that is enacted and modified by flows of information and electronic circuits and fast, information-based, transportation systems. In the last decade, studies by Peter Hall, Peter Daniels, AnnaLee Saxenian, Michael Batty, Jim Wheeler, Barry Wellman, Jeff Henderson, Roberto Camagni, Stephen Graham, Marvin Simon, Amy Glasmeier, and so many other scholars have substantiated, empirically the emergence of a new spatial structure. This structure is defined by articulated territorial concentration and decentralization in which the unit is the network. This particular model of spatial organization, which seems to be characteristic of the Information Age, is the model that I tried to conceptualize 10 years ago as the space of flows.

The space of flows

As I understand it, "space of flows" means that the material arrangements allow for simultaneity of social practices without territorial contiguity. It is not a purely electronic space nor what Batty has called a "cyberspace", although cyberspace is a component of the space of flows. First, it is made up of a technological infrastructure of information systems, telecommunications, and transportation lines. The capacity and characteristics of this infrastructure and the location of its elements determine the functions of the space of flows, and its relationship to other spatial forms and processes. The space of flows is also made of networks of interaction, and the goals and task of each network configurate a different space of flows. Thus, financial markets, high-technology manufacturing, business services, entertainment, media news, drug traffic, science and technology, fashion design, art, sports, or religion constitute a specific network with a specific technological system and various territorial profiles. So they all operate on the logic of the space of flows but they specify this logic.

Second, the space of flows is made up of nodes and hubs. These nodes and hubs structure the connections, and the key activities in a given locale or locales. For instance, Wall Street or Ginza are such nodes, as well as Cali and Tijuana in their specific trade, or Berkeley, Stanford, and MIT in computer sciences. Hubs are communication sites (e.g., airports, harbors, trains, or bus stations) that organize exchanges of all kinds, as they increasingly are interconnected and spatially related. However, what characterizes the new role of these hubs and nodes is that they are dependent on the network, that their logic depends on their place in the network, and that they are sites to process signals that do not originate from any specific place but from endless recurrent interactions in the network.

Third, the space of flows is also made of habitats for the social actors that operate the networks, be it residential spaces adjacent to the nodes, protected and secluded spaces of consumption, or global corridors of social segregation separating these corridors from the surrounding places around the globe (e.g., VIP lounges, the virtual office, computing on the run, standardized international hotels).

Fourth, the space of flows comprises electronic spaces such as websites, spaces of interaction, as well as spaces of one-directional communication, be it interactive or not, such as information systems. A growing proportion of activity is from the web and the visual design of websites, as well as the structure of an operation of their content is becoming a fundamental frame for decision making, information making, and communication.

Space of places

I have described the new spatial structure of the Information Age, the space of flows. But we really need to know that not all the space is organized around the space of flows. As was the case in the whole history of humankind, most people live, work, and construct their meaning around places. I define a place as the locale whose form, function, and meaning are self-contained within the boundaries of territorial contiguity. People tend to construct their life in reference to places, such as their home, neighborhood, city, region, or country. This is not to say that the local community is thriving. In fact, all over the world, research shows that there has been a process of individualization and atomization of place-based relationships. The loss of community is the founding theme of urban sociology, since the Chicago School. Yet you may have no community, but still refer to your place as your main source of experience. Social organization and political representation also are predominately place based. And cultural identity is often built on the basis of sharing historical experience in a given territory.

When analyzing spatial transformation in the Information Age and showing the emergence of a new spatial form (i.e., the space of flows), I emphasized the persistence of the space of places, as the most usual form of spatial existence for humankind. I also observed that, while most dominant activities were constructed around the space of flows, most experience and social interaction was and still is organized around places. When using the term "dominant activities", I am referring to (1) financial flows, (2) management of major corporations in services and manufacturing, (3) ancillary networks of firms for major corporations, and (4) media, entertainment, professional sports, science and technology, institutionalized religion, military power, and global criminal economy. Thus, I added that the constitution of the space of flows was in itself a form of domination, since the space of flows, even in its diversity, is interrelated and can escape the control of any locale, while the space of places is fragmented, localized, and thus increasingly powerless vis à vis the versatility of the space of flows. The only chance of resistance for localities is to refuse landing rights for overwhelming flows—only to see that they land in the locale nearby, therefore inducing the bypassing and marginalization of rebellious communities.

This was my analysis some time ago, which has been presented in various publications during the last decade. I still sustain most of this analysis, and I think it can be backed up empirically. However, an analysis of transformation of space in a given historical moment—that is, the moment of the dawn of the Information Age—should not be cast in stone as an iron rule of spatial development. Yes, there are two different forms of space, flows and places. Yes, the space of flows is historically new in its overwhelming prevalence because it can deploy its logic through a new technological medium. Yes, dominant activities in our society are organized around the logic of the space of flows, while most, and the most powerful forms of autonomous construction of meaning, and social and political resistance to the powers that be are being constructed, currently are around places. But, two major qualifications may be introduced:

(1) The space of flows includes some places. Indeed, the space of flows is not simply an electronic space. Electronic spaces—such as the internet or global communication media—are but one dimension, however important of the space of flows.

(2) Both electronic spaces, and the space of flows at large, are not organized exclusively around and by social/economic/cultural domination. Societies are not closed systems, they are always open processes, characterized by conflict. History, in fact, is a very tiresome experience. It never ends, against the claims of the neoliberal illusion. Wherever there is domination, there is resistance to domination. Wherever there is imposition of meaning, there are projects of construction of alternative meaning. And the realms of this resistance, and this autonomous meaning are ubiquitous. Which means, concretely, that while the space of flows has been produced by and around dominant activities and social groups, it can be penetrated by resistance, and diversified in its meaning. The grassroots of societies do not cease to exist in the Information Age. And after an initial moment of exclusion and confusion, people and values of all kinds are now penetrating and using the space of flows, the internet and beyond, in the same way that the Parisian Champs Elysees dreamed by Hausman to escape the populace of the rive gauche, have become, in the 1990s, the hang out place for the festive, and multiethnic young

lot of the Paris banlieues. While the space of flows remains the space in which dominant activities are spatially operated, it is experiencing at the same time, the growing influence and pressure of the grassroots, and the insertion of personal meaning by social actors, in a process that may alter the cultural and political dynamics of our societies and, ultimately, may alter the space of flows itself. So let me review the main dimensions of this grassrooting of the space of flows.

The space of flows and the grassroots

First, I will refer to a series of dimensions of autonomous expression of social meaning in the space of flows, with emphasis in electronic spaces, but in interaction with the space of places. First is personal interaction, people using the net for themselves and electronic mail as recuperating letter writing as a form of communication. And people are finding ways to be together with much more diversity and importance than has been the experience before in history: chat groups, multidimensional communication, cultural expressions of all kind, people building their websites. People build their fantasies, but they also experience their needs and exchange their information. They are inhabiting the space of flows and thus transforming it. Am I talking maybe about a small global elite? Well not so small, and not so elite.

A second dimension for autonomous expression is represented by purposive, horizontal communication, not just personal feelings of casual communication. Horizontal communication occurs among people and across countries, and establishes information systems that are alternative to the media. They are in fact doubling the media. There is, indeed, much gossip and irresponsible information. As you know, the news that triggered one of the latest scandals relating to President Clinton was first sent from the internet through a news bulletin, which is a one-man operation out of his home office in Los Angeles, while Newsweek was weighing the opportunity of the publication. There are people and institutions very concerned about the lack of control of information in the net. Everywhere, many governments are terrified of losing control of information, a fundamental source of power throughout history. They usually argue in terms of controlling child pornography. I think child pornography is terrible, but what happens in countries like France or Spain for instance is that it is perfectly legal to sell child pornography. It is not legal to produce the images nor to hire or kidnap the children to do it, but selling it is not a problem. But you cannot do it on the internet. Why? Because the Internet is a mass media, or so the statist argument goes. The fact is that horizontal communication in the Internet by bypassing both the media and governmental controls is becoming a most fundamental political issue, which ultimately reflects who we are collectively, as a society. And if some of us are enjoying child pornography, if we are this kind of monster, this appears reflected in the internet. The internet brings us face to face with the mirror of who we actually are. So I would rather work on ourselves rather than close down the net. The fight is against the self not against the net.

Third, there is a fast growth of networks of solidarity and cooperation in the internet, with people bringing together their resources, to live and to survive. To give an example, the senior net in the United States not only brings information (e.g., medical information to counter the monopoly of medical information by doctors) and resources together; it also develops solidarity ties between senior people, thus reinforcing the group to which all of us belong, or will belong, if we are lucky. Thus, at the time the welfare state, at least as constructed in the last half century, is being challenged economically and politically, people are reconstructing networks of solidarity and reflecting/debating about them at the same time.

The fourth dimension is social movements. The net is used increasingly by social movements, of all kinds, as their organizing ground and as their privileged means to break their isolation. The greatest example here and one that has become classic is the Zapatistas in Chiapas, Mexico. Without fully presenting the case, on which I have written in my latest book, let me remind you of some interesting facts on this social movement. Zapatistas organized solidarity groups around the world on the internet. And they very effectively used the internet to diffuse their information and to obtain interactive communication between their different solidarity groups. They also have used the internet in a protective way to fight repression when, in February 1995, there was a major military offensive that forced them to escape to the forest. They sent a message over the internet asking everybody to flood the White House with messages because at that point the White House had put our money into the Mexican bailout. A major crisis in Mexico would jeopardize the entire stability of the region, ultimately wasting United States taxpayers' money. So, in one day, over 30 thousand messages came to the White House. That does not mean that street demonstrations in front of the White House are not important, but you cannot organize them in 24 hours; and in this particular case, it was a matter of life and death in these 24 hours. This ability of the Zapatistas to work on the net does not come from Marcos as people would say, even if he was a communications professor or from the Indian communities. It came from women's groups in Mexico. In 1993, women's groups organized an internet network in Mexico to support women's solidarity funded by the Catholic church and organized instrumentally by the Institute of Global Communication in San Francisco, a group of progressive computer people out of Silicon Valley. The global communications institute and women's groups sent several people to Chiapas, where they organized an extension of the women's network that was called La Neta. La Neta is an interesting expression because, on the one hand, it is the Spanish feminine term for the net; but also in Mexican slang it means the truth. So this La Neta network branched out in Chiapas and trained a number of people in Chiapas that human rights groups were the ones who were able to link up with the Zapatistas and provide both the technological and knowledge support for their internet operations.

However, not only progressive movements are on the internet. Everybody is on the internet and our societies are on the internet. The internet has played a major role in the development of American militia groups. The internet is as real as life itself. Increasingly, global movements of solidarity, environmentalists, human rights, and women's groups are organized on the internet again on the basis of local/global connection. One of the greatest and latest examples in the United States was the Fall 1997 One Million Women March organized by two Black women in Philadelphia. There was practically no organization, no sponsorship, and yet a small group of women in Philadelphia went on the net and called a demonstration, obtaining an extraordinary level of support and mobilization. But going to a place, I think is the most interesting thing. The space of flows is not just being in the net. It is to organize in the net to be in Philadelphia on a given day—that is, using the net to control space.

Fifth, linkages are a development that we have to pay close attention to, increasing linkages between people and institutions in an interactive process. The creation of what some people call virtual cities are renewing local governments and citizen democracy. We have some relatively old experiments, such as in 1986, Santa Monica's PEN program allowing public debate between citizens—including debates on major issues such as homelessness in Santa Monica, with the homeless themselves being able to get into the debate. European cities are organizing participation in information systems. Graham and Aurigi have studied these experiments and say that they usually are one-directional information systems. So still it is not a full-fledged participatory democracy; it is more information than participation and democracy, but they are still evolving and changing.

And there is potential for much more. I am personally struck by the experience of Amsterdam's Digital City, an autonomous group originally supported by the municipality of Amsterdam. It is a private foundation that has organized a system of citizen participation and citizen interaction. You have to register to take part, anyone can visit the site, but to really participate and go into houses, you have to be registered. By 1998, they had 80,000 fully registered, participating "residents". They have activities organized around different squares: larger squares and micro-squares. Each square relates to different activities (e.g., cultural politics, sports, business, homes). People build houses, sometimes also marry, initiate recall elections, certainly become involved in debates, and from time to time link these activities to real life in a very close interaction. So the digital-city experience has shown the possibility of mobilizing the population at dramatically different levels from the most political activist to chat groups. What strikes me too is how much the group is connected to the local, political, and spatial experience in Amsterdam. On the one hand, this is a movement that grew out of the squatters movement in Amsterdam. Caroline Nevejan and Marlene Strikker, the two women who lead the movement and who lead this program, were members of this squatters movement and, in their own view, they have not changed their values much. They have continued their ability to mobilize people and change society through the new medium without abandoning the idea of the city as a place.

Even symbolically the city has ceded them as their headquarters place on one of the most historic buildings in Amsterdam, the Waag, the building that in the 16th century used to close the canals for trade when ships were arriving in Amsterdam. This building also housed the School of Medicine where illegal autopsies were being performed because of the church's repression. In that building, there is a room where Rembrandt painted his famous "Lesson of Anatomy". It is in that very room where the server of the digital city is located. I think this kind of historical continuity and this linkage between history and information flows, place and electronic networks, is representative of something new happening in the space of flows.

Another example of this linkage between institutions, civil society, grassroots groups, something that is less known because it is only in the project stage, is the Barcelona Internet Citizen Project. This project is being sponsored by the city of Barcelona and linked to a mega-project that they called Forum 2004. It is in fact a good example of connecting the global to the local, internet to grassroots. Remember that the 1992 Olympic games created a great transformation in

Barcelona. Among other things, Barcelona opened up to the sea by building a whole new neighborhood, connecting seaside promenade and beaches to the harbor. Now a group of local leaders, with the support of the municipality, have conceived a new project, an Olympics of sort: the Forum 2004, with the sponsorship of UNESCO and the pope. Over the course of six months in 2004, the project will plan to bring in half-a-million young people from all over the world into Barcelona in 2004 to discuss what to do with the world in the 21st century. And of course they need to build a city to organize this project, therefore another 20 km of seaside development.

Furthermore, the project includes the idea of linking up the world to those thousands of youths, sharing the debate on the net. For the Barcelona citizens to be apt to the task, there is a project to set up an internet Citizen center to train and diffuse the uses of the internet to people at large. Most people in Barcelona are unaware of the potential uses of the internet, so that a literacy campaigning directly linked to an event and with the purpose of participating in a global debate could just be a key trigger in bringing Barcelona as a whole into the Information Age.

As you can see, there is a gradual opening up of the Information of Age to different avenues. So through a blossoming of initiatives, people are taking on the net without uprooting themselves from their places. And through this practice, they transform both forms of the space. However, are we talking only about a small elite? Are people not being in fact massively excluded from the net? Well first of all, the recent data show there is a large number of elites, about 128 million users in 1998. Yes, data are shaky, but the same shaky data were indicating about 30 million users in 1995/1996. What seems to be a little more solid is the rate of diffusion among users, which seems to be nearly doubling every year. By the end of 2000, we should be approaching 500 million internet users. Serious experts in the communication business predict about 1 billion users by the middle of the first decade of the 21st century, considering a slowdown in the rate of diffusion when less-advanced countries and less-educated and less-affluent groups become the new frontier of expansion. The computer capacity and the telecommunications capacity is already there, the issue is how to bring people into the net. And for what?

Yet there is certainly a social bias in terms of who uses the internet. There is a gender bias, with the proportion of men to women being three to one. There is also an ethnic bias, with ethnic minorities having much lower rates of the internet use, although in the case of Hispanics in the United States, the rates of incorporation are extremely high. There is a country bias too. In fact, Scandinavia is advancing over everybody else. Finland has decided to become the first Information Society in the world. Projections are that by the year 2000 there will be more websites in Finland than Finnish people. Still, in absolute terms, there is a dominance of the internet by American users.

However, more importantly, the bias is not only in terms of use, but use for what, that is the level of education required to look for and retrieve information. I have proposed a notion that we are living in a world that is made of the interactive and the interacted. We interact but many people are just interacted. For many people, the net may become an extension of a multimedia-based, one-directional system, so that they may receive some basic information to which they just have to react, as in some marketing device. However, if we look historically into the diffusion of information and to the diffusion of technology and to the ability to upgrade the level of consciousness and the level of information, there has always been a connection between open-minded, educated social groups and the uneducated masses that through this connection become educated. As in the historic example of the development of the labor movement, printing workers were critical in that they knew how to read, where most workers did not know how to read or what to read. Printing workers were the ones that in many countries created the basis for self-training, self-development, and self-organization of these uneducated masses. And this is happening now in many countries. Low-income communities are being brought into the internet in different ways by local community groups.

I also personally know some important experiences that are highly developed as in the working-class periphery of Barcelona, an area called the lower Llobregat, in which the unions and the municipalities decided that they have to move into the Information Age and develop social struggles and social consciousness. They have created a cultural organization, and a network of internet-based, publicized activities, around a journal titled "La Factoria," which you can access on the net. Thus, they have started a process of mass education of social debate, mixing the print, the net, the city, the factory, and ultimately grassrooting the net.

Finally, even if there is still a minority of users (but a minority that is going to be numbered in the hundreds of millions), their eruption in the net, with the creative cacophony of their social diversity, with the plurality of their values and interests, and given the linkage between places and information flows, transforms the logic of the space of flows, making it a contested space. And a plural and diversified space.

Conclusion

So, whither the theory of the space of flows? Not necessarily, because this theory was always based on analyzing the linkage between electronic space and places through networks of flows. This is indeed, increasingly, the space in which most important activities operate in our societies. There is interaction, there is connection. Moreover, it remains true, I think, and can be empirically sustained that strategically dominant activities are operated essentially through the space of flows, and that global elites ensure their domination in this process, bypassing segmented, isolated localities. And trenches of resistance to the domination of flows of capital and information are being built primarily around places.

However, new dynamics are operating, dynamics of interpenetration of uniformity and autonomy, of domination and resistance, and of instrumentality and experience, within the space of flows. So, historically produced forms of space, even as complex and new, such as the space of flows, by their very existence are transformed through the process of their enactment. They become contested spaces as well, freedom is carved in their hallways, and cultural identity is built, and affirmed, in the net. So, the geography of the new history will not be made, after all, of the separation between places and flows, but out of the interface between places and flows and between cultures and social interests, both in the space of flows and in the space of places. The attempt by capital, media, and power to escape into the abstraction of the space of flows, bypassing democracy and experience by confining them in the space of places, is being challenged from many sources by the grassrooting of the space of flows.

5

What is Collective Intelligence? (1997)

Pierre Lévy

What is collective intelligence? It is a form of *universally distributed intelligence*, constantly enhanced, coordinated in real time, and resulting in the effective mobilization of skills. I'll add the following indispensable characteristic to this definition: The basis and goal of collective intelligence is the mutual recognition and enrichment of individuals rather than the cult of fetishized or hypostatized communities.

My initial premise is based on the notion of a universally distributed intelligence. No one knows everything, everyone knows something, all knowledge resides in humanity. There is no transcendent store of knowledge and knowledge is simply the sum of what we know. The light of the mind shines even where we attempt to persuade others that no intelligence exists: "educational failure", "rote execution", "underdevelopment". The overarching judgment of ignorance turns against the judges. If you are tempted to judge someone as ignorant, look for the context in which his knowledge can be turned into gold.

Intelligence is constantly enhanced. There is little doubt that intelligence is universally distributed. But facts must find some form of concrete realization. An intelligence that is frequently ridiculed, ignored, unused, and humiliated is obviously not enhanced. While we are increasingly concerned with economic and ecological waste, it seems as if we are willing to squander our most precious resource by refusing to acknowledge it, develop it, or even use it when it is found. From a school report card to a corporate job profile, from archaic management methods to social exclusion through unemployment, we are currently witnessing the deliberate organization of ignorance concerning the extent of the intelligence around us, a terrifying waste of experience, skill, and human wealth.

The real-time coordination of intelligence. This will involve communications methods that, once past a certain quantitative threshold, must be based on digital information technologies. New communications systems should provide members of a community with the means to coordinate their interactions within the same virtual universe of knowledge. This is not simply a matter of modeling the conventional physical environment, but of enabling members of delocalized communities to interact within a mobile landscape of signification. Events, decisions, actions, and individuals would be situated along dynamic maps of shared context and continuously transform the virtual universe in which they assume meaning. In this sense cyberspace would become the shifting space of interaction among knowledge and knowers in deterritorialized intelligent communities.

The effective mobilization of skills. Before we can mobilize skills, we have to identify them. And to do so, we have to recognize them in all their diversity. Officially validated skills now represent only a tiny minority of those that are active. The question of recognition is critical. Not only does it lead to improved skills administration in business and community environments, it also possesses an ethical and political dimension. In the age of knowledge, failure to recognize the other as an intelligent being is to deny him a true social identity. It feeds resentment and hostility, the humiliation and frustration from which violence is born. For when we acknowledge the other for the range of skills he possesses, we allow him to identify himself in terms of a new and positive mode of being, we help mobilize and develop feelings of recognition that will facilitate the subjective implication of other individuals in collective projects.

The ideal of collective intelligence implies the technical, economic, legal, and human enhancement of a universally distributed intelligence that will unleash a positive dynamic of recognition and skills mobilization. One of the necessary conditions for the economic rise of Europe at the end of the eighteenth century was the introduction of an effective legal guarantee for intellectual property (copyrights, licenses, patents of invention, etc.). Thus inventors could devote their time, intellectual energy, and financial resources to innovation without worrying about being stripped of the results of their efforts by those in power. Once monopoly and economic privilege were banished by law, as soon as there were methods to assign, publicly and irreversibly, the mark of a physical or moral person to a technical process, innovation became worthwhile for its own sake. Once rules were in place for the process of innovation, once it became a legitimate activity, one that was socially encouraged and economically recompensed, a scientific and industrial dynamic of immense scope was set in motion. Yet we are now faced with the necessity of making a similar transition with respect to the skills and intelligence of collectivities, for which no system of measurement currently exists, no method of accounting, representation, or legal regulation worthy of the name, although they are the source of all contemporary forms of power.

It is worth bearing in mind that collective intelligence is a universally distributed intelligence that is enhanced, coordinated, and mobilized in real time. To prevent any possible misunderstanding, I would also like to specify what it isn't. Collective intelligence must not be confused with totalitarian projects involving the subordination of individuals to transcendent and fetishistic communities. In an ant colony, the individuals are "dumb"; they have no collective vision and no awareness of how their actions are integrated with those of other individuals. But although individual ants might be "stupid", their inter action results in an emergent behavior that is globally intelligent. Yet the ant colony possesses a rigidly fixed structure; the ants are sharply divided into castes and are interchangeable within those castes. The ant colony is the opposite of collective intelligence in the sense that I am using the expression. Far from leading us in the direction of the knowledge space, the ant colony precedes the earth, it is prehuman. Any attempt to assimilate the operation of society to that of an ant colony should be considered barbarous and reprehensible.

Collective intelligence is born with a culture and grows with it. Obviously, when we think, we make use of ideas, languages, and cognitive technologies inherited from a community. But a culturally informed intelligence is no longer programmed like that of a termite colony or bee hive. Through processes of transmission, invention, or forgetfulness, heritage becomes an element of individual responsibility. The intelligence of the group is no longer the mechanical result of blind or automatic activities, for it is individual thought that perpetuates, invents, and mobilizes that of society. And yet, the intelligent community described in this book cannot be reduced to the status of conventional culture. In an intelligent community the specific objective is to permanently negotiate the order of things, language, the role of the individual, the identification and definition of objects, the reinterpretation of memory. Nothing is fixed. Yet, this does not result in a state of disorder or absolute relativism, for individual acts are coordinated and evaluated in real time, according to a large number of criteria that are themselves constantly reevaluated in context. [①] In place of the "invisible hands" of the termite colony, we have the visible hands and imaginable dynamic of expanding virtual universes. Through their interaction with diverse communities, the individuals who animate the knowledge space are, far from being interchangeable members of immutable castes, singular, multiple, nomadic individuals undergoing a process of permanent metamorphosis (or apprenticeship).

This project implies a new humanism that incorporates and enlarges the scope of self knowledge into a form of group knowledge and collective thought. The old adage "I think, therefore, I am" is generalized as a process of collective intelligence leading to the creation of a distinct sense of community. We pass from the Cartesian *cogito* to *cogitamus*. Far from merging individual intelligence into some indistinguishable magma, collective intelligence is a process of growth, differentiation, and the mutual revival of singularities. The shifting image that emerges from such skills and projects, and from the relations among members in the knowledge space, constitutes, for a community, a new mode of identification, one that is open, dynamic, and positive. New forms of democracy, better suited to the complexity of contemporary problems than conventional forms of representation, could then come into being.

---

① The knowledge tree is an illustration of the technical and social feasibility of such a project.

6

数字公平的含义、测度和实现途径研究 (2011)

赖茂生

Digital Equity: Its Implications, Measurement, and Realization (2011)

Lai Maosheng

Abstract: Digital equity is a new problem that merits high attention among modern social equity issues. This paper explores the implications of digital equity and the origin and development of the digital equity movement. Then it introduces methods and indicators for measuring social equity and digital equity, and analyzes the measurement data and research results regarding condition of digital equity (including the digital opportunity index and the digital divide index) from the relevant institutions and researchers at home and abroad over the past decade. Finally, in light of the specific situations in China and the characteristics of information science, it reviews the major obstacles, principles and possible approaches towards realizing digital equity.

Gwen Solomon 2002 年提出了数字公平的概念，认为“数字公平”指所有学生为了生活、学习、工作和未来都有适当的机会获得信息与通信技术，不管其社会经济地位、身体状况、语言、种族、性别及其他特征如何，都应当受到平等的对待。[①] 2003年，他与合作者又称："数字公平还意味着所有学习者都有机会去发展完全参与到数字时代中所需要的各种手段和能力，包括作为现在和未来的技术、传播和信息资源的设计者和生产者（不仅仅是使用者）。"[②]

1 数字公平溯源

1.1 信息公平呼声的响起

1968年，在南斯拉夫的卢布尔雅那召开的"大众传播媒介和国际了解"讨论会上，一些专家学者指出了发达国家和发展中国家间存在着新闻和信息传播不均衡和不平等的问题。会议讨论了从根本上改变这种状况的必要性。

从1970年起，在联合国教科文组织历届大会和一些国际组织召开的国际会议上，这个问题都成为引起争论的重要议题。许多第三世界国家指责西方四大通讯社的国际报道忽视第三世界国家，对这些国家抱有偏见和不负责任。美国等少数西方国家则强调新闻媒介有在任何地方自由搜集、传递和发表新闻的权利。在1970年教科文组织第16届大会上，几个发展中国家明确提出了传播媒介分布不平等的问题，要求组织更加合适和更加均衡的国际新闻传播系统。1972年教科文组织第17届大会通过的一般性辩论决议草案指出："新闻工具如被滥用，也可成为控制世界舆论的工具或成为道德、文化污染的根源。而且，如果信息传播被少数国家垄断，新闻信息的国际流通常常是单向的，这就可能导致对其他国家的文化价值的严重损害。"

1973年，第四次不结盟国家首脑会议指出，绝大多数国家已沦于少数几个新闻中心播发的消息信息的消极接受者的境地。1976年，不结盟国家举行传播问题讨论会，首次提出建立"世界新闻新秩序"。同年，教科文组织第19届大会设立了世界传播问题研究委员会。

1978年教科文组织第20届大会通过了《大众传播媒介致力于加强和平和国际了解，促进人权和反对种族主义、种族隔离和战争煽动的基本原则宣言》。同年，第33届联合国大会根据上述宣言通过33/115号决议，指出需要

① Gwen Solomon. Digital equity: It's not just about access anymore. *Technology & Learning* 2002, 22 (9): 18–24.

② Solomon Allen, Resta.Introduction: Educational technology and equity. In G.Solomon, N. Allen, P. Resta (Eds.). Toward digital equity: Bridging the divide in education 2003: xxvi-xxiv.

"在新闻自由流通及更广泛更均衡地传播新闻的基础上，为加强和平和国际了解而建立新的更公正和更有效的世界新闻和传播新秩序"，并决定成立"联合国新闻政策和活动审查委员会"。

1982 年，著名的罗马俱乐部出版了《微电子学与社会》一书，其中收录的一篇论文题为"第三世界的前景"（裘恩·拉达撰写），它指出在国家内部和国家之间存在着三大差距。第一个差距是科学技术能力的差距，当时发展中国家的科研经费总量大约仅占世界科研经费总量的 3%，发展中国家拥有的科学家和工程师的总量仅占全球总量的 13%。第二个差距是工业能力的差距，1980 年发展中国家的工业产量总量仅占全球工业产量的 9%。第三个差距是社会信息基础结构方面，当时在发展中国家每 30 人有一份报纸，每 500 人有一台电视机，而在发达国家是每 3 人有一份报纸，每 12 人有一台电视机，此外，世界图书出版总量中 83% 是发达国家出版的。而且，随着信息基础结构越来越依赖于电子学的发展，这种差距正在迅速扩大。作者最后指出，数据、信息和新的生产基础结构不应当只使少数人受益，我们不能有一个在信息方面把人划分为"穷人"与"富人"的世界。③

Leah A. Lievrouw 和 Sharon E. Farb2003 年在一篇综述中概括地反映了世纪之交有关信息与公平问题的研究状况，并提出信息公平是指在个人、社群、地区、类别或其他社会单元中公正、合理地分配或配置信息资源，使得他们有机会获得他们生活中所需要的重要的或有价值的信息。他们认为，从某种程度上讲，如果信息不能公平地分配，人们就得不到这种机会，就产生了信息不公平的现象。④我国学者朱高峰院士也指出，"信息公平"包括很多方面，远不止网络接入的问题，关键是信息获取机会的公平以及信息技术使用手段的公平。

1.2 "数字鸿沟"问题的提出

1985 年，梅特兰委员会撰写的一份具有里程碑意义的《国际电信联盟报告》（梅特兰报告（Maitland Commission Report），1985 年）明确指出，在"拥有"信息和"缺少"信息（Information Have-less）的人们之间存在着一条数字鸿沟（the Digital Divide），并指出："如果只有少数人从 ICT 中获益而绝大多数人却仍然生活在相对闭塞的环境中，是不公平的。"

---

③ 京特·弗里德里奇，亚当·沙夫，李宝恒等译．微电子学与社会．北京：生活·读书·新知三联书店，1984：230–231, 261.

④ Leah A. Lievrouw,Sharon E. Farb. Information and Equity. *Annual Review of Information Science and Technology*, 2003：499.

1995 年，美国通信和信息管理局（NTIA，National Telecommunications and Information Administration）也提出了数字鸿沟问题，并以上网的程度作为衡量标准，研究接入 Internet 能力上的差异，探讨这一差异与地区、收入、受教育程度、语言、人种和民族的关系。1998 年 NTIA 在其出版物 Falling through the Net Ⅱ：New Data on the Digital Divide 中强调美国不同社会 - 经济群体之间存在获得信息通信机会不平等的问题，描述了家庭电话、移动电话、计算机及互联网的使用，因收入、年龄、居住地和受教育程度等因素的不同而存在的巨大差异。数字鸿沟广泛存在于发展水平不同的国家之间，同一国家的城乡之间、贫富之间，受教育程度不同的群体之间、男性和女性之间、年轻人和年长者之间等。

美国商务部在其《数字经济 2000》报告中为“数字鸿沟”作了如下定义：这是一种由于地域、种族、经济状况、性别和身体状况等产生的差异。这种差异主要是指：通过互联网或其他信息技术和服务获取信息的差异和利用信息、网络以及其他技术的能力、知识和技能的差异。美国商务部的“数字鸿沟网”把“数字鸿沟”形象描述为：“在所有的国家，总有一些人拥有社会提供的最好的信息技术。他们有最强大的计算机、最好的电话服务、最快的网络服务，也受到了这方面的最好的教育。另外有一部分人，他们由于各种原因不能接入最新的或最好的计算机、最可靠的电话服务或最快最方便的网络服务。这两部分人之间的差别，就是所谓的‘数字鸿沟’。处于这一鸿沟不幸一边的，就意味着他们很少有机会参与到我们的以信息为基础的新经济之中，也很少有机会参与到在线的教育、培训、购物、娱乐和交往之中。”

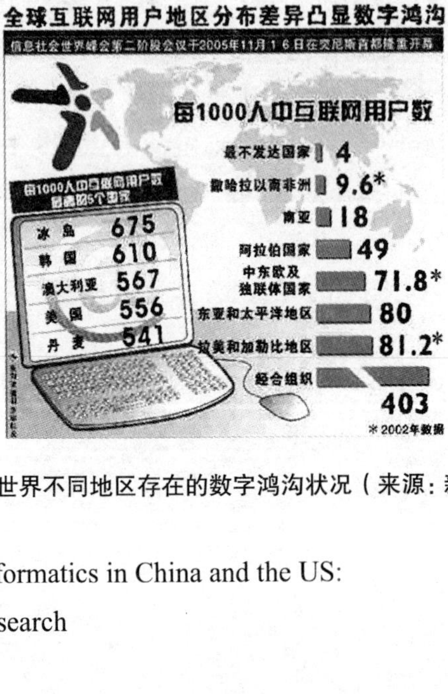

图 1　世界不同地区存在的数字鸿沟状况（来源：新华社 2005）

当今世界，经济全球化趋势日趋明显，信息网络化对国际政治经济的影响越来越大。以信息技术为代表的高新技术突飞猛进，微电子、计算机、通信与媒体技术加速融合，网络已深入到社会经济生活的各个方面，对生产力的发展起到了巨大的推动作用。信息网络化政治成为经济增长的重要驱动力量，其发展水平成为国家现代化和综合国力的一个重要标志。“数字鸿沟”实质反映了不同国家和地区在经济、科技、文化教育等方面的巨大差距。

进一步深入研究发现，“数字鸿沟”表面上是接入问题或者说是不同的群体在掌握和运用电脑、网络等数字化技术水平上的差异，实际上反映各群体在信息时代所面临的机遇差别，是网络经济社会中个人、群体获取知识、掌握创新思想的能力以致创造财富的能力差距的表现。

自 90 年代中期起，学者、教育者和活动家都使用“数字鸿沟”这个词描述由于种族、社会经济地位、性别及其他社会文化身份特征而造成的在利用计算机和互联网方面存在的悬殊差别。后来，通过考察和分析“数字鸿沟”的各种表现和原因，这些学者严肃地认识到应当摒弃简单化的物理“获得”的概念，应当从种族、性别、阶级、语言、能力和帝国主义等更加广阔的范围来分析数字鸿沟。他们把这种鸿沟描述为这些更广泛的系统性的不平等的一种症状。而且，他们开始深入考问有关资本主义、全球化、学校企业化与 ICT 对社会和教育日益增长的重要性之间的关系。⑤

1.3 数字公平观念和数字公平运动的兴起

数字公平是数字时代社会公平的一种重要的、具有代表意义的公平，正如信息社会中人们必然要争取信息公平一样。数字公平又是针对数字鸿沟和数字不平等现象而提出来的一种社会主张和社会运动。它是当今社会影响个人发展的重要因素。但是，它又超出了个人的范围，国家之间、地区之间、行业之间、组织之间、企业之间、社区或社群之间都可能存在数字公平问题。

与“数字公平”相对应的概念是“数字不平等”。美国普林斯顿大学保罗•迪马哥教授（Paul DiMaggio）对“数字不平等”的解释是：信息通信技术接入和使用方面的不平等。美国西北大学伊斯特•哈吉坦教授认为“数字不平等”是指在线不平等（Online inequality），即数字鸿沟现象中那些接入 ICT 的人群中的不平等现象，用来衡量不同的互联网使用方式对社会不平等的影响程度。荷兰的简•凡•迪克教授认为“数字不平等”最初特指物质层面的技

---

⑤ Light.Rethinking the digital divide. *Harvard Educational Review*, 2001,71(4): 709–735.

术机遇不平等，2002年后则强调社会、文化和信息资本方面的不平等。

数字公平的讨论、实践和研究不应当局限在教育领域，它涉及各个领域。因为数字化技术正在渗透和应用到各个领域，包括生产、生活、政治、经济、法律、科学、文化、教育等。在内容生产领域，数字化技术已经渗透到内容的初始创建（原创）、传播、集成、再创造、开发、展现、分销、接收、消费和用户的再创造等整个生产、消费和利用全过程，涉及原创者、出资人、生产组织者、生产线、技术提供者、出版社、内容集成商、分销商、服务商和内容消费者等。它们之间都存在公平问题，如公平拥有、公平交易、公平使用等问题。这里既有传统意义上的公平问题，也有因为数字化而引起的问题，二者可能纠结在一起，都需要解决，解决起来难度也可能更大。

目前，对数字公平的关注仅限于ICT的利用层面，且往往集中在弱势群体方面。这当然是必要的，也是一个比较突出和迫切的问题。然而，仅仅这样是不够的，因为这样容易忽视其他领域的数字公平问题，拖延这些领域问题的解决。而这些领域的问题若得不到解决，也会影响到弱势群体的数字公平目标的实现。我在2000年曾经发表过一篇小文章，谈到数字鸿沟的背后实际上是经济鸿沟、教育鸿沟、文化鸿沟在起作用。背后的这些鸿沟不解决，数字鸿沟问题也不会得到根本解决。值得注意的是，现在有的西方学者（如福山）把当前的全球经济危机和西方出现的“占领运动”归咎于技术，说罪魁祸首是技术，是技术使中产阶级的财富大为缩水，使少数人贪婪地攫取和占有了大部分社会财富，造成了金融危机和贫富悬殊的加剧。这是一种有意的张冠李戴，目的是掩盖西方制度的重大缺陷。有的西方学者就一针见血地指出是因为西方信奉新自由主义和市场原教旨主义，疯狂地追逐利润和拒绝监管，使政府不能保障社会正义和公平。不过，福山的观点也从一个方面说明了技术（代表是ICT）在今天的社会中作用之大，说明了数字公平的重要性。

起源于他们的工作的数字公平运动，虽然其范围、重点和深度不同，但是他们持续关注的是三个基本目标：(1) 挑战（质疑）计算机和互联网作为美国和世界的“伟大平衡器”的概念；(2) 揭露这些技术由于硬件、软件、基础设施、数字化素质和其他必要的资本类型的不公平分配而导致现有的不平等；(3) 扩展“数字鸿沟”的概念，将它从物理获取扩展到包括社会、文化和政治层面，以及可能导致的社会和经济方面的收益。[6]

⑥ Paul C. Gorski. Insisting on Digital Equity: Reframing the Dominant Discourse on Multicultural Education and Technology，2007：1–14.

2 "数字公平"的基础——社会公平

数字公平是人类公平观念和理想发展过程中的最新形式，是信息公平的扩展。

2.1 社会公平观念（原则）的历史发展

什么是公平，古往今来，仁者见仁，智者见智，众说纷纭。尽管不同时代和不同社会的人们对公平的感受和认识很不相同，但这些不同的感受和认识却从不同的角度揭示了公平的基本内涵。

《管子·形势解》："天公平而无私，故美恶莫不覆；地公平而无私，故小大莫不载。"《说文解字》对"公"的解释："平分之，从八从厶（厶 sī，古同"私"）。八犹背也。韩非曰：背厶为公。"（广义的公平概念）。孔子认为："丘也闻有国有家者，不患寡而患不均，不患贫而患不安。盖均无贫，和无寡，安无倾。"

在各国的法律发展史上，公平在法律制定和法律实施中占有十分重要的地位，在许多情况下，"人们往往把公平看做是法律的同义语"，法院也被称为"公平之宫"。

（1）马克思主义的公平观

马克思主义认为，社会公平是个历史范畴，具有历史性和相对性。一个社会的公平观念是由这个社会的生产关系所决定的，不同社会生产方式中的公平观念是不同的。公平是相对的，没有绝对的平等。马克思说："在现存的资产阶级社会的总体上，商品表现为价格以及商品的流通等等，只是表面的过程，而在这一过程的背后，在深处，进行的完全是不同的另一些过程，在这些过程中个人之间表面上的平等和自由就消失了。"[⑦]也就是说，这种形式上的公平是掩盖了实质上的不公平。在资本主义经济制度中，从流通领域看，无产阶级与资产阶级是平等的，他们的交换是公平的。但是，一进入生产领域，这种平等和公平就荡然无存。马克思指出："在雇佣劳动制基础上要求平等的报酬或仅仅是公平的报酬，就犹如在奴隶制基础上要求自由一样。""工人应当摒弃'做一天公平的工作，得一天公平的工资'这种保守的格言，而要在自己的旗帜上写上革命的口号：'消灭雇佣劳动制度！'"[⑧]恩格斯认为，"真正的自由和真正的平等只有在共产主义制度下才可能实现；而这样的制度是正义

---

⑦ 《马克思恩格斯全集》第46卷．人民出版社，1979：20.

⑧ 《马克思恩格斯全集》第16卷．人民出版社，1964：5.

所要求的。”[9]

(2) 西方进步学者的公平观

罗尔斯在《正义论》中提出“正义即公平”的重要思想，即一种正义理论。他既对以边沁为代表的“效益最大化”的功利主义学说进行了否定，又对以洛克为代表的“权利最大化”的自由主义进行了改造和修正，提出并论证了一个“词典式序列”的正义原则。这种序列要求首先满足序列中的第一个原则，然后才能考虑第二个原则；满足了第二个原则，然后才考虑第三个原则，以此类推。在这个“词典式序列”的正义原则中，第一是平等自由原则，第二是机会公平与差别原则。平等自由原则适用于宪政领域，对应于社会基本结构和制度，这些结构和制度必须充分保证社会所有人平等分配社会财富的基本权利，平等地享有最广泛的基本自由，即思想、言论、信仰、人身以及各项公民权利。而第二个正义原则既要求公平的机会平等，即“社会职位向所有人公平地开放”，同时也要求用差别原则来调节社会和经济的不平等。“差别原则”仅仅适用于社会经济领域，对应于经济权益的分配，即在政治领域平等自由原则下，在确保财富创造和收入机会平等的前提下，主张对社会中“受惠最少者”实行“差别待遇”，在经济利益和机会方面给予倾斜性配置。他还提出普遍的正义即公平观要求所有的社会基本善（自由权和机会，收入和财富，尤其是自尊）都必须平等分配，除非某种不平等的分配可能是符合每一个人的利益的。[10]

2.2 社会公平的当代内涵

我国权威工具书《辞海》对“公平”这个词的解释是：“作为一种道德要求和品质，指按照一定的社会标准（法律、道德、政策等），正当的秩序合理地待人处事，是制度、系统、重要活动的重要道德品质。”“公正 (Fairness)、无偏的状态、质量或者理想。”“指社会的政治利益、经济利益和其他利益在全体社会成员之间合理而平等的分配，它意味着权利的平等、分配的合理、机会的均等和司法的公正。”另外，它对“平等”的解释是：人与人之间在经济、政治、文化等方面处于同等的地位，享有同等的权利。

现代意义上的公平概念是一个经济学、社会学、法学、政治学等领域都广泛应用的范畴。它指的是一种合理的社会状态，指机会的均等、分配的公

⑨ 《马克思恩格斯全集》第 1 卷 . 人民出版社，1956 ：576.

⑩ （美）约翰 • 罗尔斯 . 正义论；何怀宏等译 . 中国社会科学出版社，2001.

正；起点的平等、结果的公正；权利的均等平等、程序的正当等等。公平集中表达了人类的社会理想，它存在于人们一切社会活动的方方面面。归纳起来，它包括社会成员之间的权利公平、机会公平、过程公平和结果公平，此外还有代内公平和代际公平。

所谓权利公平，是指公民的权利不因职业和职位的差别而有所不同，其合法的生存、居住、迁移、教育、就业等权利得到同等的保障与尊重。所谓机会公平，是指公民能普遍地参与社会发展并分享由此而带来的成果。所谓过程公平，是指公民参与经济政治和社会等各项活动的过程公开透明，不允许某些人通过对过程的控制而谋取不当利益。所谓结果公平，则主要指在分配上兼顾全体公民的利益，防止过于悬殊的两极分化，以利于共同富裕的实现。[11]代际公平是指两代人之间怎样分配积累资本和提高文明及文化水准的负担，当前这一代人对下一代人的要求应尊重到什么程度。

也有学者从民法意义上来剖析公平的不同内涵：当事人拥有平等的社会外部条件和平等的法律地位。可称为“前提条件的公平”。社会对其所有成员都一视同仁：平等地分配基本的权利和义务。每一个社会成员都能从社会那里获得同等的与其付出相对应的对待。可称为“分配的公平”。在交换过程中当事人的权利和义务基本对等和合理。可称为“交换的公平”。当出现权利与义务关系失衡时，法律应当依据正义原则和人类理性对这种失衡结果进行矫正。可称为“矫正的公平”[12]。

2.3 数字公平的现实意义

随着信息化和数字化社会的来临，社会公平的含义得到了进一步延伸和丰富。信息公平和数字公平日益成为人们关注的焦点。我们为什么要关注数字公平？

主要原因是，从原则上讲，公平的信息获取是公民取得成就和有效地参与社会活动的一种基本的和必要的条件。正如经济学家和哲学家 Amartya Sen 指出：“每一种有关社会安排的道德理论都倾向于要求某种“空间”上的平等，要求根据参与理论中某些重要变量，每个人在某些重要方面得到同等的对待。”在与信息相关的领域，“信息获取”就是这样一个重要变量或者重要的“空间”。甚至，很难想象其他的“空间”不需要以获取信息作为先决条

⑪ 公平与正义标准表述 . http://www.sina.com.cn [2006/11/15].

⑫ 赵万一 . 民法公平原则的伦理分析 . 重庆社会科学 , 2004(1).

件，包括经济机会、创造、自足、自由、安全或者心理健康。⑬

他们还从社会资本的角度来看待信息公平问题，在Sen看来，从广义上讲，社会资本是一种资本类型。它可以使人从他所拥有的社会关系中获益。而社会资本的一种重要形式是存在于社会关系中的信息潜力，即一个社会网络成员所知道的，就可以通过成员之间的互动而得到表达和共享。社会网络还是一种有价值的信息资源，因为它们大于社会关系之和，也大于组织内的互惠性交换。

今天，数字公平具有丰富的内涵：

(1) 物质层面技术机遇的公平，基础设施普及程度及使用的方便性；

(2) 教育层面：教育公平，知识资本方面的公平；

(3) 制度方面：信息公开程度，隐私保护程度，就业和职位升迁制度；

(4) 个人和家庭层面：社会成员之间、社群之间的公平，包括家庭、商业、社群等方面，不受数字鸿沟两分法的限制；

(5) 文化层面：考虑不同的文化、传统和机构情境。

3 社会公平和数字公平的评判标准

3.1 社会公平的测量标准

社会公平的衡量有标准。这个标准是历史的、发展的。公平原则具有高度概括性和含义的不确定性。公平原则并不是一个含义非常明确的概念，他本身就具有概括性、历史性和个人感受的差异性。

衡量社会公平的指标有直接测定指标和间接替代指标。直接测定指标根据不同人群的收入水平来测定公平性。间接替代指标用支出来替代收入，如通过人口和健康调查、生活标准测量调查、世界健康调查来获取相应数据，并采用主成分分析或因子分析方法测定财产指数（Asset index）。

(1) 洛伦茨曲线（Lorenz curve）

反映收入分配平均程度的曲线被称为洛伦茨曲线。如图2。

⑬ Leah A. Lievrouw, Sharon E. Farb. *Information and Equity. Annual Review of Information Science and Technology*, 2003:500.

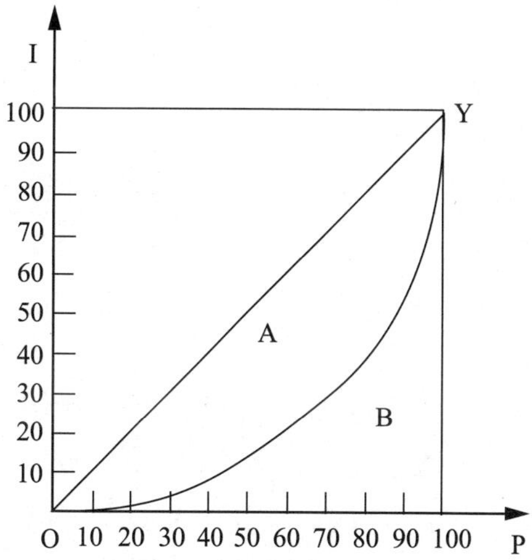

图 2　洛伦茨曲线

图 1 中纵坐标轴 OI 表示国民收入百分比，横坐标轴 OP 表示一国人口百分比，OY 为正方形的对角线（A），又叫做绝对平等线。然后，将实际收入分配情况绘入图中，得到一条实际的洛伦茨曲线（B）。它表示占总人口的一定百分比的人口拥有的收入在总收入中占的百分比。可以看出，曲线 B 与 OY 越接近，表明收入、分配越平等，距 OY 越远，表明收入分配越不平等。

（2）基尼系数（Gini Coefficient）

基尼（C.Gini）是 20 世纪的意大利经济学家，他根据洛伦茨曲线图找到了判断收入分配平均程度的指标，这个指标就是基尼系数。Gini 系数 G 的计算公式为：

$$G= Sa/(Sa+Sb)$$

根据国际通常标准，基尼系数在 0.3 以下为最佳的平均状态，在 0.3 ~ 0.4 之间为正常状态，超过 0.4 为警戒状态，而超过 0.6 以上就属社会动乱随时发生的危险状态。

（3）沃尔夫森"极化指数"

沃尔夫森（Michael C.Wolfson）1994 年在《美国经济评论》上提出测度两极分化现象的一个指标。沃尔夫森认为的两极分化，不是收入水平在两极之间差距极度拉大，而是总人口中穷人部分和富人部分都在越来越多，中等收入阶层的人数却在减少（他假设这一部分人会最终完全消失）。也就是说社会最后只剩下"有钱人"（haves）和"穷人"（have-nots）这两个有和一无所有的部分。用公式表示：

$$W=2(U^*-U1)/M$$

式中 U * 为修正了的平均收入（平均收入 ×1– 基尼系数）；U1为最贫困

的 1/2 人口的平均收入；M 为中位收入。

像基尼系数一样，其取值也是在 0（没有分化）和 1（完全分化）之间。当收入完全平等的时候，为 0 分化；当收入极度不平等的时候，也就是富人占有了全部收入时，极化也就发生了，这个时候，1/2 的人拥有的收入为 0，另外 1/2 人则占有了平均收入的 2 倍。当然，经常的情况是发生在这两极之间。

3.2 数字公平的评判标准

国际电信联盟单独或与其他国际组织合作推出了多个相关的评价指数，如：2003 年国际电信联盟发布数字接入指数（DAI），2003 年联合国教科文组织（UNESCO）发布数字鸿沟指数（DDIX），2005 年国际电信联盟发布信息化机遇指数（ICT-OI），2005 年国际电信联盟发布数字机遇指数（DOI），2007 年国际电信联盟在日内瓦举行的第 6 届世界电信和信息通信技术指标会议（WTIM）上推出信息化发展指数（IDIITU）等。下面选择介绍几种与本文密切相关的评价标准。

（1）数字鸿沟指数

根据美国商务部报告中"数字鸿沟"的定义：人们在利用互联网及其他信息技术和服务获取和利用信息时由于地域、种族、经济状况、性别和身体状况等因素的影响所产生的一种差异，研究者通常用"互联网普及率（或使用率）"、使用深度、移动通信工具的使用率、"网络准备指数"、"数字鸿沟指数"（digital divide index，简称 DDI）、"信息智商"（Information Intelligence Quotient，即 IIQ）、"网络无障碍水平"等指标来测量不同国家、不同人群、不同阶层之间的差异。下面介绍几种有关测量数字鸿沟指数的方法。[14]

① 美国电信和信息管理局（NTIA）：绝对差距与相对差距法

NTIA 的主要考察变量有 3 个，即电话、电脑、互联网的普及率。重点考察对象是收入、教育程度、地区、种族、年龄和家庭结构。在进行趋势分析时，重点使用的是绝对差距法。NTIA 方法的优点是：提出早，数据充实、完整，比较直观，易于理解。其缺点是：没有反映数字鸿沟整体状况的综合指标，在进行历史比较分析时，即在技术扩散的早期和中期，两种测算方法的结果差别很大，甚至可能得出相反的结论（从相对差距上看，数字鸿沟可能是缩小的，而从绝对差距上看，数字鸿沟反而是扩大的）。

---

⑭ Wang Youmei. 介绍几种不同的数字鸿沟测算方法 . 2010-08-01.

② 帕沃·西切尔（Pavle Sicherl）：时间差距法

由斯洛文尼亚卢布尔雅那大学法律系的经济学教授、社会经济指标研究中心创始人帕沃·西切尔 2002 年提出，用于分析欧美之间互联网普及率之间的差距。2004 年，西切尔发表了《数字鸿沟新视点》一文，进一步完善了应用时间差距法分析数字鸿沟的理论。西切尔用三种方法对两个地区的差距进行了测算。如表 1。

表 1　计算北美和西欧每千人中互联网用户差距的三种方法

时间	绝对差距（千分点）	相对差距（%）	时间差距（年）
1995	83	375	
1998	205	194	-3.0
2000	272	123	-3.3
2005	191	36	-4.2

表 1 中使用的绝对差距法，即两个地区互联网普及率的绝对差距，用二者之差表示。不同时间二者的绝对差距有所变化，呈现先期扩大后期减小的特点。1995 年为 83 点，2000 年扩大到 272 点，到 2005 年又缩小到 191 点。相对差距法即两个地区互联网普及率的相对差距，用一个地区高出另一个地区的百分点表示。由于西欧地区的年增长速度快于北美地区，所以相对差距呈现下降趋势。1995 年北美地区高出西欧 375%，到 2005 年则只高出 36%。时间差距法即两个地区在互联网普及率上的时间差距，用达到特定水平时（或在特点时间点发展水平间）的时间差来表示。测算结果表明，欧美间互联网普及率的时间差距在逐年扩大。1998 年西欧落后于北美 3 年左右，到 2005 年差距扩大到 4.2 年。

③ 法比奥拉·里卡帝尼、莫罗·法里奥：相对集中度指数

由意大利国家统计学会高级研究员法比奥拉·里卡帝尼和通信部统计办公室主任莫罗·法里奥 2002 年提出。测量了 OECD 的 29 个国家 1997–1999 年间的数字鸿沟指数，考察对象是服务器、互联网主机、个人电脑、移动电话、固定电话的普及率，并与人均 GDP 相对集中度进行了对比分析。见表 2。

表 2　1997-1999 年 OECD 数字鸿沟指数

信息技术变量	1997	1998	1999
安全服务器普及率	64.4	56.3	54.5
互联网主机服务率	56.9	51.8	45.9
个人计算机普及率	36.1	31.1	31.1
人均 GDP	31.7	31.2	30.9
移动电话普及率	35.3	29.1	24.2
固定电话普及率	16.8	16.3	15.8

④ 托比阿斯 · 休星和汉尼斯 · 塞尔霍夫：DDIX（数字鸿沟综合指数）

由德国 Empirica 公司研究员托比阿斯 · 休星和汉尼斯 · 塞尔霍夫 2002 年提出，主要考察弱势群体与平均水平间的综合差距，考察变量有计算机、互联网和在家上网的普及率，考察对象分别是性别、年龄、受教育程度、收入，并对 1997–2000 年欧盟 15 国间的数字鸿沟状况进行了测算。2004 年，他们在进一步完善测算方法的基础上，对 2000–2002 年欧盟及 15 个成员国的数字鸿沟进行了测算。如表 3。

表 3　2002 年欧盟 15 国数字鸿沟指数

	计算 机（%）		互联网（%）		在家上网（%）		合成指数（0.5A+0.3B+0.2C）
	指标值	占总水平比重	指示值	占总水平比重	指示值	占总水平比重	
全部人口平均水平	56.5	=100	50.3	=100	38.6	=100	
年龄：50 岁以上	31.7	53.4	25.1	49.8	20.6	53.4	53.3
女性	50.4	89.1	43.6	86.7	32.7	84.6	87.5
教育年限：≤15	25.9	45.9	22.3	44.4	15.6	40.4	44.3
低收入人群	17.1	30.3	11.9	23.6	8.5	22.1	26.6
合成指数（平均数）	55.2		51.1		50.1		52.9

⑤“中国数字鸿沟课题组”提出的“数字鸿沟指数”

2007 年由中国国家信息中心“中国数字鸿沟课题组”提出，其计算公式是：

$$DDI=\sum_{i=1}^{m} A_i P_i$$

式中，*DDI* 代表一国或地区的数字鸿沟总指数，其值介于 0–1 之间。*Pi* 代表要重点考察的数字鸿沟种类及其指数。在计算中国数字鸿沟时，本报告选取城乡数字鸿沟、地区数字鸿沟、性别数字鸿沟作为考察对象，主要是因为这几类数字鸿沟相对比较重要，且具有可比性，基础数据也相对完整。*Ai* 代表权重。一般来讲权重的设定应以其重要性来确定。考虑到难以判断到底哪一类数字更为重要，为不影响历史分析，在实际测算中赋予各类数字鸿沟相同的权重。由于反映的是相对差距及其变化，只要对历年计算采用相同的标准就不会影响结果分析。*DDI* 越大，说明数字鸿沟越大；*DDI* 越小，说明数字鸿沟越小。一般来讲，*DDI* 小于 0.3，表示数字鸿沟不明显；*DDI* 介于 0.3–0.5 之间，表示存在明显的数字鸿沟；*DDI* 介于 0.5–0.7 之间，表示存在显著的数字鸿沟；*DDI* 在 0.7 以上，表示存在巨大的数字鸿沟。[15]

（2）按收入划分的国家数字机遇指数平均值

世界经济论坛组织（WEF）2000 年报告《从全球数字鸿沟到全球数字机遇》认为，我们应该更好地将注意力集中于“全球数字机遇”上。这将更有利于开展那些发展中国家抓住机遇的行动，因为那是我们今天真正面临的一个前所未有的向全球数字发展的转换的机会。

由 ITU、联合国贸易发展大会 (UNCTAD) 和韩国数字机遇与促进署 (KADO) 共同创建了一个数字机遇指数（DOI）评价指标体系，于 2005 年 6 月首次正式发布。见图 3。

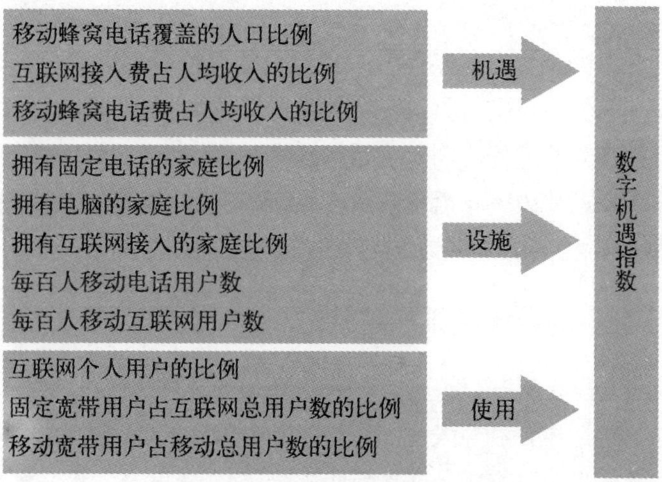

图 3　数字机遇指数评价指标体系

---

⑮ “中国数字鸿沟研究”课题组 . 中国数字鸿沟报告 2007

数字机遇指数（DOI）的主要目标是衡量“数字机遇”或者说是衡量一个国家通过吸收信息通信技术而受益的潜力。数字机遇指数（DOI）的构建基于三大因素：机会、基础设施和利用水平，指标采用的是绝对数值，而不是相对数。一些国家用该指数的方法来制作各自的信息化评估体系（指标体系见表 1）。

数字机遇指标选取移动电话和互联网接入费占人均收入的比例，即 ICT 的可支付性。基础设施指标采用了家庭普及率而不是人均普及率，能更准确地反映一个国家 ICT 接入的现状。利用度指标选取了宽带接入技术（包括固定宽带和移动宽带／3G)，可以评估市场的成熟度。

（3）信息化发展指数（IDIITU）指标体系

随着国际电信联盟的“信息化机遇指数”（ICT-OI）和“数字机遇指数”（DOI）的各自发布，各国要求统一信息化指数、进一步发展和改善信息化评估体系的呼吁开始进入信息社会全球峰会的议题。因此，国际电信联盟在 2007 年将 ICT-OI 指数和 DOI 指数两个合并，建立了“信息化发展指数”（IDIITU）。

ITU 在建立信息化发展指数（IDIITU）指标体系的概念框架时指出，一个有效的来描述各国信息社会进程的概念框架应基于以下基本的三阶段模型：

第一阶段：ICT 准备度，这反映了网络基础设施和获取 ICT 的水平；

第二阶段：ICT 强度，这反映了社会使用信息通信技术的水平；

第三阶段：ICT 影响度，这反映的是高效率使用 ICT 所带来的结果。

这三个 ICT 的相关因素不能被一项指标完全跟踪，因此，有必要制定一个综合指数。这个综合指数将这三个阶段的要素结合起来，就能衡量一个国家在构建信息社会的进程。同时，该指数应该有一定的时间框架，世界信息社会峰会的目标是到2015年后重新审查该指标体系。因为随着信息化的发展，将可能出现新的技术来取代现在包括在指标体系中的指标。

4. 数字公平的评测结果和现状分析

4.1 国际电信联盟发布的全球测量数据

2006 年，国际电信联盟发布了全球 181 个国家和地区的“数字机遇指数”（DOI）的测量结果的完整版。其更新版本于 2007 年发布。本文表 4 是其中的节选部分，表 5 是中国与世界上高、中、低收入水平国家之间的数字机遇指数比较。

表 4　2005 ／ 2006 年度部分国家或地区数字机遇指数排名

	经济体	机遇	基础设施	利用度	数字机遇指数
1	韩国	0.99	0.74	0.67	0.80
2	日本	0.99	0.73	0.58	0.77
3	丹麦	0.99	0.84	0.43	0.76
4	冰岛	0.99	0.73	0.49	0.74
5	新加坡	1	0.71	0.45	0.72
6	荷兰	1	0.72	0.41	0.71
7	中国台湾	0.99	0.75	0.38	0.71
8	中国香港	1	0.71	0.40	0.70
9	瑞典	0,99	0.72	0.38	0.70
10	英国	0.99	0.70	0.39	0.69
	芬兰	0.99	0.65	0.44	0.69
	挪威	1	0.66	0.41	0.69
	卢森堡	0.99	0.69	0.39	0.69
	以色列	0.98	0.60	0.48	0.69
	中国澳门	1	0.69	0.37	0.69
	瑞士	0.99	0.66	0.40	0.69
77	中国	0.92	0.28	0.16	0.45
	全球平均				0.40

表 5　中国与不同收入水平国家间的数字机遇指数比较（2004）

	人均国民收入（美元）	每百人电话主线	手机普及率（%）	互联网普及率（%）	PC 普及率（部／百人）	DDI 合成指数
低收入国家	510	3.3	4.8	2	0.8	
中低收入国家	1580	19.2	25.5	7	3.8	
中高收入国家	4770	22	49	13.3	9.9	
高收入国家	32040	55.8	76.6	48	50.4	
中国	1290	24.1	25.9	7.23	14.1	
DDI- 中国 / 低收入国家	-1.53	-6.30	-4.40	-2.62	-16.63	-8.20
DDI- 中国 / 中低收入国家	0.18	-0.26	-0.02	-0.03	-2.71	-0.96

续表

	人均国民收入（美元）	每百人电话主线	手机普及率（%）	互联网普及率（%）	PC 普及率（部/百人）	DDI 合成指数
DDI- 中国 / 中高收入国家	0.73	-0.10	0.47	0.46	-0.42	0.07
DDI- 中国 / 高收入国家	0.96	0.57	0.66	0.85	0.72	0.73

基础数据源自：Information and Communications for Development 2006: Global Trends and Policies, The World Bank.

测量结果表明，涵盖的 181 个国家和地区数字机遇指数存在很大差距：

• 从收入水平看，低收入国家 / 地区的平均值是全球平均值的一半，还不到高收入国家的三分之一，见图 4。

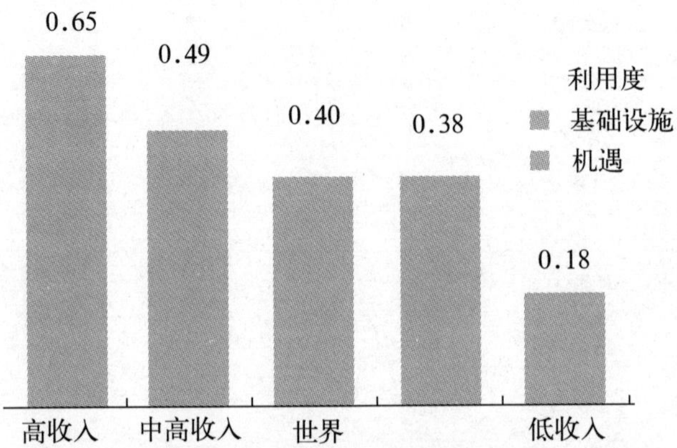

图 4　按收入划分的国家数字机遇指数平均值

• 从区域看，欧美的平均数字机遇指数高于世界平均值，亚洲等于平均值，而非洲则远低于平均值，见图 5。

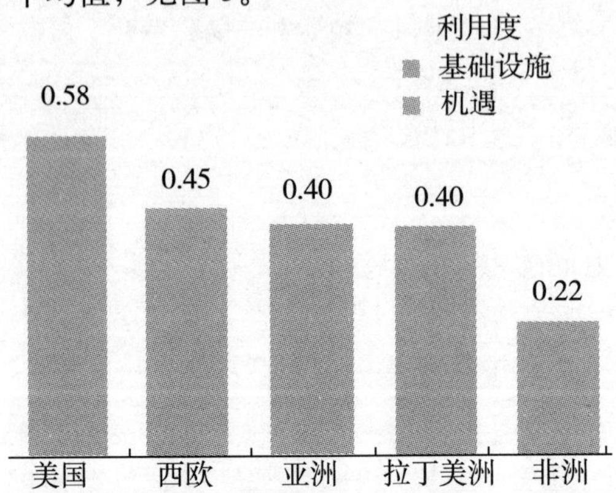

图 5　按地区划分的国家数字机遇指数平均值

2004–2006 年期间，全球数字机遇指数平均值提高了 0.05，其中高收入国家和中高收入国家分别提高了 0.06 和 0.07；中低收入国家和低收入国家分别只提高了 0.05 和 0.04，虽然这些国家基础设施建设的改善提高了基本电信接入和可支付性，但与高收入国家的差距反而在加大。

4.2 中国有关机构发布的数字鸿沟指数

国家信息中心“中国数字鸿沟研究”课题组发布的《中国数字鸿沟报告 2007》提供的中国数字鸿沟测量数据的部分综合数据见图 6。

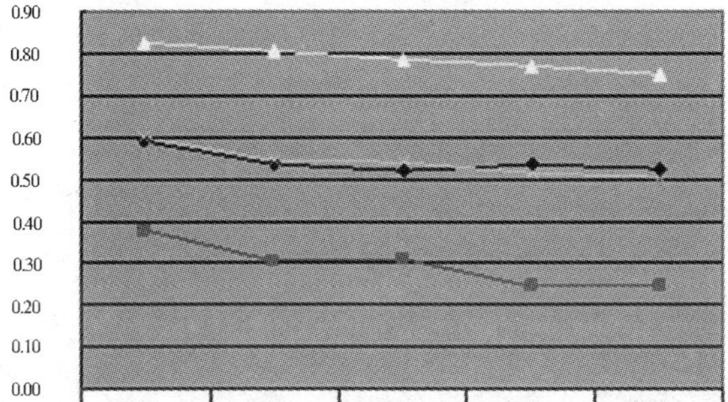

	2002	2003	2004	2005	2006
地区数字鸿沟总指数	0.59	0.53	0.52	0.54	0.53
性别数字鸿沟总指数	0.38	0.30	0.31	0.25	0.24
城乡数字鸿沟总指数	0.83	0.80	0.78	0.77	0.75
中国数字鸿沟总指数	0.60	0.55	0.54	0.52	0.51

图 6　2002–2006 年中国数字鸿沟指数变化（来源《中国信息年鉴 2007》）

2007 年地区数字鸿沟总指数为 0.53，即最低地区的信息技术综合利用水平落后于全国平均水平 53% 左右，表明地区之间仍存在着明显的数字鸿沟。从总体变化趋势看，2006 年以前地区数字鸿沟呈逐年缩小趋势，2001—2006 年地区数字鸿沟指数下降了 16% 左右。2007 年地区间数字鸿沟比上年有所扩大，主要原因是计算机和彩电方面的差距有所扩大。

2007 年城乡数字鸿沟总指数为 0.65，即农村信息技术应用总体水平落后于城市 65% 左右，表明城乡之间存在着明显的数字鸿沟。从分类指标看，城乡数字鸿沟主要体现在计算机和互联网方面，固定电话和移动电话方面的差距居中，彩电方面的差距最小。从变化趋势看，城乡数字鸿沟呈缩小趋势，2002–2007 年城乡数字鸿沟指数下降了 12.2%。由于农村信息技术扩散启动相对较慢，城乡数字鸿沟缩小的速度还不够快。

表 6 是王敏晰和李新两位研究者去年发表的最新数据。[16]

⑯　王敏晰，李新 . 浅析西部地区应对“数字鸿沟”的策略分析 . http://www.hi138.com.

表6　中国东、中、西部地区数字鸿沟状况

地区	人均 GDP 指数	人均报纸订阅指数	电话普及指数	因特网普及指数	人均电信业务指数	人均电信基建投资指数
东部	149.4	138.37	141.44	197.30	181.90	156.4
中部	78.3	90.18	80.20	44.89	70.66	67.4
西部	61.4	67.65	57.85	32.00	49.01	64.8
全国	100.0	100.00	100.00	100.00	100.00	100.0
相对差异系数（%）	72.2	135.60	88.70	383.90	142.00	119.7

4.3 其他有关“数字鸿沟”的测量数据

联合国的报道说，在互联网技术飞速发展的今天，全球有超过 8.5 亿人被“排斥”在信息社会之外，这其中大部分人在非洲。因此，非洲在信息与通信技术发展方面，还有很漫长的路要走。报告认为，“不能获得和利用信息与技术是造成贫穷的原因之一，非洲走出困境的唯一方法是尽快参与到信息与科技社会当中去”。

表7　阿拉伯世界的数字鸿沟

国家	人口总数（2006）	互联网出现时间	上网人数（2000）	上网人数（2006）	网民占总人口比例（2006）	网民增长率（2000-2006）
阿联酋	3,870,936	1995	735,000	1,397,200	36.09%	90.10%
阿曼	2,424,422	1995	90,000	245,000	10.11%	172.22%
巴基斯坦	3,259,363	1998	35,000	243,000	7.46%	594.29%
巴林	723,039	1992	40,000	152,700	21.12%	281.75%
卡塔尔	795,585	1996	30,000	165,000	20.74%	450.00%
科威特	2,630,775	1992	150,000	700,000	26.61%	366.67%
黎巴嫩	4,509,678	1995	300,000	700,000	15.52%	133.33%
沙特	23,595,634	1998	200,000	2,540,000	10.76%	1170.00%
叙利亚	19,046,520	1997	30,000	800,000	4.20%	2566.67%
也门	20,764,630	1996	15,000	220,000	1.06%	1366.67%
伊拉克	26,628,187	1999	12,500	36,000	0.14%	188.00%
约旦	5,282,558	1994	127,300	629,500	11.92%	394.50%
阿尔及利亚	33,033,546	1994	50,000	1,920,000	5.81%	3740.00%
埃及	71,236,631	1993	450,000	5,000,000	7.02%	1011.11%
吉布提	779,684	1999	1,400	9,000	1.15%	542.86%
科摩罗	666,044	1995	1,500	20,000	3.00%	1233.33%

续表

国家	人口总数（2006）	互联网出现时间	上网人数（2000）	上网人数（2006）	网民占总人口比例（2006）	网民增长率（2000-2006）
利比亚	6,135,578	1998	10,000	205,000	3.34%	1950.00%
毛里塔尼亚	2,897,787	1997	5,000	14,000	0.48%	180.00%
摩洛哥	30,182,038	1995	100,000	4,600,000	15.24%	4500.00%
苏丹	35,847,407	2000	30,000	2,800,000	7.81%	9233.33%
苏马里	12,206,142	2001	200	90,000	0.74%	44900.00%
突尼斯	10,228,604	1991	100,000	953.000	9.32%	853.00%
合计	316,744,788		2,512,900	23,439,400	7.40%	832.76%
全世界水平	6,499,697.060		361,000,632	1,086,250,903	16.71%	200.90%

来 源：Gabriel Accascina. Information and Communication Technologies for Development in the Arab States[EB/OL]. [2008-01-22].UNDP,2002. http://www.undp.org/

曹文忠 陈瑛 制作（新华社10月13日发）

图 7　美国数字鸿沟加深：不同人群在线购物者比例

许多相关研究和实测数据都清楚地表明，在较高和较低的社会经济群体之间长期存在着信息获取和使用方面持续和显著的不平等，而且它又被经济和社会领域普遍存在的不公平所加剧。长期以来，信息资源和信息技术主要都是按照支付能力和市场基础来分配的，这种状况不改变，数字不平等将持续下去，且可能扩大。因此，政府和公共部门必须继续努力去保证信息资源在社会中得到更公平的分配。

5 实现数字公平的障碍、原则和途径

5.1 实现数字公平的主要障碍

(1) 难以获得最新的硬件、软件和连接性。

(2) 随着表现在联机内容中的知识越来越丰富，人们获得有意义的、高质量的和文化上相关的内容越来越困难，因为市场上出售的内容资源很昂贵，不能代表少数民族族群的文化，大部分网络内容资源都是需要较高的文化水平才能阅读的，那些没有这种机会的将会被进一步边缘化。

(3) 难以得到那些懂得如何有效地使用数字化工具和资源的教师。这涉及教育的信念、文化、教学法和受教育者的社会经济状况问题。

(4) 难以获得能受到那些具有远见和支持技术变革的领导支持的系统。

5.2 实现数字公平的原则

在美国联邦政府教育部资助的数百个相关的全国性项目中，有几十个技术项目的负责人在 1999 年创立了数字公平网络（The Digital Equity Network），目的是确定数字公平战略和资源并加以传播和传递。该网络确定了 7 条实现数字公平原则：

原则 1：可公平地获得硬件、软件、接入和连接网络；

原则 2：可公平地得到具有使用技术资源的教师来讲课；

原则 3：可公平地获得高质量的数字化的科学内容资源；

原则 4：可公平地获得文化上相关的内容资源；

原则 5：可使学生公平地获得自己创建内容的机会；

原则 6：领导者主动地支持数字公平；

原则 7：学习气氛应鼓励不懂技术的教育者参与到技术决策中。

本文认为，国家的法律和制度是维护和实现数字公平的基本保障。实现数字公平必须具备现实的社会经济条件和切实可行的政策措施。需要处理好公平与效率之间的关系，既避免差距悬殊，又要防止平均主义倾向。

5.3 实现数字公平的途径

第一，提高全社会的数字公平意识。

第二，加强相关制度的建设，努力消除各种体制性障碍。

第三，大力加强基础教育，创造一个公平的起点。

第四，进一步扶持信息产业发展，提高广大人民收入，逐步做到普遍服务。

第五，继续大力推进经济社会各领域的信息化建设，加强信息基础设施建设，加强相关标准规范的研究、制定和实施。

第六，加强信息素养和信息质量教育。

在实现数字公平的过程中，我们还会面临诸多的挑战，例如，需要大力提升部分弱势群体的文化素质；在信息传播和利用过程中有意识形态的制约，还存在信息爆炸和信息犯罪的危险。

对于情报学来说，需要把实现信息公平的途径从传统的关注系统和服务层面的管理和分配问题的研究和政策分析，扩展到研究不同个人和社会群体之间的兴趣、目标、实践和复杂的社会关系，以便更深刻地解释人们是如何获得、理解和使用信息的。需要有更多的基础研究去了解非传统的、社会性信息资源（如社会网络），了解如何去帮助不同的个人和组织去设计及使用资源，更好地适应人们的价值观。这就需要有一种创新性的、灵活的方法，去假定和验证人们的信息需要、信息使用和信息源，从文献和系统深入到关系、文化实践以及思想在社群中的传播模式。

5.4 值得注意的几个问题

第一，许多研究和调查结果表明，如果人们缺乏理解和使用可获得的信息资源的能力和意愿，即便是最严格地分摊式分配资源也没有意义。因此，相关政策的制定和实施必须认真评估人们使用他们可获得的信息资源的能力和意愿，提高人们的信息意识，努力使可获得的内容与人们的生活和工作在情境上相关和有意义，同时为他们提供更多的学习机会。有证据表明，一些重要的互联网用户已经成为“互联网的辍学者”，因为他们看不到在线信息的有用性和价值。类似的现象也可以在一些民族社群或语言社群中看到。研究工作和政策制定应当指导人们如何识别各种不同社群所需要的基本信息，并创造条件保证这类信息的可获得性。

第二，数字公平的实现在很大程度上取决于人们的价值观，如是否支持信息资源的开放存取，社会崇尚公益事业的风气，信息内容和信息服务行业的社会责任感等。因此，促进数字公平的教育和培训工作必须融入价值观方面的内容。

第三，如前所述，公平的信息获取是公民取得成就和有效地参与社会活动的一种基本的和必要的条件。这个条件不具备，就会影响到社会的流动性。提高社会流动性，就要减少家庭背景、社会背景等因素造成的代际不平等，消除长期动态的不平等，提升社会活力，促成经济长期增长，建立一种具有数字包容（digital inclusion）性的和谐社会。

第四，需要更多地了解影响人们的信息需要和兴趣的社会和生活情境。无疑，研究特定群体（主要是专业人员、学生和研究人员）的信息搜寻模式的工作已经做了很多了。但是这些研究还应当扩展到包括更复杂的日常生活情境。这些情境不是静态的，人们可能居住在或者迁移到同时存在多种情境的环境中，所以，重要的是理解人们如何跨越这些不同的情境，情境之间如何相互影响，以及这种运动中的任何共同的因素。[17]

6. 结语

“数字公平”是现代社会公平问题中值得重视的一个新问题。它的起源可以追溯到 20 世纪 60 年代至 80 年代广大第三世界国家呼吁建立世界新闻信息新秩序运动，然后是 90 年代世界各国对数字鸿沟问题的关注，然后逐渐演变成一场追求数字公平的运动。数字鸿沟或者数字不平等现象是客观存在，不仅发生在发达国家和发展中国家之间，而且也普遍发生在任何一个国家或地区的内部。它是信息社会或者数字时代中的一种新的社会分化，新的社会矛盾，是社会不公平现象加剧的一种新的表现形式。随着信息化和数字化社会的来临，社会公平的含义得到了进一步延伸和丰富。从原则上讲，公平的信息获取是公民取得成就和有效地参与社会活动的一种基本的和必要的条件。目前，有关衡量社会数字公平或者数字鸿沟状况的方法的研究取得了一定成果，建立了若干种指标，并有了一些实测数据，表明数字公平问题是比较严重的，并具有迫切性。解决数字公平是当今社会的一个新课题，它涉及许多方面。本文提出解决此问题的基本原则是：国家的法律和制度是维护和实现数字公平的基本保障。实现数字公平必须具备现实的社会经济条件和切实可行的政策措施。需要处理好公平与效率之间的关系，既避免差距悬殊，又要防止平均主义倾向。解决的途径可以有多种。同时认为在解决过程中要注意人们获取和使用信息的意愿和能力问题，价值观问题，影响人们信息需求的环境问题，以及要把实现数字公平与加强社会流动性紧密联系起来。

---

⑰ Leah A. Lievrouw, Sharon E. Farb. Information and Equity. *Annual Review of Information Science and Technology*, 2003:499.

7

创建有中国特色的信息社会——2011 北京大学“社群信息学”暑期学校通讯

阿卜杜·阿尔卡利麦特　凯特·威廉姆斯　闫慧　韩圣龙

一、为什么社会之中存在数字鸿沟？作为一个科研、教学领域，同时又和政策制定和社区发展实践密切相关的领域，“社群信息学”如何帮助我们解决这个问题？

二十一世纪是信息革命的时代，数字技术正在政治、经济和民生等领域改变着我们的社会。网民在社会中是“一等公民”，因为只有网民可以及时地获取信息，同时可以以一种民主的方式来表达自己的观点。每个买得起电脑的人都会毫不犹豫地购买电脑。每个孩子都想要使用电脑来获得更好的教育，从而有一个更好的职业前景。每个商人和农民都希望通过使用电脑在市场竞争中获得优势。每个看过这篇文章的人都会同意上述观点。（参见 http://firstmonday.org/htbin/cgiwrap/bin/ojs/index.php/fm/article/view/2576/2306）

数字鸿沟意味着并不是每个人都是网民，并且社会中有很多人不会用电脑、买不起电脑、不上网获取信息。对我们来说，这是个危机，因为这将降低社会发展速度、提高社会发展成本，并阻碍社会进步。这是社会中存在的各种不平等的一种表现。城乡之间、地区之间、族群之间、小企业和大型企业之间、低收入人群和大学生之间，等等，都存在着数字鸿沟。这种不平等必然成为学术研究和社会政策关注的问题。

学术研究和政策规制所关注的主要领域是公众计算。公众计算是指向目前被数字孤立的人们提供电脑和普及电脑知识的过程。这些人包括各个年龄层次的人，尤其是贫困人口中的儿童，因为儿童的数字孤立对社会来说是巨大损失。

第一类公众计算机构是本地社区图书馆。每个图书馆都是一个信息中心，但是直到现在，很多图书馆里的信息还只是图书、杂志和报纸。今天，电脑是生产、获取和共享信息的工具。但是仅仅在图书馆中安装电脑是不够的，因为人们需要有使用这些电脑的技能和动机。我们需要相应的政策，使得图书馆变成一个公众计算中心。

这意味着我们必须使用新的方法来培训图书馆员。二十一世纪的图书馆员必须学习相应的电脑知识，这样的话，他们才能够帮助社区成员成功跨越数字鸿沟，成为网民（参见 http://forums.pku.edu.cn/ci2011）。

城镇和乡村的每个社区都需要一个公共社区技术中心，这样才有可能下一代人跨越数字鸿沟。在二十一世纪，电脑使用技能和二十世纪及以前的时代中的读写技能一样重要。

尽管没有明确指出，“十二五”规划在很多方面谈到了社群信息学。离开基于公众计算中心的社群信息学，将没有“社会信息化”。这是在信息革命早期我们能够服务于所有人的主要手段。

我们将在下一节通讯介绍美国在社群信息学领域的成功的和失败的经验和教训。

二、美国在社群信息学领域有什么经验？在创建有中国特色的信息社会的时候，我们可以从美国的实践中吸取哪些教训？有哪些研究结果值得探究？

在美国的实践中，我们可以发现两种趋势：私有的和公众的，或者市场和政府的 / 非营利机构。市场通过技术革新使人们可以拥有电脑，可以在家里和工作场所上网，因而促进了电脑的普及。但是这种依赖于高收入的自顶向下的过程事实上加剧了数字鸿沟问题。实际上，这是一个歧视性的过程，如果被起诉，电信企业将败诉，因为电信企业的商业模式拒绝向贫穷社区提供服务，这在美国是不合法的。

政府意识到这种新技术的重要性并且下拨了补贴，这样，每个学校和图书馆就可以使用互联网。这被称作 E-rate 项目，但是它提供的网络连接速度没有达到国际标准（参见 http://en.wikipedia.org/wiki/E-Rate）。现在几乎所有图书馆都在修改他们的预算，以购买更多的电脑设备、软件和更高质量的网络接入服务，以及数据库和电子图书。

民间社会机构（例如教堂、社区中心、社交俱乐部等）开始建立社区技术中心，并向他们的工作人员和社区居民讲授电脑使用知识。

公众计算共有四种：商用（比如星巴克无线网接入）、政府（比如公立学校和公共图书馆）、大学校园和非营利机构。这些公众计算场所存在于每个城市（参见 http://uac.utoledo.edu/Publications/public-computing.pdf）。

对公众计算的最大影响来自于美国政府对金融危机和对大型银行和公司的政府救助行为的立法。2009 年的美国恢复和再投资法案中，70 亿美元将被用于建设一个新的全国性的网络基础设施，特别是为各个社群中的基础社会机构提供网络接入。这个项目是 BTOP。（参见 http://www2.ntia.doc.gov/）

针对低收入群体的公众计算的研究发现，给他们一个机会，低收入社群可以通过网络来帮助和支持社群及社群成员。在资金有限的情况下，社群可以利用其社会资本来实现社群的发展。有一个相关社群案例研究（http://people.lis.illinois.edu/~katewill/ci-in-china/readings/alkalimat%20williams%202001%20cyberpower.pdf）。还有一个关于公共图书馆的研究中有部分相关研究（http://people.lis.illinois.edu/~katewill/ci-in-china/readings/ williams%20IM%20paper%20june%202011.pdf）。

在二十一世纪，成为网民可以让人们找到更好的工作，有更好的社会流动性。如果社区居民都成为网民，社区可以发展得更快。美国是个两重社会，一方面，它的网民跻身于世界上最优秀的网民群体；另一方面，美国社会也存在数字鸿沟。在上述背景下，社群信息学在美国成为一个学术研究领域以及社群行动主义关注焦点。

三、北京大学信息管理系举办了“社群信息学暑期学校 2011”。这个暑期学校是如何在美国经验的基础上举办的？学生们在暑期学校课程里学习内容是什么？这个暑期学校对中国的发展、缩小数字鸿沟并最终走向信息社会有什么好处？

北大信息管理系获得北大研究生院的资助举办了社群信息学暑期学校。暑期学校有四位教师，两位来自美国伊利诺伊大学香槟分校，一个来自南开大学，一个来自北京大学。

社群信息学暑期学校有一个网站，网站上有教师介绍、课程大纲，以及每次课的课程阅读材料（http://forums.pku.edu.cn/ci2011）。

学生们可以在课堂上听教师讲课，学习教师提供的 ppt 幻灯片，观看田野调查录像，进行小组讨论。课后，学生们可以和教师们进行每周一次的面对面交流。此外，学生们被分为九个研究小组，每组三到四人。他们将对以下 9 个地点进行实地调研，研究它们作为公众计算场所，在多大程度上和我们的社群信息学相关：

a. 北大南门当泽网吧

b. 西单星巴克咖啡

c. 朝阳区安贞街道社区图书馆

d. 大兴区图书馆

e. 民间流动图书馆

f. 国家图书馆

g. 科学院图书馆

h. 中国农业大学图书馆

i. 北京大学图书馆

学生们学习了若干数据收集方法，使他们能够收集关于数字鸿沟的详细数据。他们研究了中国社区活动的实例，这些活动试图通过公众计算建立桥梁，帮助人们跨越数字鸿沟。这些实例反映了公众计算的不同表现形式。这些方法包括田野调查法、介入观察法、问卷调查法、深度访谈以及焦点小组讨论法。

学生们学习了由伊利诺伊大学的两位教师提出的 D-7 方法：

a. D1 = Definition，即研究问题的定义

b. D2 = Data collection，即数据收集

c. D3 = Digitization，即数据的数字化

d. D4 = Discovery，即数据分析的发现

e. D5 = Designing，即设计如何规范化和展示研究结果

f. D6 = Dissemination，即研究结果的发布

g. D7 = Difference 即研究活动给社会和科研文献带来的变化

学生的研究结果将被汇编成一个论文集，供包括北大信息管理系以及教育部等所有对此感兴趣的机构和个人查阅。

我们也将收集学生的反馈评估，了解此次暑期学校的优势和不足，帮助我们更好地规划今后的暑期学校，提升社群信息学的研究和实践活动。

四、在 2011 社群信息学暑期学校的基础上，我们未来的计划是什么？社群信息学领域中中美研究人员的合作是否应该继续？什么样的活动是双赢的？

我们认为社群信息学是一个重要的研究领域，也是为解决数字鸿沟带来

的普遍社会问题而进行政策制定和实践活动所关注的焦点。美国在这一领域有所进展，最近有一个国家项目致力于为地方社区提供高速互联网接入服务，并让公众可以使用社区技术中心。2011 年暑期，我们在北京大学信息管理系讲授社群信息学课程，把社群信息学介绍到中国。

我们在自己的实践活动中积累经验，这个夏天，我们想证实在不同国家环境下持续发展社群信息学以及中美合作以至于全球化合作的必要性。在当地建立一个和谐的国际环境很重要，人们可以更直接地进行合作，从而可以更好地理解我们面临的共同问题，寻求通用的解决方案。

我们的第一个计划是持续开展已经成功的活动：

a. 通过会议以及对研究单位的学术互访来促进研究生的培养和研究经验的分享

b. 在两国间以及国际层面继续举办专注于社群信息学理论和研究的暑期学校

c. 继续合作发表学术出版物，包括会议论文集、期刊论文和专著

我们还计划开展一系列需要更高层次合作的和来自中美双方更长期资助的项目：

中美两国都已经建立了各自的国家统计数据集。一个建立国家级的兼容数据集的合作项目对测量两国是如何在社区层次解决数字鸿沟问题是很有帮助的，尤其是从公众计算的角度来看。（这方面研究请参见：http://firstmonday.org/htbin/cgiwrap/bin/ojs/index.php/fm/article/view/2576/2306。）

确切地说，关于学校和图书馆的公众计算服务的数据集对于考察各国是如何将其公民培训成网民这一过程来说是至关重要的。下面是美国的一些案例，来自美国图书馆：http://www.ii.fsu.edu/Solutions/Public-Libraries-The-Internet，来自美国学校：http://nces.ed.gov/fastfacts/display.asp?id=46。

当然，我们还需要更多的关于公众计算的一般数据。我们在美国进行了如下调查，俄亥俄州托莱多市：http://people.lis.illinois.edu/~katewill/ci-in-china/readings/williams%202004%20public%20computing%20toledo.pdf，伊利诺伊州尚佩恩－厄巴拿市：http://people.lis.illinois.edu/~katewill/echambana.pdf。对更多的美国城市以及中国的城市进行这样的调查是非常重要的。

随着中美合作的持续，我们将建立一个可持续的学者网络和数据库。之后，和我们已经有个人联系的其他国家（包括加拿大、日本、古巴、英国、墨西哥、特立尼达和多巴哥、牙买加、南非、印度、法国和德国）的学者的加入将使我们的社群信息学项目变得更加国际化。

Toward Building the Information Society with Chinese Characteristics (2011)

Abdul Alkalimat, Kate Williams, Yan Hui and Han Shenglong

PART I: Why is the digital divide a serious problem in society? How can "community informatics" help deal with this problem as a field of academic research and teaching, as well as a field of policy development and practice in community development?

1. The 21st century is the time of the information revolution by which digital technology is transforming society from the market to the government to everyday social life. The netizen is the first class citizen in every society because only the netizen has access to all of the information in a timely manner, and can express their ideas in a democratic manner. Everyone who can afford to own a computer gets one immediately. Every child wants to use a computer to achieve a high standard in education and to aspire for a good career. Every business person and farmer wants to use a computer to gain an advantageous position in the market. Everyone who can read this message knows all of this very well. (See http://firstmonday.org/htbin/cgiwrap/bin/ojs/index.php/fm/article/view/2576/2306)

2. The digital divide means that not everyone is a netizen, and that large sectors of society lack computer skills, lack access to computers, and do not go online for information sharing. This is a crisis because it slows development, is costly, and prevents the society from moving rapidly to achieve a high standard of living. This is a great manifestation of all forms of inequality in society. The rural is more digitally divided that the urban areas, some regions more than others, some ethnic groups more that others, small business more than large corporations, low income jobs versus university students, etc. This inequality must become the subject of academic research and social policy.

3. The main focus for research and policy formulation is the area of public

computing. Public computing is the process whereby access to computers and computer literacy training is made available to people who are currently digitally divided. This includes people of all ages, but especially the children of the poor and isolated populations as this is the most serious loss of talent for the society.

4. The first institution that fits this definition is the local community library. Every library is an information center, but up to now this information has been books, magazines, and newspapers. Now it is the computer that is the tool for information access, information development, and information sharing. But it is not enough to put computers into the library, because people have to have the skills and motivation to use these computers. We need policy for every library to become a public computing center.

5. This means a new approach to the training of librarians. The 21st librarian must have additional courses in computer applications so that they can be active agents of change in their jobs by mobilizing the community to march over the digital divide to become netizens. (See http://forums.pku.edu.cn/ci2011)

6. There is need for public community technology centers to be created in every neighborhood, in every urban and rural village so that the digital divide can be ended within one generation. Computer literacy is as important in the 21st century as the ability to read and write was in the 20th century and before.

7. The 12th Five Year Plan for Development calls for community informatics without mentioning the term. There can be no "domestic...informatization" without community informatics based on public computing centers. This is the main way we can serve all of the people at this early stage of the information revolution.

8. Our next communication will cover some lessons about community informatics from the experience of the USA. There are great lessons to be learned from both successes and failures.

PART II: What has been the US experience with community informatics? What are the lessons that can be learned from the US to build on in developing the information society with Chinese characteristics? What research results need to be studied?

1. There have been two tendencies in the US experience, the private and the

public, the market and the government/non-profit sectors. The market facilitated the expansion of computer access through technological innovation that led to personal ownership of computers, and home and work connectivity. But this was a top down process that fed on high incomes and actually created the digital divide. In fact this was a discriminatory process that led to court decisions against telecom redlining because the telecoms illegally built a business model that refused to offer services to poor communities.

2. The government recognized the importance of this new technology and provided subsidy so that every school class room and every library would be able to afford connectivity to the Internet. This was called the e-rate, but it provided speeds that did not keep up with global standards. (See http://en.wikipedia.org/wiki/E-Rate). Now almost every library is changing their budget every year to allocate more and more to computer equipment, software, and better connectivity. This includes replacing the purchasing of books to subscribing to data bases and ebooks.

3. The social institutions of civil society (eg. Churches, community centers, social clubs and neighborhood organizations) began to set up community technology centers to transform their organizational structure and teach computer literacy to their staff and constituency.

4. There are four basic types of public computing: commercial (e.g. Starbucks wifi), government (e.g., the public school and public library), the university campus, and the non-profit sector. These types of public computing sites are in every city. (See http://uac.utoledo.edu/Publications/public-computing.pdf)

5. The greatest impact on public computing is being carried out as part of the national legislation regarding the financial crisis and the bail out of the large banks and corporations. In the American Recovery and Reinvestment Act of 2009 over $7 billions was allocated to build a new cyber infrastructure for the entire country, especially providing connectivity to anchor social institutions in every community. This program is called BTOP (See http://www2.ntia.doc.gov/).

6. The major finding of research in public computing for low income groups is that given a chance the community will help itself, will use its own networks for help and support. With limited funding the social capital of the community will be invested for their own community development. This has been demonstrated in

a community case study (See http://people.lis.illinois.edu/~katewill/ci-in-china/readings/alkalimat%20williams%202001%20cyberpower.pdf) and also as part of studying how people cross the digital divide in the public library (See http://people.lis.illinois.edu/~katewill/ci-in-china/readings/williams%20IM%20paper%20june%202011.pdf) .

7. In general the findings are that becoming a netizen in society is the best 21st century door way to better employment and social mobility for individuals, and that a community develops faster when its residents are netizens. The US is a dual society with its netizens among the best in the world, but it is limited by its digital divide. This is the context for the rise of community informatics as an academic filed of study and a focus for community level activism.

PART III: There is a "Community Informatics Summer School 2011" being hosted by the Department of Information Management at Peking University. How is this summer school building on the US experience? What are the students learning in this course? How will this benefit the development of China to narrow the digital divide and become an information society?

1. The Department of Information Management got the financial support from the graduate school of Peking University to host a summer school in Community Informatics. There are four course staff, two from the University of Illinois, one from Nankai University, and one from Peking University.

2. The summer program has a website that identifies the instructors and provides a syllabus and assigned background readings for each lecture: http://forums.pku.edu.cn/conference_blue/index.php?hy_id=17.

3. The students heard lectures, were exposed to power point slides, videos of field research, mini discussion groups, and extended office hour discussions with their instructors every week. In addition they were organized into nine research teams of 3–4 students each. They studies the following locations to examine the extent to which they were public computing sites carrying our community informatics:

   a. Dangze Cyber Café

   b. Starbucks Coffee at Xidan

c. Anzhen Street Community Library of Chaoyang District

d. Daxing District Library

e. Civilian Mobile Library

f. National Library Information Commons

g. National Science Library Information Commons

h. Library of China Agricultural University

i. Peking University Library

4. The students are learning several data collection methods that enable them to gather detailed data about the digital divide. They are studying specific examples of the Chinese experience in community programs that are building bridges to end this digital inequality through public computing. Each example reflects a different definition of public computing. Their methods include ethnography and involved observation, survey and in-depth interviewing, and focus groups.

5. The students projects are being organized around the innovative D-7 Method being developed by the two faculty from the University of Illinois:

a. D 1 = Definition of a research problem

b. D 2 = Data collection

c. D 3 = Digitization of the data into electronic files

d. D 4 = Discovery by analyzing the digitized data

e. D 5 = Designing how to format and present research results

f. D 6 = Dissemination of research results

g. D 7 = Difference in society and the scientific literature based on this research

6. The student research is being aggregated into a bound printed volume of proceedings for evaluation by all interested parties, including the Department of Information Management, The Graduate School of Peking University, and the Ministry of Education.

7. We are also gathering student evaluations so that we can learn from the strengths and weaknesses of this course to assist us in planning future summer schools and activities to promote community informatics research and practical activities.

PART IV: What future plans are being proposed based on the 2011 Community Informatics Summer School? Should the collaboration between scholars in China and the US continue in the field of community informatics? What kinds of activities might prove to be mutually beneficial?

1. We have argued that community informatics is an important field of study, and a focus for policy and practical activity in dealing with the pervasive social problems caused by the digital divide. There has been some development of this field in the US, including the recent national project to connect local community institutions with high speed Internet connections and provide public access to community technology centers. During this 2011 summer we have introduced the field of community informatics during a course taught at the Department of Information Management at Peking University. There is much more to do.

2. As we have learned from our experience this summer we want to affirm the necessity to continue to develop community informatics in each national context and at the global level of China/US collaboration. It is essential to build a harmonious global environment at the local level, people collaborating directly with each other in order to understand that we all have common problems for which we can seek common solutions.

3. Our first proposal is that we continue what has been successful:

   a. Exchange of scholarly visits to foster research training and sharing of experiences in conferences and campus based research units

   b. Summer school courses that focus on the theory and research of community informatics in both countries and on the global level

   c. Joint scholarly publications, including conference proceedings, journals articles, and book length anthologies

4. We also propose that several new projects be developed that require more advanced collaboration and multi-year funding from both China and the US:

   a. National statistical data sets have been developed in both the US and China. It would be very useful to have a joint program for developing comparable data at the national level to measure the trends in how each society is overcoming the digital divide at the community level, especially in terms of public computing. (For research toward this end see the following article: http://firstmonday.org/htbin/cgiwrap/bin/ojs/index.php/fm/article/view/2576/2306).

b. Specifically, data sets on the public computing services of schools and libraries would be critical to how all people in each society are being trained to become netizens. Some examples from the US, on computers in us libraries: http://www.ii.fsu.edu/Solutions/Public-Libraries-The-Internet; and in schools: http://nces.ed.gov/fastfacts/display.asp?id=46.

c. And of course we need more general data on public computing. We have done such surveys in Toledo, Ohio (http://people.lis.illinois.edu/~katewill/ci-in-china/readings/williams%202004%20public%20computing%20toledo.pdf) and in Champaign-Urbana, Illinois (http://people.lis.illinois.edu/~katewill/echambana.pdf) It would be very important t to have such surveys on more US cities and on Chinese cities as well.

d. And, as the China-US collaboration continues and builds a sustainable network of scholars and databases, then our community informatics project can be globalized by including other countries in which we already have individual contacts including Canada, Japan, Cuba, England, Mexico, Trinidad-Tobago, Jamaica, South Africa, India, France, and Germany.

Part II
RESEARCH

8

Community Informatics (2009)

Kate Williams and Joan C. Durrance

Abstract

Community informatics is an emerging field focusing primarily on the interaction between local communities and information technologies and a more particular focus within social informatics. It is rooted in library practice, most notably the outreach that led to information and referral (I&R) services, as well as other innovative practices, for example the community technology center and the community network, aimed at strengthening communities faced with the digital era and its attendant disruptions and opportunities. Community informatics research and teaching is carried out at a growing number of library/information schools and elsewhere, as appropriate to this interdisciplinary endeavor.

Community informatics is an emerging field that encompasses both study and practice, although the focus here is on the former. Loader (2000, cited in Keeble and Loader 2001) has described it as navigating the interaction between *transformation* as expressed in information technology and *continuity* as expressed in a local, historical community. This is a specification of Kling's (1999) definition of the field of social informatics, of which community informatics is a part: "the interdisciplinary study of the design, uses and consequences of information technologies that takes into account their interaction with institutional and cultural contexts." While social informatics historically most often concerned itself with business and government settings, community informatics looks at a third realm of social activity, the community. The concept of community and the tensions within that concept, set in the context of the nascent information society, are the basis for the core ideas of community informatics. Community informatics practitioners can be found in public libraries, community technology centers, community networks, and in an increasing range of community and economic development activities, employed in the private, public, or non-profit sectors. Researchers come from the disciplines of library and information science, communications, community development, computer science, informatics, sociology, urban and regional planning, and other fields. Fortunately, the discussion in this encyclopedia entry is informed by the fact that one author (Durrance) comes to community informatics through library practice and scholarship, and the other through community practice and study of the digitization of society, or social informatics (Williams 2005). This allows the entry to trace multiple paths that have led to a single, if fuzzy-bounded, interdisciplinary field. By all accounts, however, the starting point is very much the local, historical community.

Community as the basis for community informatics

Most scholars have defined information technology very concretely as a particular, if evolving, set of digital tools and applications. But defining and understanding community is a challenge that has productively engaged more than a century of scholars. With the last major wave of US migration from country to city, the fate of community within the metropolis occupied a generation of scholars, who themselves referenced the scholarship of those who had earlier grappled with the meaning of the European migration to the cities. The earlier discourse was very much driven by the ideas of Marx, Tönnies, and Durkheim, while the Chicago School (including among others Frazier, Mead, Park, and Wirth) was the most influential in the United States.

Community is variously defined in the social sciences and has been examined in many of its guises in community informatics literature. Most often, it refers to a population living within certain geographic boundaries (geographic community), and this gives rise to a local history and culture which is the context for whatever else happens. This definition is bolstered by the fact that planning and funds flows are channeled according to those boundaries and political battles are often fought within these jurisdictions. This can be seen during the 1980s when various cities implemented community technology projects. (For a comparison of four cities, see Guthrie and Dutton 1992.)

But there can be communities within these geographic communities, as for instance the communities of interest that contended—homeless and their allies, and local business and real estate interests—within Santa Monica's Public Electronic Network (Rogers, et al 1994). Or Bishop, et al's (2001) work on a Web tool for local African-American women working on health issues. And there are communities with a particular geographic, historical origin that are now spread across large or small distances. Diasporic communities have taken to the Internet to maintain close ties with people far away, for example Trinidadians (Miller and Slater 2000). And one's community may be spread across a single metropolis (see chapter 1). Wellman, in fact, later proposed (2001) and then tempered his assessment (2002) that every individual with their ties now represents a distinct personal community, more or less place-based.

Benjamin (2001) used a recursive definition of community—"people living in a geospatial area who define themselves as part of a community"—in order to analyze why some telecenters succeed and others fail to attract local involvement. This definition has a history in ethnography and acknowledges that communities are quite often self-identified or socially identified.

Human activity itself has been theorized as taking place in communities (Lave and Wenger, 1991). Rheingold (1993) documented the arrival of the virtual community and the cell phone based social network (2002). Rheingold's online or phone based communities interact in particular ways with the local, the historical community. Online discussion lists, games, and other social computing phenomena have generated interesting work that enriches and is enriched by community informatics perse.

There are tensions and overlaps between these various communities. The field of community informatics, by studying the interaction between transformation and continuity, between information technology and local community, is building up a picture of how the social, historical places we live in are evolving as we move from the industrial age to the information age, with particular attention to social and digital inequalities. Moreover, it has done this very much based on practice, both inside and beyond libraries.

Roots of the field outside the library: The social informatics perspective

Setting aside for the moment the important role of libraries and library scholars in community informatics, several other interrelated but distinct social trends have also given rise to and continue to shape the field. These can be summed up as the network society, the hacker ethic, and the digital divide.

For some time now the network society has been unfolding on and in local communities. What does this term mean? It means that today society is characterized by networks rather than organizations; flexible production with a flexible workforce; an economy that is globally coordinated in real (or chosen, as with e-mail) time. A new space has been identified that contrasts with the space of place, that is, the geographic communities where we live and breathe. This new space is the space of flows that is based on digital tools and systems; in other words, the sum total of all the communications and transportation flows that link the global, mobile, network of human networks (Castells 1996). The world's economies, east and west, adopted digital technologies even as they experienced the economic crises of the 1960s and 1970s; what has resulted is spaces of place that are threatened, because they are mostly bypassed, by the space of flows. In the industrialized countries, one can think for example of the Rust Belt in the United States or vast stretches of the North of England as thus threatened. Other spaces of place, Silicon Valley, for example, have certainly not been bypassed, and yet even there the space of flows has left toxic dumps for the space of place to cope with.

Faced with this, local governments responded with digital initiatives of their own. Among many: In 1989, Santa Monica, California, offered its residents free online discussion lists, accessible in public libraries or from home, and access to city officials, as mentioned above (Rogers, et al 1994). In 2000, Lagrange, Georgia, offered its entire population free cable Internet (Youtie, et al 2002).

An interesting reflection in academia of this space of place—space of flows or network-communities tension was the 1996 colloquium that became the edited volume *High Technology and Low Income Communities* (Schön, et al 1999). This arose from a dialogue between two mutually exclusive groups in urban planning at MIT, one focused on opportunities for Information and Communication Technology (ICT) and the other on low-income communities. They recruited Manuel Castells to the event and produced a proceedings volume that discussed, but did not name, community informatics.

On the heels of early experimentation, the second social trend that has given rise to community informatics is the discourse and the activity around the concept of the digital divide. This emerged in the mid 1990s as a popular phrase for the gap between people who access and use information technology and those who do not (Williams 2001). In the United States, the Department of Commerce was an early implementer of both research and policy on this. The department launched a (continuing) series of survey reports on individuals' access to and use of computers and later the Internet and other particular tools such as cell phones.

In the realm of practice, the same agency within the Department of Commerce began more than a decade of annual rounds of grantmaking (Telecommunications and Information Infrastructure Assistance Program (TIIAP), later the Technology Opportunities Program, or TOP) to organizations in local communities to support their community technology projects. The Department of Commerce initiative was rooted in the economic imperative to develop a market for computers and for e-business and to develop a skilled workforce via education and public provision of information technology. Such experiments as TOP were echoed by private and other public funders, including technology companies and even the National Science Foundation, which helped Playing to Win launch the nationwide Community Technology Centers Network. One could certainly say that the dot-com technology bubble fueled the digital divide discourse in the United States, with corporations supporting local and national projects.

A third social trend giving rise to community informatics can be summed up as the hacker ethic, which took hold as computers and software became a hobby and a profession. In contrast to the media's definition of hacker as thief, the hacker ethic is the practice of building computers and writing code for the fun of it, for the creativity of it, and for the community-building. This is what Himanen (2001) calls "the spirit of the information age". The hacker ethic expressed itself in the origins of the personal computer out of the milieu of the Homebrew Computer Club and in the production of Linux and other such software. It also expressed itself in projects where hackers joined up with others to produce tools such as:

- PLATO, where by 1972 hackers and teachers were writing online courses for all levels of students (Woolley 1994).
- Berkeley Community Memory, the public terminals established in 1973 that provided an online bulletin board for all passers by (Felsenstein and Aboba 1994).
- Community technology centers such as Playing to Win, opened in 1983 by math teacher Antonia Stone in a Harlem housing project (Stone 1986), and

- Freenets or community networks such as the Cleveland Free-net, which began life in 1984 as St. Silicon's Hospital and Information Dispensary, an online communications tool for doctors and patients (Bluming n.d.).

The community network and community technology center phenomena each grew into international movements, with associations, publications, and annual conferences for practitioners. Community technology projects emerged out of the grassroots—as in Toledo, Ohio (Stoecker and Stuber 1997, 1999; Alkalimat and Williams 2001; Williams and Alkalimat 2004) and inner-city Wilmington, North Carolina (Mele 1999)—and blossomed in both virtual and actual space. Community network developers soon connected with librarians and library scholars, for reasons given below.

Roots of the field within libraries

Urban social unrest provided the backdrop for librarians developing new approaches to service that resulted in the creation of early community information services. The riots of the late 1960s marked the beginning of change in the nation's urban libraries. The decay of the inner city had resulted in a mismatch between the services that agencies such as public libraries offered in the mid-1960s and the needs of a changing population. Librarians had traditionally used library circulation figures to measure their effectiveness in the community. As the middle class left the nation's major cities, urban libraries suffered a drastic drop in circulation. At the same time researchers found that, "citizens are uninformed about public and private resources, facilities, rights, and programs... and frustrated in their attempts to get information required for everyday problem solving". (Kochen and Donohue 1976, p. 20)

By the early 1970s, the federal government had provided funding for both the development of information and referral (I&R) services and a series of educational programs and guides aimed at helping professionals gain skills in developing I&R services (Cronus and Crowe 1971; Long 1975; Croneberger 1976). The federal government's active fostering of the development of I&R services by various institutions drew in both practitioners and academics, including a group of pioneering urban libraries and a small cadre of LIS researchers (Kochen and Donohue 1976; Childers 1984; Durrance 1984).

Academics who focused on community information in the 1970s worked with practitioners through associations and consultancies, analyzed practice, contributed articles and reports, made public presentations and developed academic curricula in the established LIS programs at Syracuse University, the University of Maryland, Drexel University, and the Community Specialist Program at the University of Toledo.

Clara Jones, then Director of the Detroit Public Library and its first African-American leader, argued at the time that:

> The welfare of the public library is inextricably interwoven with the destiny of the city, the financial dilemma of libraries being one manifestation of characteristic urban ills. Although we are a predominantly urban nation, there is widespread indifference or resignation to the desperate plight of cities... It seems increasingly evident that we can no longer depend solely on the traditional cornerstone of public library service to adults—reference work, reading guidance, and programming—to stimulate sufficient interest and satisfy a broad enough range of needs. (Jones 1976, pp. 85–86)

The purpose of I&R was to provide a link between a person with a need and the resources in the community that would meet that need. To accomplish this, pioneering I&R staff created community information files, provided information about community services, and engaged in active question negotiation. Information and referral services, considered essential to avoid fruitless agency ping-pong–people seeking services bouncing from one office to the next in an environment where social services by hundreds of agencies and nonprofit organizations were delivering social services. Information and referral work was considered by many to be a radical departure from standard public library services.

At their outset, I&R services were also confusing and lacked definition (Childers 1984). The Alliance for Information & Referral Services in 1973 defined I&R and outlined a set of activities including: file development, simple and complex information giving, actively helping clients make contact with a resource (referral), working with the client to overcome obstacles (advocacy), and assuring that clients actually reached the appropriate resources (follow-up); some of these were divergent from traditional library practice. In the late 1970s, Childers conducted a bench-mark study of I&R in public libraries and found that while public libraries in his study embraced the information role, for the most part they did not engage in referral and follow-up (Childers 1984).

In spite of the limitations in adopting the I&R model in the 1970s, library engagement in the community-focused information services discussed above laid the groundwork for the public library's community-focused roles in the digital age and the beginnings of academic response to community problems.

By the 1990s, librarians and library scholars were ready to join forces with the grassroots activists, local government staffers, foundations and other nonprofits, and businesses who were experimenting with technology in communities. A particular series of three conferences helped to catalyze the community networking movement. The Ties that Bind conferences (1994, 1995, 1996) were sponsored by Apple Computer's Library of Tomorrow Project and the Morino Foundation. They brought together a wide range of individuals and groups to foster community networking (Hallman 2006). The encompassing goals of these conferences were:

> to provide information and case studies on the types of community networks that have proven viable, including economic, collaborative, and technical models; to help individuals representing schools, non-profits, foundations, businesses, media, and government agencies realize how community networking can be used as a tool to help advance the goals and needs of the community; to understand the importance of community networking in the formation and effective use of the National Information Infrastructure; to understand the emerging context—the social, economic, technical political, and sustainability issues which characterize the challenges and potentials for Community Networking. (Cisler 1995)

These conferences, led by Steve Cisler of the Apple Library of Tomorrow, resulted in the creation of the Association for Community Networking and strongly influenced the encompassing thought processes that resulted in the development of the community informatics framework.

A major study funded by Institute of Museum and Library Services (IMLS) and conducted in 1999–2000 by Durrance & Pettigrew found that community information provision had undergone major change as a result of Internet adoption by libraries. They found increased use of networked community information, a variety of digitization projects, a strong Internet presence, adoption of digital reference, increased collaboration between libraries and other community organizations, and, as a result of these innovations, increased visibility and community support (Durrance and Pettigrew 2000, 2002).

One noteworthy example of library-community information projects is the

Tallahassee FreeNet (TFN), Florida's oldest community network. It was started in 1993 by faculty from the Florida State University supercomputer center. Quickly the LeRoy Collins Leon County Public Library became an operating partner and the TFN became one of the nation's first library-university community networking projects. Tallahassee FreeNet's mission statement reflected the aims of all the early collaborative community networks:

> TFN is more than an operator of an information system. It is the agent guiding Tallahassee and to some extent Florida, into the Information Age. Therefore, it is further the mission of TFN to precipitate community cooperation that is the basis for having community-wide electronic communication. (TFN n.d.)

University contributions

During the 1990s, a number of universities, armed with excess computing power and aware of the digital disparities between the universities and communities, worked with local agencies to form community networks. Several of the long-lived projects among these are worth noting:

1. The Community Networking Initiative (later joined with the Alliance for Community Technology) at the University of Michigan School of Information and Library Studies, now School of Information. The University of Michigan Community Networking Initiative (UM-CNI) began with support from the W. K. Kellogg Foundation in 1994. This project enabled faculty and students to take a leadership role in Internet-based community networking (see for example, Durrance 1994). A collaborative venture involving the UM-CNI, the Flint Public Library, the Mideastern Michigan Library Cooperative, the Library of Michigan, and the Apple Library of Tomorrow Program created in 1995 the Flint Community Networking Initiative, a model public library Internet training laboratory featuring an extensive training program first for staff and later for community members—especially teens—and an ongoing community-focused Internet presence in Flint. Today the Alliance for Community Technology carries out a variety of teaching, research, and service projects.

2. Prairienet and the Community Informatics Initiative at the University of Illinois at Urbana-Champaign Graduate School of Library and Information Science. Prairienet, a partnership between the university and local community members and nonprofit organizations, was founded in 1993. It

seeks to:

> promote equity of access to computer resources for everyone in the community; facilitate information and resources sharing in support of community development efforts; empower individuals by teaching computer skills and providing access to the Internet; and strengthen community organizations by assisting them with access and the sharing of information (PrairieNet Community Network 2005).
>
> The Community Informatics Initiative focuses on research and teaching, especially through Prairienet and its other community partnerships, among them the East St. Louis Action Research Project and the Puerto Rican Cultural Center in Chicago (Bishop and Bruce, 2005; Bruce and Bishop 2007).

3. Blacksburg Electronic Village at the Virginia Polytechnic Institute and State University. This program is connected to researchers in architecture and design (and later information architecture) as well as human-computer interaction. This collaboration included the Town of Blacksburg and a major communication company in order to bring high-speed Internet and social computing to the community. Planning began in 1991; the Blacksburg Electronic Village became operational in 1993. It has been an international model for networked community through its innovative collaboration and citizen involvement (Cohill and Kavanaugh 1999).

Emergency of community informatics as a unifying concept

Allowing for the caveats summed up by Stoecker (2005), a loose network of scholars can today be seen to comprise a core of community informatics research. The scaffolding of the field features two processes that have contributed to drawing together scholars via conferences, proceedings volumes, and at least one journal. The first of these two processes is the series of seven Dimensions in Advanced Computing (DIAC) conferences sponsored by Computer Programmers (later Professionals) for Social Responsibility since 1987; this has generated both proceedings volumes and edited books (most recently Day and Schuler 2003 and Schuler and Day 2004). Dimensions in Advanced Computing's organizer Doug Schuler, a cofounder of Seattle Community Network, launched an undergraduate program in community informatics and authored *New Community Networks: Wired for Change* (1996).

The second process has been anchored in the north of England, where Brian Loader and others have generated a flow of edited and authored volumes (Keeble and Loader 2001; Loader 1997; Loader and Hague 1999; Loader and Thomas 2000; Loader and Dutton 2002; Loader, et al 2003; Loader and Keeble 2004), several conferences, and the quarterly journal *Information, Communication and Society* (since 1998), all while guiding several community technology projects.

Other integrative processes are: 1) the work of Gurstein (2000) defining community informatics and bringing particular attention to work in Australia, Canada, and elsewhere; 2) the annual Community Informatics Research Network meetings; 3) the broader biennial Conference on Communities and Technologies; 4) the also more broad but still highly useful conferences of the Association for Internet Research (annual since 2000) and; 5) the journals *First Monday* (launched 1996), *The Information Society* (1981), *Journal of Computer Mediated Communication* (1995), *New Media and Society* (1999), and the *Journal of Community Informatics* (2004).

New directions

As technology has evolved, converged, and diffused, the binary concept of the digital divide has revealed itself as containing multiple digital *inequalities* bearing deeper analysis. (For a recent example see Mossberger, et al 2007.) Four trends are worth noting: datasets, globalization, a turn towards theory, and a recent expansion of community informatics curriculum in library information science schools.

First, academic and policy researchers have produced hundreds of case studies, and the color and texture of these continue to be highly valuable. The multitude of studied and not-yet-studied community informatics projects and practices and the need for research to guide policy present scholars with an opportunity to standardize our approach to case studies and to collect and analyze larger datasets. This will allow us to generalize and confirm trends in communities. Second, related to this, is the imperative to study community technology as a global phenomenon rather than a national one. The search for community development through technology, for community sustainability in the digital age, is turning up lessons in one part of the world that others cannot afford to ignore.

Third, as researchers turn increasingly to theorizing as well as describing, our work on communities can be usefully placed alongside the work of others on the informatics of our government, education, and business sectors. A number of theoretical concepts and frameworks are already proving powerful in this regard: information use, community inquiry, civic intelligence, social networks and social capital (Williams and Durrance 2008), and the public sphere among them. These summations will help community informatics and others scholars to revisit and update our conceptions of the Information Society, which first took shape with very little actual data from the localities where we all live.

A fourth trend is not within the research but relies on it: the expansion of community informatics and community information in the curricula of the library and information science schools. The iSchools conferences are playing a role here, offering sessions focusing on community informatics. Today courses in this area are taught at the graduate level at 7 of the 57 library and information science programs in the United States and Canada. It is expected that such efforts will grow, in and beyond the LIS programs.

9

Social Capital and Cyberpower in the African American Community: A Case Study of a Community Technology Center in the Dual City (2001)

Abdul Alkalimat and Kate Williams

Introduction

This chapter is about the community technology center as a new organizational basis for democracy and social inclusion in the information society. We present a theoretical framework and an empirical case study, concluding with some reflections on democracy and cyber-organizing.

Background

Historical inequalities condition new social developments. [①] In virtually every society at the dawn of the twenty-first century, polarities of income, class, color and space are translating into a digital divide. [②] This divide is between those who can access and use phones, computers and the Internet and those who cannot. There are economic, cultural and also spatial dimensions to this divide, because, for example, the lower-income inner-city community is excluded structurally and physically, living in unmarked but well-defined neighborhoods with different or fewer resources.

---

① In an earlier publication we discussed continuing social inequalities in the information revolution. See Alkalimat, et al 1995.

② See the URLs for the Department of Commerce and the Benton Foundation.

Digital-divide measures usually focus on individual or household access. However, the digital divide also involves social applications of technology and the content of networked information. Government surveys provide the most authoritative data to date on access. United States government statistics indicate 1998 household rates of access as: telephones 94.1 per cent, computers 42.1 per cent and Internet use 26.2 per cent. At the highest income levels (annual household income of $75,000 or more) computers are in almost 80 per cent of the households, with little difference between Blacks and Whites at this income level. But on the whole the digital divide is also a color divide. In their latest study, the US Department of Commerce stated, "The digital divide has turned into a 'racial ravine' when one looks at access among households of different races and ethnic origins." (National Telecommunications and Information Administration 2000)

In addition to home and work, people access computers and the Internet in public settings including government institutions (such as libraries and schools), commercial enterprises (such as copy shops and private business schools) and other venues making up the public sphere. [3] The community-technology center (CTC) is a generic name given to a computer lab open to the public. Especially with recent government and private funding, CTC's are multiplying. They have formed into associations often funding related, at the local, state and national levels. Toledo, Ohio, the location of this study, is typical, with three associations at work, sometimes in co-ordination. [4]

The actual development of public computing labs far exceeds the membership of the various associations. Preliminary results of a census of public computing in Toledo indicate numbers exceeding 120, and generally for every competitive funding opportunity applicants far outnumber grant recipients (Williams and Alkalimat 2001).

Theoretical framework

Our general research focus is on community-technology centers in urban poor communities, especially communities of color. Our specific research question for this chapter is this: How does social capital structure power in a community-technology center (CTC) and influence its programs and effectiveness for local

---

③ See Bertot and McClure (2000) for the use of library computers to access the Internet; Williams (2000) presents data on Internet service being provided by libraries in Ohio.

④ See URLs for CTCNeT, OCCCN and CATNeT.

residents?

Excerpted Mission Statements

Local	
Coalition to Access Technology and Networking in Toledo (CATNeT) Founded 1996 22 members	...to contribute to the empowerment of low-income citizens and community-based organisations by providing or facilitating access to the technological tools that are more routinely available to our community's more affluent citizens and organisations.
State	
Ohio Community Computing Centers Network (OCCCN) Founded 1995 39 members	...dedicated to expanding access to technology in Ohio's low-income communities...Supports the efforts of centres that provide free public access to computers and the internet for members of their communities.
National	
Community Technology Centre Network (CTCNeT) Founded 1990 400+members	...provide opportunities whereby people of all ages who typically lack access to computers and related technologies can learn to use these technologies in an environment that encourages exploration and discovery and, through this experience, develop personal skills and self-confidence. ...offers resources...[to] facilitate telecommunications, print, and in-person linkages enabling members to benefit from shared experience and expertise. ...a leading advocate of equitable access to computers and related technologies; it will invite, initiate and actively encourage partnerships and collaborations with other individuals and organisations that offer resources in support of its mission; and it will strive, in every arena, to bring about universal technological enfranchisement.

Table 1. Community technology center associations: Toledo, Ohio and US

Historical context

This research question is anchored in theoretical concerns about how the organization of society establishes the context for and conditions the sustainability of the African-American freedom struggle. We are interested in how public computing can play a role in this freedom struggle. This struggle has been the theme of the Black experience, involving the dialectical interplay of social forces internal and external to the Black community. This dialectic is sometimes hidden under the ideological banner of nationalism versus integrationism, but the objective dynamic is that all organizations and movements of the Black freedom struggle use resources from both internal and external sources, as well as facing obstacles from both. The success of an organization or movement depends on its resources being more powerful than the obstacles it faces.

Thus the two concepts of community and power are the main foci of the scientific literature that sets the context for our research question. Citing this literature, we formulate a theoretical framework for the case study and provide the basis for interpretation of our results.

The African-American community is rooted in a history of struggle (Alkalimat, et al 1986). It came into being as the result of the global expansion of capitalism by means of four centuries of the slave trade. It has experienced three fundamental historical stages: slavery, tenancy and industry. Each of these stages has ended and transitioned into the next on the basis of disruptive processes: the Atlantic slave trade, the emancipation process from slavery and the mass migration from the rural agricultural south to the urban industrial north. Beginning in the 1970s, another disruptive transition became apparent, as suggested by the new concepts used to describe the crisis: unemployment became structural, and permanent unemployment, homelessness emerged, stagflation, etc. The economic expansion and political expansion of democratic inclusion that lasted from the Second World War through the 1960s was ended and a reversal began (Figure 1).

		Politics of reform and transformation	
		–	+
Expanding economy	+	1950s	1960s
	–	1980s	1970s

Figure 1. Structural parameters for Black middle class advancement, 1950–90

In his study of the Black middle class, Landry (1987) suggests a conceptual map of decades. The 1950s was a decade of expanding economics but an absence of reform politics. The 1960s ushered in reform politics on top of economic expansion, and the Black middle class grew and advanced. In the 1970s, reform politics continued but the economy stalled, the Black middle class held steady. The 1980s, with neither an expanding economy nor reformed politics, was another decade of relative incremental growth for the Black middle class. This meant that the 1960s saw an unprecedented and short-lived growth of the Black middle class.

Community context

The 1970s and 1980s also produced unprecedented poverty in the inner cities of the United States. Wilson advances three concepts that sum up changes in the social organization of Black community life during this time: social buffer, social isolation and concentration effect (Wilson 1987). These concepts capture the crisis facing Black people being marginalized through the birth process of the information society. Wilson (1987, pp. 56–88) states his argument:

> I believe that the exodus of middle- and working-class families from many ghetto neighborhoods removes an important 'social buffer' that could deflect the full impact of the kind of prolonged and increasing joblessness that plagued inner-city neighborhoods in the 1970s and early 1980s ... Thus in a neighborhood with a paucity of regularly employed families and with the overwhelming majority of family having spells of long-term joblessness, people experience a social isolation that excludes them from the job network system that permeates other neighborhoods ... The social transformation of the inner city has resulted in a disproportionate concentration of the most disadvantaged segments of the urban Black population, creating a social milieu significantly different from the environment that existed in these communities several decades ago.

As a result, the last quarter of the twentieth century gave rise to a new Black middle class and a new impoverished class.

The old Black middle class contained entrepreneurs, service professionals and farmers. The new Black middle class has almost no farmers, and the service professionals have become overwhelmingly employed by the state. Over 70 per cent of Black women with college degrees and 50 per cent of Black men with college degrees work for government (Landry 1987: 116–22). This process started during Reconstruction after the Civil War, when government employment was the main avenue open to Black upward social mobility. It continues today, as affirmative action applies only to employment in the state and in those private firms with government contracts.

While charting the main feature of what he calls the 'network society', Castells analyses unprecedented urban poverty on a global scale. He argues that the new impoverishment and social exclusion is a systemic feature of this period.

> This widespread, multiform process of social exclusion leads to the constitution of what I call, taking the liberty of a cosmic metaphor, the black information holes of informational capitalism...Social exclusion is often expressed in spatial terms. The territorial confinement of systemically worthless populations, disconnected from networks of valuable functions and people, is indeed a major characteristic of the spatial logic of the network society. (1998, pp. 162, 164)

Elsewhere, applying this analysis to the United States, he describes the informational city as a dual city.

> By dual city, I understand an urban system socially and spatially polarized between high value-making groups and functions on the one hand and devalued social groups and downgraded spaces on the other hand ...The power of new information technologies, however, enhances and deepens features present in the social structure and in power relationships. (1998, p. 27)

In this context we apply the concept of social capital to the inner-city African American community. [⑤] Social capital, contrasted with physical capital (for example machines) and human capital (for example education), describes the social relationships, expectations, obligations and norms that facilitate productive human activity. [⑥] Putnam measured US social capital over the twentieth century. Collecting longitudinal data on American participation in all sorts of organized groups, he found that since roughly 1960 there has been an across-the-board decline in social capital. His thematic metaphor is that people used to bowl in organized leagues, and now are 'bowling alone'.

Putnam makes a distinction between bonding social capital, relationships within a group, and bridging social capital, relationships that link a group with others. These two types of social capital together make up the social capital of any given social group:

> Bonding social capital is good for undergirding specific reciprocity and

⑤ Orr (1999) presents a useful case study of Black social capital in a historical study of Baltimore school reform in which he discusses bonding and bridging social capital as intergroup and intragroup relations of Blacks and Whites.

⑥ For definitions and literature review on social capital see Resnick (2000), Feldman and Assaf (2000), and Putnam (2000).

> mobilizing solidarity. Dense networks in ethnic enclaves, for example, provide crucial social and psychological support for less fortunate members of the community ... Bridging networks, by contrast, are better for linkage to external assets and for information diffusion ... Moreover bridging social capital can generate broader identities and reciprocity, whereas bonding social capital bolsters our narrower selves. (2000, pp. 22–23)

The distinction between bridging and bonding social capital plays a particular role when a community lacks key resources, for instance, money:

> among the disadvantaged, 'bridging' social capital may be the more lucrative form. All told, people in economically disadvantaged areas appear to suffer doubly. They lack the material resources to get ahead, and they lack the social resources that might enable them to amass these material resources. (Putnam 2000: 32)

Discourse

The concept of the public sphere has been debated since its historical exegesis from European intellectual history by Habermas (1989), Calhoun (1992) and Negt and Kluge (1993). The public sphere is a social ecology for relevant discourse that shapes policy, public opinion and the dominant intellectual themes of an era.

Dawson critiques Habermas in such a way that we can connect Putnam to our focus on the dual city (Dawson 1994). Habermas concludes that the public sphere of capitalist society is a bourgeois phenomenon, but Dawson utilizes a concept from feminist theory to argue that the Black community has always had a subaltern counter-public as the social basis for resistance: 'An independent Black press, the production and circulation of socially and politically sharp popular music and the Black church have provided institutional bases for the Black counter-public since the Civil War' (Dawson 1994, p. 206). After articulating an analysis of the same economic transformation discussed by Landry, Wilson and Castells, Dawson states: 'the ideological and political restructuring that accompanied this transformation was decisively accomplished in the 1980s by a number of extraordinary conservative regimes including those of Margaret Thatcher, Helmut Kohl and Ronald Reagan' (Dawson 1994, pp. 213–214). He then asks what continues to be a relevant research question in and after the same period discussed by Landry, Castells and Wilson: 'The question before us becomes, what is the basis in the 1990s for restructuring an oppositional subaltern public in the aftermath of a rightist backlash of historic proportions' (Dawson 1994, p. 215). In sum, our approach to community examines the dual city (Castells) for social capital (Putnam) in the socially isolated Black inner city (Wilson) to produce a Black counter-public sphere (Dawson) by means of a community-technology center.

Social movements

Morris analyses the institutions that the Black counter-public relied on during the civil rights movement in a case study of the Montgomery, Alabama, bus boycott movement in the 1950s led by Martin Luther King (1984). He employs an 'indigenous perspective' use of resource mobilization theory to define the Black movement: 'Resource mobilization theory emphasizes the resources necessary for the initiation and development of movements. They include formal and informal organizations, leaders, money, people, and communication networks' (1984, p. 279). Landry describes how the Montgomery movement was: 'led by a young middle class minister, Martin Luther King Jr., but was sustained by poor Blacks of the city, domestics, garbage collectors, and unskilled laborers as well as Blacks of other classes' (Landry 1987, p. 71). Landry's data on this broad-based mobilization supports Morris in arguing the primacy of internal resources.

Morris anticipated Putnam's distinction between bonding and bridging social capital:

> The basic resources enabling a dominated group to engage in sustained protest are well developed internal social institutions and organizations that provide the community with encompassing communication networks, organized groups, experienced leaders, and social resources, including money, labor, charisma, that can be mobilized to attain collective goals ... The significance of outside resources, in this view, lies in the help they can give in sustaining movements. However, our evidence suggests that they are not a causal determinant. (1984, pp. 282–283)

Cyberpower

Jordan advances the notion of cyberpower and identifies three interrelated regions of cyberpower, 'the individual, the social, and the imaginary' (1999). Cyberpower—the effect of online activity on power—can be measured and mapped. We use three definitions of these types of cyberpower:

- *individual*: gaining skills and connections for oneself
- *social*: gaining skills and connections for a group
- *imaginary or, as we have renamed it, ideological*: gaining skills and making connections in order to advance the imaginary: a vision, a movement, an ideological purpose.

Jim Walch (1999, p. 23) argues for a research agenda in this area:

> A new, 'wired' political community is emerging, a net-polis. The contours and nature of this political community are only in formation, nebulous. The task of research is to study what is happening, why, and what possible patterns might emerge. A major concern—for politicians, scholars and citizens—is maintaining democratic values in cyberspace: equal access, responsibility, representativity, public control and accountability.

There is an emerging research literature on the community technology center. Researchers with the Educational Development Center have documented that users of CTCs gain computer-related job and job-hunting skills as well as advances in the areas of employment, learning, increased confidence and sense of community (Mark, et al 1997, Chow, et al 1998, 2000). Breeden, et al found that CTCs are popular with all ages, provide a wide variety of benefits and offer management and sustainability challenges to their operators (Breeden, et al 1998). The Department of Commerce has published three dozen case studies of CTCs funded by their Technology Opportunities program (formerly TIAAP) (National Telecommunications and Information Administration 2000).

Somewhat in advance of the nationwide spread of CTCs, a sequence of studies by Bertot and McClure (with others) quantified the continuing expansion of public computer access across the nation's public-library outlets. [7] Lentz, et al (2000) observed computer users at seven CTCs and public libraries and found that environmental factors such as layout and staff behavior can structure access to technology in ways that sometimes discourage users. From a background of building and studying community networks as well as CTCs, Bishop (2000) outlines design recommendations for technology literacy projects in low-income communities: a community-wide approach, reliance on native talent rather than outsiders as staff, working through existing human networks for outreach and adopting a 'discovery' approach to educational goals.

---

⑦ Bertot and McClure (2000). Previous studies were released in 1994, 1996, 1997 and 1998.

CTCs elsewhere in the world can also be found in the research literature. Relating to evaluation, Hudson (2000) has proposed a tele-center typology, which includes a range of services (phone, fax, computers, Internet, print matter, training, copying, design and research services) reflecting the developing world's simultaneous leap into all forms of telecommunications. In the UK, the PAT 15 report, issued by one of the Policy Action Teams reporting to the government's Social Exclusion Unit, reviewed progress in community technology to date and recommended that by April 2002, 'each deprived neighborhood should have at least one publicly accessible community based facility to complement any home access' (Policy Action Team 15 2000, p. 6). Gurstein (2000b) and Loader (1998) are among those who have identified community informatics as a strategy whereby information technology helps develop communities as well as individuals.

The global construction of the Internet has led to cyberpower as a tool in the fight for human survival and freedom. Marginalized and socially silenced groups have used information technology to build support and global media attention (Dyer-Witheford 1999). Such groups are found in East Timor, Nigeria, Congo, Yugoslavia and South Africa. Three particular examples illustrate high levels of bonding social capital utilizing information technology to escape social isolation and leap into connectivity with a global abundance of bridging social capital.

First, *Wilmington, North Carolina* (Mele 1999). Faced with a demolition/reconstruction plan that threatened their apartments and their community, residents of the Jervay Place public housing project purchased Internet service for computers already in use in a resident training center and expanded their library-based research to include listserv participation and email communications and the publication of a well-received Jervay website. With the help of online contacts, they produced a counter-plan for redevelopment of the housing project in the interest of current residents and negotiated their way into the planning process.

Second, *Chiapas, Mexico* (Cleaver 1998; Ronfeldt and Martinez 1997). Upon the implementation of NAFTA, the Zapatista National Liberation Army came out of the jungle to take over a series of towns in the state of Chiapas and make indigenous voices heard at the national level. Friends and reporters posted news about the Zapatistas on the Internet, and more than a dozen support websites and listservs were set up, in various languages. Once the Zapatistas and their allies began to use the Internet directly, they were able to mobilize seven thousand people from around the world to two conferences held in Chiapas and in Spain and to continue to provide 'counter-information' side-stepping local news blackouts.

Third, *WTO* (Vari 2000; Tabb 2000). The 1999 WTO protests in Seattle were the results of email mobilizing, and the Seattle Independent Media Center posted on the Web moment-to-moment reports on the demonstrations and the police response. The resulting global visibility fuelled subsequent protests, workshops and teach-ins. Indymedia.org, which received 1.5 million hits during the week in Seattle, now has thirty local spin-off sites. Al6, which organized counter-events to the Washington DC IMF/WTO/World Bank meeting, can perhaps best be described as a networked movement center, with listservs, web pages linked to those of cooperating organizations, online donation mechanisms etc.

Our general theoretical model is summed up as:

Social capital → Community technology center → Cyberpower

Our thesis is that the social capital invested in a community technology center determines its role in the community and the continuing freedom struggle. Community-technology center outcomes will be expressed in cyberpower. The overall question is whether social capital and cyberpower are creating a new Black counter-public in the information society.

Method

This study is an example of what the African-American psychologist Kenneth Clark (1989) called involved observation. In his study of a social-action agency in Harlem, New York, he played two roles simultaneously, executive director and researcher. He recruited another social scientist to help him debrief and escape the blinders of his own subjectivity. This is very different from the detachment required of participant observation. The two authors here are volunteers and board members at the center involved in planning and implementing programs. We have used our two viewpoints to triangulate towards objectivity. We have also discussed this analysis with staff, volunteers, and other board members.

In addition, we made use of the center's archives, benefiting from cooperation with the center as a whole. The archives include 18linear feet of papers in files and binders and a number of electronic documents. Part of our work was assembling and inventorying this material for the center: minutes and handouts from board and staff meetings, financial records, day-to-day program records and program plans and reports. It is testimony to the care taken from the beginning days of the center that staff preserved these records. We also conducted interviews with key participants. In turn, we discussed research findings with board members, staff and volunteers, whose input only helped improve the study.

Historical narrative

The object of our case study is the W.J. Murchison Community Center, a center which today carries out tutoring, community gardening, support for other community groups and most of all computer classes and open computer time. The center has seventeen PCs and is located at street level on a smaller arterial street in African-American central Toledo, Ohio. The community garden is one block away, across from Martin Luther King Jr Elementary School. Half of the computers are networked to the Internet. An average of two hundred people use the center each month, and more than 170 have user IDs for which they paid $5 annually, $10 for families.

According to the 1990 US census, 70 per cent of households in the surrounding area live at or near federal poverty levels and 70 per cent are female-headed. Ninety-seven per cent of residents are African-American. The area has lost population over the last forty years. Many of the mostly wooded houses, built around 1900, are boarded up. The city has also torn down abandoned houses. Inhabited houses may be broken down or freshly painted and carefully maintained. Yards may be overgrown with weeds or rich with flowers and trimmed hedges. The community is also dotted with vegetable gardens with greens, tomatoes and an occasional stand of corn.

Nine churches are located within half a mile, more beyond that radius. These churches serve both community residents and people who live in the generally more affluent and newer African-American communities to the west, many of them with ties to the old community. Hair salons, little stores selling candy, soda, junk food and beer, and 'big box' auto-parts stores, dominate the local economy. McDonald's is the morning coffee spot for older men in and from the community. The absence of a grocery store has been a political issue for some time.

Interstate 75, a major highway linking the southern and northern United States, slices the Toledo Museum of Art away from the community. The museum does not conduct any outreach in the area, although the founder, Edward Drummond Libbey, a local glass magnate, stipulated that admission to the museum was to remain always free, and built a wing that has long housed art classes for the general public, classes which many older white Toledoans remember fondly.

In 1998, in a well-publicized move against drug dealing, Toledo's mayor declared martial law on a side street next to the center. The police moved in and set up guard stations limiting people's access to their homes and preventing guests from visiting. This prompted a brief debate. After a few months the city removed the concrete barriers and martial law was lifted. In 2000, the federal government allocated over $4 million to gentrify parts of the area, continuing a nationwide pattern of depopulation preliminary to a (real or promised) return of the middle class to the central city.

Stage one: Church

Bishop W.J. Murchison is pastor of the nearby St. James Church, which he founded in 1967. A retired construction worker and contractor originally from Alabama, he and his wife Sister Dorothy Murchison live six blocks away from the center. She sings and has for many years organized youth choirs at St James and across Toledo. She is also known for her grassroots fundraising: bus trips to nearby outlet malls, gospel concerts, birthday calendars, banquets and especially her 'brownies' funds (pennies).

In 1992 crack cocaine swept through the area, snatching up many vulnerable individuals of all ages and settling into buildings that became crack houses. For Bishop, who had always emphasized the church's ministry to youth, this recalled Ecclesiastes 3: 1-8, especially 'A time to plant, and a time to pluck up'. He experienced a vision, which was to found a community center. As he puts it, 'We were about to lose a generation'.

With crack tearing through the families of his own congregation, it was natural to draw together a group of church members to implement his vision. His own niece Deborah Hamilton, saved since her mid twenties, was among the group; her husband Gary was staying clean after a recent run-in with crack. Bishop also recruited a younger minister, Dr. C. E. Reese to administer the effort. Remembering the early days of the center, Sister Murchison references another Bible verse, Proverbs 18: 29: 'Without a vision, the people perish'.

In 1993, partly because drug-treatment agencies had already set up nearby, the group decided to focus on prevention—agreeing in one early handout, 'If the mind is replete with substance of the positive nature, then the need for further stimulus becomes a moot point.' Dr. Reese outlined the center's first mission statement: 'Awareness ... Education ... Outreach'. The center's programs got under way in the basement of St. James Church.

Programs consisted of counseling, job preparation and computer skill training. By 1994, there were two donated Wang word processors. When both computers were in use, participants practiced keystroking on keyboards hand-drawn on particleboard. This work was driven by their religious faith and loyalty to the programs of the church, and their hunger for education and advancement.

In 1994 Dr. Reese left Toledo, and the board asked Deborah Hamilton to become the executive director. Members recall four reasons: she had a college degree, she knew how to use computers, she had served as secretary of the board and she was a staunch member of the church.

Guided by Mrs. Hamilton's self-study on organizational development, the board became a fundraising committee. In the tradition of the Black church, a series of projects kept bringing money in, several hundred dollars at a time, and the organization always had close to $2000 saved up. An effort to recruit a grant writer began, and in early 1995 a volunteer began to work with Mrs. Hamilton on a Community Development Block Grant proposal.

By February 1995, the board was so encouraged by the programs and the fundraising that, when Bishop suggested for a second time that for $100 the center could rent part of a small building he built and owned on Lawrence Street, it agreed. Moving out of the church was a marker of the start of a second stage in the life of the Murchison Community Center.

Stage two: State

Although it was rejected, the 1995 CDBG grant submission, done in communication with the responsible city agency, was a learning experience for the center. What the center began to learn was how to jump through the hoops set by the state, the government bureaucracy. Once the funding started to flow—$44,000 in 1996, $25,000 in each of 1997, 1998 and 1999—it dwarfed the funds raised through the social networks of the board members, i.e. church members, and defined the terms under which the center operated for the next stage of its life.

For example, the second mission statement of the center made no reference to the first, and was developed by Mrs. Hamilton and a center volunteer with the aim of fitting the requirements of the CDBG grant application process. Within a year this volunteer joined the staff of CDBG and was assigned for some time as the CDBG liaison to the center. Since then, she has continued to look out for the interests of the center and provide valued unofficial advice.

CDBG is a program established in the 1980s when so many 1960s Great Society federal funding streams to impoverished communities were cut off. In their place, President Reagan and Congress directed a much smaller amount of funds through the Department of Housing and Urban Development to be doled out by city and county authorities according to federal guidelines. Thus CDBG provided federal funds, but local officials directed the flow.

Another example of an external authority setting the agenda for the center came when Mrs. Hamilton and a few others were working into the wee hours one night on another government grant proposal. They were stumped when it came to writing a needs statement, and read the suggestion: 'conduct a needs assessment of your community such as by means of a survey.' They had never surveyed the community. The grant process used the same language of 'needs assessment', so the idea of conducting a survey took hold.

In fact, most of them had been raised or had raised their own children in the community, but the exercise of a survey captured the attention of the center for several months. The board settled on twelve questions, and eventually 116 surveys were gathered. It isn't clear what use was made of the information, gathered in response to external bureaucracies rather than as an outgrowth of the center itself Echoing the critique of John Kretzmann and John McKnight, the questions themselves portray the community as a collection of needs rather than a collection of resources that can be mobilized (Kretzmann and McKnight 1993).

When the local CDBG office rejected the center's 1995 proposal, it further recommended that the center should partner with a start-up Community Development Corporation. CDCs were again a product of the 1980s, which saw an epidemic of homelessness. By the 1990s in Toledo, CDCs had carved up the inner city and were taking the lion's share of CDBG funding. This money subsidized them in building and occasionally renovating small areas of inexpensive housing, and then selling with great fanfare.

The neighborhood had been mostly left out of the 'gold rush'. Roosevelt Revitalization Corporation and the center, in these tracts, were to partner and submit one proposal for 1996. This process again took attention away from the grassroots fundraising that the board had been focusing on, but the joint proposal was funded and stage two was really under way.

Within two months of the grant period, Roosevelt proved unready to start work. Mrs. Chestnut, now representing CDBG, recommended that the two organizations should split, with the center getting the funds, because programs were already under way and governance well established. Roosevelt would go back to the drawing board. A new term, leverage, came to the board as Mrs. Chestnut explained why the city had funded the center. The funds ($44,000) were to be used to lever other dollars, so that the center would not remain 90 per cent CDBG-funded. The city, the board learned, had funded the center, first as part of the now-suspended Roosevelt partnership, second, as a fresh effort in census tracts 25 and 26 (which no doubt covered a CDBG gap) and, third, because the grant focused on job development.

Not only did the CDBG office recommend policy directions, but also they required a complex of procurement, personnel, program and financial policies, procedures and reporting that the center had to master. One of the most onerous was the process of reimbursement. The monthly activity reports were to include every document produced that month plus a quantitative and descriptive report on each area of program activity. These reports were required before a monthly check was sent. Then, every expenditure had to be documented, every check copied, and submitted monthly to CDBG. Several weeks later a check would arrive for all approved expenses. Disputed or incompletely documented expenses would be delayed one month or more. In order to provide service the center had to obtain a line of credit, which it did, with the personal assurance of Bishop Murchison and his construction business track record.

Financial administration became particularly difficult given that the payroll and all book-keeping was being done by an older member of the church who was in bad health for more than a year, making any change a sensitive matter. By October 1998 the indebtedness ballooned to more than $11,000.

As a result of the reporting requirements, programs were documented as never before, and a monthly number, reflecting the number of people participating in center programs, was reported. The total number hovered around fifty-five per month during 1997–8.

As soon as the first CDBG grant began, three new board members were elected and an assistant director and program coordinators, all working part-time, were hired. The terms of the grant did not allow for a full-time salary for Mrs. Hamilton, so she continued to work a full-time day job and volunteer her time to the center, taking occasional payments that just about equaled her travel and incidental expenses. The new individuals were either not members of St James or were more loosely tied to the church; the staff members, only one from St James, worked during the day or after school hours rather than in the evening when the board met, so the close personal ties that the board had used to keep the center together began to loosen.

The role of the board changed during this time. What had been an active fundraising committee became a bureaucratic group that approved policies and financial reports. Meetings were held almost weekly over 1995 and early 1996; then monthly meetings became the norm. Near-perfect board-meeting attendance also became a thing of the past. The 1997 strategic plan, for instance, was the result of only four of twelve board members attending a session with a paid consultant and a representative from the city's plan commission. These two people wrote up the strategic plan.

Accompanying this shift, staff rather than volunteers carried out programming during this time. For example, a children's program that started out with arts and crafts with one volunteer followed by a rap session with another, Mr. Hamilton, was converted into that same volunteer doing arts and crafts as paid staff, with various 'guest speakers' following the arts and crafts. With the program carried out as a job rather than a church youth mission, speakers were often unskilled or absent, and the effect on the kids was not nearly as powerful, because there was no ongoing relationship with any adult outside of the arts and crafts leader. Eventually the program was arts and crafts only, with the modest supplies and skills of the staff member, who worked days as a security guard.

Computer classes continued over the years, with different projects to buy or get machines donated. The board investigated but then declined to pursue a 1996 opportunity to apply for $80,000 from another CDC to build a computer lab. The reason noted in the board's minutes was 'not enough room'. That same night the board adopted a slogan for the center: 'Knowledge is Power'. It is a curious reflection of the balance of power in the organization: the conservatism of staff, succeeding in nixing a plan to bring in computers which they did not know how to use, and the determination of the St James members. Donated computers were sought in lieu of the $80,000, and the organization connected with a more gradual citywide effort to bring computers into the community known as CATNeT.

CATNeT—the Coalition to Access Technology and Networking in Toledo—formed as a collaboration between the University of Toledo's Urban Affairs Center and a local subsidized housing agency related to the Catholic Church; this agency had won a US Department of Housing and Urban Development Neighborhood Network grant to build labs at six apartment complexes. With only one donated computer materializing for the center over the first year of the connection, Mrs. Hamilton could not make it a priority to attend meetings, which were held during her workday.

Stage three: University

In early 1998 a University of Toledo (UT) Africana Studies course called the Poverty Seminar invited Mrs. Hamilton to speak. The seminar was discussing the question of 'ending poverty once and for all', and made a special effort to look for ways to use computers and the Internet to end poverty and to bring participants up to date on the Web, email, etc. The Murchison Center attracted students' interest as a site teaching computers in a low-income African-American community.

Soon after Mrs. Hamilton visited the seminar, the seminar organized a 'Day of Dialogue' on 'Ending Poverty versus Ending Welfare' and recruited center staff to host an event. More than five hundred people attended three panel discussions held that day. The locations—a soup kitchen in the Black community, a local farm workers' union in the Latino community and the largest auditorium on campus—attracted a wide variety of people and helped to bond the organizers—the Africana Studies program and the Murchison Center.

Summing up the event, the seminar decided to approach the Murchison Center about a partnership. The seminar would start meeting at the center and in exchange would contribute some volunteer time to the center and its programs.

While the students collected data about the community, the seminar helped the center in a number of ways. Most of these were summarized in a written letter of agreement between the director of Africana Studies and Deborah Hamilton:

- computerize accounts and train staff in Quicken
- design and help pay for a newsletter

- provide after-school tutoring for elementary schoolchildren
- send student techs to troubleshoot and teach computer classes.

Work on the accounts led to some work on grant proposals, and a university representative joined the board of the center. Data gathered and discussed in the seminar, together with the tutoring experience, led to a focus on mathematics and the proficiency tests.

During this time the programs of the center that the university was not involved in dwindled to a point where the assistant director complained that the center was being used by just three families, as a babysitting service. A gap emerged between the more middle-class staff, who themselves worked other jobs were looking for other work to supplement their part-time work at the center and the people from campus who were 'fresh legs' and brought from the seminar process a sense of mission similar to the church founder. Different from the paid staff, the university group aimed to partner with poor people rather than deliver services to them. The university group was also more diverse: Blacks, Asians, Whites, multiple faiths, experience with national social movements against racism, AIDS, nuclear weapons, environmental pollution and the death penalty, and 1960s, Gen-X, and hip-hop in personal style.

The community research by the students turned up the fact that almost no local elementary students were passing the math proficiency tests, and everyone recognized that math skills are a ticket to high-tech, high-paying jobs, where African-Americans are underrepresented. Moving past the original partnership, UT and the center launched a program of practice testing and tutoring, taking place in the center, in the school and on the university campus. A similarly oriented summer youth program followed. The center's assistant director distanced herself from the partnership without participating in any meetings and soon left the center, but Mrs. Hamilton continued to hold the university volunteers in high regard, because of the focus on computers, the resources coming into the center and the education she was getting along the way. One component of this was a group trip to the Black Radical Congress in Chicago, which was her first exposure to Black Power as a movement.

The Black Radical Congress gathered together Black academics and social activists to rally African-Americans who were critical of the mainstream efforts of elected officials and the conservative orientation of the Million Man March, which opted for atonement rather than activism to change state policy. The main tool used by the BRC in creating this counter-public has been and continues to be the Internet via listservs discussions involving fifteen thousand subscribers.

The university's seminar approach carried over into program management. Work was evaluated in meetings that included staff, volunteers and parents. For instance, after discussing various approaches to discipline, the group developed an axiom: 'Discipline is a result of engagement'. In other words, policing kids who are not interested in an activity was not effective. The kids had to be drawn into an activity that would absorb their attention, the way video games did at home or learning PowerPoint did at the center. This would have to involve reasoning with children and making a convincing case for whatever activity was at hand.

Both administration and programming at the center were changing, but not only as a result of the university involvement. Bishop Murchison was pressing on with building a new center across the alley from the old one, and it was finished in June 1999. He invited the director of Africana Studies to give the keynote address at the grand opening, a gathering of more than three hun dred people in front of and inside the new center. The Bishop had designed the facility with a distinct room for a computer lab, and small grants finally came in to allow the center to fill the lab with eight new computers. Slightly used computers were donated by UT, as were volunteer time and a student worker who kept the PCs up and networked. The center also hired three parttimers at wages lower than the earlier staff: two Africana Studies graduate students and a computer-savvy father from the neighborhood who had joined the practice proficiency testing.

In August 1999 the board acknowledged the changes in the center's programs when it added the phrase 'community based cyberpower' to the mission statement and added 'strengthening the nearby school' to the center's goals and objectives. Over the next year the board voted in three people who came out of the new activities. One of these was an information-technology staff person at the University of Toledo and the other two were grandmothers who got involved along with the grandchildren they were raising.

Fifteen hours a week of computer classes, tutoring in the schools, and practice math tests became the programming. The number of people served monthly climbed steadily from roughly fifty-five to more than 250 by early 2000. Parents—predominately grandmothers raising grandchildren—were recruited into the tutoring and testing activities and began to help make decisions and implement programs.

Several of them had computers or wanted computers, and an electronic discussion list was implemented via the online service e-groups. With a free electronic discussion list via www.egroups.com and two donated computers placed temporarily at grandmothers' homes, four people from campus and four from the community were able to stay in touch and make decisions. An average of sixty-two messages were posted per month. One-third of the messages came from the non-university list members, who were not accustomed to typing or to broadcasting their ideas. A breakthrough came when one grandmother succeeded in using e-groups to assign out tasks for a barbecue. This was done from her home without any direct assistance from others.

The center's computer classes ranged from elementary (Adult Basic Computing) to advanced, particularly when a new UT course, 'The Black Church', set a requirement for students to build a web page for a local church. Cyberchurch, as it came to be called, evolved into a mainstay offering at the center. One of the students stepped forward to teach it.

This did not come without struggle. Board members representing local agencies within the government bureaucracy kept aloof from the center. One expressed strong disagreement with the center's programs. Elements at King School became defensive about new forces in the PTO and attempted to steal the PTO election. A controversy broke out over a passage in a report published by the center, a passage that one grandmother ultimately labeled a 'wake-up call':

- Year after year... the King Cougars win the city basketball tournament. Last year the tem was undefeated 28–0.
- Also last year, no 4th or 6th grade King student passed all five proficiency tests. Nine per cent of 4th graders and 7 per cent of 6th graders passed the math test.
- But with support and study, King students can excel in math just like they do in basketball. The test scores show how much the entire school (students, parents, teachers, administrators, and community) has to change to meet TPS's (Toledo Public Schools) stated goal of 75 per cent passing.

A crisis came in spring 2000 when the CDBG grant proposal was twenty minutes late and as a result, rejected. The center's testimony before the city council—

delivered by the director of Africana Studies—did not change matters. The center drew strong approval from long-time liaison workers at CDBG, who had read the detailed monthly reports and saw the center's tremendous growth trajectory. New people were brought on to the board and are at work raising funds.

As of now, the watchword at the center is 'sustainability,' both in terms of funding and in terms of people. The university forces brought a movement mentality to the center, which supplanted the relatively careerist or workaday orientation of stage two. The state edged out the tight group of ideological St James Church leaders of stage one. The goal is to move firmly into a stage four, where the broader community itself is in the driver's seat at the Murchison Community Center. At that point StJames Church, the state and the univer sity will all have to move into new supporting roles. The center is now an island of connectivity in the community; as it moves forward it will be poised to become just one station on the modern underground railway, one node on a network into the information-society promised-land.

Analysis

The historical narrative of the Murchison Center is summed up in Table 2. Each stage is named after the form of social capital making the critical contribution in the life of the center at that time. This has been a cumulative process, so at present there are four kinds of social capital on the board: church and community (bonding) and state and university (bridging) social capital.

Stage	*Facilities*	*Budget*	*Partners*
Church (1992–5)	St James Church basement, 1520 Hoag Street (July 1992)	Under $4,000 per year, raised by grassroots fundraising projects: $1,000 or more in account	Roosevelt CDC (local start-up)
State (1995–8)	1610 Lawrence (February 1995)	Average $30,000 per year, 90% from CDBG: line of credit briefly tops $11,000	CDBG, Lucas County Human Services Department, CATNeT
University (1998 to present)	1616 Lawrence (July 1999)	Average $35,000 per year, primarily grants, contracts, grants, user fees, small donors	University of Toledo, PASS charter school, Toledo GROWS, OCCCN, CTCNeT

Table 2. Historical stages of the Murchison Center, 1992–2000: Facilities, budget, partners

As noted above, this pattern of social capital is highly suggestive of a broader pattern that has been repeated at various stages of Black community development and the freedom struggle. Innovation takes place on the basis of initiatives generated within the Black community. The state steps in, either to stop what is new or to reconfigure it in line with agency specifications and funding requirements. This process suggests a process of spontaneity followed by institutional co-optation. For instance, in 1964 the Mississippi Summer Project initiated by the Student Non-violent Coordinating Committee (SNCC) started a network of 'Freedom Schools' to intervene in the early childhood development of poor children. In 1965 the federal government took this project as inspiration for a federal program called 'Operation Head Start'. In this case a state bureaucracy replaced a movement.

Several scholars have studied the intervention of the state to block the new tactics of the 1960s civil rights movement. Doug McAdam (1999) found that the state was interested not in advancing the movement but in preserving 'public order'. Piven and Cloward (1979, p. 231) found that 'in the wake of the student sit-ins and the freedom rides the Kennedy administration attempted to divert the civil rights forces from tactics of confrontation to the building of a Black electoral presence in the South'.

The difference in the case of the Murchison Center is the continuity of leadership. Throughout the history of the Murchison Center, continuity ensuring the stability and growth of the center has rested on its founder, Bishop Murchison, and its founding institution the church, which has supported the third continuity in the form of Mrs. Deborah Hamilton. Mrs. Hamilton has been executive director, mostly without pay, since 1994. Bishop Murchison has attended 94 of 107 total board meetings of the center.

Attendance at meetings is a solidly documented empirical indicator of social capital. Putnam bases his social capital argument on a decline in attendance: 'In short, in the mid-1970s near two-thirds of all Americans attended club meetings, but by the late 1990s near two-thirds of Americans never do' (Putnam 2000, p. 61).

In Figure 2 we present data on attendance at board meetings from 1992 to 2000. Board attendance is aggregated by the background of the board member and charted from 1992 to 2000. There is a general pattern consistent with our conception of three stages, basically 1992–5, 1995–8, 1998–2000. Overall there has been a sharp decline in the relative importance of attendance by board members representing bonding social capital. Church members have been replaced by the state and the university. Part of this is subtle, as three board members are both church members and government employees. One of these individuals works as a claims examiner for the Ohio Bureau of Employment Security; another is a security supervisor with the Lucas County Department of Human Services (the welfare department).

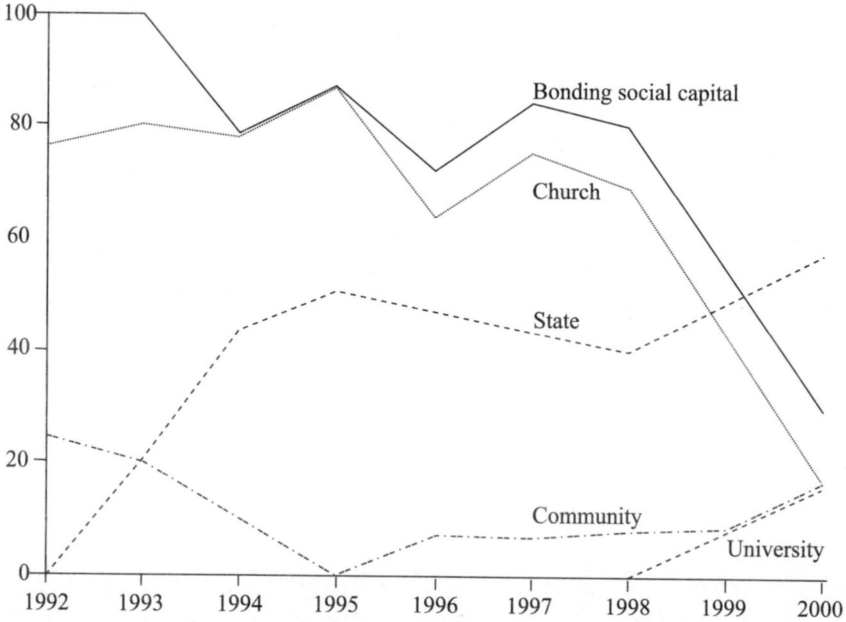

	1992	1993	1994	1995	1996	1997	1998	1999	2000
Number of board meetings	3	2	2	35	20	12	11	13	10
Number of participants	4	5	9	8	13	12	10	11	18

Church: Attends St James Church
State: Works for government agency
University: University student or faculty
Community: Private sector employment, lives in area served or is participant in programme:
Bonding social capital: Church, lives in area served or is participant in programme

Figure 2. Social capital: Attendance at board meetings by institutional affiliation, 1992–2000, as percentage of total, by year

The mission statement of an organization is a good indicator of its ideology. As noted above, the first Murchison Center statement reflects church language along with the grassroots slogan of 'Awareness, Education, and Outreach'. The second statement speaks the language of bureaucracy, but the slogan 'Knowledge is Power' also adopted during stage two expresses the orientation of Bishop Murchison and

St. James Church, reflecting the historic Black commitment to education and to struggle. Stage three brought a new concept from the technologically oriented poverty seminar: community-based cyberpower.

> Stage 1, church:
> Prevention is designed to focus upon [the] central city [with] Axiology/value ... Metaphysics/reality ... Epistemology/knowledge Awareness ... Education ... Outreach. (May 1993)
>
> Stage 2, state:
> Knowledge is Power (October 1996)
>
> Our mission is to educate, counsel, and provide the necessary training to alleviate the problems of underemployment, drug/alcohol abuse, peer pressure, and violence. We are committed to enhancing the overall social and economic growth of the neighborhood residents in our service area. (February 1997)
>
> Stage 3, university:
> Knowledge is Power (continued usage)
> Our mission is to educate and provide community support to alleviate the problems of underemployment, drug/alcohol abuse, peer pressure, and violence. We are committed to enhancing the overall social and economic growth of the neighborhood residents in our service area. Our main tool for change is community-based cyberpower.
> Community based cyberpower: community empowerment and organising using computers and the Internet. (August 1999)

The board and its changing ideological orientation connect with the program activities of the center and related participation. Figure 3 charts attendance at different programs from 1997 to 2000. Computer related programs begin to grow in mid-1998 with the technical support and teaching input from campus. Tutoring and practice testing in cooperation with parents and the university began in January 1999, but figures were not incorporated into monthly reports until October 1999. This in itself is a reflection of the bureaucratisation of the center, to the point where new developments were not swiftly incorporated into reporting. Reporting was seen as solely for the state and not for internal records. University volunteers had a big impact on mobilizing the community to participate. Demarcation between stage 2 (state) and stage 3 (university) is visible.

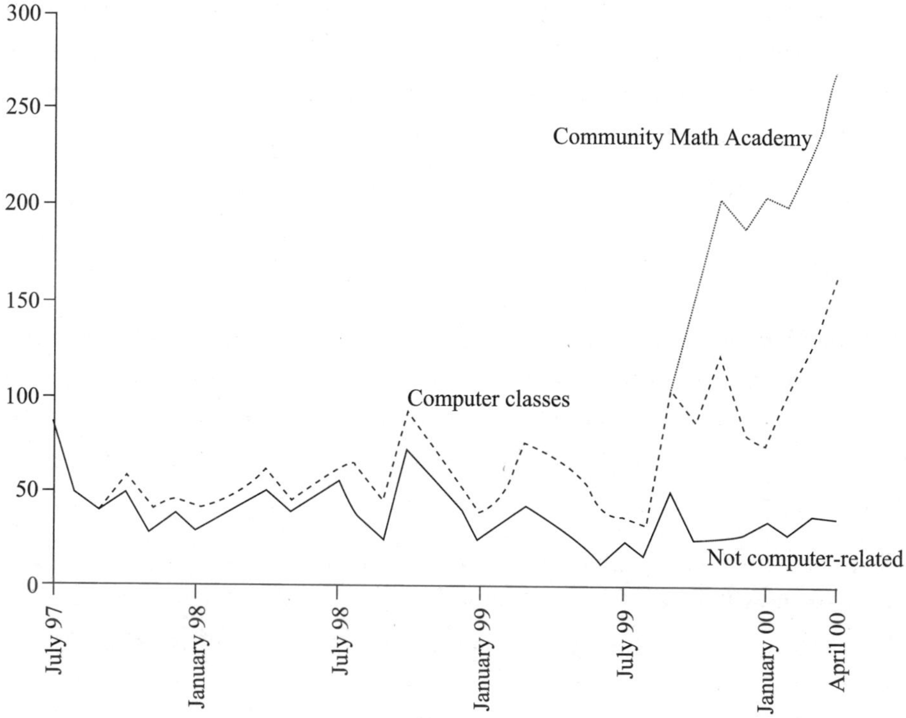

Figure 3. Attendance at different programs from 1997 to 2000

A closer look at the center's program offerings—computer classes and otherwise—allows us to identify the cyberpower that emerged from the social capital and other inputs that went into the center. Cyberpower was an outcome, but also, we will see, a further input into the center.

Individual cyberpower

As soon as the center acquired computers, adult beginners were taught to use the computer, to type, and to produce resumes. Once educational games were available on CD-ROM, children came in to do that as part of tutoring. By 1999, when computers had modernized and more computer-savvy staff and volunteers were on hand, these jobs and/or school-related classes grew more sophisticated. By 1999, adults were learning Adult Basic Computing (Windows and Wordpad), Word, Excel; children were using CD-ROM games but also learning Kids Basic Computing, Word, PowerPoint, and being guided through using educational websites.

The individual power that resulted was seen in adults' job-skills development and job-hunt successes, their individual mastery over the software. It was also seen in their moving to teach others, either the student sitting at the next computer or a whole room of students, as they moved from learning to teaching a class. At this point individual cyberpower becomes social cyberpower.

Social cyberpower

Long before 'community-based cyberpower' was part of the Murchison Center mission, it was in evidence. The first sign of this was in 1994 when Mrs. Hamilton explained her 'field promotion' from board secretary to executive director. 'I had been to college and I knew computers'. At that point computer knowledge was seen as something to be shared with the community. According to Mrs. Hamilton, the board at that time was looking for her not just to word-process letters but to teach others.

When the Community Math Academy began in January 1999, a local father began to volunteer at the monthly practice proficiency tests. When attendance at these was taken, it included not just name and phone but also email. His email address was piesqd@[...]. Pi is the ratio between the diameter and the circumference of a circle. Asking about this creative screen name, other volunteers learned that he was a UT student, a working engineering technician and, for the neighborhood, an early adopter of computers. Within a few months he volunteered to teach the evening Word/résumé-production class. Soon after he was promoted to computer lab manager. He computerized attendance records so that the monthly quantitative reports were produced by Access instead of by pencil and paper.

The Community Math Academy itself was a product of and a generator of social cyberpower. As we have said, students in the UT Poverty Seminar had found the Murchison Center's computer lab in an online listing on the CATNeT site, and the partnership that resulted came from the shared attitude that computers were a key to Black community empowerment. Where the seminar managed to show its participants the Web and perhaps get a few people HotMail accounts, the Community Math Academy went further, using e-groups to cement its volunteer leadership core and thus build social cyberpower. This involved some private computers as well as some loaners that went into people's homes, although they then decided to return the loaned computers and get their own more powerful units. In addition, center staff and volunteers' contacts with school officials were by email instead of phone or letter-writing, which was either unsuccessful or cumbersome.

A year after first inquiring about it, the Community Math Academy was able to make use of the school's computerized automatic phone message system to notify parents about the practice proficiency tests. In this way the voice of the newly elected King PTO delivered a message to six hundred King families. Just as with the loaner computers from the university, this board of education system was a case of bridging social capital and bonding social capital investing together in building the center's programs.

Perhaps the pinnacle examples of social cyberpower are the two classes, Cyberchurch and Cyberschools, which began in 1999 and 2000 respectively. Here, though, we cross over once again, as social cyberpower becomes ideological cyberpower.

Ideological cyberpower

The university brought to the scene the language of the digital divide, the Black liberation struggle and the community technology movement. This language expressed, clarified and advanced what the center was already doing to some extent. The ideology of community uplift using computers, rooted also in the concept 'Knowledge is Power', was elaborated in the day-to-day work, the plans and the mission statement of the center. Embedded here was an ideological orientation towards the community as a set of assets as well as needs, best evidenced in the last sentence of the mission statement developed by the Community Math Academy (emphasized below). The goal of 'ending poverty once and for all' was an early critical ideological issue.

> The Community Math Academy aims to improve the math skills and change the math attitudes of young people in central city Toledo. We see math as an academic subject and a tool for social transformation. We see math as part of ending poverty once and for all.
>
> The academy is a project of UT, the Murchison Center, and King School. We join with children and their parents to conduct educational activities in the school, the community and the home. *Parents are the leaders of the academy because parents love their children and, more than anyone, determine their futures.*

Operating as it did over the Internet as well as through face-to-face meetings and sessions, the Community Math Academy program was itself an instance of ideological cyberpower. But two classes, Cyberchurch and Cyberschools, began in 1999 and 2000 respectively and also illustrate the ideological cyberpower generated through the center.

Cyberchurch emerged as an assignment in a university course on the Black Church. When each student went to complete a website for a local church, they came to the center to build their site. This class then took on a life of its own, with word of mouth bringing more students, one student stepping forward to teach it, and more skills and web space being applied. The course assignment originated as an idea that the director of Africana Studies sold to the instructor for Black Church. The instructor, a local pastor and high school guidance counselor, had pastored in various Toledo churches for twenty-seven years, and provided his church space to the local Black Panther chapter when it formed. While the website building assignment in his course was a burden to him at first—he was asking students to do something he hadn't done—one day after hearing a lecture by the director he told him, 'I've heard you talk about this "eBlack" many times, and I always agreed. But now I really, really get it! I have it so much on my mind that I'm thinking of taking out all the pews in my church and using folding chairs, and getting in some computers. It can still serve on Sundays but can be a lab the rest of the time'. His plans began to unfold.

The ideological content of this form of cyberpower is the vision that, if the Black church is online, then a good portion of the Black public sphere can be kept intact as our personal, cultural, political and spiritual lives move into cyberspace, as more and more Black people get online. If the Black church is intact, then the Black liberation struggle has that important institution, with all the social capital embedded therein, to rely on.

While Cyberchurch was a class that expresses the dynamic combination university social capital (bridging) and church social capital (bonding) within the context of the center, Cyberschools had a slightly different origin. It originated from a combination of university social capital with community social capital (bonding), again within the context of the center.

Murchison's Community Math Academy project put the center and its volunteers, especially the university students, in close proximity to King Elementary School. The CMA, especially the involved parents, who were all grandmothers, attended the school's PTO meetings, seeking more parent involvement. CMA volunteers worked in the schools as classroom teacher aides and after school as tutors. As a result, new officers were voted in as PTO leaders.

The King PTO had two members who were a couple with one son in the school but had been unable to organize parents to do more than bake sales and an annual book sale. The Murchison Center began to do outreach to get more parents to the PTO meetings. Thus the annual election brought in a full slate of PTO officers with new energy and a plan to build the library up, participate in practice proficiency testing and so on.

Cyberschools was begun to support these parents and others like them. Like Cyberchurch, it meets one night a week. Cyberschools sessions are dedicated to two things: organizing to get more families to practice proficiency tests, and helping local PTOs get their plans and contact information posted on to web pages devoted to their schools and their families, plus email.

PTOs across the country have web pages and use email to keep parents in touch and organized. But these PTOs do not often appear to be in the Black community. With computers moving into homes and workplaces, anyone can take advantage of the Internet to organize. Not only that, the websites that Cyberschools takes people to explore include the Toledo Public Schools, the teachers' union, the University of Toledo, the Ohio Board of Education (which posts information about schools, testing, standards, the Ohio 4th Grade Guarantee (no fourth-grader failing the reading test will be advanced to the 5th grade) and more. So the Internet is a source of information as well as a communication tool used by parents to impact children's experience in public schools. Parent involvement is proved to be perhaps the deciding factor in student and school success.

Implications

We are now able to elaborate further the theoretical framework emerging from our analysis. We will move beyond the particularity of this case study to conceptual implications for our general research focus, community technology centers in urban poor communities, especially communities of color. First e will concentrate the lessons of this case study into several propositions that in turn can serve as guidelines for further research. Second, we will discuss the implications of this research for the public sphere, especially the Black counter-public sphere.

The first point is that these centers are social organizations, and therefore part of the structure of social relations in a community. This understanding requires a paradigm shift from the current dominant trend to study individuals who pass through the center, to the centers themselves as social units.

A second point is that the digital divide has to be understood as a community attribute, part of a broader phenomena called public computing. The digital divide as community descriptor can be determined by how extensive and effective are the local organizations, which provide and promote public computing.

A third point is that the CTC as community organization is the locus for the concentration of resources. These resources can be conceived as different forms of capital:

- *physical*: buildings and equipment
- *human*: staff
- *financial*: budget
- *social*: social background and ties of board members and the organized partnerships of the organization.

A fourth point is that social capital is the key. Bonding social capital is the fundamental resource that makes something belong to a community. Without this form of community wealth and legitimacy the organization is an artificial construct. Bridging social capital is essential in acquiring temporary resources and external support. Whenever bridging social capital is dominant, the organization is in crisis and in danger of dying or being transformed as an extension of external interests rather than the interest of the original community and its bonding social capital.

A fifth point is that the investment of these resources produces a social value, cyberpower. There are three forms of cyberpower:

- Individual cyberpower: new human capital
- social cyberpower: collectives engaged in cyber organizing
- ideological cyberpower: ideas and policy promoted by individual and social cyber power.

A sixth and final point is that the success and sustainability of a center is a function of whether point five loops back and feeds into the capital resources of the organization. The organization produces bonding social capital or it fails the litmus test of success and sustainability.

On the basis of these six points it is critical to raise the issue of democracy and social inclusion of people who are living in the social isolation of the poor part of the dual city. The existence of a democratic system is not merely the actions of individuals at the polls. Democracy requires informed citizens who are socialized and live in a complex set of overlapping social networks. Each network is an interest group, and multiple memberships mean multiple interests, sometimes congruent and sometimes in conflict. This complexity is the basis for democratic discussion and compromise. We argue and compromise because while we have differences with others, on other issues we share common interests.

Building sustainable democratic equality in the information age means more than how many individuals are online. The key is to stabilize and support people working with information technology in the form of social organizations rooted in the legitimate social capital of the community. The key is to invest all forms of capital to produce social capital for the socially isolated inner city Black poor. In turn, this investment should be utilized to produce Black cyberpower. Powerlessness, especially the lack of cyberpower, is anathema to democracy in the information society.

10

Social Cyberpower in the Everyday Life of an African American Community: A Report on Action-Research in Toledo, Ohio[①] (2004)

Abdul Alkalimat

Introduction

What will the experience of the African American community be in the information age? This is a critical question as it appears more and more that the social transformation underway utilizing information technology is permanent, and increasingly redefining standards for social life: literacy, job readiness, upward social mobility, and social power. Most African Americans were not among the early adopters of this new technology and therefore appear to be beginning the 21st century in much the same way as the 20th century, not at the cutting edge of economic development. This reality can be changed.

This chapter reports on an action-research project designed to explore the ways in which the everyday life of a community can become the content of its virtual community identity, and by so doing create a bridge over the digital divide. The project is based in Toledo, Ohio (USA) and is a joint effort by the Africana Studies Program at the University of Toledo and the Murchison Community Center. The field work for much of the research reported here was done by

① Partial support for this project came from the Urban Affairs Center and the College of Arts and Sciences at the University of Toledo.

the first masters' degree graduates in eBlack Studies, Africana Studies based on information technology. They continue to work together in the Murchison Center as executive director, Americorps VISTA volunteer, and volunteer teacher.

The Murchison Center began in 1992 as a program of the St. James Baptist Church. It has become a full service community technology center, with 20 networked workstations, cable internet connection, and capacity for printing and multimedia. The program includes after school tutoring and adult classes four nights a week. The annual budget of the Murchison Center has been about $30,000, not including VISTA funding, which pays several volunteers just under $800 per month. There have been stages when the decisive influence on the center was the church, the government, and then the university. Each stage was cumulative, so that previous influence and contributions were not lost. Current transformations appear to be towards greater community influence and inputs to the Murchison Center (Alkalimat and Williams 2001).

The local community is the kind of neighborhood where people are usually locked out of the access and training needed to be an active part of the information society. As master's student, center co-founder and executive director Deborah Hamilton described the area, It is located in central city Toledo where the community...is 70% poor or near poor. Ninety-seven per cent are African American in the immediate area (census tracts 25 and 26, Toledo, Ohio). The 1990 median income is $12,400 and $15,400 respectively in both census tracts. Single mothers head more than 60% of the households. One fourth of the residents are under 13 years of age. (Hamilton 2002, p. 13)

Overall, Toledo is a metropolitan area of over 500,000 people, 20 percent of whom are African American. It has a shrinking manufacturing base historically linked to the auto industry headquartered in Detroit 50 miles to the north. Its irony in the global economy is that Toledo produced the classic World War II Jeep that was vital in the war against Germany. Now today Daimler-Benz owns the plant, which produces the Jeep Cherokee. Toledo's capital used to be local, community based, and big enough to finance local projects like building a major art museum (1901), university (1872), and manufacturing, especially glass and auto components. Now most of the big capital is absentee-owned.

Toledo has had considerable effort put into developing community level technology resources. Two 1996 initiatives led to the formation of a local organization called Coalition to Access Technology and Networking in Toledo or CATNeT.② A local housing manager got a Housing and Urban Development grant to build and staff several computer labs in private apartment complexes, and a local academic researcher got involved with a State of Ohio initiative, the Urban University Neighborhood Network. The network started with 9 labs and now has a membership of 34 labs (Stoecker and Stuber 1997). A recent survey to locate all of the public computing in Toledo found over 250 public access sites including schools and libraries (Williams and Alkalimat 2004). In addition, the Toledo labs are active in a statewide organization (Ohio Community Computing Network)③ and a national organization (Community Technology Centers Network).④

The Toledo model shown in Figure 1 proposes how a socially excluded community can be transformed into a networked community, able to mobilize cyberpower to advance its interests. In the model, the transformation from a historical community to a networked community is catalyzed by cyberorganizers and by the organizing and mobilizing impact of the content and interactivity of cyberspace. This is how the actual social organization of the community can create or cooperate with cyberorganizers to build an existence in cyberspace. The process intensifies as the community becomes more engaged in using information technology and dependent on the new opportunities of an entire community sharing a virtual

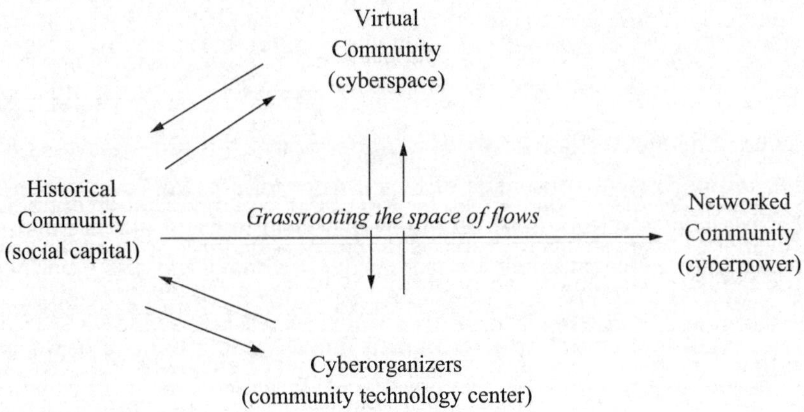

Figure 1. The Toledo model

② http://uac.utoledo.edu/metronet/catnet/.

③ http://www.occcn.org.

④ http://www.ctcnet.org.

collectivity. It is precisely this collective that will learn how to act, first in cyberspace like sending mass emails or signing a petition, or swarming emails, then by leaving cyberspace and taking action in the real world. Both of these actions, virtual and actual can be called cyberpower as the key staging area for the collective action was in cyberspace.

We will now use this four part framework to report on four of the cyberpower projects. Cyberfamilies is a project to utilize the existing practice of research for family genealogy to build a database beginning with individual extended families to network and link-up an entire community. Cyberhair is a project based on databases of beauty salons, combs, and information resources about hair care and design. Cyberchurch is a project to build a dynamic database of church websites, and extend that into a comprehensive virtual community of individual churches and the entire religious community. Cyberschools is a project to use cyberspace in two ways, as a directory of individual school web pages, and a site for a community wide campaign to pass a state mandated proficiency test. This is a work in process.

Actual experience	*Virtual experience*	*URL*
Neighborhood	Virtual Dorr Street	http://www/murchisoncenter.org/dorrstreet/
Family	Cyberfamily	http://www.murchisoncenter.org/cyberfamilies/
Church	Cyberchurch	http://www.cyber-church.us
School	Cyberschool	http://www.murchisoncenter.org/cyberschool/
	First Saturday	http://www.murchisoncenter.org/firstsaturday/
Business	Cyberhair	http://www.murchisoncenter.org/cyberhair
CTC	Murchison Center	http://www.murchisoncenter.org

Table 1. The historical community: The actual experience and its virtual representation (the Toledo Model)

Cyberfamilies

Historical community

The family is generally regarded as a core institution of every society. It has been the vehicle for procreation and social reproduction–people have babies to replenish the community by creating a family, and then in turn rely on the family to socialize the children to become members of society. The research focus on the Black family, especially on changes in Black family organization, has charted the Black family from its origins in Africa through the destructive terror of slavery, sharecropping tenancy, and industrial city life. Within this, the most persistent debate has been over the relative importance of slavery in understanding the persistence of family disorganization today.

This leads to one of the main obstacles in building a family database. There are limited records of biological parenting under slavery. Although a slave culture did emerge and provide a counterweight to the system, official records regarding family continuity were based on the slave owner and not the slave. In addition, family relations without formal legal marriage, and generally without documentation, presents a problem for anyone researching family history. On the other hand, it is precisely these problems that lead people to value the successful attempt to reconstruct family networks.

Cyberfamilies pointed up a big difference between lineage as tracing one's origins versus family history as tracing one's socio-biological network, inclusive of all its many branches and hubs. A lineage network will include the shortest available distance between two points in a family network, but a social network includes all available branches. Some family members seek historical meaning by linking with a particular ancestor, others by linking with broad social forces in society and the world. In my own family, the progenitor is Free Frank, a slave who bought himself and 19 other family members. The family points to him as the main frame of reference. The question is, How are you related to Free Frank? On the other hand, during family gatherings people might have spoken of the role the family played in different wars, of the different professions and industries people worked in, cities where different family hubs were located, and so on (Simpson 1983; Walker 1983).

The family has been a hot topic in cyberspace, even for African Americans who are not online to the same extent as other ethnic groups. We identified two main kinds of genealogical sites designed for African Americans: general genealogical sites on African Americans, and research databases such as the census, government records and so on, including a great deal of information on specific families.[⑤] In addition, many personal websites have some kind of reference or link to family content. The people who make up the content in most of these sites often do not know that information about them is available in cyberspace. This is public information.

---

⑤ See the following: http://www.afrigeneas.com, http://www.prairiebluff.com/aacemetery, and http://freedmensbureau.com

Cyberorganizer

The cyberorganizer for this project is Pauline Kynard. Ms. Kynard completed her undergraduate degree in Africana Studies while working as Director of the Art Tatum Resource Center in African American Culture of the Toledo-Lucas County Public Library, Kent Branch. She developed the Cyberfamilies project as her undergraduate thesis project. The project is now a formal collaboration between Africana Studies at the University of Toledo and the Art Tatum Center.

The first stage was to identify one or more families who met three criteria: basic research materials have been collected, a family member is willing to work with the project as liaison with the family, and the family agrees to have this information freely available on the cyber families web site. Working with her on their respective families are another undergraduate major in Africana Studies representing the Jaynes family, and my sister who had started a web project on our McWorter family. The three families were different in their approach to family history, but each already had completed a great deal of research. The Kynard and Jaynes families are large families settled in Toledo for three generations. The McWorter family is part of the official record of African Americans in the state of Illinois from the 1830's.

Cyberspace

Ms. Kynard worked with each family to organize available material and assist in additional research. When discussing the digitization aspect of the project it was necessary to discuss continuing research on the family. Once she has gathered and codified the information the task was for the Africana Studies Media Lab to write software for a database to express the full branching of a family social network. The working model enables every person in the network to become the center of an investigation that can follow every branch of the network that we have information for. It is a matter of statistical calculation to determine how many links we are away from each other. The most celebrated finding is that people are no more than six connections away from each other in actual reality, but the way that cyberspace has been constructed any given web page is 19 clicks from any other, but this finding only applies to the 24% of cyberspace that is available via simple surfing (Barabasi 2002: pp. 25–40, 165). Clearly our actual social lives are more connected than our representations in cyberspace. But this need not be the case.

Each individual in a family network has a page. This places them at the center of kinship links to the broader network, through their parents and their children. Each individual is at the same time at the center and the periphery of an expanding network of humanity, going back into history and forward into the future. Stable communities will be more closely connected, but over generations most groups are likely to be much closer than people think.

Networked community

The first outcome from the pilot stage of this project is that Ms. Kynard was asked to prepare a CD for the Jaynes family reunion. This project has now become an organizing activity in the family to digitize their history and current make up. Secondly, she is preparing a slide-lecture presentation on the project for community groups interested in genealogy. And, the library is considering expanding its uploading functions such as is required by the cyberfamilies project, i.e., giving more importance to creating digital libraries of local content.

The project is moving to an institutional process that will create a new generation of family cyberarchivists, e.g., students in school. Plans have been developed to implement a module for graduating seniors at the local Black high school to develop digital family history. They will have the option to contribute their family information to the database of cyberfamilies. As the families interconnect then the identity of the network will shift from family in a narrow sense to community in a broad sense. We will discover as never before the logic of kinship and be able to transform it as a network into a communications channel for cyber activity. The latent social cyberpower of this dormant network will be activated. This will be its digital awakening and engagement.

Cyberhair

Historical community

Taken together, hair care and hair design are an important part of social life, culture and identity in every society. In the Black community they are especially critical because African hair has unique qualities for hair sculpture and because there is a long tradition of African American cultural excellence in this activity. The hair salons are centers of economic, cultural and social action. Doing hair is rooted in deep cultural economics, encompassing family labor, barter with friends, or doing it by oneself.

The beauty salon was created to provide a service in the urban Black community, especially in the 20th century. As a result of proletarianization, African American families became smaller, family networks were de-territorialized, and many services became commodified. The salons became centers of cultural production and economic exchange as well as "third places", sites of public discourse that form a hub serving across a dense network of families, friends and acquaintances. Transgenerational interlocking networks of families and churches are vehicles for discourse. Beauty salons are a vital part of the African American public sphere.

The main icon of the Black woman as entrepreneur is Madame C. J. Walker (1867–1919), founding leader of the Black hair care industry. She invented a new chemical process for hair care and design. But her impact went way beyond this. She recruited and trained a corps of hair care workers thereby giving beauticians a greater professional profile. This was the most stable form of independent business ownership for Black women in the 20th century. She provided significant financial and moral support to the writers, artists, and institution-builders who became known as the "Harlem Renaissance". She also did so with the political militants of the "New Negro" movement.

However, today the political economy of the Black hair care industry is changing. One major example is the retailing and wholesaling of Black hair care products. In Toledo there is one Black hair products distribution company over 40 years old. Over the last ten years Asian business interests have opened at least four megastores, each with more than ten times the floor space and product selection. Salons located in the major malls and department stores now include Black people in their market. This has led to a tension between the traditionally more networked, "conversation-intense", and slower beauty parlor in the community and doing hair as a commodity in a time-driven, mass market, mall environment.

The beauty salon in the Black community has historical roots but is in a state of crisis. There is some hope for the future, however, as the main Black high school has a growing cosmetology program. Enrollment there is greater than that in many of the more high tech areas that lead to a college major in engineering and computer science. Enrolling in cosmetology is also evidence of a desire to get a skill and possibly be self-employed and able to support oneself and a family.

Cyberorganizing

The Cyberhair project emerged in three stages: a conference, a class project, and a MA thesis project. The conference defined the project, the class began the enumeration of salons, and the thesis work built the Cyberhair website, "Black

People's Hair".

A symposium—"Black Peoples Hair: A Symposium on the Political Culture of Everyday Life" ⑥—was during the first year of the UT Africana Studies program on March 6–7, 1997. This brought Black studies to life for UT students, many of whom were first in their families to attend college, a day when art historians who focus on African hair, hair braiders, and students could bring their knowledge together. The conference was scholarly, with presentations on the mutual influence of African and African American hairstyles over the last five centuries. It was practical, with hair braiders demonstrating their work on volunteers. And it was emotional and personal, with participants sharing stories of their struggles with their hair and their identity.

The conference set the framework for the Cyberhair project in three ways. The project would focus on cultural production rather than cultural performance. It would advocate Panafricanism as a cultural approach. And it would advocate the adoption of information technology as a technological foundation.

The Africana Studies program then organized an undergraduate course called "Cyberspace and the Black Experience" ("Africana Studies 4900" 2000). Along with readings and seminar discussions, the course initiated a practical research project to build a database of Toledo's African American beauty salons. Here a debate emerged over whether it was a "politically correct" action to study places that were hostile to a positive Black identity, meaning did anything other than natural hairstyles. The one sister in the class with "trendy locks" was opposed to going to the beauty salons for this reason, but the others who all wore styles more in the mainstream of Black Toledo agreed that this project would make a big impact on the overall Black community. They were responding to the design of the assignment, to build a cyberresource that might motivate people to become computer literate and cross over the digital divide.

The one young man in the class took up the task of completing the database as his masters project in Africana Studies. In his thesis, Brian Zelip explains his situation:

> I am a white male. Every salon I went to was a Black salon. 78% of the salons were owned by women. All of the salon owners were in their mid-30's or older, whereas at the time of the research I was 24 years old. ... It was anticipated that the research being carried out by me would be faced with

⑥ See http://www.murchisoncenter.org/cyberhair/conference.htm

some degree of resistance and non-cooperation. (Zelip 2002,p. 88)

He bases this on the social meaning of color, gender, hair and age. However, he then attributes his success to how these barriers were overcome: the salon owners' respect for the research sponsors (UT Africana Studies and the Murchison Center) and for his knowledge of the African American community and culture. Zelip had been a hip hop dj on the campus radio station.

Cyberspace

The website was built around the 1997 hair conference, the database of beauty salons, and a collection of images of Afro combs. This anchored the digital identity of virtual Black hair in the actual space of cultural production rather than cultural performance. Beauty magazines stress cultural performance–gorgeous women, lots of documentation of spectacular events, product ads, and celebrities. The magazines are like dream books to guide stylist and the customer. In contrast, Cyberhair's emphasis on cultural production targeted the universal experience of everyday life.

The Africana Studies Media Lab digitized a collection of combs from the US and elsewhere that the author gathered over a 35 year period. The process of organizing the digitized images facilitated our discovery that the Afro comb has passed through four historical stages: traditional, industrial, Panafrican, and global. The combs began in traditional society (made of wood), underwent further development in industrial society (metal), took new forms during the struggles for national liberation (wood, metal, and plastic), and now reflect the reality of globalization (extruded plastic).

Networked community

In the project, students become cyberorganizers, relying on the historical community of salon owners, stylists, and customers to help build the site and determine its future evolution. Out of fifty salons, seven owners were found to have active email addresses, but none of the shops had a computer in the salon for business or the public. But as a result of contact with our project several salon owners and stylists have taken computer classes at the Murchison Center.

Zelip went on a study tour of South Africa and took the opportunity to document hair care practices. On one occasion he found a beauty salon next to a cybercafé. The hair stylists had never been online. He gathered them in the cybercafé to view

Black People's Hair on the web. When he returned to Toledo, he showed slides of the South African experience to the stylists who were in the site. This is a small example of cyberspace creating a Panafrican experience at the grass roots in the 21st century.

Survey data collected by students identified a small number of salon owners who are interested in making efforts to use computers and the Internet. The Murchison Center set aside computers to place into salons, and a masters student from the University of Michigan School of Information joined the project as cyberorganizer to carry out the installation and support of the PCs. This will enable the project to support the use of software for the salon as business, and the Internet and the World Wide Web for customers. In the future we will investigate the possibility of uniting an intensely individualistic group of entrepreneurs into a collectivity to serve common interests.

Cyberchurch

Historical community

The church is the most comprehensive social institution in the African American community. It provides a total experience based on its embodiment of culture, ideology, social organization, economic development, leadership, ritual, and a moral order. It is important among the social cyberpower projects because it also has had a long history of adopting new advances in communications technology. Today one can experience the Black church in person, on the radio, on television, in print, on video, CD, DVD, the Internet and the World Wide Web. The actual church takes up regular time each week and provides host space for many community activities. It seems only a matter of time before the church in cyberspace will rival the traditional gathering of a congregation.

Our survey suggests that there are at least 300 churches that primarily serve African Americans in Toledo. This constitutes the most powerful set of leaders, real estate interests, ideological consensus, and mass mobilization in the Black community. However, the church has to adapt to the new technology if it is to serve youth as they become cyberactivists. When we began our project less than 10 churches had their own web page reflecting the community wide impact of the digital divide. When the church adopts a new technology it also has the role of infusing it into other community activities as well. It is in this sense that Cyberchurch is a pivotal project.

Cyberorganizing

Cyberchurch began as a research assignment in an Africana Studies course on the Black church. Reverend Al Reed, a local minister with a social activist background, was recruited to teach the course once a week every Saturday morning. This schedule was set to allow for non-traditional working students to enroll in the course. Each student was assigned to gather church information for a web page. We began without allot of computer literacy. However, the majority of students became comfortable and fluent with basic computer software and aspects of the web. In fact, out of this course, a couple of students even became teachers at the Murchison Center and leaders of the Cyberchurch project.

A second process was outreach to church leadership to attend free computer literacy orientation sessions offered weekly by the Africana Studies program. The main result of this has been a greater interest in the project. Many of the participants in the early morning outreach sessions also began attending evening workshop sessions. The process of building a virtual community was itself becoming a meaningful social group meeting on a face-to-face basis. These discussions were important for several reasons: they became focus groups to get community feedback on the project, they educated people about the project and got them to buy into the plan, and it allowed for students to emerge and make the transitions from student to community worker.

The project plans four progressive levels in the expansion of the Black church into cyberchurch. Level one is a church in the online church directory, with a web page containing publicly available information about the church, including a photo. Level two is a church that has supplied information about its staff, organization, calendar, and program and that has at least ten of its members with email signed up to a Cyberchurch electronic discussion list. Level three is a church web site with sound files, and/or video of at least one sermon and one song by the choir. Level four is a church with its own community technology center.

An action-research team called the Toledo Spiders carried out the data collection for level one. This team was made up of undergraduates and led by a graduate student in Africana Studies, all paid with federal work-study funds. The team used digital cameras and tape recorders to document conferences and churches as part of the Cyberchurch project. The project began to take off as people were motivated to get their own church online, and community organizers began to see this as a positive organizing project. The Murchison Center staff is currently organizing to visit each church to make direct contact with the church leadership. Unless a church member has participated in Cyberchurch classes, this visit is generally the first notice the congregation has of the project, which is usually followed by a regular announcement in the printed church bulletin distributed every Sunday.

There are five main lessons from this work: First, standardization of a main template for the project solved problems created by first trying to use freeware and free web hosting with people with low computer literacy. Second, emphasis on email seems a more democratic way to build a networked community while building a main web location as a virtual base of operations. Third, early adopters of this program were church seniors, but the critical mass for the church to become a networked community will be the youth. Fifth, student workers have to be mentored in terms of technical skill, attitude, and time management. Lastly, the greatest resource in building a cyberorganizing project is the bonding social capital that sustains participation.

Cyberspace

The general plan for the page is to combine the feature of a general portal with a database of individual church web pages. Again, our emphasis is on cultural production. We are approaching the church in terms of sites of cultural production (churches, seminaries, and publications) and tools of production (holy texts, hymns, and theologians). Linking all of this together can create an environment embracing all organized religious activity. One sister attending a Cyberchurch session responded to this design with a smile on her face saying, "My Lord, if we can all get together like this in cyberspace then we can all be in the same church".

On the site, each church's web page is based on a standardized template. The page allows for voluntary submission of information to start the process of a church being added to the database. Confirmation by the Cyberchurch team is necessary before any information is posted.

The logic of this structure follows an intervention by cyberorganizers into the internal organization of the church resulting in the church becoming itself a cyberorganizing force within the community. The cyberorganizer can join the church or just work with it, but also there will be church members who have or gain the skill who become cyberorganizers as well. In fact it is not too early to see the emergence of a new field for church professionals, cyberministry. The digital archive of the Black church experience will constitute its historical identity, and digital interaction will become a major vehicle for collectivizing religious experience.

Networked community

The church as a networked community can come into existence as each of the four levels of the cyber church project is achieved. The key is level two, when church members join the electronic discussion list. With more than 250 churches at level one now, level two may result in more than 2,500 people on an emailing list. We are currently in the process of building level two and the mailing list. The Cyberchurch team meets in a working session once a week. They will constitute the editorial collective for a newsletter based on a unified church calendar. This will be sent out as an email message, while the annual calendar will be archived on the web site. While starting out as a mailing list, the role of cyberorganizing in this case is to building a discussion list.

A community organization in Chicago has also joined Cyberchurch, adding Chicago churches to the site. On a national level, the project has been joined by the National Society of Black Engineers [7] with more than 300 local college chapters of African American students in engineering and computer science.

The project is also networking the existing resources in the community. Five women who have become cyberorganizers in the cyber church project are also now the webmasters for their respective churches. Several churches have started labs on their own, and have affiliated with CATNeT.

Cyberschools

Historical community

The school as a social institution and a site for social change has always been an important part of the African American community. Free Black communities established schools before the Civil War in the 18th century, and then universal public education was established during the Reconstruction in the South in the 19th century. A third level was reached in the 1950's and 60's, when the school became a key battleground in the 20th century. Throughout these high points were critical shifts in the political orientation of the Black public sphere. There

---

⑦ http://www.nsbe.org.

were different great debates that dominated public discourse: the emancipation debate (including the abolitionists, the Civil War, and the Reconstruction), the self-determination debate (the alternative views of people such as Marcus Garvey, Booker T. Washington, and W. E. B. DuBois), and the Black liberation debate (especially the alternative perspectives of Malcolm X, Martin Luther King).

Schools are vehicles for socialization. Each school level with a simultaneous experience (for example, the students in one high school at one time) constitutes a generation. This same group will share social experience throughout their life cycle. The schools in Toledo had a functional fit with the economy when industrial mass production required lots of workers with general skills. People graduated from high school into the factories and got good, often lifelong, jobs. In the 1960's, Black youth were overcoming lower rates of success, but by the 21st century the process has been reversed. At this stage of deindustrialization, the Toledo schools have become dysfunctional, falling far short of expected levels of achievement. The teachers are mainly white, and the students are mainly Black. The economic interests of the union are discussed independent from the quality of education facing the children and their parents. The school is the primary battleground over whether the future of the current generation of Black youth is to be part of the information society or delinked in isolated lower-income inner city "forbidden zones".

Cyberorganizing

There have been three stages to this project:

1. The Community Math Academy: a two year long initiative at the Martin Luther King Elementary School focusing on "parent power" and information technology;

2. Cyberschools: a networking from the base of one school to create a web portal for a groups of schools;

3. Online practice proficiency test: a web page with new practice math tests every month from September to March.

The core group of the CMA included eight people, four cyberorganizers based in the university (one faculty and three graduate students) and four grandmothers based at the Murchison Center and the surrounding community. Every person in the group had a computer or was provided a refurbished one through a program of the Murchison Center. The CMA established a discussion list. We knew it was working when one of the grandmothers used the list to organize a community barbeque. Michelene McGreevy was the student cyberorganizer on this project and she based her master's thesis in Africana Studies on her work (McGreevy 2002).

Our first initiative of after school tutoring in the Murchison Center led to meeting with parents and grandparents with a concern for school reform. Their focus was on the school where everything seemed to be going wrong. The parents were demobilized and the teachers' union did not have a positive relationship with the community. The CMA became active in building the local Parent-Teachers Organization. When we joined, the meetings were called and attended by a husband and wife team of parents with little or no support. CMA's involvement led to increased attendance by parents at meetings. A consequence of this was that conflict arose, prompting the need for a contested election. During this period, the appointment of a new principal precipitated a change in school administration. Parent involvement in these meetings was not encouraged as the new regime sought to gain control.

In response to this the project shifted focus from the actual to the virtual, to building web pages for schools to recruit parent, teachers, and students to unite in an effort to take virtual control of their schools by defining them in cyberspace. The initial focus was on building web pages for each school, going well beyond the administrative page on the main web site of the Toledo Public Schools. This was aimed at making the school a transparent user-friendly seeming place. We also wanted to demonstrate the power of machine assisted community memory. One example of this is that when the local Black high school won the city championship in basketball it was in the newspapers for one day and that was the end of it. We put up a web page on it and it remains there today as fresh as ever to bolster the local spirit of excellence.

This second stage shifted from a focus on a high school and its nine feeder schools to a focus on the high school alone. There was positive recognition of each new page of local content, but as the school and the local community leadership did not promote the necessity of building a virtual identity this was a good but not very utilized community resource. Our attempt to digitize the bonding social capital was a highly valued but seldom used resource. The missing element was support from the local school culture, especially the legitimacy of support from parents and teachers.

The third phase of this project focused on the crisis of poor academic achievement as measured by low scores on state mandated proficiency tests. These annual tests cover five subject areas, and are given to three grade levels (4th, 6th, and 9th). It is now necessary to pass these tests or be held back to repeat the grade level until you pass the test.

We began giving practice proficiency tests in math every first Saturday. The project grew from nine students to 400 students. The tests are composed based on official state guidelines by a student community teacher work team, and the tests are monitored and graded by a collective of college student volunteers. Now the first Saturday practice tests are online and available for access to everyone. [8] The tests are a major battlefront in education, as the state is requiring more testing. Our project is designed to mobilize people in the struggle for good test scores. Some people will be helped in the short run and their children will get higher scores. In the longer run we are building a social process that can be linked to other efforts for school reform.

Cyberspace

Each stage of this project has had a corresponding representation in cyberspace. A webliography of links served as a resource for the tutoring activity. Cyberschools was a portal with a common template for web pages about each of the 10 schools. The tests online are for printing and administering, with a separate answer sheet for immediate review and study. Each of these cyberspaces is useful: global, local, struggle for good test scores.

Networked community

We have positioned two paths to networking in this project, the digitization of local school culture and the digitization of test preparation. One is a focus on the local, the particular differences of each school, while the other is global, and points to the universal struggle faced by all students. As computer literacy becomes universal in the high schools then both paths will be used, but under these circumstances the use of the online tests has had the greatest result as it maximizes the potential of a small group to meet the needs of a very large group. The proficiency test is a state level law hence our project online is of immediate use to everyone in Ohio.

The greatest potential for new cyberinitiatives lies within the high schools in the

---

⑧ http://www.murchisoncenter.org/firstsaturday/.

USA. There is widespread availability of computers and high speed Internet access. The youth are wellsprings of creative energy. Our work is but a prelude to the revolution being born among the hackers, gamers, texters, and all the other smart mobs that Howard Rheingold (2002) has helped bring to our attention.

Conclusions

Just as there are many bridges across the digital divide, there are alternative ways for a community to become networked. There at least five models: 1) early utopian community free-net projects, 2) experimental communities like Netville, 3) dot-coms built for mass participation like eBay, 4) Social movements and political campaigns, and 5) public computing for social cyberpower. We have reported on action-research in Toledo, Ohio involving a project to implement and study the public computing model, based at the Murchison Community Center.

Our approach focuses on four factors: historical community, cyberorganizers, cyberspace, and the networked community.

1. The historical community: We have found the content of the historical community in the institutional structures that sustain and reproduce the community. We have concentrated on the family, the church, the school, and the beauty salon as key institutional contexts. In addition to digitizing the content of institutional life, two other points of focus emerged. The first is to pay attention to the antagonisms that the community faces because these struggles create the social future of the community; and the second is the recruitment of emerging cyberorganizers from the indigenous activists that keep these institutions going. The search is for the ways in which social cyberpower contributes to the sustainability of an institution and the overall community.

2. The cyberorganizer: Social cyberpower is associated with public computing, especially the school, the library, and the community technology center. Organizing forces for actual social struggle in this way is emerging as a new field for research and curriculum development as there is a growing need for the kind of work reported in this article. We anticipate that information technology will induce changes in the fundamental methods of social research and social activism alike. The challenge is for academic programs to learn how to link research and practical experience. The land grant college system did it for agriculture and mass production industry, and

now we need to do it again in terms of information technology.

3. Cyberspace: The work thus far has emphasized collecting and uploading content into dynamic databases that are configured to assist poor communities in organizing efforts for their own behalf. In addition, all of our databases must be configured to interface with each other so we will in fact be reaching higher and higher levels of collectivity.

4. Networked community: We have merely put basic ingredients together for the virtual reincarnation of a community. The magic of cyberspace's future will be created as more of humanity gets online. It is in this context that the virtual struggle for the future is on. In general what is at stake is the fundamental social structure of cyberspace, and that is one of the most critical factors that will be influencing democracy and quality of life. We have the polar opposite choices of the corporation or the community. Our action-research is to learn about and work for the community paradigm as the future of the information age.

11

A Census of Public Computing in Toledo, Ohio[①] (2004)

Kate Williams and Abdul Alkalimat

This chapter reports on research designed to identify every public computing site in the city of Toledo, Ohio. In addition to describing these sites, we analyze their social environment. Our goal is to explore how different social processes are influencing the informatization of society and the persistence (or not) of the digital divide.

Three bridges across the digital divide

The digital divide is a concept about inequality that grabbed the imagination of scholars, activists, policymakers, and all varieties of hardware and software producers. (A good overview might include Norris 2001, the Benton Foundation's http://www.digitaldividenetworkorg, the Pew Internet and American Life reports at http://www.pewinternet.org, and Williams 2001.) Being wired started out as an interesting innovation for scientists and the military and now has become a systemic norm for social and economic life. Moreover, social and technological change makes the digital divide a moving target. The digital divide concept, explicitly or not, is now at the heart of most discussions about workforce development, architectural and urban planning, youth and social welfare, and all levels of education (Schön, Sanyal, and Mitchell 1999). The fundamental

① The authors acknowledge the support of the Alliance for Community Technology at the University of Michigan, The W.K. Kellogg Foundation, and the Urban Affairs Center and Africana Studies program at the University of Toledo.

assumption is that computer literacy is a requirement for being a first class member of society (National Research Council 1999; Williams 2003).

The most frequently cited measures of the digital divide focus on access (by ownership or some other means) and use. There are multiple and related conceptions and measures (National Telecommunications and Information Administration (NTIA) 1999a, 2002; Loader 1998; DiMaggio and Hargittai 2001). Elsewhere we advanced the concept of cyberpower, a measure of to what extent individuals, groups or institutions are able to wield power with information and communications technology or ICT (Alkalimat and Williams 2001).

There are three ways people bridge the digital divide to access and use information and communications technologies and even have the possibility of cyberpower. They may use a computer (with or without Internet) at home; we call that *personal computing*. They may use ICT on the job; we call that *private computing*. Market forces drive personal and private computing, involving individuals as consumers or as workers, respectively. But there are many other places where people can access and use computers and the Internet: universities, schools, libraries, cybercafes, and so on. New ICTs are being introduced as well. On one block in Boston, several shops and cafes offer free wireless access to anyone who has a laptop and wireless network card (Bray 2002). On New York City streets as well as in many airports, a public telephone-like booth offers web browsing and email (Emling 2002). As part of its plan to combat the digital divide, the city of Atlanta is rolling out a mobile computer lab on a bus (Holsendolph 2001), building on earlier rolling computer labs in Indianapolis (Drumm and Groom 1998) and elsewhere. All these settings for using ICT apart from home or work we call *public computing*.

Outside the US, public computing is at least equally important. Franchise convenience stores in Japan linked to their corporate partner are the site of e-commerce opportunities for their customers using a public access terminal hooked up to the infrastructure previously used only for store-corporation communications. Beijing is reported to have 2000 cybercafes used heavily for games, chatting, email and web. In Britain a recent initiative to provide public access computer in libraries is linked with community digitization work. India's telephone shops often also provide an online computer. Cuba has a string of youth computer clubs where the public learns on networked computers and where teams of people write software; they have also begun setting up public browsing rooms (salas de navigación). Mexico created a small sensation recently when it agreed to purchase from Microsoft rather than adopt a set of open source software tools for the nation's public schools; and the Gates Foundation has been active in the US and abroad funding the installation of public computing to serve what it sees as marginalized communities. A 1998 survey reported that Canadian reliance on school and "public sites" for accessing the Internet increased at lower income levels.

Public computing is a major aspect of how space is and will be allocated in society. This is a collaborative process involving professionals such as architects, urban planners, social service agencies, librarians, and educators as well as advocates or activists, be they politicians, community interest groups, or social movements. This process of designing public computing into urban spaces is one theme running through a stream of books published out of MIT over the last decade by a set of public intellectuals of the information revolution, scholars and cheerleaders for their versions of the future. (Thus from MIT's departments of architecture, artificial intelligence, computer science, and the Media Lab, in chronological order, we saw Brand 1987; Mitchell 1995; Negroponte 1995; Dertouzos 1997; Gershenfeld 1999; Mitchell 1999; Dertouzos 2001; Brooks 2002.) Magazines from MIT's own *Technology Review* to the trade-oriented *Archi-Tech* (Turkel 2002) address this problem of designing smart spaces.

Figure 1 compares personal, private, and public computing using data from US federal surveys (Williams 2001, using data from Kominski 1999; NTIA, 2000). By 1990, more than half of K–12 students had ICT access in school. By 1997, more than half of adults had access at work. By 2000, more than half of American households had a computer at home. Figure 1 suggests that the greatest and certainly the earliest equality of access might be found in public computing. The quality of that access—part of which is expressed in the social environment of a given public computing site—is an important determinant of digital equality. But before we can evaluate the quality of a public computing site we have to know it exists. Many public computing sites are invisible even to their neighbors and thus overlooked at the many levels of research, policy formation, and practice. Our method, explained below, can be applied to bring these sites into plain view so that research, policy and practice can be more informed.

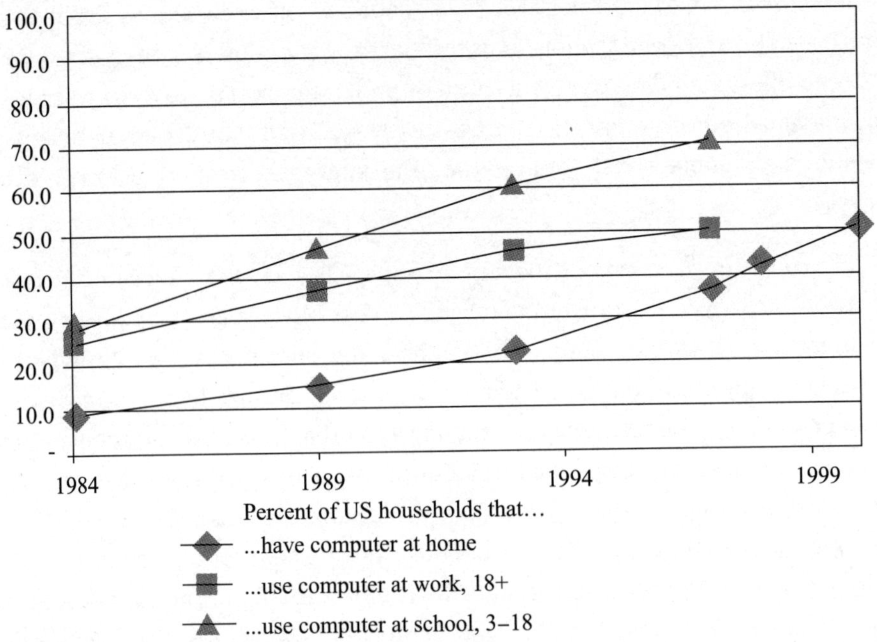

Percent of US households that...	...have computer at home	...use computer at work, 18+	...use computer at school, 3–18
1984	8.2	24.6	28.0
1989	15.0	36.8	46.0
1993	22.8	45.8	60.6
1997	36.6	49.8	70.8
1998	42.1		
2000	51.0		

Figure 1. Operationalizing personal, private, and public computing. Source: Williams 2001, using data from Kominski 1999; National Telecommunications and Information Administration 2000.

Two social processes

We are concerned with how democracy will fare in the transition to the information society, and this has been another thread through the literature (Toffler and Toffler 1995; Schuler 1996a; Lévy 1997; Miller 1996; Lee 1997; Perelman 1998; McChesney 1999; Walch 1999; Rifkin 2000; Hodges 2000). The early adoption of information and communications technology followed the dynamic of the marketplace, taking place at high income levels and in occupations related to the military, science and technology, banking and finance, and the media.

But two social processes are at work. Society functions with and within the world's markets and also depends on a democratic tradition. This tradition, encoded in laws and cultural practices, can complement or counterbalance the impact of the market on national policy and on the life chances of those with the least—people with marginal or no employment or dependent on low incomes. We are accustomed to the interplay between these two traditions of social life and social change, the market and the democratic public sphere.

The strength of the market is that innovation in search of profit drives change. With regard to ICT, new hardware and software, new uses and applications, are being produced constantly and prices tend to fall. While not a natural law (see Chapman 2004), Moore's law—every eighteen months, chip capacity doubles and chip prices fall by 50 percent—is holding true into the twenty-first century. The problem with the market is that we see persistent and even worsening inequalities that threaten the fabric of society (Kelly 1998; Schiller 1999; Gilder 2000).

The strength of the democratic tradition is that its emphasis on equality mediates against alienation and social conflicts. But at the same time, poverty nurtures the legacies of intolerance and authoritarianism that undercut the trust and stability necessary for democracy to be sustained.

From the earliest public computing projects—Community Memory in Berkeley, California; Playing to Win in East Harlem, New York City, and the Cleveland FreeNet in Ohio, for example (Schuler 1995)—to the relatively recent federal eRate legislation, the US has seen considerable democratic activity designed to provide ICT access for all. As we will see, public computing itself expresses the interplay and contradictions between forces of the market and forces for democracy. This can help us to understand prospects for the digital divide.

The social environment of public computing

People enter virtual space—to browse the Web or a play a game of virtual Solitaire—via technology that is located in actual space (Lévy 1997, 1998, 2001). That space is a social environment, the result of a confluence of social forces, institutions, and histories. People negotiate their way through and into social spaces when entering a public computing site, and operate in social space when online.

The social environment of public computing includes four aspects. First, is the hardware and software configuration. Second is the institution which hosts a given public computing site. Third is the immediate surrounding community. Finally, each community is located in a larger territory or macroenvironment: a city, country and region. This social environment in turn impacts and shapes our use of ICT and of cyberspace.

Castells (1989, 1996, 1997, 1998, 1999; Castells and Hall 1994) has categorized various macroenvironments according to their position in the global transition to the networked society. Relying on Castells, we see three categories: the technopole, the unconnected areas, and the dual city.

In the technopole, almost everyone is connected to and with ICT. In the world's unconnected regions, almost everyone is generally delinked from ICTs. In the dual city, some communities and strata of people are connected, and other communities and strata are not. Most of the world's industrial cities in transition to the information society are dual cities. So are most national capitals, even if the only ICT-connected are the armies, the NGOs, the state and supranational institutions, and the inevitable business and luxury hotels.

Castells and Hall (1994, pp. 10–11) discuss four kinds of technopoles: industrial complexes, science cities, technology parks, and certain regions with a comprehensive technopolis program for regional development. Their summary points to three main functions of these cities: reindustrialization, regional development, and synergy for innovation. Castells (1998) also advances the concept of the Fourth World, the world's delinked regions and countries. He explores (1999) how the typical "informational city" is a dual city and asks whether and how the digital and other social divides in such a place can be reversed. There are many empirical measures being discussed in these works, but it appears that public computing is not in the picture.

Examining Toledo, Ohio, as a dual city, we have pursued two research questions. What are the public computing sites? What is the social environment of public computing?

Public computing: The national picture

There is a growing body of research literature on the process of informatization of US society. Here we scan this literature with four questions in mind:

1. To what extent are people using ICT?

2. What has been the impact of government policy on public computing?

3. What has been the contribution of the community technology center?

4. What trends provide leading models for change?

People using ICT

The US Department of Commerce released its latest digital divide report in 2001. As of fall 2001, the number of people using the Internet in the US was increasing by 2 million people per month. Overall, 66 percent of individuals use computers, 54% use the Internet, and 45 % use email. Among children age 5–17, 96% use computers (NTIA 2002).

		Computer use		Internet use	
		October 1997	September 2001	October 1997	September 2001
Gender	Men	53.8	65.5	24.3	53.9
	Women	53.3	65.8	20.2	53.8
	difference	0.5	(0.3)	4.1	0.1
Employment	Employed	61.7	73.2	28.5	65.4
	Unemployed	24.8	40.8	12.4	36.9
	difference	36.9	32.4	16.1	28.5
Household income	$75,000 and above	80.8	88.0	44.5	78.9
	Less than $15,000	29.8	37.3	9.2	25.0
	difference	51.0	50.7	35.3	53.9
Ethnicity	White	57.5	70.0	25.3	59.9
	Black	43.6	55.7	13.2	39.8
	difference	13.9	14.3	12.1	20.1
Education	College degree	74.3	84.9	41.4	80.8
	No high school diploma	7.9	17.0	1.8	12.8
	difference	66.4	67.9	39.6	68.0

Source: National Telecommunications and Infomation Administration, 2002

Table 1. Percent of US population using computers and the Internet

Table 1 shows data from the Department of Commerce report (NTIA 2002) to summarize trends among selected population strata. Each of these population strata increased its use of computers and the Internet during the 1997–2001. The digital divide between men and women practically vanished. But the other paired strata show a different trend, as the shaded cells in the table highlight. For white/Black and college degree/no high school, the digital divide in both computer use and Internet use widened. For employed/unemployed and >$75,000 income/<$15,000 income, the computer use gap narrowed, but the internet use gap widened. Eventually, all strata could be on par. But the widening divide in the interim is troubling because late adopters have a different relationship than early adopters with the technology—and with the economy and society that are structured around this technology.

Government public computing policy

Government policy with regard to public computing has resulted in expanding funds for schools, libraries and community centers. Where there is quantitative data, we see different rates of ICT availability across the population within the overall trend of increased ICT availability to all.

The eRate, which provides technology funds for schools and libraries, has amounted to a $6 billion investment in public computing since it was implemented as part of the 1996 Telecommunications Act. In 1994, 35 percent of US schools were connected to the Internet; by 2001 99 percent were. Table 2 Kleiner and Farris 2002 summarizes trends among selected types of schools. Each of these types of schools has more school Internet and more classroom Internet in 2001 than in 1994. But as the bold face numbers in the table indicate, certain gaps widened: between high and low minority-enrollment schools and between schools with high and low percent of students receiving free lunches (the most measured indicator of student poverty). In minority/poor schools, Internet access tends to be more limited to libraries, computer labs, or computers used only by teachers and administrators.

		Schools with Internet		Classrooms with Internet	
		1994	2001	1994	2001
Minority enrollment	6% or lower	38	99	4	88
	50% or higher	27	98	2	81
	difference	11	1	2	7
Percent of students receiving free lunch	35% or lower	39	99	3	90
	75% or higher	20	97	2	79
	difference	19	1	1	11

Source: Kleiner and Ferris 2002

Table 2. Percent of schools and classrooms with Internet access

Library provision of computers and Internet is nearly universal, with 95.7% of the country's libraries having Internet connections, 94.5% making Internet connections available to their patrons, and an average of 8.3 workstations per library location (Bertot and McClure 2000 p. 25). The Gates Foundation has set out to boost public computing in library branches located in low income communities, and in a study of Toledo libraries, we found that each library branch did provide public computing, but that the branches with more ICT were located in communities that were more white, with higher income, and more educated. So our small local study of libraries suggests a trend similar to the schools and to ICT use across the population (Williams 2000).

The Pew Public Internet Project has been issuing a stream of empirical reports which include data on public awareness of public computing. They report 51% of the adult population knowing of a public place to use computers and get on the Internet (whites 53%, Blacks 44%). Among computer users, awareness increases to 63%. Of various sites they mention libraries (42% aware of these), schools (2%), cybercafés (1%) and copy centers (1%) (Horrigan 2001 p. 26). Gordon, et al (2002) report a survey in which 76% of Americans agree that "public access to computers and the Internet will help to narrow the gap between the haves and have-nots in our society," and a "substantial majority" of those surveyed are willing to pay to guarantee public access computing.

Community technology centers and community networks

The community technology center (CTC) is a more varied category than schools and libraries and has so far included technology centers in community centers, apartment complexes, churches, and trade unions. A combination of grassroots efforts and federal funds (Department of Education, Commerce, Housing and Urban Affairs, and NSF), state funds (in Ohio, for instance, via settlements against Ameritech as part of its agreements with the state's public utilities commission; (see Children's Partnership, http://www.techpolicybank.org/ohdesc.html, and Ohio Community Computing Network, http://www.occcn.org/history.html), and private funds has resulted in the proliferation of these organizations. Today a number of CTCs are organized on the national, state, and local levels. The Community Memory project mentioned above, where computer hobbyists installed a public access terminal outside a shop in Berkeley, is perhaps the earliest community technology site (Farrington and Pine 1997). Community networks, which originated before the Internet to network home computer users together, were early originators of

CTCs, placing terminals in laundromats and elsewhere to broaden access beyond computer owners (Bishop 1993; Agre and Schuler 1997).

Ohioans work in active CTC associations at all three levels. CTCNet (more than 650 members; http://www.ctcnet.org) was launched in 1994 based on the experience of the early CTC Playing to Win, established by Antonia Stone in New York City Ohio Community Computing Network (more than sixty-six members; Angela Stuber, personal communication, 2002; see also http://www.occcn.org) formed in 1995 to oversee the allocation of funds for community technology projects from a settlement against Ameritech for unequal phone-service provision across the state. CATNet, based at the Urban Affairs Center of the University of Toledo, formed in 1996 and has a current membership of forty centers (http://www.uac.utoledo.edu).

Model cities for public computing

The national projects mentioned above could certainly be taken as models. But on a smaller scale, a number of cities have taken the initiative to overcome a digital divide identified between communities and organizations. These cities have set out to create and shape public computing. Some are technopoles and other are readily identifiable as dual cities:

- Technopoles such as Austin, Seattle, and Portland, Oregon
- Government cities such as Nashville, Atlanta, and Washington, D.C.
- University towns such as Blacksburg, Virginia, and Urbana-Champaign, Illinois
- Diversified cities such as New York and Boston.37
  (S. Levy 1998 and Sassen 2002 provide two among many approaches to categorizing and ranking cities with respect to informationalization.)

Noteworthy among these cities is Seattle, where public computing is a major thrust for city government. The city department of information technology is implementing Citizens Technology Literacy and Access programs, providing funds, and conducting research aimed at making Seattle a "technology healthy city" (http://www.cityofseattle.net/tech/). Seattle is the home of Microsoft Corporation and also the highly successful Seattle Community Network, which played an early role in public computing by installing and supporting computers in libraries, laundromats and other public locations.

The city has created an online directory which links to 132 Seattle CTCs (http://

www.cityofseattle.net/tech/techmap/). In a recent survey, 82% of residents reported having access to the Internet, 72% having home Internet access. The 10% reporting access only outside the home report using the Internet at work (81%), school (76%), an Internet café (62%), a community center (39%), or a public library (34%) (Information Technology Indicators Residential Survey, 2000, p. 24).

Method

Our method depends on surveys, key informant interviews, statistical analysis, and keeping our eyes open as involved actors in the city under study. But in order to recruit students to responsible positions within the research project, we reconceptualized our method as the D6 method. This served to orient inexperienced young people both to what scientific research is about and to the specific tasks of researching public computing in Toledo. Several of the students then used the D6 method in their master's theses (Hamilton 2002; McGreevy 2002; Zelip 2002).

We call the method the D6 method because it has six parts, each beginning with the letter D: definition of the problem, data collection, digitization, discovery, design, and dissemination. Table 3 describes the basic activities associated with each concept.

Table 3. D6 method

Definition	Defining the problem,summing up the relevant literature, and formulating the research question and/or hypothesis
Data collection	Operationalizing the variables,drawing a population sample,collecting data regarding the variables
Digitization	Inputting,scanning,otherwise putting the data on the computer,organized in a useful way
Discovery	Analyzing the data to test the hypothesis or answer the research question
Design	Laying out the data and the analysis in text,tables,and figures in order to convey the findings to various audiences
Dissemination	Sharing the findings with the various audiences as widely and effectively as possible

D1, Definition of the problem

Our definition of the problem came as much out of experience as it did the research literature. Dealing early on with technology as a potential solution to social problems, with technology as ubiquitous on major campuses but hard to find off-campus, we experienced the importance of public computing. We searched constantly for places where people could get online, and eventually became involved in a community technology center (Alkalimat and Williams 2000). The large datasets such as the NTIA surveys have not placed much emphasis here, but the literature close to everyday practice with technology tells many tales that suggest its value to people seeking work, social connections, even political impact (McKeown 1991; Mark, Cornebise, and Wahl 1997; Chow, et al 1998,2000; Williams 2001).

D2, Data collection

We collected data in the setting of an academic department and a community technology center, using students who worked in both. The students were paid by the Federal work-study program and/or were earning academic credit through enrollment in the University of Toledo course "Cyberspace and the Black Experience"(Africana Studies 4900, 2002). Data collection included a phone survey, visits to sites, and the use of various digital devices-camera and tape recorder.

We created a list of all of the potential sites for public computing that we could find. Our starting point was the telephone as a near universal feature of organized public life. In the United States nearly 90% of the entire population has at least one telephone at home, or lives with a few block of a public phone. We assumed that organizations would have a phone, and used the phone directory as the starting point in our enumeration.

We constructed a list of organizations to contact using the hard copy yellow pages, an online yellow pages then available for free at www.555-1212.com, several local directories, news clippings, and personal leads. We identified 96 yellow page categories as relevant to our search, based on personal familiarity and on our review of the research and policy literature about community computing and other forms of public computing (available from the authors). The daily newspaper, for example, mentioned a children's hospital providing computers for patients to use, so for that reason alone we included hospitals as a category for potential sites. We called coffee houses because we knew of at least one cybercafé in town.

After compiling a list of more than 1,578 organizations that might host public computing sites, we began canvassing them by telephone to find out who actually did provide computers for nonstaff to use. Students made most of the calls. Each call began as follows: "Hello I'm calling from the University of Toledo researching computer use in the area. Do you have any computers for (the public/your members/parishioners/students/or other relevant term for that institution) to use?" We made on the average of three attempted calls before recording the site as a no response. These calls were made over 18 months during 2000 and 2001. As we made the calls, we also located the addresses and verified that exactly 1,578 of the organizations were actually within Toledo city limits. Those outside the city were omitted from the dataset. We also contacted institutions that we estimated would host multiple sites (the public library, public schools, Catholic schools, and so on) and gathered data from them in person.

D3, Digitization

Digitization began when we used the online yellow pages to build our call list and continued building a database of our call data. We also used geographic information systems software for geolocating the possible and actual sites.

D4, Discovery

Discovery proceeded using GIS software (ArcView) to map the location of the public computing sites and the demographics of Toledo, and using a statistical package (SPSS). We made use of class sessions and team meetings to discuss results periodically.

D5, Design

Design involved writing this paper and producing a website (http://www.communitytechnology.org/toledo) that will provide information about the public computing sites in a searchable database. The University of Toledo Urban Affairs Center plans to publish our findings.

D6, Dissemination

In addition to disseminating the book and the website via academic and online channels, we will present findings to a growing network of business and community leaders who are interested in a technology plan for Toledo to advance new-technology-related local industries and boost the skills and connectivity of the local and future workforce.

Enumeration and analysis of data

Our search for public computing in Toledo, Ohio found 253 sites hosted by a variety of institutions, as shown in table 4 below. We coded these 253 public computing sites as community, government, commercial and university, according to their host institutions. *Government* public computing sites are those located in public institutions, a direct reflection of public policy and political forces. *Community* public computing sites are those hosted by non-governmental, not-for-profit organizations. These represent the diversity of civil society. *Commercial* public computing sites are those operating for a profit, in response to market opportunities. *University* public computing sites are those established at colleges and universities. While they will always be fewer in number, they will likely be the most technology-intensive public computing facilities in any community. Each type of public computing has its own economic imperatives, social dynamics, and spatial realities or demographics.

Schools—K–12 public	92
Public libraries	14
Apartments, hotels, and other group residences—public	2
Government offices	1
Total government	109
Schools—K–12 private	29
Schools—preschools and child care—nonprofit	8
Schools—other	1
Churches and temples	29
Civic organizations—other	12
Civic organizations—youth	4
Civic organizations—seniors	6
Apartments, hotels, and other group residences—nonprofit	4
Civic organizations—unions	3
Museums and parks	2
Hospitals and health care centers	1
Total community	99
Schools—preschools and child care—for profit	13
Schools—trade—for profit	10
Apartments, hotels, and other group residences—for profit	15
Copy shops, cybercafés, stores	4
Total community	42
Schools—universities and colleges	3
Total university	3
Grand total	253

Table 4. Public computing in Toledo, Ohio, by host institution

As Table 4 indicates, schools are the largest number of sites in each of the four categories. So government sites are primarily schools and libraries. Community sites are primarily schools, churches, and community centers. Commercial sites are primarily schools and apartment complexes.

Table 5 below provides an overview of the response rates that led to the enumeration in Table 4. We can use these figures to estimate the actual count of public computing sites in the city. Of the 1,578 potential hosts we sought to ask, we got yes or no responses from 761, or 48 percent. Of these, 253 (33%) reported that they do host public computing. The 817 sites we could not contact may or may not host public computing. So we calculate that between 16 percent (253 out of 1578) and 33 percent (253 out of 817) of the institutions on our list of 1,578 do host public computing. We believe the sites we could not contact are less likely to host public computing. As a result, we chose to settle on a rate of 20 percent, and estimate that Toledo is likely to have 316 public computing sites.

	Potential host institutions	No, do not host public computing	Yes, host public computing	Yes as percent of all responses	No response	Response rate, percent
Government	138	21	109	84%	8	94%
Community	935	270	99	27%	566	39%
Commercial	501	216	42	16%	243	51%
University	4	1	3	75%	-	100%
Grand total	1,578	508	253	33%	817	48%

Table 5. Contact data on public computing in Toledo, Ohio

Toledo is a "rust belt" industrial city, historically connected to the auto and glass industries. The 2000 US Census (http://www.census.gov) reports its population as 313,619, 23.5 percent African American. The distribution of the population is similar to other Midwestern cities: the Black population is concentrated in the inner city and people with higher incomes live near the periphery or in the suburbs. Toledo also has a working-class east side, home to many Latinos and to a concentration of Toledoans of Hungarian descent. This demographic pattern allows us to identify four areas: East Toledo, a commercial downtown, the inner city, and the outer city. Toledoans call the outer city the North, West and South Sides. The map below shows these four areas. Shaded areas represent poverty rates of greater than 25 percent. With this in mind, we can examine the four types of public computing uncovered in our enumeration.

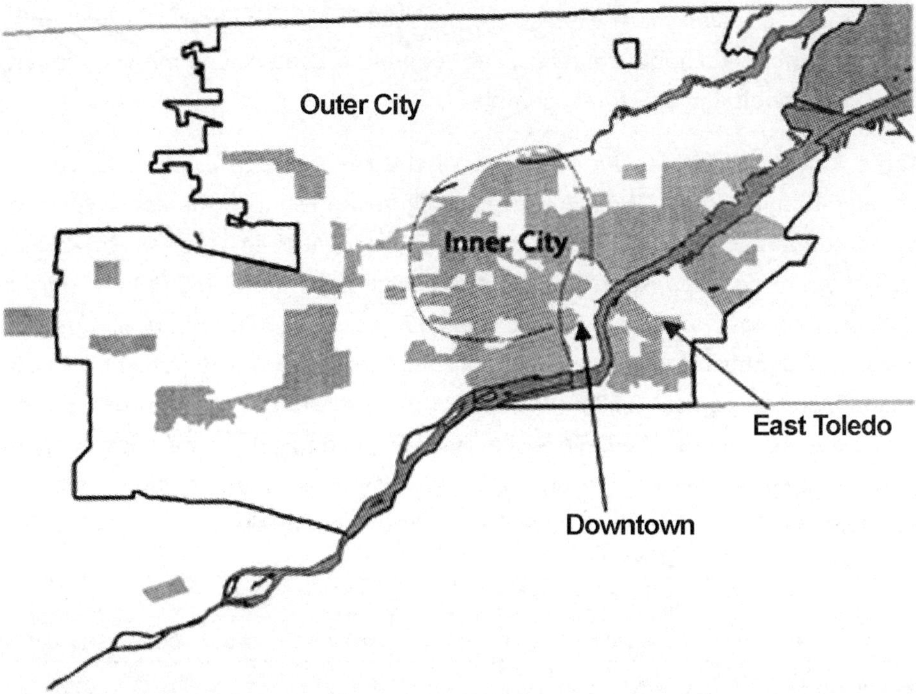

Figure 2. Four areas of Toledo, showing census block groups of 25 percent or higher poverty rates in shaded grey.

Government public computing

Of the 109 government public computing sites mapped in Figure 3, 92 are public schools and 14 are public libraries. There are also two computer labs operated by the county's public housing administration, and one county tax assessor's office. This office provides computers for the public to use to search the county's real estate databases.

Toledo is a city with five overlapping school systems: the Toledo Public Schools (TPS), Washington School District (an autonomous district wholly within the Toledo district), the Catholic schools, charter schools, private schools, and an emerging but tentative statewide virtual school system of online schools. Except for the virtual high schools, all of these are surrounded by suburban school systems. In Toledo Public Schools there are eight high schools, eight junior high schools, and forty-four elementary schools (http://www.tps.org). There are over 37,000 students, of whom 46 percent are African American, and 7 percent are Latino. On the other hand the staff is only 20 percent Black. The legacy of segregation persists, such that the high schools fit into three groups. One school is mainly Black (95% Black), three schools

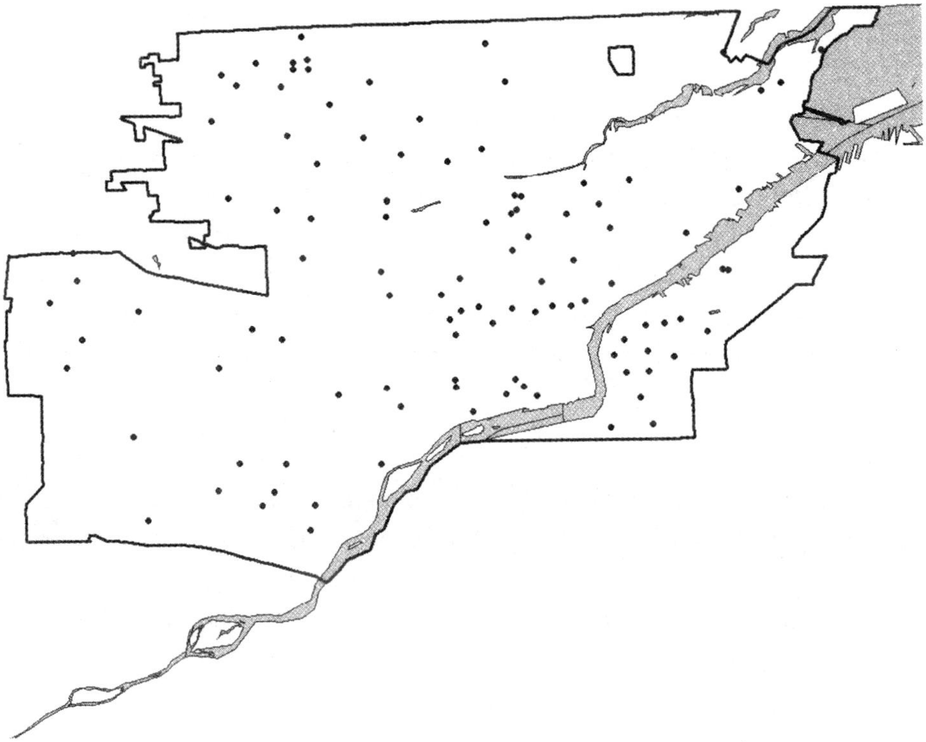

Figure 3. Government public computing sites

are in the middle (Blacks making up 61, 56, and 51% of enrollment), and four make up the third group (26, 24, 19, and 13% Black enrollment). Thus the school system suffers from de facto segregation based on class and race. The Supreme Court of Ohio has ruled that the current arrangement of school districts in Ohio is unfair as it produces major inequities in funding levels for different school districts, especially ones like Toledo (DeRolph v. State, 2000, 88 Ohio St.3d, http://www.catalyst-cleveland.org/06-00/DeRolph.htm).

The technology transformation of the public schools got a boost when a bond issue passed in 1994 providing additional funding. A technology commission was set up within TPS that also included telecommunications industry representatives. The period from 1995 into 2001 was a period of rapid technological development. The State of Ohio invested over $800 million in K–12 technology. A TPS official reported that the system grew from about 4,000 client computers to its current size of 10,000 clients, and the figure would rise to 15,000 within a year and a half ("Toledo Public Schools: NetApp Scores an A+ for Improving Content Delivery", 2000). As of early 2001, every elementary classroom had about five networked computers, and almost every school has at least one computer lab for the entire school.

Many organizations are attempting to expand technology access in the schools and enhance training. The State of Ohio has SchoolNet and SchoolNet Plus which offer funding and training (http://www.osn.state.oh.us/home/). They fund support for Tech-Prep programs for students going into technical careers, but this functions primarily in the suburbs of Toledo. Federal and state funds are channeled through the University of Toledo to other programs like Prep-Tech, Excel, and Gear Up, which are designed to enhance the educational achievement of either at-risk or minority students.

The public schools' computer labs service the student body of each school. In the past the Toledo Public School System has had an open door policy, e.g., the lighted school concept involved having an open school for community use one night a week. This is no longer commonplace, and would certainly not involve the use of the computer labs. In contrast, some of the suburban schools do exactly this, running computer classes in the evening for the public. Another important feature of the computer labs is that Toledo Public Schools invested in reading and math drill software (Computer Curriculum Corporation, http://www.ccclearn.com) and have avoided providing Internet access in the labs in order to drive teachers to make full use of the software. However, many TPS teachers are not trained to use the diagnostic powers of the software to customize test questions to the strengths and weaknesses of the individual student. The district runs free classes on the software in the summer but few teachers take the course.

The public library sites are all part of the Toledo-Lucas County Public Library (http://www.toledolibrary.org). In addition to the fourteen sites in Toledo, there are four branch libraries in the suburbs. There are approximately 250 computers in the system dedicated to Internet and/or database access, children's software, or word processing functions are available. The library sought and won several grants from the Gates Foundation to acquire computers to equalize the access of lower income communities, and these computer were allocated primarily to the most needy branches, as mentioned above (Williams 2000).

The library has a part-volunteer, part-paid program of Web Wizards who assist patrons in using the Internet. Printing used to be free but for the last year has cost 10 cents a page. In general, the Wizards and the general library staff help anyone who comes in with this technology. In answer to the state requiring a plan to protect children from pornography, children have to have their parent's signature and be issued a card before going online at the library.

Public schools and public libraries are located in all neighborhoods of the city. They are government agencies and fall under the mandate of the 14th Amendment that requires equal access under the law for all citizens. Our sense is that this government mandate, even supplemented by private initiatives, is not yet enough to overcome the disparities of race and class.

Community public computing

There are a total of ninety-nine community computing sites. These are mapped in Figure 4. The host institutions are non-profit organizations, neither commercial nor government, although they may receive public funds. There are thirty-eight schools and preschools, twenty-nine churches, twenty-eight community facilities or centers of various kinds, and four apartment complexes.

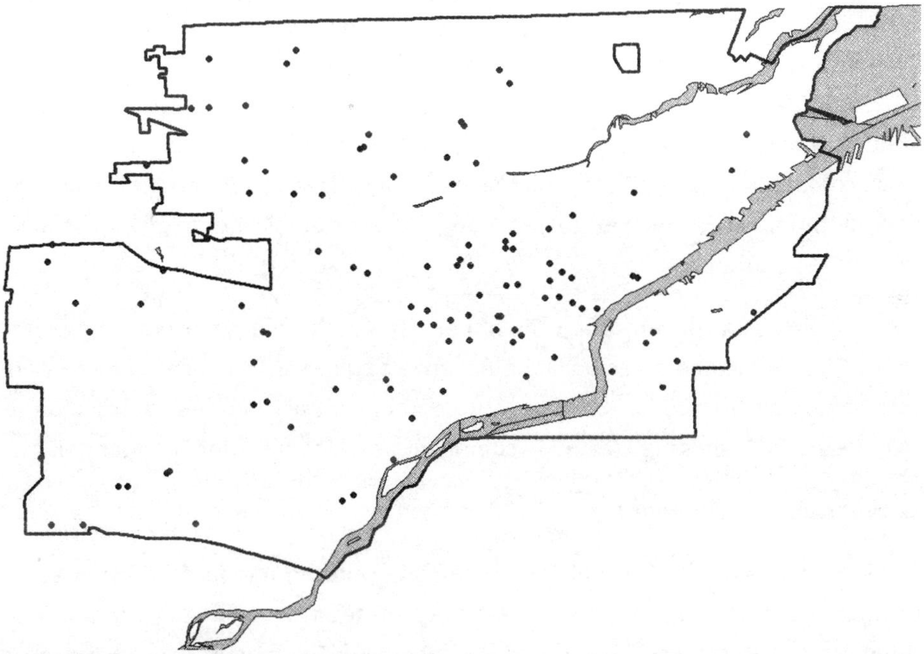

Figure 4. Community public computing sites

Of the thirty-eight schools, twenty-two are part of the Catholic Diocese of Toledo. As elsewhere in the US, many of the European immigrant populations were Catholic and built churches in what was a smaller city. In a sense, the Catholic schools 55 are a parallel system to Toledo Public Schools as well as link to their respective churches. But these schools are tuition based, so they represent a form of community schooling oriented to those who can pay. As such, they are more friendly to parents, community, and congregation. In most Northern US cities, about 10 percent of students attend Catholic schools; for Toledo the rate is an unusually high 20 percent (Patrick McGuire, personal communication, 2002).

The twenty-nine churches include seventeen different Christian denominations. The highest representations are Lutheran (ten), Baptist (seven), and Catholic (three). In many cases these are churches with affiliated schools, but they have computer access for church use.

The rest of the community public computing sites consists of community centers oriented either to the general public or a specific constituency. They include community centers for the general public (e.g. Wayman Palmer YMCA, W. J. Murchison Community Center, Adelante), for seniors (e.g. Alpha Community Programs, Eleanor Kahle Senior Center), for youth (e.g. Boys and Girls Clubs, Black Data Processing Associates), for union members (Farm Labor Organizing Committee, Toledo Federation of Teachers, Police Patrolmen's Association), for museum visitors (Center for Science and Industry and the Toledo Museum of Art) and the Medical College of Ohio hospital. The last two are unusual: the museum has a computer in its K–12 resources center that is used by children and teachers, and the hospital has a PC set up in a lounge near its physical therapy department for inpatients to use.

The map shows a concentration of community sites in the inner city along with sites in higher income areas near the northwest suburbs. The community centers with computers are primarily dedicated to poorer central city populations, and the remainder of the sites are located in communities which can afford computer labs.

Commercial public computing

There are forty-two commercial public computing sites in Toledo. Of these twenty-three are commercial schools and preschools, fifteen are apartment complexes, three are Kinko's copy shops and one is a cybercafé. The map in Figure 5 makes it clear that these public computing sites are either in the downtown area or in the outer city, especially in the western part of the city.

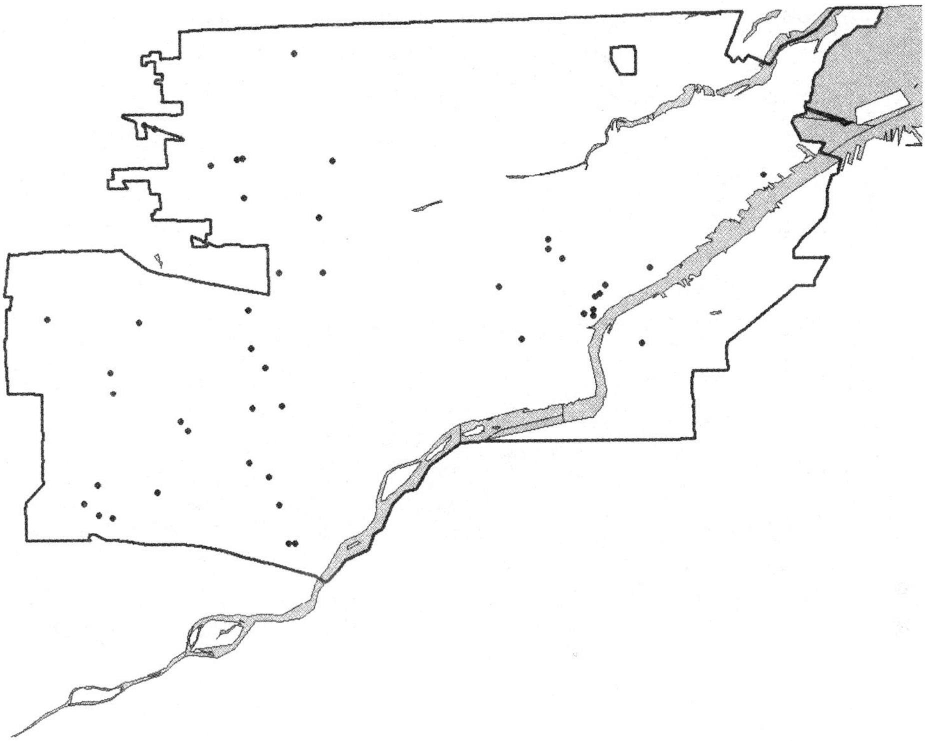

Figure 5. Commercial public computing sites

Several of the apartment complexes belong to the same owner, who won a Department of Housing and Urban Development grant to set up computer labs and thus improve his apartments. He has helped to grow the CTC association in town, CATNeT.

Kinko's is a copy shop that developed a business model and a reputation around public computing. Their sites are near the suburbs and the University of Toledo campus. The cybercafé is also near campus.

Commercial sites are far fewer than government or community sites. This might reflect a lack of effective demand from the local population, or a lack of imaginative capital from Toledo entrepreneurs.

University public computing

Three universities and colleges in Toledo provide computer labs for their students: the University of Toledo, the Medical College of Ohio, and Mercy College of Northwest Ohio, a nursing and allied health college. Each of these institutions is oriented towards educating professionals and technical workers. UT and MCO are located in outer Toledo, and Mercy College is located in the inner city near what was once a hospital complex. (See Figure 6.)

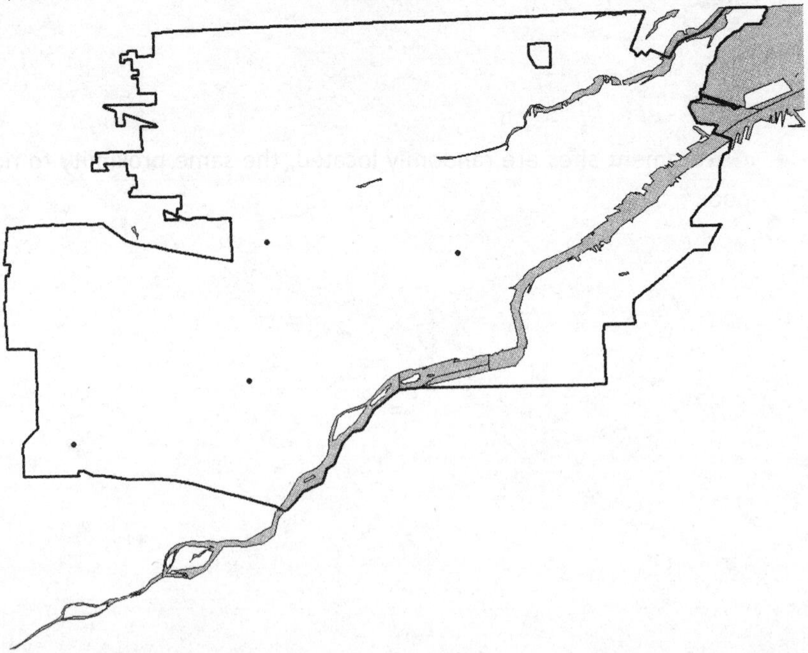

Figure 6. University public computing sites

Their computer facilities are open only to students or rare one-time public events, with two important exceptions. Mentioned above is the computer available for patients at MCO hospital. UT's women's studies program operates a women's computer lab as part of their support to un- or underemployed women in Toledo.

The university and college facilities are possibly the most advanced public computing sites in the city. For instance, the UT business school is a wireless zone for laptop access to the network. Many departments provide specialized hardware and software. UT also teaches computer classes of all kinds in several off-campus labs downtown.

The university is an important partner for public computing. UT faculty helped start and continue to work with CATNeT, the local association of community technology centers. A larger group of faculty is also proposing a sociology minor in social informatics. This program would link with public computing across the city in order to place interns for potential future employment, conduct research, and collaborate for advocacy and policy formulation.

Social environment of public computing

We hypothesize that the four kinds of public computing fit three patterns in relationship to the social environment:

- Government sites are randomly located, the same proximity to rich and poor.
- Community sites are located close to the opposite ends of the social spectrum, the rich and the poor having community sites but not the middle strata.
- Commercial and university sites are located according to market demand, closer to upper income and students.

As the maps indicate, our data suggest this pattern, but weakly. We expect that a broader dataset would make a more compelling case.

The marketplace has a direct impact on the location of commercial and university sites. There are however, two important particularities. University sites combine upscale owner occupied single family homes with low cost apartment complexes for students. Further, a large concentration of ICT users live in relatively affluent suburbs (Sylvania, Perrysburg, Maumee, etc), which transforms this urban pattern into a metropolitan one.

The U-shaped pattern of the predicted community public computing sites may prove to be the best countermotion to the market as a foundation for democratic traditions. The role of the church and other institutions of bonding social capital is to give poor and working populations a basis for collective consciousness and action, including self-empowerment projects with ICT.

Government public computing sites are a result of public spending that reflects increasing commitment to an ICT transformation of education at all levels. As Figure 7 below indicates, the informationalization will be equal, but the level of access and use is a matter of available state revenue and relative level of commitment. In times of expanding revenue, an egalitarian state is a major factor, but in dire times the impact can be relatively negligible.

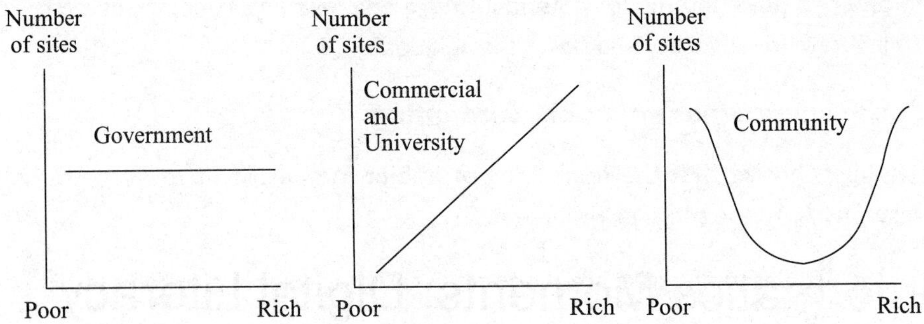

Figure 7. Modeling the distribution of public computing. Government computing sites distributed equally across poor and rich communities, commercial and university sites distributed more to rich, community sites distributed more to poor and rich, leaving out the middle income.

In general, changes in hardware and software will dramatically impact what we mean by public computing, especially the increasing use of wireless, voice recognition, broadband, and technology convergence (phone, computer, TV, music, camera, and so on). But we will still have the basic four categories of public computing. In each case, we are interested in the rate of adoption and pattern of use, and then in what cyberpower—people's ability to use ICT to achieve their goals—results in. (Alkalimat and Williams 2001 elaborates on the concept of cyberpower as an outcome of a community technology center.)

We are arguing that the stream of technical innovation is a force banging against society, and like the beginning of a game of billiards, the balls are scattering. Each type of public computing expresses a structural force—an aggregation of institutions, people, and spaces—constituting a power dynamic. It is the configuration of all the power dynamics of a society that determines the likely course history will take.

We envision two stages of future research. The first stage involves confirming this description of public computing and measuring variation in different urban and rural areas, as well as in different countries. In the second stage, we and others will examine what is going on in public computing sites, what users are doing, and what forms of cyberpower emerge. The stakes are high; we believe they extend to the nature of democracy in the information age.

12

Informatics Moments: Digital Literacy and Social Capital in Civil Society and People's Everyday Lives ① (2012)

Kate Williams

Abstract

The informatics moment is the moment when a person seeks help in using some digital technology that is new to him or her. This paper examines the informatics moment in people's everyday lives as they sought help at a branch public library. Four types of literacy were involved: basic literacy (reading and writing); computer literacy (use of a mouse, buying a computer), library literacy (navigating online catalogs and databases), and domain literacy (most commonly and urgently, looking for work in a world where practically all job postings and applications are online). Social capital is also associated with many of these informatics moments: people seek help from those with enough skill who are close at hand, approachable, and familiar, and they collaborate with others in their networks to do so. Understanding the informatics moment could accelerate people's (and society's) anxious transition

---

① The author wishes to thank Aiko Takazawa for her research assistance, as well as other contributors to the research, firstly the CyberNavigators, Roberto Pang, Amy Eshleman, and Mary Dempsey at Chicago Public Library; other members of the Community Informatics Research Lab at the University of Illinois, especially Abdul Alkalimat, Aaron Fleisher, Hui Yan; Aysha Marsh, and transcriptionist Sarah Meadows; and volunteers Samantha Lester and Matt Hampel. The research was funded by the Institute for Museum and Library Services and enabled by the cooperation of the Chicago Public Library.

to an inclusive digital age.

Background and purpose

This study identifies and describes a phenomenon taking place in Chicago's branch public libraries—the informatics moment—and its relationship with social capital. This moment has two meanings, one empirical and one abstract. Empirically, it is a moment when a library patron is seeking and getting help using a computer or the internet. Abstractly, the informatics moment is a phase in the transition of a society or a social sector to the information age, with all the dislocations and transformations that are entailed in introducing digital tools and infrastructure.

The informatics moment is a new term that we have coined. The term places this work within the i-schools—the professional schools and centers of research on the interaction of people, information and technology which were organized in the late 1990s and since (Larsen 2010), in response to the emergence of the digital age. It also places this work under the rubric of social informatics, which Kling (1999) sums up as emphasizing and exploring the social context of computer use, to the point of coining its own new term "socio-technical systems" in order to reconceptualize the computer. The term also draws on concepts of the information revolution and the network society (Castells 1996).

As observed in this study, the informatics moment has a structure and a process. The structure consists of the technological infrastructure of the public access computers provided in the library (and also as this study will help to show, an emerging human infrastructure). The process consists of the interaction of the patron with a staff member called a CyberNavigator as the patron uses the computers. In this moment, the patron is bridging a digital divide that he or she faces in trying to do something. In fact, the CyberNavigator faces the digital divide with the patron, as they quite literally face the computer screen side-by-side.

The new term "informatics moment" aims at shifting the attention of both scholars and practitioners to the agency of those involved. We can understand this by comparing it to another widely used term: the digital divide. This term was first used in 1996 (Williams 2001). It served (and continues to serve) to galvanize a great deal of time and money around the world. The digital divide is most typically defined as the gap between those who use computers and those who do not. Experience with and scholarship on this phenomenon, also referred to as digital inequality, has shown that it is both multidimensional and changing. The focus on the informatics moments looks at the digital divide from the perspective of the person or persons experiencing it. It relies on the CyberNavigator staff—who also experience the digital divide—as witness and participant, but emphasizes the agency of the person seeking (and by and large getting) help. He or she sets out to do something that involves computers or the internet, and he or she seeks help. [②]

Empirically, this study collects data about informatics moments that last a few minutes, an hour, or perhaps through multiple encounters in the public library. Any particular informatics moment as experienced in the library may be successful or may end in frustration.

As of 2008, 16,671 US public library outlets (central and branch locations) were serving 97 percent of the population (Henderson, et al 2010), thanks in large part to the long-standing practice of local tax support that has made US libraries both free and permanent. [③] Some 3 percent of Americans reside outside of the taxing district or service area of any library; but many people are close enough to travel and choose to pay an annual fee for user privileges ($50–$200 in several Illinois locales, for example). American libraries provide local residents with free book lending, reference assistance, information and referral services, study and meeting spaces, and free access to computers and the internet. Helped again by tax dollars (particularly the federal eRate subsidy), 99.8 percent of public libraries provide on average twelve public access computers per location (Bertot 2009). Fifteen years of surveys and analysis of public access computing in the libraries by John C. Bertot and his colleagues have detailed the structural aspect of the informatics moment in the branch public library. More recently Bertot (2009) has used interviews and library visits to investigate the social and institutional implications of information technology in libraries. Complementing that work, this study examines and theorizes on the IT help-getting and -giving moment that (almost always) takes place sitting in front of the library's public access computers.

Those computers are used for life's necessities as well as for homework, leisure, and

---

② Some (Clement and Shade 1998) have identified seven dimensions to the digital divide, others (Dimaggio and Hargittai 2001) five, and most recently one more scholar (Dijk 2005) has identified four. All noted the role of help in surmounting the digital divide, using different terms: social facilitation (Clement and Shade 1998), social support (Dimaggio and Hargittai 2001), and social resources/learning from others (Dijk 2005).

③ US public libraries are popularly considered free, and many of them have the word "free" in their name, because local residents can use them (and borrow materials) without cost apart from small charges for printing, overdue items, and the like. Local taxpayer support keeps the libraries funded, so technically they are not free.

life-long learning. Forty-two percent of those using library computers nationwide did so for formal education (doing homework, attended remote classes, or applying to school), and 40 percent did so for employment or career purposes (Becker, et al 2010). It is also relevant that a study of recent change in digital reference questions discovered that "people seem to turn to public libraries when they face a difficult question. ... In addition, unsuccessful searching of the Internet seems to motivate people to ask questions in the libraries. Librarians face the challenge of developing their skills for answering questions of increasing complexity" (Numminen and Vakkari, p. 1257).[④]

Others have examined the process of surmounting the digital divide in a community. A disregard for community members' own predicaments, knowledge, connections, and goals set a technology training program on a course to reproduce and reinforce the digital divide (Kvasny 2006). The ethics of libraries are to start from and support the patron's own objectives and requests (American Library Association n.d.). So, to recap, relying on the model in Figure 1 below: This study examines the process whereby people in their everyday lives bridge some digital divide they face, making use of public access computing in the branch library and seeking and getting help there.

Our interest here is to empirically investigate how the local community—ordinary people in their everyday lives—is navigating the information revolution. We turn away from a consideration of deficits (the digital divide) to a focus on the process of crossing that divide (the informatics moment). The branch public library is a rich site of informatics moments: people using the public access computers and seeking (and getting) help in doing so. What does the informatics moment look like in this setting?

So the first objective in our research is to understand the informatics moment. But our second objective it to understand and how social capital affects the process and outcome of the informatics moment. Social capital is defined here as the resources that people access through their social networks rather than on the marketplace or through bureaucratic channels (Lin 2001).

Social capital is a meaningful factor, or independent variable, in several ways. First,

---

④ Piritta Numminen and Pertti Vakkari define digital reference service as "an Internet-based, professional question and answering service [whereby] users address their questions to the service typically through Web form, e-mail, or chat" (Numminen and Vakkari, p 1250).

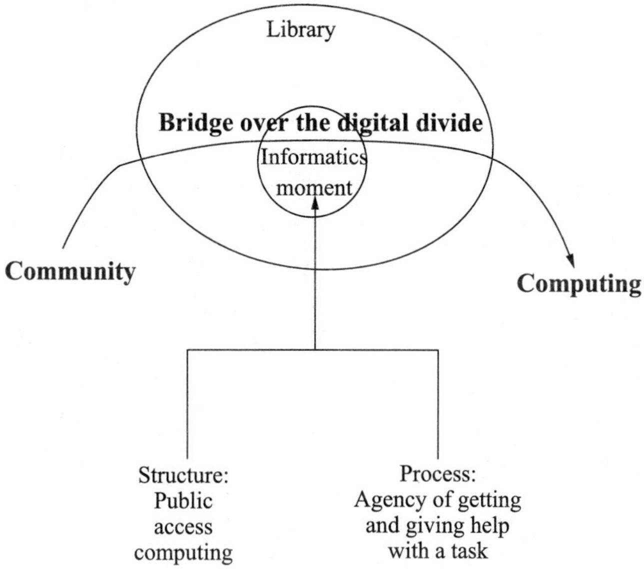

Figure 1. Process components of the informatics moment

this takes up digital divide theory (referenced above) which has proposes social support as a key aspect of the digital divide. In other words, people with less or no access to or use of digital tools are very often those without connections to people who would support their use of those tools. Second, social capital has been found to be one of the widest used frameworks for understanding sustainability of technology in community settings (O'Neil 2002). The search for meaningful theory that can summarize our experience with technology use in communities requires that we continue to test this framework in more and wider settings. Research on community use of information technology suggests a *positive* role for social capital in helping individuals and groups overcome digital inequality (Alkalimat and Williams 2001; Williams and Durrance 2008). And finally, social capital has already been recognized as both a factor and an outcome in the public library (Kranich 2001; Vårheim 2007). The present study asks, then: What role does social capital play in the informatics moment?

As Figure 1 shows, help seeking and help giving are part of the informatics moment. The library and its staff are a neighborhood bureaucracy available to the public. In what way might this entail social capital? A bureaucracy is quite often necessary but not sufficient in providing resources (Lin 2001; Lin, et al 2001). Translating this to the branch library, the patron may get help in the informatics moment not only because the bureaucracy works, but also because social capital is in play.

To understand the informatics moment in people's everyday lives and the role of social capital, we chose the setting of the branch public library in Chicago, Illinois. This afforded us a window on hundreds, even thousands of informatics moments, because the library fields a staff of CyberNavigators and facilitated them participating in the study as key informants. The CyberNavigator's job is to support people in their informatics moments, so the study includes data about the informatics moments in which the CyberNavigator participates, not the informatics moments when a patron gets help in some other way. But with the CyberNavigators the study gained participants with an average of twelve months' experience of a great number of informatics moments.

As of summer 2010, the CyberNavigators program operated in forty of the library's seventy-four locations. CyberNavigators are recruited by the library and hired by the Chicago Public Library Foundation to work for twenty hours a week at $14 per hour. They are assigned to a particular library to help people use the library's public access computers and internet, in coordination with other activities in that library.[⑤]

Table 1 provides some demographic information about the CyberNavigators. In open-ended questions they also reported owning and using smartphones, microphones, DJ equipment, webcams, and gaming devices as part of carrying out dozens of digital tasks including vlogging, fixing friends' cellphones, making movies, paying bills, and reading comics online. In sum, the CyberNavigators are upwardly mobile, plugged-in Chicago natives, the young netizens who have been identified as the leading force in the information revolution.

A particular selection criterion for CyberNavigators is "good with people", and that means people in specific Chicago neighborhoods. Managers interview candidates with particular branch library assignments in mind and often the candidate hired has a personal history with that neighborhood. Depending on time of year and how many are hired at one time, training may consist of shadowing another CyberNavigator for a few days, or attending a small group training which focuses on library policies and the library's online resources. Ongoing one-day training sessions every six months alert CyberNavigators to new resources.

---

⑤ A history of Chicago Public Library's public access computers and the CyberNavigator program itself is outside the scope of this article, but available from the author.

Characteristic	Percentage*
Average age (years)	27
Gender (male; %)	50
Roots:	
Born in Chicago	68
Attended Chicago elementary schools	84
Attended Chicago high schools	81
Language:	
Help people in Spanish as well as English	32
Help people in Mandarin or Cantonese as well as English	8
Ethnicity:	
African American	48
Latino	25
European American	20
Asian or Asian American	5
Education:	
Completing or completed a bachelors degree or higher	91
Currently enrolled in college/university	49
professional or preprofessional field	47
Social science or humanities	34
Science or technology	20
New to working in Chicago Public Library	81
Digital tools and skills:	
Computer at home	97
Broadband at home	89
Have contributed to Wikipedia	15
Have written a computer program	12

* Unless otherwise noted.

Table 1. Demographics of the CyberNavigators

As the title of this paper reflects, literacy theories (Lankshear 1997; Eberle and Robinson 1980; Williams 2003; Scribner 1994; Cope and Kalantzis 2000; Heath 1994; Nagle 1999; Finn 1999) as well as domain theory (Hjorland 1995) and learning theory (Lave and Wenger 1991) were invaluable in helping parse the complexities of the informatics moments observed in this study. This study affirms these theories and demonstrates the power of applying them to digital settings. In order to explain this smoothly, these theories are discussed in greater detail alongside the empirical findings, in section 3 below. In this connection we also celebrate the librarian who managed the North Pulaski Branch and joined with a patron in 1981 to set up the first public access computer in Chicago Public

Library. He attributed his motivation to "the belief that computers are becoming so commonplace that learning how to use them is almost as important as learning how to read and write" (Dewey 1983, p. 21). Certain methods were adopted from social informatics (Orr 1996) and sociology (Burawoy 1991; Burawoy 2009; Clark 1965); these are discussed in the next section.

Method

Data for this study was collected in four ways: via documents, ethnographies, focus groups, and questionnaires. With limited resources, the ethnography required decisions on sampling; the focus groups and questionnaires targeted the entire population of CyberNavigators.

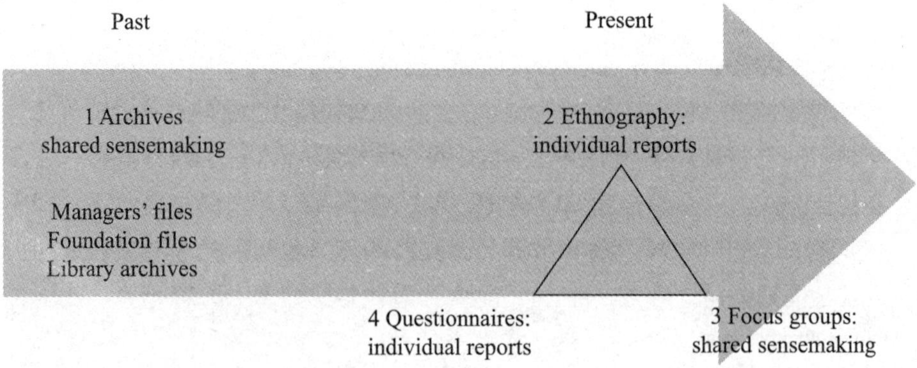

Figure 2. Four types of data collection for the study

This methodology triangulates from three sources of data about the present, informed by sources from the past. (See Figure 2.) In other words, each subset of data is used to validate the others, yielding a rich description.

Files and archives

The Chicago Public Library and its foundation made available the administrative files on the CyberNavigators program from the mid 1990s on. We also queried the library's archive for earlier documents. Administrative files amounted to three boxes of files which contained press clippings about the program; related articles; promotional materials; and internal planning and evaluation documents that recorded significant discussions about the program as it came into existence and evolved. It was possible to access these files because library administrators had an ongoing interest in learning from the program.

The CyberNavigator manager also shared internal reports and facilitated the research in many ways. The library's archives staff provided at least one key historical document.

Unit of analysis, unit of observation, and sampling

The unit of analysis is the informatics moment; the unit of observation is the CyberNavigator. He or she is to a certain extent a proxy for the branch library and the community served. As of 2010, forty of Chicago's seventy-nine public library locations had CyberNavigators on-site. For the focus groups and the questionnaires, we set out to study the entire population of forty. Thirty-seven CyberNavigators answered the questionnaire and twenty-seven participated in focus groups (93 percent and 68 percent response rates, respectively).

Limited resources dictated sampling for the ethnographic work. Two sites were included from each subdivision of the library system (South, Central, and North). As part of a research program that focuses on underserved communities, this study excluded libraries serving more affluent areas. As a result the six sites in the sample are more representative of Chicago's population with regard to income, that is, lower income. To represent the population ethnically and catch any differences across ethnicity, locations were selected that serve major ethnic groups of Chicago: African-American, Mexican, Puerto Rican, Chinese, and Polish. This is important given Chicago's ethnic diversity: 37 percent of the city's population is African American, 36 percent speaks a language other than English at home, and 22 percent is foreign born (US Census n.d.).

Ethnographies

We carried out week-long ethnographic observations in six branch libraries. According to Michael Burawoy (1991, 2009) our theories, our questions, allow us to do ethnography. We cannot possibly perceive everything, so we look for specific aspects of a culture, setting, or social process and use our limited perceptions to test our beliefs. So it is better to be explicit and conscious about the theories and questions we take into the field. Ethnography complements other social scientific methods such as surveys or interviews.

To implement this approach, our ethnographies were highly structured by a set of questions that the field notes had to answer. To start, the focus of the field workers was on the patron-staff (or patron-observer, see below) interactions. From the study's field handbook:

For every request for help, or [staff/CyberNavigator] interaction with a patron, note down:

Time of day?
What did the patron ask about?
What was the patron trying to do?
Who did they ask for help?
What language did they use?
Did they seem to know the CyberNavigator?

Those of us on the study also practiced involved observation following Kenneth Clark (1965). He directed a community organization and developed social scientific findings from that experience. Leading the work of that organization, trying to effect social service delivery and social change, yielded a great deal of data. The check on his subjectivity was his regular discussions—debriefings—with an uninvolved research colleague. Likewise, we aimed not to be outside, impartial observers. We thought of ourselves, and explained ourselves to staff, as learning by shadowing, and we all shared a commitment to seeing Chicagoans across their various digital divides. All of us helped the CyberNavigator at times. This meant that if he or she was busy and a patron was seeking help, we provided that help or referred the patron to another library staff person. In this way, allowing for the short time in the field, we observed and we also became insiders. Since demand frequently outstrips resources, this was the only ethical approach that respected the setting and the community: to assist with current practice while carrying out research to serve future practice.

In total, six people carried out the ethnography. Each person spent three to five days in a library location, jotting notes each day and typing them up each evening. To encourage reflection and stimulate serendipitous findings in this first stage of the fieldwork, a day's notes had to include one paragraph on each of the following topics:

1. The most interesting moment
2. The greatest problem
3. The greatest solution

At the heart of the notes were the descriptions of 157 interactions with a patron seeking help. We hand-coded these interactions. The three daily reflective paragraphs helped to shape the focus group agenda and the survey questions.

Focus groups

A total of twenty-seven CyberNavigators participated in six focus group discussions. These discussion groups ranged in size from two to seven people and averaged 4.5 people per group. These focus group discussions were guided by Julian Orr's study of copier repair technicians (1996). He found that stories were central to their work; telling each other stories helped them do, make sense of, and enjoy their work. If we could gather stories from the CyberNavigators, we reasoned, it would help us understand the informatics moment.

In the process of recruiting the focus groups, we asked participants to think about and bring one best story and one worst story from their experiences as CyberNavigators. To start the discussions, everyone shared at least two stories. As with Orr's copier technicians, these stories were fun for participants to hear. They validated their experiences. They were the same, and different. They were causes for mourning and celebration of the patrons and the communities, many in crisis, and also of the CyberNavigators themselves. And unlike the copier technicians, who shared their repair stories every day on the job, the CyberNavigators were in their own branches twenty hours a week and hadn't had the chance to sit down together. They themselves recognized this, as one transcript recorded:

> CyberNavigator: This is therapy! You're paying us to have therapy.
> [*Everyone laughing and talking at once.*]

The stories tumbled out in vivid detail.

The ethnographic work showed the pressures of the informatics moment for the staff: always on call, providing public service in distressed communities, in the branch library but not quite *of* the branch, since they were paid by the Chicago Public Library Foundation and supervised by their own manager first, and by the branch manager second. So another line of questions was: How would you make your job better? How would you make the program better, along various dimensions: technology, space, training, and so on? Once the focus groups were transcribed, we identified and hand-coded 598 distinct chunks of narrative.

Questionnaires

Thirty-seven CyberNavigators completed questionnaires. Twenty-seven of these were self-administered at the focus group sessions, ten others at a CyberNavigator training soon after. Participants answered eighty open- and closed-ended questions. Some questions were adopted from an earlier study of social capital and community technology use (Williams 2005); others were developed from the ethnographic data. Questions covered demographics; technology use; technology help given and received; and social capital. Taken together, the documents, ethnographies, focus groups, and questionnaires resulted in both texts and data—narratives and numbers—that the research team analyzed.

Findings and discussion

What does the informatics moment look like in the setting of the Chicago Public Library? What role does social capital play? There are two overarching findings:

1. The informatics moment involves four types of digital literacy work.
2. Social capital is a positive influence on the informatics moment.

Four types of digital literacy in the informatics moment

The informatics moment, as observed in this study, centers on a helping interaction between someone seeking to use computers and the internet and a helper in the public library. The ethnography suggested literacy as an organizing concept for these interactions, using the following definition but also including nontext records (images, sound, etc.), "technological literacies may be defined as social practices in which texts (i.e., meaningful stretches of language) are constructed, transmitted, received, modified, shared (and otherwise engaged), within processes employing codes which are digitized electronically, primarily, though not exclusively, by means of (micro)computers" (Lankshear 1997, p. 141).

The helping interactions recorded in the ethnographies break down into three types. Answers to the questionnaires added one more type and the focus group discussions provided more detail on all four. Four main types of literacies are involved in the informatics moments:

Basic literacy, that is, reading and writing. None of these appeared in the ethnographic data;
Computer literacy, using the computer and applications running on it;
Library literacy, using technologies and systems that are specific to Chicago Public Library or to libraries in general; and
Domain literacy, using technology in order to carry out tasks in specific domains of modern life.

Quite often one informatics moment has several of these literacies embedded in it. When this was apparent, we coded for domain literacy first, then library, then computer, and then basic. The result of coding of the informatics moments that the field team observed can be seen in column four of Table 2. Basic literacy help getting was not observed, but the CyberNavigators reported in the questionnaires that they did indeed provide such help (column three in the table).

	Percentage of CyberNavigators Providing Help with This at Least Weekly (N=37) (1)	Informatics Moments Observed (2)
Basic literacy		0 (0%)
Reading text	90	
Writing text	76	
Computer literacy		51 (32%)
Using a mouse or browser	100	
Setting up or using e-mail	97	
Producing a document	87	
Using social network sites	52	
Learning computers in a structured class	48	
Playing games online	38	
Library literacy		64 (41%)
Printing	100	
Making or changing a computer reservation	100	
Using the online catalog	87	
Using the library's databases	73	
Domain literacy		42 (27%)
Searching for work	94	
Doing non-job-seeking research	89	
Applying for work	87	
Producing or updating a resume	79	
Using other government websites	68	
Doing homework	67	
Applying for or checking on government benefits	50	
Seeking news or cultural information	46	
Doing e-commerce	23	
Seeking health information	19	
	19	

Table 2. Types of informatics moments

As Table 2 shows, the four types of literacy were operationalized in the questionnaires as various tasks that patrons seek help with. The CyberNavigators reported how often—daily, weekly, monthly, or less than monthly/never—they helped people with these tasks. The last column in the table indicates how often the four literacies were observed in the ethnographies. Some kinds of help are given more often than others ("at least weekly", column three in the table). Narratives from the focus groups tell more about basic literacy, computer literacy, library literacy, and domain literacy in the informatics moment. They are presented roughly in order from the most foundational.

Basic literacy.—People who cannot read or write do not often make their illiteracy plain for all to see. They hide their illiteracy out of a fear and often desperation that is based on an intelligent understanding of their vulnerability in a text-based world. They overcompensate and create distractions (Eberle and Robinson 1980). Their sense of fear and shame is perhaps perpetuated by the "state of grace" school of literacy theory, which holds (completely incorrectly) that people who cannot read or write also cannot reason logically or think abstractly (Williams 2003, p. 14; Burawoy 2009, pp. 20–21).

This helps to explain why the ethnographies did not reveal basic illiteracy. The focus groups, however, told of patrons who say, "Can you just type it for me?" Among the "worst stories" CyberNavigators told, one theme was "They don't want to learn, they just want you to do it for them", In these situations, CyberNavigators reported frequently helping by doing rather than by teaching, because the hard-luck stories of the patrons—these moments are usually tied to applying for jobs—were compelling. A librarian commented that it's very hard to draw lines between helping, teaching, and doing. A more common strategy is to explain that job hunting involves several steps—introduction to the computer, then email, and so on, and thus moving the patron into a sequence of help sessions, sometimes including the printing of job-search resources. This entails domain literacy (more below) and reflected how the types of literacy in an informatics moment can be layered over each other.

A total of 90 percent of Cybernavigators help people read something at least weekly; 76 percent help people write something at least weekly. Not being able to read will prevent a person from using computers or the internet, except perhaps to play video games. Many patrons we observed, who were not asking for help, were looking at Youtube; could it be some of them were *limited* to Youtube, because most websites require more reading?

Teaching people to read and write has been a priority in Chicago Public Library for many decades; even when they ended direct literacy services in 1996, the library continued to host efforts by partner literacy organizations (L.K. 1996). How could illiteracy have disappeared? Data in this study is *suggestive* of illiteracy. Between patron need and CyberNavigator frustration, it could be helpful to train the CyberNavigators in spotting illiteracy so that a different intervention could be applied than attempting to press on past a possible foundational problem. As the CyberNavigators often say, every job today requires an online application. For some manual or semiskilled labor, applying may require more literacy than the job itself. On the other hand, the information-age job transformation can mean that the same job, driving a long-haul truck, for instance, now requires working with a laptop in the cab.

Computer literacy.—A rich definition of computer literacy can be drawn from a synthesis of work from computer science, education, and literacy studies (Williams 2003):

1. Having contemporary skills (e.g., browsing or text editing);
2. Knowing foundational concepts (e.g., networks);
3. Possessing intellectual capabilities (e.g., evaluating sources);
4. Understanding computer literacy as an aspect of life in an information society;
5. Being familiar with at least the basics of computer programming;
6. Practicing computer literacy that is tailored to individual needs, interests, goals;
7. Being part of the community of people who can use IT, which means knowing a) how to keep learning, b) who or where to go for new concepts and skills (including software help features and online sources) and c) how to solve problems with others in that community;
8. Not assuming that someone with computer literacy is better than someone who isn't computer literate.

Each of these eight aspects is in evidence in the informatics moments in the library. Part of what makes this remarkable is that the public access computers in Chicago Public Library are very limited and locked down. Most machines provide only Internet Explorer. From that browser window, patrons can surf, open .pdf documents, view word processing files, interact with forms, watch videos, and initiate a print job. There is nowhere to save files except "on the cloud", that is, on corporate servers (e.g. Google Docs), unless the CyberNavigator shows you a trick to saving in the Temp folder. The machines wipe all user data upon logging off. From one dedicated machine in every location, patrons make or change a reservation. From another machine, they forward a print job to the printer. At three locations (Harold Washington downtown, Sulzer on the North Side, and Woodson on the South Side), public computers also provide Microsoft Office and flash drive functionality so patrons can open, create, and save documents, including from the web.

Focus group comments from the CyberNavigators demonstrate how each of these eight aspects of computer literacy appears in the library's informatics moments.

1. *Skills*. Most basic of these is using the mouse: "[I first tried to teach with online mouse exercises] and I'm like: 'Dude, this is awful.' Like, patrons hated it, I hated it. So I take them to Yahoo games. I'm like: 'All right, pick your favorite game. Let's go play.' And there they are, going: 'Oh, this is fun,' and then they just, like, learn it so much faster."

2. *Concepts*. The concept of electronic mail that you come to a computer to check, that waits for you only—and your password—is fundamental. This story demonstrates how informatics moments are not always completely successful, and is also an example of the CyberNavigator solving the universal problem of forgotten passwords:

   [I'll explain to a patron that companies] are only going to respond to you, you know, via email. They're going to respond to you via email, and you need to be able to respond and have a conversation back and forth via email. And they're like: "Well, I don't even use it that much. I don't even have a computer." I was like: "Well, you're always welcome to come here during library hours so you can use your email address." "Well, I don't even know how to login and logout." And I'm like: "Well, I'll be here. [...] and you have to save your username and password." [...] But the good thing is that I've created a format—I've made it that it's their first initial, last name, and then last two ___.

3. *Intellectual capabilities*. In this story a patron learns an online service that is critical for his community and then assumes CyberNavigator–type responsibility for others who need it:

The truth is, if you're filling out a Circuit Breaker [applying to a state grants program for seniors and disabled], you probably have some hard luck stuff going on in your life. Period, you know? But there was this guy. He would come into our branch, and he asked me for help filling out a Circuit Breaker one day. [...] then he comes back, like, later in the week and he's like: "Hey, remember me? I'm back. I got more Circuit Breakers." And I was like: "OK." Turns out, in his world, he was, like, the Circuit Breaker Man. [...] he took a lot of pride and joy in being able to help his friends and family get their paperwork done.

4. *Understanding computer literacy as part of life in the information society*. The two examples above illustrate the informatics moment as a leap in the patron's understanding and practice, accepting computers in their life. Contrary to the frustration detailed above, many stories were told of email success. The patrons and the CyberNavigators (several explained a similar approach) explicitly agreed to collaborate on passwords in a way which secured the password for the patron. In effect, patrons are constructing their own IT support network by agreeing to rely on the CyberNavigator in this way.

5. *Familiarity with at least the basics of computer programming*. The data only supplied one instance of this, but this story is important in two ways. First, Word Macros are a programming language that is available to any Word user if they can navigate it. Second, programming is an activity that only four of thirty-seven CNs report doing. Third, it illustrates that library staff are passing through informatics moments alongside the patrons: "Even the branch librarian, like, sometimes she gets stuck in Microsoft Word, and she's trying to work in Word Macros, or something, things like that, and she'll be like: 'Oh, the CyberNavigator!' And luckily, I do know how to do it, but they do expect me to know. It's like, that's your job, that's what you're supposed to know."

6. *Practicing computer literacy tailored to individual needs, interests, goals*. This story alludes to the fear people have who cannot use computers—much like those who cannot read and write, and understand the power that computers, like written text, has over our lives. It also shows, again, the paradigm shift—patrons find entirely new ways to approach a task: "A lot of people come in, and they have a big anxiety about using the

internet. And I'm just like: 'OK, go to Google and talk to Google like you were talking to me. What exactly do you want to do?'... That's rewarding to me, you know, in a way because it's just like: 'Oh, OK. I didn't even think about that.'"

7. *Being part of the community of people who can use IT, practicing continuous learning, knowing how to find help, and helping others.* In this example someone has crossed the digital divide and the CyberNavigator is happy to have her in her own help network: "She started out being afraid of, like, breaking the internet. Wouldn't even touch the computer. ... [It] took a little over two weeks before she was able to get the hang of, like, the whole thing. ... Then she's so excited ... [and] the best part of it was that she actually started schooling me on little things."

   Circuit Breaker Man above is another example of this. Other stories featured patrons coming in groups of two or more and helping each other, or being strangers and helping each other or the CyberNavigator.

8. *Not being better than people who aren't computer literate*. The development of a helping network, as above, expresses this last aspect of computer literacy. In talking about their own skills, the CyberNavigators returned time and again to the core skill: patience. Respect for the patron navigating the informatics moment was critical. One CyberNavigator had adopted a slogan he told his patrons in order to teach them patience and respect for learners: "Practice makes permanent."

Library literacy.—Library literacy means the skills and knowledge to use the particular systems in the library, particularly Chicago Public Library. Any library's public access computers and online resources have particular and multiple systems or interfaces that are often complicated by budget limits or rules laid down by multiple parties: publishers, vendors, software companies, local and federal government, as well as the library itself. Patrons as well as staff have to learn these, and sometimes relearn them, if usage isn't frequent. Thus library literacy includes knowing how to navigate the two systems put in place to manage the scarce resources of computer time and printing. A pay-as-you-go printing process starts at the patron's workstation but finishes at a printing station. And software for reserving computer time runs on another workstation, as well as on staff machines. Then there are four tools for accessing the library's online offerings: the library website, the catalog, the databases, and downloadable books and other media.

These tools run on at least six different platforms, or software, depending on how the databases are delivered.

1. *Printing*. New computer users can print wildly; every public computer lab has to deal with controlling costs. Chicago Public Library has in place a complex system that only daily users can remember and all staff spend time supporting patrons:

   That print system is the worst thing, seriously. It's just too complicated for new people. New people come in, you know, you got to print from over here. They're already having a problem because the print button on the screen [Internet Explorer] doesn't work. So they have to go to File, then Print. Then they come over to you: "Where's it going to come out at?" Now let's take your library card and go to the circulation desk [to pay]. Then after they do that, still, nothing's going to come out 'cause there's too many steps. [*Assents from other CyberNavigators*] It's too extra.

2. *Reservations*. Likewise, time on the computer is scarce and hard-won. A "worst story" of a CyberNavigator was the day two men got into a fight over their reservations. This story illustrates the cooperation required to manage reservations, which are made and changed by patrons and staff—except at some branches, not the CyberNavigator, because of their foundation-not-library status: "So I can't cancel reservations for people. I can't look up reservations for people that they made on the computer. But I was able to do that at my first branch. So it's kind of handicapping me at my new branch cause then I have to go a clerk and say, 'Hey, can you cancel this for me?'"

3. *Library website*. The library's website is complex and content comes from the central administration. This is an example of a resource that CyberNavigators have to stay on top of, even for basic information.

   I had a patron call not so long ago. They're like, "I saw on the website that these are your hours." And I'm like, "My hours are on the website?" They're on the website. Everyone's hours are on the website. [*Another CyberNavigator: What website?*] The CPL website. They're on there.

4. *Online catalog*. This is an area where other library staff are poised to help a patron. The handing off of patrons between library staff and the

CyberNavigator adds another level of complexity to the supporting of their informatics moments: "The cool times are when, you know, like, you help a student find an article or there's a really long line in the computers, and someone thinks that they have to get on the internet, and I'm like: 'No, we can use the catalog for that!'"

5. *Databases*. Here, again, the informatics moment calls for a librarian, because he or she will be trained and expert at database use:

   This high school student from ___ came in the other day, and she knew how to use the computer. Like, I could have showed her, like, you know, database stuff on the computer. [...] But, like, again, going back to efficiency and, like, not giving people the runaround. Am I going to be able to give her, like, the fastest way online to, like, find age-appropriate, or whatever, information for school about cottonwood trees? Heck no. I took her to the children's librarian, you know? I'm like: "This is a reference query."

6. *Downloadable books and other media*. Here the CyberNavigators are limited to explaining, not demonstrating or teaching, because the downloading runs on software which does not function on the public access computers.

Domain literacy.—Identifying this type of literacy makes references to the concepts of multiliteracies (Cope and Kalantzis 2000; Heath 1994; Nagle 1999), and to domain analysis work (Finn 1999). The multiliteracies concept emerges from findings that a person can be highly literate in one setting but not in another. School-sanctioned literacy skills and unsanctioned literacy skills are not always transferable—for instance, writing a term paper and writing a rap lyric (Heath 1994). Learning is situated—someone can do arithmetic in the supermarket, but be stymied in a high school math class (Lave and Wenger 1991). Information science is overlooking the issue of domain: information flows in one domain can be very different from those in another, and in order for new information systems to effectively serve various domains the information scientist must attend to a domain's particularity (Hjorland 1995).

Applying the concept of domain here highlights the fact that patrons bring tasks that require a certain amount of domain expertise. The CyberNavigator's expertise varies, but quite often life experience rather than specific training or education is the basis for their helpgiving. Here is an example from a CyberNavigator who is not a lawyer or paralegal: "A lady had just lost her son, and her grandchild—his children's mother came and grabbed him and took him to Indiana. She had no way of getting in touch with her grandson, so I helped her get through the legal parts online and everything, and finally, she got custody. By the way, she started signing up for my basic internet class!"

In another example, a CyberNavigator—who is in college for a psychology degree, but no more—guides someone through an extended informatics moment towards a job. Job seeking is such a leading activity at the library's computers that staff and administration have created an online resource guide, and CyberNavigators are getting a half-day orientation to it:

> One of my best success stories was a young lady I was assisting with job searching. And it went from learning how to use the computer, then she wanted to do a resume, and then from resumes to applying for jobs online. And she was coming out of a [battered] relationship. She wanted to have her own identity, her own income, and she went from, like, not really having a job or having a lot of experience, but I was able to utilize just her volunteer experience ... to articulate it into a resume format. And we applied for a job, and she actually got the interview and the job and everything. She was like: "This is, like, the most money I ever made in my life," and she's like: "I would never have made it if it wasn't for you," and everything, and I just felt good because she was looking for something and she got it.

The next story from the ethnographic observation echoes the same themes, but it is explicit that the CyberNavigator's expertise is from his own job-seeking experience. He is not a career counselor, but rather a valued peer helper:

> A woman wanted to apply for a management position at McDonald's. She had an advertisement for McDonald's employment: "Apply now! www.mcdonald..." The McDonald's website requires you to enter all your resume information as well many questions about past experiences and so on. The patron has the information, handwritten. The CyberNavigator helped her, reading it out loud and teaching her how to use a mouse and how to click. In the middle, when it asks for social security number, he then told her, "You need to fill in the all the blanks, there are 60 questions you have to answer." He also offered her an extension of her computer reservation time, past 60

> minutes. The CN suggested either go to the shop directly and tell them you applied online or call them. He told me later, I learned that from experience helping and from my own experience. And he is just 21 years old!

All library staff work together to help:

> At one point I was wasting a lot of time trying to help the person, like, write an objective in their resume. What goes in an objective? So one of the librarians, she does a resume workshop. She sits down with the patrons. She has, like, a mock resume—objective, experience, stuff like that—and she had books and everything and flyers, and from a certain time to a certain time she assists people with resumes. Then when they're ready to actually type it up and put it on the internet, I help. We work hand in hand.

As many examples have shown, quite often one informatics moment entails several types of literacy. The best examples, as above—and far and away the most common, since job losses have spiraled in the US and nearly all job applications are on the internet—is the job search.

The informatics moment draws on social capital

A book-length visual-sociology study of a rural repair shop explains how a fundamental aspect of work done at the repair shop is building and maintaining community (Harper 1987). A branch library is like that small shop, and the patrons in their informatics moments are seeking a repair so that they can go about their task. While the public library is structurally a government bureaucracy, sometimes its best work is done via social capital (Kranich 2001; Vårheim 2007) and the present study found social capital at work in the informatics moment.

Table 3 presents the operationalization and the measurements of social capital in this study. Three types of social capital are identified: the social capital of the CyberNavigators; that of the community, which includes the patrons; and that of the library staff. These types of social capital are documented in a modest portion of the observed informatics moments (19 percent, 22 percent, and 7 percent, respectively) and more deeply documented in the surveys and focus groups. Certain forms of social capital are very much in action; others are not. From this emerge six main findings.

1. *Names and recognition are key*. As with reference interactions (Durrance 1983, 1995), informatics moments are associated with the parties knowing

	Percentage of CyberNavigators Experiencing This at Least Weekly (*N*=37) (1)	Informatics Moments Observed (2)
CyberNavigator...		30 (19%)
Knows patron's name	95	
Recognizes patron	84	
Brings own laptop to use in helping patrons	35	
Allows patron to use CyberNavigator's laptop to get help	30	
Helps someone he or she knows from outside work	16	
Sees or gets together with patrons outside work	14	
Community		34 (22%)
Patron knows CyberNavigator's name	95	
Patron referred by someone other than library staff	78	
Patrons come in twos, threes, or more for help	54	
Library		11 (7%)
Librarians connect CyberNavigator to patrons seeking help	100	
Guard connects CyberNavigator to patrons seeking help	84	
Paraprofessionals connect CyberNavigator to patrons seeking help	81	
Library staff helps patrons (not including printing/reservations)	76	
Library staff sees or gets together with CyberNavigator outside work	3	

Table 3. Experiences of CyberNavigators, Community Patrons, and Library Personnel and Informatics Moments Observed

each other's names or recognizing each other: "I grew up locally, go to church down the street, so they either know my name, or a lot of them at first called me Circuit Breaker Lady." Many references are made to regulars, patrons who come every day or enough to be known. Regulars on occasion help smooth a rough moment or even help another patron. One CyberNavigator began to encourage this in order to accelerate progress. Again, this is like the repair shop operator (Harper 1987), or like waitressing work (Rose 2004); the bureaucracy or the business is the substrate for the growth of social capital, to the extent that this is understood, valued, and feasible.

2. *Private laptop use is another measure of social capital.* Given anyone's sense of urban crime, a remarkable one-third of Cybernavigators bring their own laptops and even help patrons use these laptops. This "going the extra mile" is sometimes frowned upon by branch managers but it gets around the obstacle of library computers that are overbooked and locked down with few applications. Related to this is the practice of CyberNavigators putting their own hands on patrons' laptops—"It's against the rules but people do it, cause sometimes you just have to"—in order to help.

3. *Most CyberNavigators are known in the library, not outside in the community.* They aren't a *visible* community resource. We investigated other public computing sites near the libraries and generally these were unfamiliar to the CyberNavigators, even though sending patrons there might help them and lighten the load at the library. One CyberNavigator recognized this, relating approvingly that at another branch, "People from all the local agencies meet once a month, keep each other informed so that referrals can be made".

4. *Given that, however, the community is clearly networked into its CyberNavigator.* They know his or her name, they are referred by non-staff, they come in family and other groups. This takes some time: "Once I helped someone, then others began to ask questions", and "I've only been here three weeks so it's slow still; at my old branch patrons knew me".

5. *Are some community members excluded from help in their informatics moments because they are not networked even indirectly with the library or the CyberNavigator*? One CyberNavigator estimates that 30 percent of his help is to regulars, and two of the six ethnographers saw such a stream of regulars that they wondered if word of mouth through existing networks was enough to reach the whole community.

6. *The library staff per se is actively collaborating with the CyberNavigator.* They refer patrons and they help patrons themselves. There is also conflict, but by and large the public library is embracing the public computing library, as these stories demonstrate:

> The staff respects me and my job, so if I know something, like, I even see them telling patrons the same thing I tell them now, because they, they listen. They watch. And we talk. So, you know, it's good information because giving patrons outdated computer advice, it does make you cringe. You have to find a way to say, hey, buddy. You know, before the patron gets out the door, but not in a disrespectful way.
>
> [The guard] sits right next to the reservation station so she just hears me doing things and I talk to her cause I stand right next to security. So she knows basically more about how to make [an] appointment for somebody with me.
>
> Now that [we've settled into a working relationship] the clerks are assisting with printing or making reservaions, and they normally won't interrupt me if I'm in a session.
>
> If patrons start a sentence with 'computer,' the staff directs them to me.

Finally, this field observation:

> I'm too old to learn, the librarian said. Then the CyberNavigator comforted the librarian with a story of a seventy-year-old patron who has gotten good at the computer. The librarian and the CyberNavigator keep a close warm relationship.

All in all, social capital appears to be closely associated with successful informatics moments, that is, people being able to get the IT help that they need to complete tasks which are quite often urgent. The library provides this resource by activating a social network: staff-CyberNavigator ties, CyberNavigator-community ties, library-community ties, and within-community ties. The close-up view afforded by this study validates social support as a component of the digital divide, affirms past findings for a positive relationship between social capital and IT use, and validates the public library as a resource for growing social capital and thus maintaining community.

Summary of findings

People experience informatics moments when they seek help to do something with information technology. This is their moment of bridging a digital divide. In the setting of Chicago Public Library, they are helped in these moments by a

CyberNavigator.

The informatics moments observed in the library entail one or more of four different literacies: basic literacy, computer literacy, library literacy, or domain literacy. These informatics moments succeed, that is, the collaboration between patron and CyberNavigator are successful: people looking online for jobs get them, people who were afraid of computers become computer users and even cybernavigators in their own right. Their gratitude expresses the paradigm shift, the giant leap, they have made: they return to say thank you, they press food and other gifts on the CyberNavigators, they even try to pay them.

People also recommend the CyberNavigator to others, and this is just one way that social capital is involved in the informatics moment. The CyberNavigator becomes familiar and trusted by patrons and staff based on a track record of success in helping and his or her approachability.

In sum, in their informatics moments, people get help via their social network: local people they know recommend the CyberNavigator; library staff recommend the CyberNavigator; and they turn to the CyberNavigator. They seek and get help from someone who is both close and approachable: a particular person in their own neighborhood library. In this moment and at its best, the library represents both government- and community-based social capital at the same time; this is understood in the library profession (Kranich 2001) and beyond (Putnam 2003), although professional, paraprofessional, and security guard training does not necessarily cover this aspect of library work.

One particular focus group moment is worth recalling in shifting to future considerations: the comment "You're paying us to have therapy!" followed by laughter all around. The very finding that stories of the informatics moment tumbled out in such vivid detail suggests that staff providing this service may be more than ready to examine their work, learn from it, and help make a better public library.

Designing the branch library of the future: A call for theory

After witnessing hundreds of informatics moments unfolding before them, staff and patrons at one branch library began to talk: Will the library be a temple to books? A friendly place to use computers? Will it be both? As their CyberNavigator explained, "I think, actually, we get used more than the librarians. Like, especially at my branch because I feel like nobody goes to the library for books anymore. Everything seems to be online. So it would only make sense that, you know, with books came the librarian, and with computers came the CyberNavigator, you know?"

Certainly both electronic and physical books are circulating, and additional data we have collected from the traditional library staff will shed more light on this. But it does appear that by their words and deeds, the creators of the CyberNavigator program—senior administrators, managers, and frontline staff—are designing the branch library of the future.

Practice can proceed further if informed by robust theory. The informatics moment in people's everyday lives merits closer examination and wider understanding if we are to accelerate it. Libraries are grappling with this moment. A 2009–2010 national survey asked public libraries if they carried out technology training (Davis, et al 2010):

> Informal point-of-use assistance, 76.6 percent of libraries
> Formal technology training, 37 percent
> One-on-one technology training sessions by appointment, 23.5 percent
> Online training material, 21.7 percent
> No training offered, 10.9 percent

How effective these activities are, who staffs them, and to what extent libraries are keeping ahead of demand, is not terribly well known. Yet 76.6 percent of public libraries means close to 13,000 outlets nationwide.

Interviews with state library staff and surveys of thirty-five public libraries found that supporting patrons who need help with IT is just part of the major challenge of public access technologies (Bertot 2009). A key solution emerging from that analysis is building "a community approach to public access with the library as one of the foundational institutions" (Bertot 2009, p. 88, and similarly p. 89). By partnering with its foundation and its branches' friends groups to raise funds and hire a special category of staff, Chicago Public Library has sustained a critical service for patrons. At least three library schools and one community college—Dominican University, University of Texas (Roy, et al 2010), University of Illinois, and Champaign's Parkland College—mobilize students as volunteer CyberNavigators in their local libraries, because staff cannot answer patron demand and educators recognize CyberNavigating as a new skill that their graduates need. The social capital reflected in institutional ties like these, as well as the social capital and successful informatics moments documented in this study, point to a vital library service *and* the resources to sustain it.

A particular direction for future research is further theory-building regarding these findings in the context of the literature on the reference encounter. This can clarify how the informatics moment is a continuity, but also something new, as the data from Chicago Public Library suggests.

Other helping professions and our information society as a whole also need an understanding of the literacy and the social capital involved. The informatics moment is in fact quite ubiquitous. Who has not either helped someone use computers, or been helped? Within and beyond the branch public library, there is something hopeful to be learned about our information society by looking closely at these interactions.

13

Community Informatics in Lao Shao Bian Qiong Areas: Informatics of Happiness: Thoughts on ICT Applications in China's Backward Rural Areas (2011)

Chen Jianlong

1 Our choice

The building of a new socialist countryside is an important component of China's 11th Five-Year Plan for national economic and social progress and also a historic task in our modernization process. Like many others, we keep asking ourselves what we can do. With this simple but beautiful wish in mind, we embarked on a tough and dedicated journey, hoping that we could help.

We started our research with farmers and herdsmen in Lao Shao Bian Qiong Areas (the old revolutionary base areas, autonomous areas inhabited by ethnic minorities, remote border areas and underdeveloped areas). In the summer vacation of 2007, my students and I stayed in the mountainous countryside of Jingning She Autonomous County in Zhejiang Province. We worked together with the local people and interviewed them friendly to gain some observations. One year later in the mountain villages in Fuping County, Hebei Province, we measured the local digital opportunity and visited farmers who used Internet for date marketing. In the 2009 summer vacation, we went to the Ningxia Hui Autonomous Region to visit the rural information service stations, information workers and related government officials. In this summer vacation we visited the pasture area in Sonite You County of Inner Mongolia to understand the local work and life, communicating with local herdsmen.

The rural area is a thread-bound book of ancient simplicity. While reading, we cherish it and constantly reflect upon its content. Farmers are like a brief and clear picture book. While reading, we find it fascinating, simple yet profound. Agriculture is like a popular and convenient e-book. While reading, we follow the page numbers and soon put all the pages behind us. Who often read ancient books? Picture books? Or e-books? Who is reading an ancient picture book? An ancient e-book? Or who is reading an electronic picture book? And what kind of book are we reading? The answer is that we are trying to read an ancient picture book, because we pay attention to the farmers and herdsmen living in rural areas. We are meanwhile trying to read an electronic picture book, because we pay attention to farmers and herdsmen still working in agricultural sector. It is therefore fair to say that we are trying to read an ancient electronic picture book, because we focus our attention on the rural, vulnerable groups in need.

2 Lao Shao Bian Qiong areas and community informatics

Lao Shao Bian Qiong Areas refer to the old revolutionary areas, autonomous areas inhabited by ethnic minorities, remote border areas and underdeveloped areas. The old revolutionary base are those set up under the leadership of the Chinese Communist Party during the Second Chinese Revolutionary Civil War and Anti-Japanese War periods in over 200 poverty-stricken counties of 24 municipalities and provinces nationwide. Autonomous areas inhabited by ethnic minorities are where ethnic minority groups live in compact community. China now has 155 autonomous areas with 5 autonomous regions, 30 autonomous prefectures and 120 autonomous counties, involving altogether 639 counties and municipalities. Remote border areas refer to the county-level administrative divisions along the border line. Apart from the 56 border farms and ranches of the Xinjiang Production and Construction Corps, we have another 134 border counties in total. Some national authority developed the Comprehensive Development Index based on the three indices of development level, vitality and potential. Accordingly underdeveloped areas are counties whose Development Index ranks among the last 20%. It is obvious that Lao Shao Bian Qiong Areas are featured large population, large proportion of our nation's territory, small economic output and weak development foundation. It has already become a specific task of our regional policy to facilitate the development of Lao Shao Bian Qiong Areas in China's 7th Five-Year Plan. Some say that our development of a comprehensive well-off society hinges on the poverty elimination and prosperity of these areas.

Community Informatics is increasingly recognized as an emerging interdisciplinary subject. The study of community has a long history. As many scholars focused their research on the complicated and profound influences of ICT on individuals, some pace-setters began to notice the far-reaching influence of ICT on the organizational structure, activity form and conduct norms of a community. As a new research domain and also a new term, community informatics was born due to the rapid development of ICT and its wide application in human life. In 2000, *Community Informatics: Enabling Communities with Information and Communication Technologies* compiled by Michael Gurstein was published, and caused big echoes worldwide as many scholars joined in community informatics research and practice. At that time, Michael Gurstein wrote that community informatics studied how ICT could help achieve a community's social, economic, political or cultural goals. As ICT evolves, humans also develop an increasingly better understanding of community informatics. But one thing for sure is that community informatics studies the relationships among people in the community, ICT and information, for instance how people can acquire, process and use information through ICT application, how the available technology and information can be used and exert influence on the people and the work and life of their community, or how the community can achieve development by using information and technology. Obviously, those ICT-failed communities are more likely to catch researchers' attention. That being said, community informatics is duty bound to enable vulnerable groups to share the benefits of information civilization.

We can see clearly that informatics in Lao Shao Bian Qiong Areas presents a specific and fascinating research subject to community informatics, which theoretically explains why we chose those areas to study.

3 My thoughts

After analyzing community informatics and related human information behavior theories in conjunction with the results of our four in-depth and hands-on investigations, we developed a preliminary understanding of the status quo and development goals of ICT application in our backward rural areas.

Status quo of ICT application in backward rural areas is summarized into the following four points (see Figure 1).

First, the People. Generally speaking, inhabitants in backward rural areas have low intellectual level, little information awareness and literacy. This is due to the fact that literacy and science education in those areas is underdeveloped, although those people have rich local and ethnic cultures. The situation is compounded by the many poorly-educated young and middle-aged working all the year round as migrant workers.

Second, the Technology. Though communication technologies centered on mobile phones have fully covered backward rural areas, the modern information technologies (in particular the Internet) for information acquisition, processing and utilization still fail those areas. Mobile phones become popular by convenience and affordability, while fixed line phones application is contracting due to a multitude of reasons. The local inhabitants obtain information mainly through traditional channels such as interpersonal communication, television and radio broadcasting, very few using Internet. Our survey in 2008 on rural residents' access to government websites in 253 poor old revolutionary regions also proved that.

Third, the Information. The information demand (endogenous demand) of residents in backward rural areas in their work and life is small, simple and explicit, while local governments and the outside world have been a strong information provider (exogenous demand), in the hope of lifting those areas out of backwardness. For local cultural and lingual considerations, governments are very much committed to providing locally-shaped information services to meet the limited demand. Only in very few cases, the inhabitants would use information services outside their county and they even have difficulties in fully and correctly understanding the services.

Fourth, the Interaction. It's fair to say that the people, technology and information have weak or even no linkage. Currently, rural inhabitants mainly rely on local governments and specialized cooperatives to obtain information. Rarely, an individual would use modern information technologies to acquire or provide information.

Notably rural residents seem content with the status quo, which must be changed to drive economic and social progress as well as narrowing rural-urban and digital gaps. However, we ought to be patient. With the attempt to construct a new socialist countryside, community informatics has unique values in backward rural areas.

We look forward to the day when inhabitants in Lao Shao Bian Qiong Areas enjoy relatively high intellectual level and information literacy, when application of information and communication technologies is equally emphasized, when endogenous and exogenous information demands see a balance, and when people, technology and information are seamlessly linked in and out of the community (see Figure 2). This is an essential goal of ICT application in rural areas.

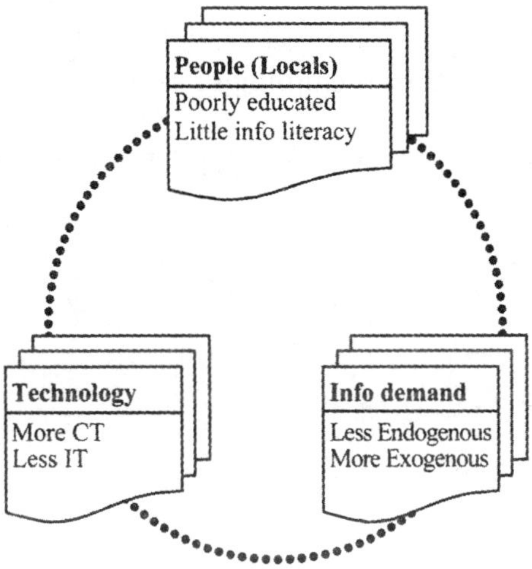

Figure 1. Status quo

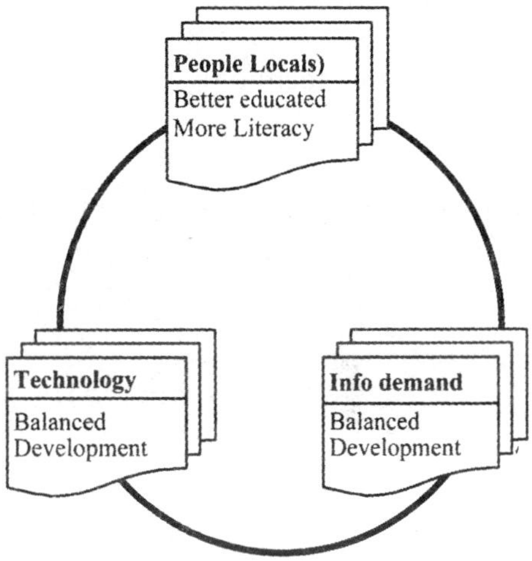

Figure 2. Development goal

To meet the goal, we shall step up our efforts in improving people's education levels and information literacy. We're pleased to find many governments and civil organizations have led this effort and scored enormous achievements. We have also seen some supporting policies issued for the economic and social development in Lao Shao Bian Qiong Areas and the important role of local successful individuals. However, more efforts have to be made to improve people's information literacy so as to spur effective demands of ICT and information content.

To meet the goal, more efforts should be made to reduce the cost of electricity, information and communication technologies, and increase accessibilities of information technologies, especially the Internet so that their passion for new knowledge and skills can be unleashed.

To meet the goal we should consider the pressing problems in local people's work and life. We should focus on the information needs of the residents to help them develop more information demands and better understand the information content so that they can be motivated to improve information literacy and use more information technology.

To meet the goal we need to have in-depth researches on the conflicts between rural residents' passiveness and activeness, recourse and self-help, material and spiritual wealth, information need and demand as well as information awareness and ability. We should take into account the interaction between people, technology and information, and integrate the three elements first at community and then at the individual level. With all these efforts we may provide local residents with accessible, affordable and valuable information and technologies service.

Realizing this goal will definitely boost the economic and social progress in Lao Shao Bian Qiong Areas and bring life happiness to local people. Therefore community informatics in Lao-Shao-Bian-Qiong Areas is informatics of happiness.

14

Toward Global Measurement of the Information Society: A US-China Comparison of National Government Surveys[①] (2009)

Kate Williams and Yan Hui

Abstract

To be global, digital and inclusive, we need comparable measures of ICT use around the world. To contribute to this, this research note analyzes what questions the Chinese and the US governments ask in their large, long-running surveys on the topic of computer and Internet use. The process and content of these surveys point up agreements, differences, and silences. Based on this, we propose nine basic questions that can be standardized and used in all country surveys of ICT use to create a coherent global dataset.

Introduction

Our current experience of globalization is founded on the broad and transnational use of digital technologies. But scholarship regarding this use is often limited to the national scale at best. As a result, we risk drawing parochial conclusions

① The authors would like to thank Maosheng Lai; Salvador Rivas; the members of the Community Informatics Research Lab; and, various faculty, staff and students at the University of Illinois GSLIS Research Showcase for their valuable feedback.

that trail behind actual social life. This paper demonstrates how to use today's "invisible college" (Price, 1963; 1986; Lievrouw, 1990) together with the power of the Internet to surmount this problem. It aims for a global science which can then inform global—and in turn national—policy, especially with regard to standardization. Bollen, et al (1993) present a useful summation of the measurement issues involved in standardizing global data. James (2009) proposes a simple solution to the problem by using just two indicators that are widely available for a number of countries: number of Internet users and number of cellphone subscribers. What greater detail can we get?

In order to govern, allocate resources, and plan, all governments who can do so investigate their population's use of computers and the Internet. The US and China are two interesting cases: each a global power, one the purported birthplace of all things digital and the other the world's largest production house and consumer market. (Important contextual discussion of how the Chinese society in the age of the Internet can be found in Qiu 2009 and Yang 2003.) This paper presents findings from an initial comparison of two national survey efforts, the US Current Population Survey computer and Internet use supplements (10 surveys over 1984-2007) and the China Internet Network Information Center's Internet development reports (22 surveys over 1997–2008).

Examining and comparing the two surveys' process and content points up agreements, differences, and gaps. The questions asked in China and the US suggest nine questions that could augment existing efforts towards global standardization in measuring country-level access to and use of information and communications technologies (ICT). We also invite other researchers to contact us and use our English-language collection of the questions asked in the two surveys.

Methodology

The term "invisible college" refers to the communiques and the travels that have connected the world's intellectuals for at least several hundred years. It is invisible compared to the visible research institutions dotted around the planet and the journals and books published online and off-line. As an example, this study was enabled by an e-mail inquiry from one author to the other. This led to a visiting position at the University of Illinois with funding from the China Scholarship Council. Comparisons and exchanges between China and the US were one of our research interests. For this study we collected the surveys, translated from Chinese into English as needed, and reformatted the digital content into a large spreadsheet for analysis.

The US surveys are available online.② China's Internet Development Reports are also comprehensive and freely available online③, although the questionnaires themselves are not. We used the reports to backwards-engineer the questions and translate them into English. We excluded all questions concerning demographics and other non-ICT topics. We thus built a database, essentially two tables in a spreadsheet, from the inferred Chinese questions and the US questionnaires.

Frequency, length, and size of the surveys

	US	China
Oct 1984	7	
Oct 1989	9	
Oct 1993	11	
Nov 1994	10	
Oct 1997	16	
Oct 1997		5
Jul 1998		13
Dec 1998	26	
Jan 1999		15
Jul 1999		24
Jan 2000		34
Jul 2000		38
Aug 2000	26	
Jan 2001		42
Jul 2001		42
Sep 2001	31	
Jan 2002		43
Jul 2002		37
Jan 2003		42
Jul 2003		51
Oct 2003	29	
Jan 2004		47
Jul 2004		51
Jan 2005		52
Jul 2005		39
Jan 2006		16
Jul 2006		24
Jan 2007		22
Jul 2007		11
Oct 2007	3	
Jan 2008		10
Aug 2008		10

Table 1. National surveys by month administered, showing number of questions

② As of June 2009, The US Computer and Internet Use supplements to the Current Population Survey from 1990 to present are available at http://www.census.gov/apsd/techdoc/cps/cps-main.html. Earlier surveys are documented at http://www.census.gov/population/www/socdemo/computer.html.

③ Information about the surveys done by the China Internet Network Information Center since October 1997 is available at http://www.cnnic.net/index/0E/00/11/index.htm.

As Table 1 indicates, the US survey began in 1984; the Chinese survey in 1997. They vary in length, with on average 17 ICT use questions (US) and 30 (China). Over time, both the US and the Chinese surveys get longer and more detailed, as indicated by the number of questions, and then shorter. For the US, the length increases sharply in 1997 and 1998, and shrinks precipitously in 2007. US markers over this period include the 1994 Clinton-Gore information superhighway/digital divide policy push, the 2000–2001 dot-com bust, and the 2001 start of the Bush presidency.

In China, the survey appears to lengthen from 1997 to 2004, and then becomes shorter over the years 2005–2008. We say appears because as "backward-engineers" of the surveys themselves, we are estimating the survey length from the questions for which data is publicly reported. As we finished this paper, CNNIC fielded their July 2009 survey, which included 99 questions about ICT. It is likely that both the US and China package and sell their data to commercial interests.

An additional comparison can be made in the frequency of the surveys. The US survey has been conducted 10 times over 23 years. The Chinese survey is done every six months. The US survey has been carried out alongside the much smaller but far more frequent Pew Internet and American Life surveys, which were first fielded in March 2000 and have continued several times a year. ④

Size and representativeness of the surveys

	Households	Household members		Individuals in armed forces	Total individuals
		Adults	Children		
Oct 1984	59,000	169,786	51,482	0	221,268
Oct 1989	59,600	180,123	52,667	0	232.790
Oct 1993	57,000	110,365	32,764	517	143,646
Oct 1994	54,000	107,506	32,110	568	140,184
Oct 1997	48,000	95.105	27,755	389	123,249
Oct 1998	48,000	95,061	27,490	384	122,935
Oct 2000	48,000	94,984	26,449	312	121,745
Oct 2001	57,000	111,778	31,098	424	143,300
Oct 2003	57,000	109,650	29,932	276	139,858
Oct 2007	55,000	106,349	27,169	444	133,962

Table 2. US survey response, from Current Population Survey

As Table 2 shows, the US survey is carried out by telephone interviews with more than 48,000 households. Generally everyone in the household is interviewed,

④ For more information, see the Pew Internet and American Life Project history, available at http://www.pewinternet.org/Static-Pages/About-Us/Project-History.aspx.

sometimes by proxy. To have adequate data about households without landline telephones, households with a demographic profile that matches households without telephones are oversampled. (According to the 2007 American Community Survey, 94.6 percent of US households have landline telephones; in the 2000 Census that figure was 97.6 percent.) Thus the US surveys are designed to be representative of the entire US population. The US survey began with a large N of 221,000 individuals, then dropped to an average of 135,000 +/-12,000 individuals during the period 1993 to 2007.

	Online survey respondents	Telephone survey respondents		Total sample
		A+C1	B+C2	
Oct 1997	Questionnaires online and in *Computer World* newspaper			1,802
Jul 1998	2,494	0		2,494
Jan 1999	>22,000	0		>22,000
Jul 1999	52,549	0		52,549
Jan 2000	202,432	0		202,432
Jul 2000	573,902	3,679		577,581
Jan 2001	26,667	62,620 and 6,000 face to face interviews		95,287
Jul 2001	78,342	52,700		131,042
Jan 2002	64,627	52,700		117,327
Jul 2002	14,592	4,800		19,392
Jan 2003	29,948	49,600		79,548
Jul 2003	19,096	4,800		23,896
Jan 2004	16,760	49,600		66,360
Jul 2004	17,883	7,200		25,083
Jan 2005	23,506	49,600		73,106
Jul 2005	18,136	5,000	4,000	27,136
Jan 2006	24,068	32,106		56,174
Jul 2006	16,332	7,200	4,000	27,532
Jan 2007	20,183	32,325		52,508
Jul 2007	21,714	7,500	5,000	34,214
Jan 2008	69,559	31,802	4,000+10,498	115,859
Jul 2008	0	7,000	2,000+7,000	16,000

Table 3. China survey response, from CNNIC. A+C1 indicates residents with household telephones including a "handy phone", a reduced price cell phone; B indicates college students boarding at school; and, C2 indicates residents without home phone but with cellphones.

As Table 3 shows, the Chinese survey began with 1,800 respondents and has fluctuated from a high of 578,000 at the peak of the dot-com boom to a recent low of 16,000. It has used online, print, telephone, and face-to-face surveys. As of December 2008, 340,804 million people, nearly 30 percent of individuals in China, had household phones including the "handy phone", a reduced price cell phone, and 641.23 million, over 50 percent of individuals, have cell phones.[⑤] The CNNIC assumes that individuals without any phone are not online. With this assumption and with the large online response, it is possible that the survey is missing more than 12 percent of Chinese people and is not representative of the whole population.

Content of the surveys

	US	China
Oct 1984	7 (100%)	
Oct 1989	2 (22%)	
Oct 1993	2 (18%)	
Nov 1994	6 (60%)	
Oct 1997	5 (31%)	
Oct 1997		5 (100%)
Jul 1998		8 (62%)
Dec 1998	19 (73%)	
Jan 1999		7 (47%)
Jul 1999		13 (54%)
Jan 2000		19 (56%)
Jul 2000		14 (37%)
Aug 2000	1 (4%)	
Jan 2001		6 (14%)
Jul 2001		2 (5%)
Sep 2001	15 (48%)	
Jan 2002		8 (19%)
Jul 2002		7 (19%)
Jan 2003		6 (14%)
Jul 2003		17 (33%)
Oct 2003	4 (14%)	
Jan 2004		5 (11%)
Jul 2004		7 (14%)
Jan 2005		9 (17%)
Jul 2005		20 (51%)
Jan 2006		4 (25%)
Jul 2006		12 (50%)
Jan 2007		10 (45%)
Jul 2007		3 (27%)
Oct 2007	0 (0%)	
Jan 2008		2 (20%)
Aug 2008		0 (0%)

Table 4. New questions in each survey

As Table 4 indicates, each time a survey is offered, some questions are reused, others are revised or dropped, and new questions are inserted. Both countries innovate and adjust to new technologies. The surveys of December 1998 in the US and July 1999 in China almost at the same moment reflect both innovation (many new questions) and breadth (many questions altogether).

⑤ Ministry of Industry and Information Technology of People's Republic of China, available at http://www.miit.gov.cn/n11293472/n11295057/n11298508/11912660.html.

	US	China	US as %	China as %
Uses	46	310	27%	46%
Connecting	35	37	20%	6%
Places	34	25	20%	4%
Ownership	29	0	17%	0%
Attitude	12	209	7%	31%
Devices	9	15	5%	2%
Frequency	7	50	4%	7%
Identity	0	17	0%	3%
Discourse	0	5	0%	1%
All questions	172	668	100%	100%

Table 5. The Chinese and the US survey questions reflect nine aspects of computer and Internet use

As Table 5 shows, nine categories emerged from a coding of all the survey questions. The US survey emphasizes ICT uses, details of connecting to the Internet, places people use ICT, and ownership of digital tools. The Chinese survey emphasizes ICT uses and people's attitudes towards all aspects of ICTs. Perhaps reflecting a socialist ideology, there are no questions about ownership. On the other hand, while China quite steadily maintains a question about "netizens"—with small shifts in the definition of this term—the US survey does not conceptualize or name people who use the Internet. Following from this, the US does not ask people what they know about computers and the Internet, while China asks people if they know certain technological terms from the current discourse.

Global standardization: Towards a model questionnaire

	US	China	ITU	OECD
Uses	√	√	√	√
Connecting	√	√	√	√
Places	√	√	√	√
Ownership	√		√	
Attitude	√	√		
Devices	√	√	√	√
Frequency	√	√		√
Identity		√	√	
Discourse		√		

Table 6. Compared to two other existing frameworks for global standardization of data collection, the US and Chinese surveys cover more of the nine aspects. Note: ITU = International Telecommunications Union; OECD = Organization for Economic Cooperation and Development.

As Table 6 indicates, the International Telecommunication Union (ITU) survey poses questions on ICT uses, connecting, places, ownership, devices, and identity (ITU, 2007), while the Organization for Economic Cooperation and Development (OECD) survey poses questions on ICT uses, connecting, places, devices, and frequency (OECD, 2009a, 2009b; OECD Working Party on Indicators for the Information Society, 2009). Neither of them asks about attitude or discourse. But both organizations are engaged in an ongoing search for standardized data. ⑥

	Model question
Uses	How do you use computer/the internet?
Connecting	What mechanism do you use to connect to the internet?
Places	Where do you use computer/the internet?
Ownership	What computer/internet devices do you own?
Attitude	What is your attitude towards computers/the internet?
Devices	What computer/internet devices do you use?
Frequency	How often do you use computers/the internet?
Identity	Are you a netizen?
Discourse	What computer/internet related concepts do you know?

Table 7. Nine questions comprise a model survey that could be asked worldwide

The questions in Table 7 could be asked worldwide with control variation appropriate to the country, but yielding comparative data. The identity question expresses both practice and self-conceptualization. The discourse question addresses not skills but knowledge, part of mastery of the new tools and the new society. The questions taken together incorporate the US focus that is rooted in the digital divide origins of the US survey: who is connected, where, what are they doing. And they incorporate the Chinese focus on their population's experience and attitude towards the digital age, conceptualized neatly and powerfully as the netizen. ⑦

Our technologies are clearly global, but why do we need globally comparable data? Because without it, international and national policy lags behind. Governmental and other agencies need data to implement useful programs and services. Commercial interests need data to understand their markets. And civil society

---

⑥ For example, a number of papers are posted at http://www.itu.int/ITU-D/ict/papers/index.html.

⑦ For comparable terms used in the US literature, see Howard, et al, 2000 on netizens and Mossberger, et al, 2007 on digital citizenship, both cited in Buente, 2009.

needs data to inform its debates and actions on issues which are quite typically both local and global. On all these fronts, ICT and the continuing invisible college enable global, data-driven practice.

15

Statistical Report on Internet Development in China (January 2012)

China Internet Network Information Center (CNNIC)

Preface

To achieve an comprehensive understanding about Internet Development Situation in China, China Internet Network Information Center (CNNIC) organized relevant Internet network organizations to jointly carry out a survey on Internet Development Situation upon the decision of the competent department of the State through discussion in 1997, and CNNIC issued the first *Statistical Report on Internet Development in China* in July the same year. To normalize and systemize the survey work, CNNIC decided to issue *Statistical Report on Internet Development in China* in every January and July since 1998. The report provides constant survey and study on the internet users scale, structural features, network application and the environment of Internet security, and rigorously and objectively reflects the Internet development situation in China, and provides an important basis for governmental departments and enterprises to grasp the development trend of Internet and make decisions. Therefore, it has been emphasized in every circle and quoted widely both home and abroad.

To date, CNNIC has successively issued 28 national statistical reports on Internet development situation, this report is composed based on the 29th national survey on Internet development, inheriting the contents and style of the previous reports.

Data collection for this report achieved great supports from the government, enterprises and all sides of the society. Under the guidance of Ministry of Industry and Information Technology and other State departments, each survey was conducted successfully; with the close cooperation of Internet organizations and websites and medias supporting the survey, etc, collection of basic resource data was completed in time.

Among them, Netease Youdao Information Technology (Beijing) Co., Ltd and Tencent Search Technology R & D Center provided help for the access of webpage data.

East.net(China)Co., Ltd., HiChina, Sinonets Co., Ltd., Beijing Innovative Linkage Technology Co., Ltd. , Beijing Xinnet Digital Information Co., Ltd., CE Dongli Technology Company Limited, Guangdong Todaynic.com International Limited (former Zhuhai Todaynic.com Internet Information Technology Co., Ltd.), Chinasource Internet Service Co., Ltd. , Longtop Online Co., Ltd. (former XiaMen Bizcn Computer & Network Co., Ltd.), Xiamen 35.com Technology Co,Ltd., Beijing BonRee Co., Ltd., and ChinaCache Communication Technology Co., Ltd.

We hereby express our sincere acknowledgement to them! And meanwhile, express our gratitude to the internet users that received the 29th Statistical Survey on Internet Development Situation!

Summary

1. Basic data

- As of the end of December 2011, the scale of Chinese internet users is more than 5 hundred million, to 5.13 hundred million. The newly added internet users over a year are 5,580 ten thousands. The Internet penetration rate stepped up to 38.3% compared with those at the end of last year, increased by 4%.

- There are 356 million mobile phone internet users in China with an increase of 5,285 ten thousand compared with that at the end of 2010. The proportion of the mobile phone internet users has covered 69.3% of the total internet users.

- Home computer broadband internet users reached 392 million, covering 98.9% of the home computer internet users.

- There are 136 million rural internet users, covering 26.5% of the total internet users with an increase of 1,113 ten thousand compared with that at the end of 2010.
- Internet users at the age of 30–39 increased remarkably, up 2.3% compared with those at the end of 2010, to 25.7%.
- Internet users with junior high school education keep rising, from 32.8% to 35.7%.
- 73.4% internet users access to Internet with desktop, down by 5% compared with those at the end of 2010. Internet users using mobile is up to 69.3%, whose use ratio is continuously close to traditional desktop.
- In 2011, average duration for net citizens to surf internet is 18.7 hours per week with an increase of 0.4 hour compared with that at the end of 2010.
- Up to the end of December 2011, there were totally 7.75 million domain names in China, in which, there were 3.53 million .CN domain names totally. There were 2.30 million Chinese websites.

2. Trend and features

Scale growth of Internet users into platform

In 2011, internet users increase by 55.8 million for a year, with penetration rate enhanced by 4%, and the speed slowing down compared with the improvement of 6% every year on average since 2007. In the past five years, among the crowd categories pushing the rapid increase of internet users scale, Internet penetration is about to top. However, it's hard for the crowd of other ages and education levels to accept Internet with the same speed for the young and highly educated group. Therefore, the overall scale growth of internet users go into platform period.

Turning point occurring for number of .CN domain name and website in China

As of the end of December 2011, there were totally 3.53 million .CN domain names, up to 0.7% compared with June in 2011. After downfall of total number of Chinese websites for more than one year, it rises again to 2.3 million currently. In China, the number of .CN domain name and website sees steady rising after completion of downtrend.

Online news utilization ratio dropped rapidly

Utilization ratio of online news keeps going down in recent years, especially in

2011. Increasing rate of online news users just reached 3.9%, 367 million, utilization ratio dropped from 77.2% to 71.5%.

E-commerce application continues to grow steadily

E-commerce applications including online shopping, online payment, online banking, and travel booking keep steady trend in 2011, in which, the online shoppers reached 194 hundred million, up by 20.8% compared with the end of last year. Online payment users and online bank users for the whole year increase by 21.6% and 19.2%. Currently, the users are 1.67 hundred million and 1.66 hundred million respectively.

Significant change for Internet communication of internet users

On the one hand, microblog develops rapidly by using of nearly half internet users, covering 48.7%. On the other hand, traditional communication applications see a sharp decline: E-mail utilization ratio from 54.6% in 2010 down to 47.9%, forum / BBS from 32.4% down to 28.2%, and blogs and personal space down from 64.4% to 62.1%.

Significant increase in online video users

There is a good development trend for online video industry. The subscribers increased 14.6% over the previous year, reaching 325 million. The utilization ratio is improved to 63.4%. It's the fifth application following the instant messaging, search, music, and news for Chinese internet users.

I Introduction to the survey

I. Survey methodology

(I) Survey on individual Internet users

1.1 Survey population

Permanent residents at the age of 6 or above who have fixed-line telephones (including home phones, personal handy phones and dormitory phones) or cell phones.

1.1.1 The sample size

Among the overall 60,000 samples for the survey, there are 30,000 residential fixed-line telephone users and mobile phone users respectively, and the samples cover 31 provinces, autonomous regions and municipalities directly under the Central Government in Mainland China.

1.1.2 The categories of the population

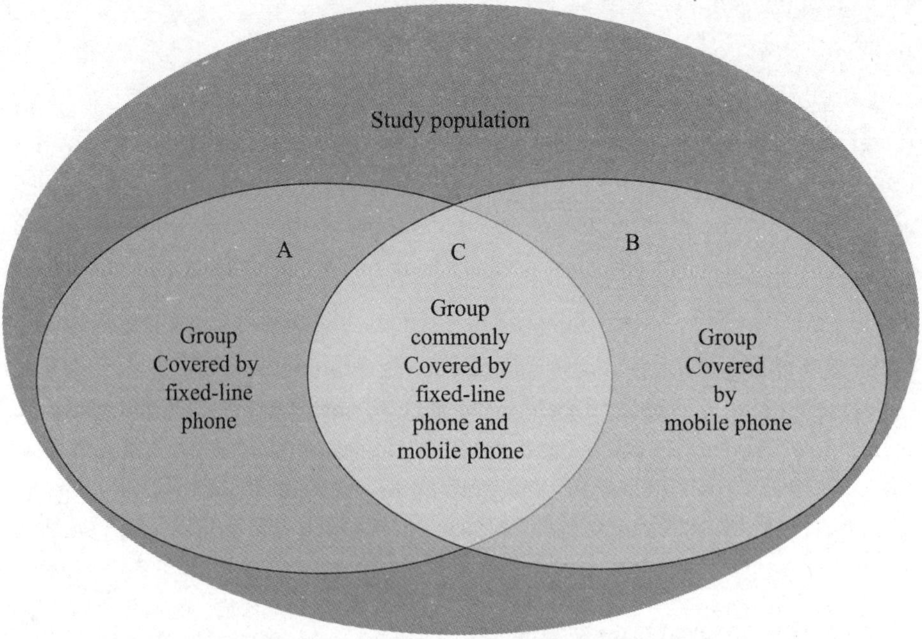

The survey population is divided into three groups as follows:

Group A: population only covered by fixed-line telephone (phone is used in above picture. Please keep consistent) (residents covered by home phone, personal handy phone users, college students covered by dormitory phone and other dormitory phone users);

Group B: population only covered by cell phone;

Group C: population covered by both cell phone and fixed-line telephone (the house phone users and cell phone users are overlapped to some extent and the overlapped part is called Group C), C= A+B.

Due to the overlap, the users in Group C may be sampled repeatedly, which will increase the chances of this Group being included in the sample. The estimation bias resulting from this problem will be corrected based on the double sampling theory.

1.2 Sampling methods

1.2.1 Two-stage stratified random sampling

To begin with, both the fixed-line and cell phone population is subdivided into 31 segments (strata) based on the 31 provinces/autonomous regions/ direct-controlled municipalities (referred to province hereinafter). The sample size of each province is decided by the square root of last year's sample size.

Within each province, every city/region/county (referred to city hereinafter) is selected, and self-weighting sampling is adopted. The sample size of each city is decided by the ratio of 6 and older population with fixed-line telephone in this city to the same population in the province.

1.2.2 Methods to ensure equal probability sampling

The telephone number in each city is selected according to the following methods:

First, select all the central office codes. Second, produce a number of random four-digit numbers according to the size of valid sample in this city. Third, combine the codes and the numbers to form a phone number pool. Finally, order the phone numbers in the pool randomly, and the interviewing phone number will be chosen from this pool.

1.3 Survey contents

The survey mainly concentrates on the quantitative and structural feature of Internet users, online conditions, web applications, attitudes of Internet users towards internet and non-user background in China. The content of survey includes whether interviewees surf the internet, their background, internet access behavior of Internet users, online depth and online experience, etc.

1.4 Survey administration

The survey is conducted through Computer-Assisted Telephone Interviewing System (CATI).

1.5 The Difference between the survey population and the target population

According to our 2005 research, the number of Internet users who do not use any telephone was very small. We believe that the number will keep decreasing along with the development of telecom industry in China. For instance, the number of phone users of our country in the end of 2005 was 740 million, while the total number exceeded 1.2 billion, with popularizing rate hit 94.2 pieces/hundred people ① by the end of November, 2011. Thus, the hypothesis underpinning this survey is that the number of Internet users uncovered by any phone is negligible.

(II) Online survey

Online survey focuses on the situation of typical Internet applications. CNNIC carried out an online survey during December 1–31, 2011. A questionnaire was placed on the website of CNNIC and questionnaire linkage was set on the websites of government media, the national ICP/ISP websites and provincial portals to ask Internet users to be actively involved in the filling of questionnaire. After the recollection of such questionnaire, validity testing of questionnaire was carried out by technical methodology to exclude invalid questionnaires. There were 32,772 copies of valid questionnaires received for such online survey.

(III) Online automatic search and the report data

Online automatic search is used to collect the quantity of the domain names, websites and geographic distribution, etc., while statistical data for reporting mainly include number of IP addresses and international network bandwidth.

1. Total Number of IP Addresses

The statistical data for IP address sub-province derive from IP address databases of Asia-Pacific Network Information Center (APNIC) and CNNIC. Sub-provincial data are obtained by adding data that have been registered in both databases and could be judged what provinces the addresses belong to according to relevant provinces. As the utilization of address allocation is a dynamic process, the statistical data are only for reference. Meanwhile, Ministry of Industry and Information Technology, the competent authority of IP addresses, also orders Chinese IP address allocation units (such as China Telecom) to report the number of IP addresses owned by them for each half-year. To ensure the accuracy of IP addresses, China Internet Network Information Center (CNNIC) will make comparison and verification on the statistical data and reporting data from APNIC.

2. Total number of domain names and websites in China

The number of domain names and websites in China are obtained by the sum of the following parts of data:

The first part is the number of domain names and websites under .CN, which can

① Source: http://www.miit.gov.cn/n11293472/n11293877/n14395765/n14395861/n14396152/14400045.html.

be obtained by online automatic search by CNNIC; the second part is the number of generic top-level domains (gTLD) and websites in China, which is assisted and provided by registrars of all types of generic top-level domains. These data include: number of all types of generic top-level domains (gTLD) and websites under domains; number of generic top-level domains (gTLD) and websites classified according to .COM, .NET and .ORG; number of generic top-level domains (gTLD) and websites classified by the province of the registrar.

3. Number of international network bandwidth

Ministry of Industry and Information Technology, through the report system, obtains timely the number of international network bandwidth connecting all operators and other countries or regions. These reporting data are incorporated in the *Statistical Report on Internet Development in China.*

II. Definition of terms in the report

Internet users: The Chinese citizens at the age of 6 or above who have used the Internet over the last six months.

Mobile Internet users: It includes but not limited to the Internet users who have used cell phones to connect and access the internet over the last six months.

Computer Internet users: Internet users accessing to and using Internet by computer in the past six months, but not limited to those accessing to Internet only by computer.

Home computer broadband Internet users: Internet users accessing to and using Internet by broadband (xDSL, CABLE MODEM, optical fiber access, power line access, Ethernet, WIFI, etc) among those accessing to Internet by computer at home in the past six months, but not limited to those accessing to Internet only by broadband.

Rural Internet users: It includes the Internet users who mainly live in the rural area over the last six months.

Urban Internet users: It includes the Internet users who mainly live in the urban area over the last six months.

Youth Internet users: It includes the Chinese Internet users below 25. [②]

② According to Youth towards the Year 2000 and Beyond passed by the 50th UN conference on December 14, 1995, the youth is classified to be age group from 15 to 24. The group aged 6 to 24 herein is called Youth group.

IP address: One of the basic internet resources used to identify the computers on the internet, servers or other devices on the internet. Internet can be only connected only by acquiring an IP address (no matter how the IP address exists).

Domain name: The domain name in this report only refers to ASCII domain name, which is a character string composed only by numbers, letters or hyphens and divided by points (.) and a hierarchical sequential Internet address mark corresponding to the IP address.

The domain names include two types: one is the country code top-level domain (ccTLD), e.g. the domain ending with .CN to indicate China; the other is the generic top-level domain (gTLD), e.g. domains ending with .COM, .NET and .ORG.

Website: It refers to the web site with the domain name itself or "www.+ domain name" as website, which includes the web site under China national top-level domain .CN and generic top-level domains (gTLD). The register of such domain name is located in the territory of China. For the domain name cnnic.cn, it has only one website and its corresponding website is cnnic.cn or www.cnnic.cn. In addition, websites with such domain name as suffix such as whois.cnnic.cn, mail.cnnic.cn can only be seen as different channels of the website.

Scope of survey: Unless otherwise indicated, the data in this report only refers to that of Chinese Mainland, not including Hong Kong, Macaw and Taiwan.

Deadline of survey data: The deadline for data of this statistical survey is December 31, 2011.

II Scale and Structural Features of Internet users

I. Scale of Internet users

(I) Overall scale of Internet users

By the end of December 2011, the total number of Chinese Internet users has been over 500 million, to 513 million. The new Internet users throughout the year are 55.8 million. Internet penetration increases 4 percentage points compared with those at the end of previous year, to 38.3%.

For the growth of Chinese Internet users in the past five years, from 2006 when Internet penetration rate rose to 10.5%, the scale of internet users has seen a rapid growth. The average annual penetration rate is enhanced to about 6 percentage points, especially in 2008 and 2009. The annual Increment of Internet users is close to 90 million. In 2011, there is a sign of slowing growth.

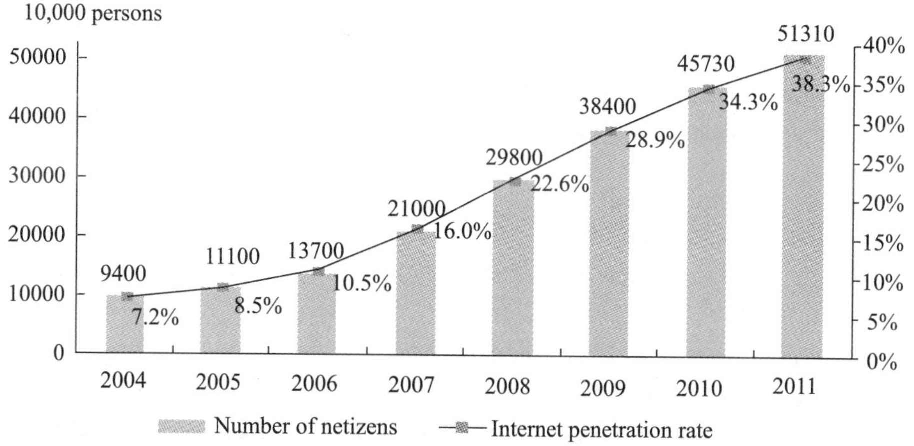

Figure 1. Scale and popularizing rate of Chinese Internet users

Currently, Internet penetration rate is less than 40% of all the people, so there is a very wide space for growth of Internet users. Considering age, education level, income level and other factors, the people with condition access to Internet and skill have been transferred to internet users. Next, there will be great difficulty for the growth of Internet users scale.

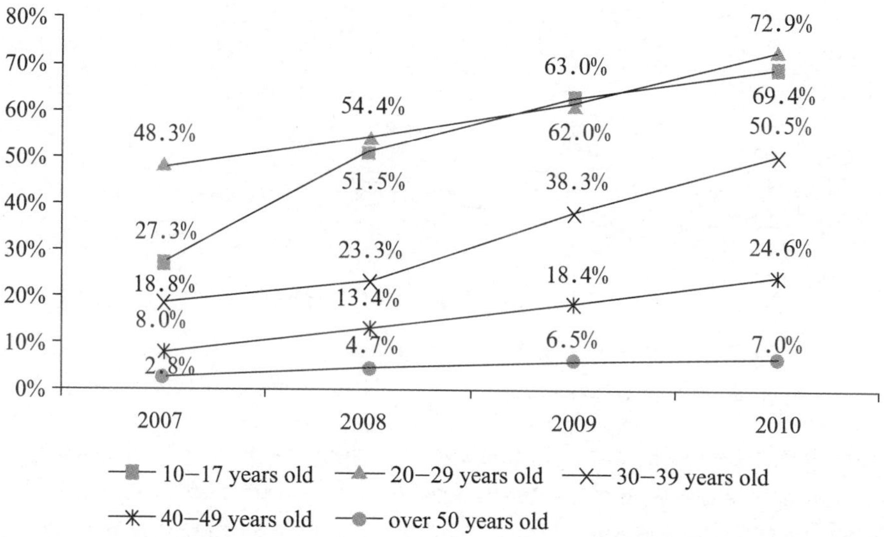

Figure 2. Internet popularizing rate for population of all ages in 2007–2010 (Population of all ages has not been released yet in 2011 China Statistical Yearbook. Relevant data is lacking.)

For age, in the past five years, the utilization ratio for the group of 10-29 years old keeps rising, close to high level currently. There is a limit for the enhancement space of such group in the future. The utilization ratio of Internet for the population above 50 years old changes a little. The utilization ratio of Internet for the population 30-39 years old rises gradually, so there is certain growth space. It will become main group for internet users growth of the next stage.

For education background, the Internet utilization ratio for population with junior college degree or above reached to 96.1% in 2011, in saturation generally. In the past five years, the penetration rate of population with high middle school degree rose significantly at most. In 2011, proportion of Internet users was more than 90%, to 90.9%. For the population with primary education and below, Internet penetration rate is always slow. Overall, in the past five years, among the populations that helps rapid growth of internet users scale, Internet penetration is about to peak, meanwhile, it's hard for population of other ages and education levels to accept Internet with the same speed of young and highly educated groups. In the future, the growth rate of Chinese overall internet users will enter a plateau.

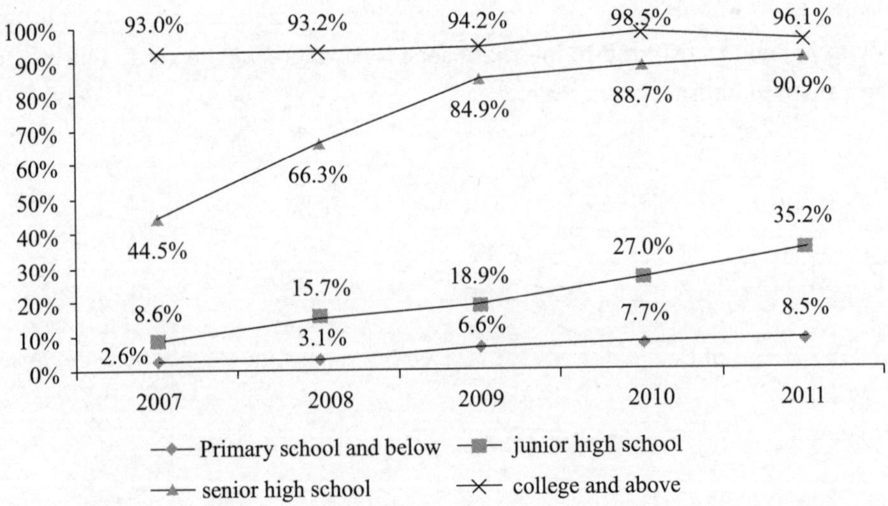

Figure 3. Internet penetration rate of population with all educated levels in 2007–2011

Thus, it can be seen that reducing the threshold of Internet access and use, encouraging elderly people, low-educated people and later acceptor for new technologies will be the important conditions to further push the expansion of internet users scale in China. In 2011, our government sturdily pushed forward the transition development of communication industry, positively promoted construction of broadband network infrastructure, and accelerated the development of new technologies and type of operation. Up to November 2011, subscriber access to Internet broadband in China reached 155 million. 3G network has covered all counties and most towns of the state[③]. The continuous completion for hardware facility provides a good external environment for deep popularization of Internet.

(II) Scale of home broadband internet users

By the end of December, 2011, the number of Internet users using home broadband[④] for Internet access has reached to 392 million, covering 98.9% of internet users using home computers for Internet, basically the same with the last year.

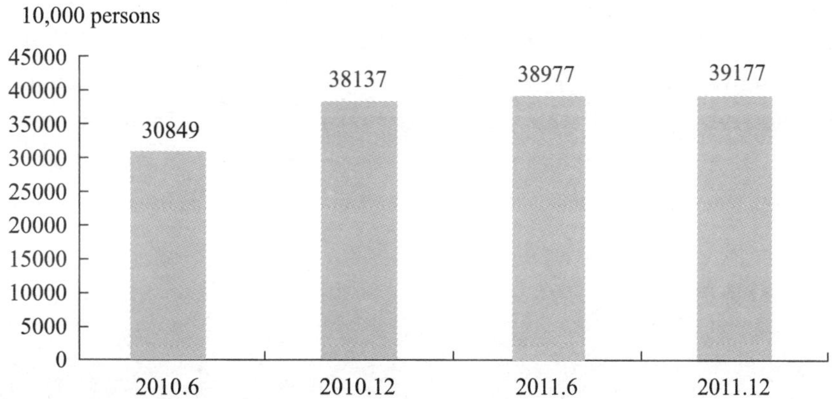

Figure 4. Scale of home broadband Internet users

(III) Scale of mobile phone Internet users

As of the end of December 2011, the scale of Chinese mobile phone users reached 356 million, an increase of 17.5% year on year. The growth is slowing compared with the previous two years.

In 2009, mobile phone users increase as high as 98.5% mainly because operators lower the network traffic charge to stimulate the burst of scale of mobile Internet users and fight for users. By 2010, the promotion effect of reducing traffic charge is gradually digested by market. The growth speed of mobile Internet users reduced

③ Source: website of Ministry of Industry and Information Technology of the P.R.C , http://www.miit.gov.cn/n11293472/n11293877/n14395765/n14395861/n14396152/14404568.html

④ Home broadband internet users refer to those using broadband (xDSL, CABLE MODEM, optical fiber access, power line access, WIFI, etc) to access to Internet.

substantially.

In 2011, the increasing speed for overall size of mobile internet users declined because operators put marketing focus on terminal in the hope of obtaining more mobile phone users by popularizing smartphone. Internet-friendly smart phone attract partial users to apply mobile Internet. Due to current high price, the population using smart phone mainly focuses on high-middle end crowd and existing internet users. For the overall size of mobile phone internet users, the promoting of smart phone is not particularly obvious.

In the future, innovative applications will be the main force driving the growth of mobile internet users. Currently, the penetration rate of mobile internet users in phone users is only 36.5%. The insufficient demand on surfing the Internet with cell phone is the main reason for most of mobile phone users failing to access to mobile Internet. With the popularity of smart phones, a large amount of smart phone internet users provide the basis for outburst of mobile Internet application. Internet service providers have begun to make overall arrangement for mobile Internet. The fierce competition will definitely give birth to innovative applications that meet the needs of sub-group and further promote mobile phone Internet users into the next round of high speed growth cycle.

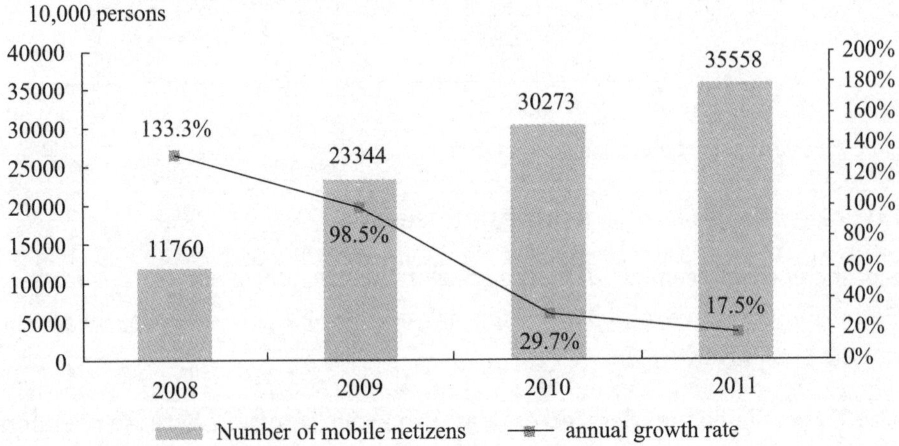

Figure 5. Scale of mobile Internet users

(IV) Scale of internet users in province

In 2011, the scale of internet users in all provinces rises significantly. There are 21 provinces with internet users over ten millions among 31 provinces (municipalities and autonomous regions) in Chinese Mainland. At the same time, regional difference of Chinese Internet development continues. Internet penetration rate in Beijing is more than 70%, to 70.3%, while in Yunnan, Jiangxi, Guizhou and other provinces where Internet penetration is low less than 25%.

Province	Number of internet users (ten thousand)	Penetration	Growth rate	Ranking of penetration	Ranking of internet users growth rate
Beijing	1379	70.3%	13.2%	1	9
Shanghai	1525	66.2%	23.1%	2	1
Guangdong	6300	60.4%	18.3%	3	2
Fujian	2102	57.0%	13.7%	4	8
Zhejiang	3052	56.1%	9.5%	5	23
Tianjin	719	55.6%	10.9%	6	17
Liaoning	2092	47.8%	9.2%	7	25
Jiangsu	3685	46.8%	11.5%	8	15
Xinjiang	882	40.4%	7.7%	9	28
Shanxi	1405	39.3%	12.4%	10	10
Hainan	338	38.9%	11.4%	11	16
Shaanxi	1429	38.3%	10.3%	12	22
Shandong	3625	37.8%	8.8%	13	26
Hubei	2129	37.2%	11.9%	14	11
Chongqing	1068	37.0%	7.9%	15	27
Qinghai	208	36.9%	10.4%	16	20
Hebei	2597	36.1%	18.2%	17	3
Jilin	966	35.2%	9.5%	18	24
Inner Mongolia	854	34.6%	14.4%	19	6
Ningxia	207	32.8%	18.2%	20	4
Heilongjiang	1206	31.5%	7.0%	21	29
Xizang	90	29.9%	10.8%	22	19
Hunan	1936	29.5%	10.8%	23	18
Guangxi	1353	29.4%	10.4%	24	21
Sichuan	2229	27.7%	11.6%	25	14
Henan	2582	27.5%	6.8%	26	31
Gansu	700	27.4%	6.9%	27	30
Anhui	1585	26.6%	13.9%	28	7
Yunnan	1140	24.8%	11.7%	29	13
Jiangxi	1088	24.4%	14.5%	30	5
Guizhou	840	24.2%	11.9%	31	12
Nationwide	51310	38.3%	12.2%	—	—

Table 1. Scale and growth speed of Internet users scale in province in 2011

Compared with global Internet penetration rate (30.2%) in 2011, there are 21 provinces that exceed such level, with one increased compared with those at the end of 2010.

Among 21 provinces, Internet penetration degree in 12 provinces such as Beijing, Shanghai, Guangdong, Fujian, Zhejiang, Tianjin, Liaoning, Jiangsu, Xinjiang, Shanxi, Hainan and Shaanxi etc exceeds national average level. Most of those provinces concentrate in the east coast. Among them, due to sharp zooming of number of population in Shanghai and Guangdong Province in the sixth population census data, the number of internet users calculated by the data increases significantly, resulting in the growth speed of internet users scale ranked the first and second place Shanghai and Guangdong in 2011.

The Internet penetration rate in 9 provinces such as Shandong, Hubei, Chongqing, Qinghai, Hebei, Jilin, Inner Mongolia, Ningxia, and Heilongjiang etc is higher than global average, but lower than Chinese overall Internet penetration. The Internet users in Ningxia and Hebei grow fast, of which, Internet penetration in Ningxia exceeds global average for the first time in 2011.

There are 10 provinces with Internet penetration lower than global average, including Tibet, Hunan, Guangxi, Sichuan, Henan, Gansu, Anhui, Yunnan, Jiangxi and Guizhou, most of which are less developed central and western region provinces.

II. Access mode

(I) Internet facility

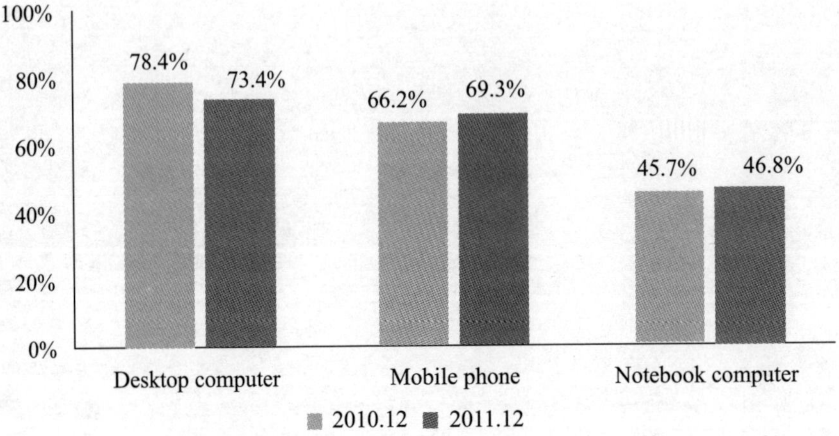

Figure 6. Internet access facilities of Internet users

In 2011, there was 73.4% internet users using desktop, 5 percentage reduced compared with those at the end of 2010. Mobile phone Internet users are up to 69.3% and notebook computers up to 46.8% slightly. With lower utilization of desktop computers, the utilization ratio of mobile phone is constantly approaching to traditional desktop computers.

(II) Access location

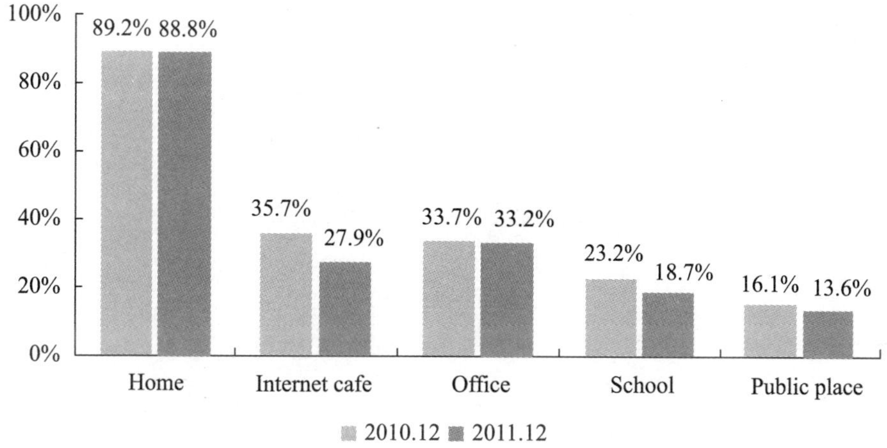

Figure 7. Locations that Internet users access to Internet

In 2011, the proportion of Chinese Internet users at home and unit keeps stable, 88.8% and 33.2% respectively, generally the same with those in 2010.

The proportion of internet users in school and cybercafé lowers significantly, in which, the Internet users in cybercafé only occupy 27.9%,7.8% down compared with those at the end of last year.

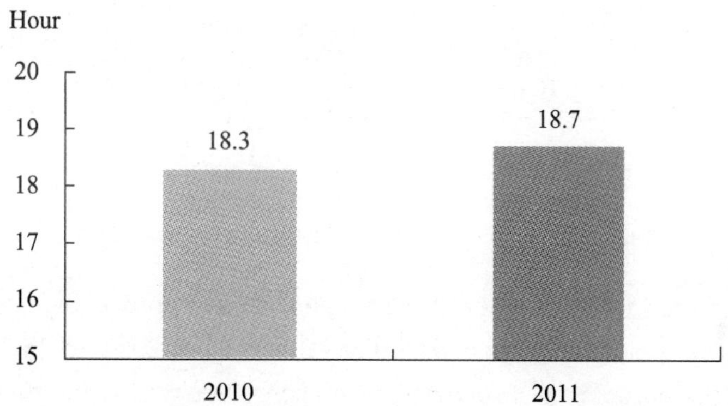

Figure 8. Average weekly online time of Internet users

(III) Online time

In 2011, the average time of Internet users spending on Internet is 18.7h, increasing 0.4h compared with that at the end of 2010.

III. Properties of Internet users

(I) Gender structure

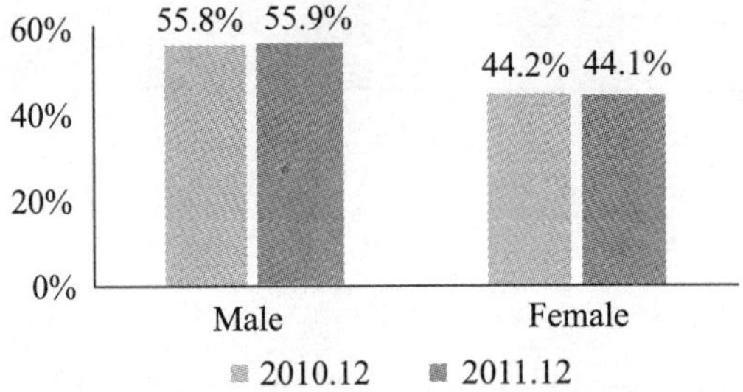

Figure 9. Gender structure of Internet users during Dec 2010 to Dec 2011

As of the end of December 2011, the ratio of Chinese male internet users is 55.9%, 11.8% higher than female Internet users. The proportion of gender generally keeps stable compared with that in 2010.

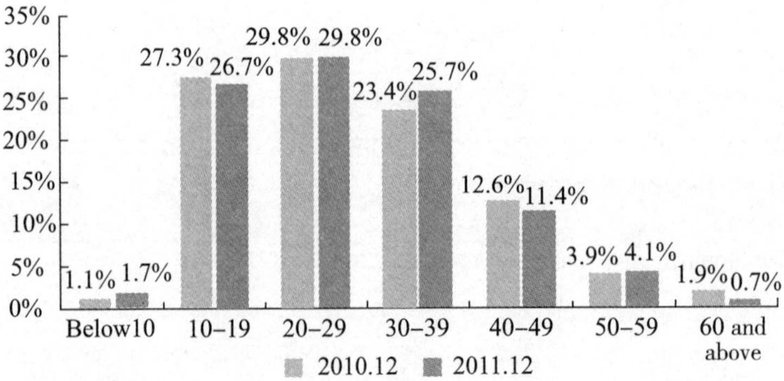

(II) Age structure

Figure 10. Age structure of Internet users during Dec. 2010 and Dec. 2011

In 2011, the proportion of Internet users aged 30–39 improves significantly, rising 2.3 percentage points compared with that at the end of 2010, to 25.7%. In recent two years, the proportion of such age group continues to rise. Internet users aged 40-49 increases slowly; therefore, the proportion in Internet users declines. The proportion for 10–19 and 20–29 year-old Internet users is generally the stable compared with that at the end of 2010.

(III) Educational structure

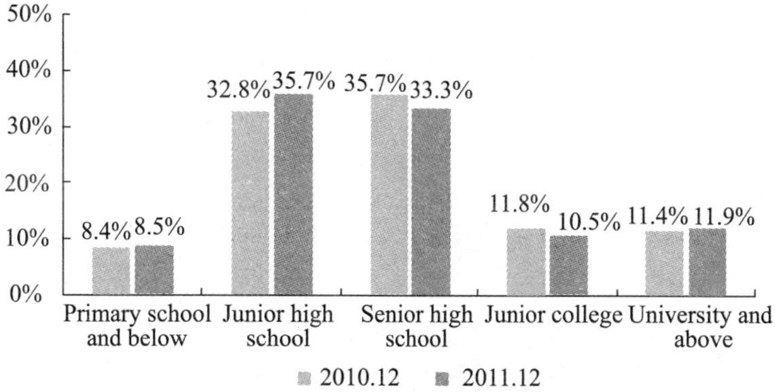

Figure 11. Educational structure of Internet users during Dec 2010 and Dec. 2011

Internet users continues to penetrate to poorly educated population. In 2011, Chinese Internet users with middle-low educational degree had been increasing continuously. The proportion of internet users in 2010 with junior high school education and below rose from 32.8% to 35.7%. Internet penetration of such educated people is lower. The proportion of Internet users in the future will be further enhanced. The proportion of internet users with high school and college education will continue to decline.

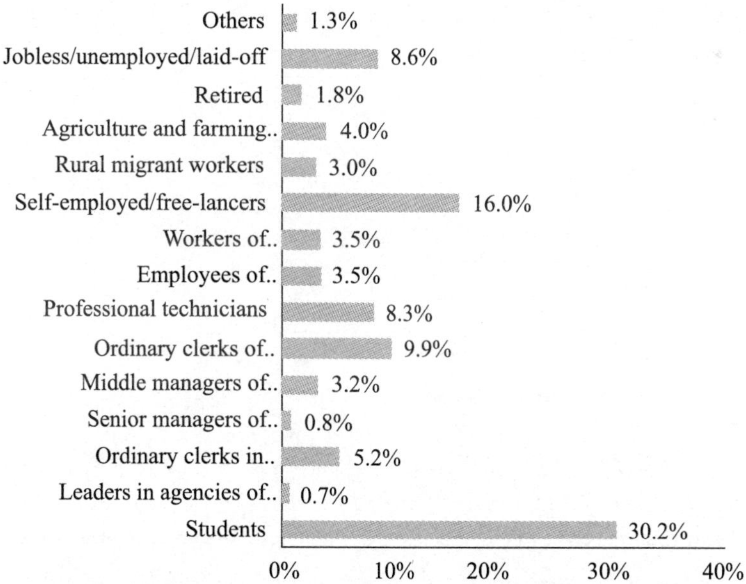

Figure 12. Occupational structure of Internet users December, 2011

(IV) Occupational structure

Students cover the largest proportion among the Internet users, as high as 30.2%, followed by self-employed/free-lancers. In corporation, senior management occupy 0.8% of overall Internet users, middle management 3.2% and general staff 9.9%. In the agencies of the Party and government, leaders and general staff account for 0.7% and 5.2% respectively. In addition, professional technician occupies 8.3%.

(V) Income structure

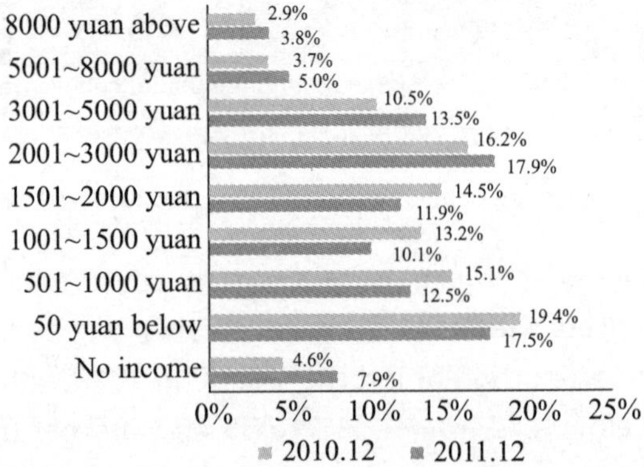

Figure 13. Individual monthly income structure of Internet users during Dec. 2010 and Dec. 2011

In 2011, the Internet users group with income above 2,000 yuan increases significantly, from 33.3% in 2010 to 40.2%. At the same time, the proportion for Internet users without income rises from 4.6% to 7.9%.

(VI) Urban-rural structure

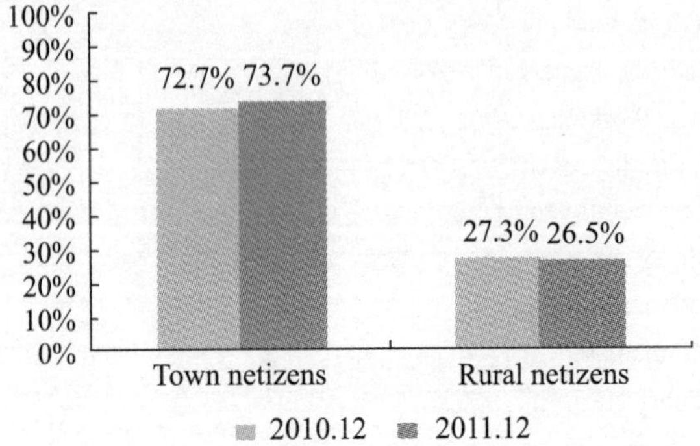

Figure 14. Urban-rural structure of Internet users during Dec 2010 and Dec. 2011

In 2011, the number of Chinese rural Internet users reached 136 million, increasing by 1113 ten thousand compared with those in 2010, accounting for 26.5% of overall Internet users. Compared with 2010, the ratio of Chinese rural Internet users declined 0.8%, with growing rate still lower than the town.

In recent years, the proportion of Internet users in rural areas is at low levels, caused by accelerated Chinese urbanization, flocking of rural residents in cities and other change factor of overall population structure. However, insufficient computer for rural people and Internet use skill are important obstruct for development of Internet in rural areas. In 2011, 57.8% of rural non-Internet users said "do not know how to use computer / network" is the reason for them not to surf the Internet. Such proportion is 45.7% in non-Internet users in town. When Internet access condition is greatly improved, it's an important tool to narrowing development gap between urban and rural areas by enhancing network use skills and awareness of farmers.

III Basic Internet Resources

I. Overview

By the end of Dec 2011, the number of IPv4 addresses had reached 330 million in China. China has 9398 blocks/32 IPv6 addresses.

There are totally 7.75 million domain names in China, in which, the number of .CN domain names rallies, to 353 ten thousand, increasing by 0.7% compared with that in June 2011. Undergoing dramatic declining in 2010, the total number of Chinese website steadily increased to 2.3 million.

International export bandwidth reached 1,389,529Mbps, increasing 17.5% compared with that in June 2011.

	June, 2011	December, 2011	Half-year growth volume	Half-year growth rate
IPv4 (piece)	331,626,752	330,439,936	-1,186,816	-0.4%
IPv6 (piece /32)	429	9,398	8,969	2090.7%
Domain name (piece)	7,861,400	7,748,459	-112,941	-1.4%
In which CN domain name (piece)	3,502,288	3,528,511	26,223	0.7%
Website (piece)	1,830,100	2,295,562	465,462	25.4%
In which website under CN (piece)	931,869	951,609	19,740	2.1%
International export bandwidth (Mbps)	1,182,261	1,389,529	207,268	17.5%

Table 2. Comparison of basic Internet resources of China during June 2010 and Dec. 2011

II. IP address

By the end of Dec 2011, there were 330 million IPv4 addresses in China, grew by

19.0% compared with those at the end of 2010.

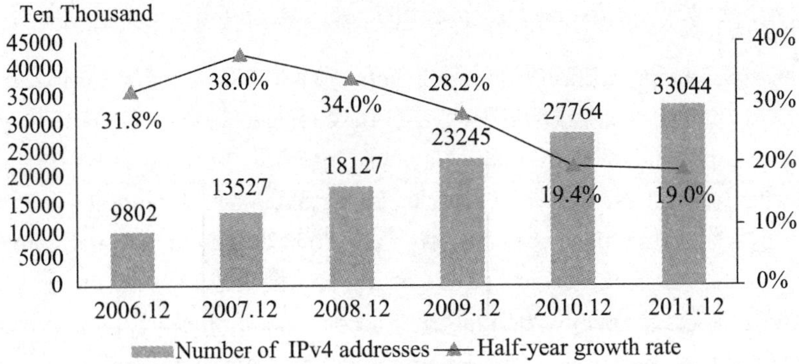

Figure 15. Variation of IPv4 address resource in China

As of the end of December 2011, China has 9398 blocks/ 32 IPv6 address, increasing greatly compared with the same period in 2010. IPv6 is the starting point of development for next generation of Internet, with significance solving resource depletion of IPv4 address, becoming foundation of other technology development, and supporting development of networking, cloud computing and other emerging Internet industry. Facing this opportunity, our government attaches great importance to it and actively promotes the development of relevant strategies. In December 2011, the State Council held executive meeting to study and deploy to accelerate development of next-generation of Internet industry, clarify route chart of developing next generation of Internet, propose to carry out IPv6 small-scale commercial Internet before the end of 2013, and conduct large-scale deployment and commerce in 2014–2015. This plan will accelerate development pace of Chinese IPv6 and next generation of Internet industry, and improve international competitiveness of China in a series of emerging Internet industries.

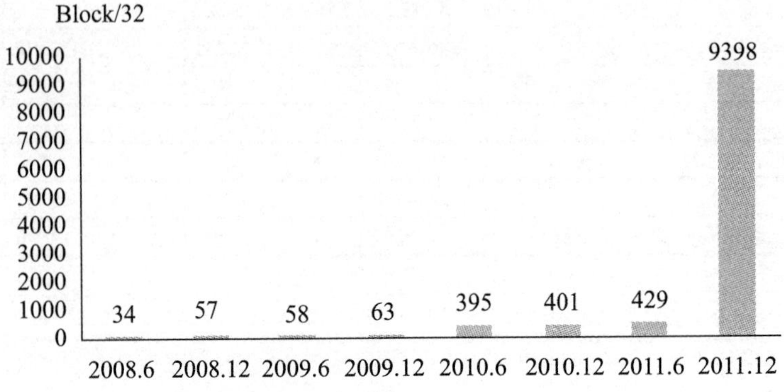

Figure 16. Change of IPv6 address Resource in China

III. Domain name

As of the end of December 2011, total domain names dropped to 7.75 million, in which, .COM domain names are 3.64 million, accounting for 47.0% of total domain names in our country .CN domain names are 3.53 million, accounting for 45.5%.

	Quantity (piece)	Proportion
COM	3,644,147	47.0%
CN	3,528,511	45.5%
NET	467,939	6.0%
ORG	107,862	1.4%
Total	**7,748,459**	**100.0%**

Table 3. Number of classified domain name in China

Among CN domain names, the secondary domain names ended with .CN account for 64.5%, followed by .COM.CN domain name, for 27.2%.

	Quantity (piece)	Proportion
cn	2,275,971	64.5%
com.cn	960,753	27.2%
net.cn	130,913	3.7%
gov.cn	51,185	1.5%
adm.cn	50,961	1.4%
org.cn	51,428	1.5%
edu.cn	3,910	0.1%
ac.cn	3,364	0.1%
mil.cn	26	0.0%
Total	**3,528,511**	**100.0%**

Table 4. Number of classified CN domain name in China

IV. Website

As of the end of December 2011, China has 2.30 million websites[⑤]. After the state strengthened security management for Internet field in 2010, number of Chinese websites declined, while overall quality improved. On this basis, the quantity of website had a steady rise in 2011.

V. Webpage

As of the end of December 2011, there were 86.6 billion webpages in China, increasing 44.3% compared with that at the same period in 2010.

---

⑤ Refer to the websites accessed by domain name registrator in China, including the websites accessed in and out territory.

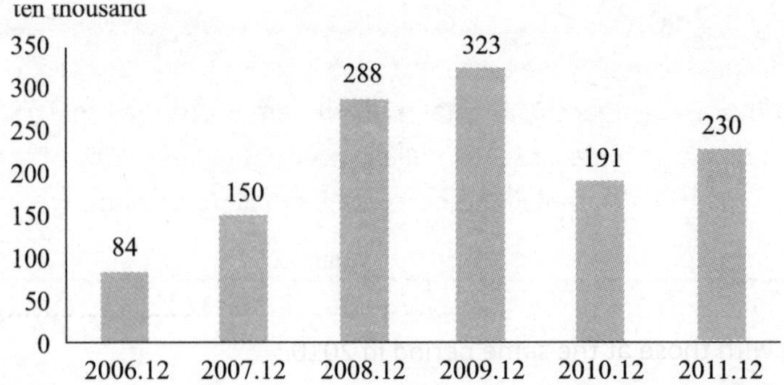

Figure 17. Variation in the number of websites in China. Note: Websites under .EDU.CN are not covered in the data.

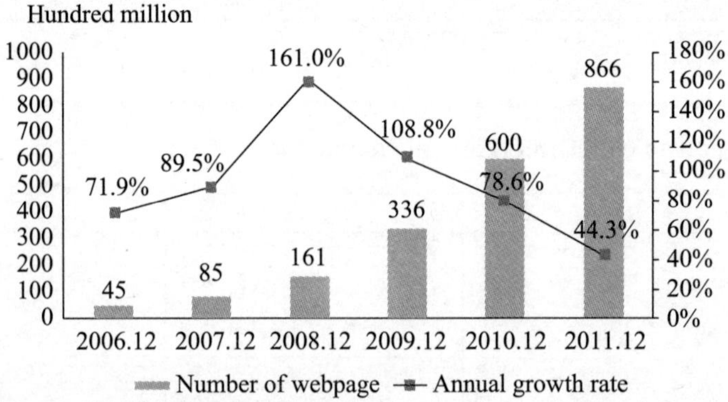

Figure 18. Variation in the size of website in China

	Unit	2010	2011	Growth rate
Total number of webpages	Piece	60,008,060,093	86,582,298,393	44.3%
Static webpages	Piece	31,908,739,278	59,364,979,522	86.0%
	Proportion	53.17%	68.56%	—
Dynamic webpages	Piece	28,099,320,815	27,217,318,871	-3.1%
	Proportion	46.83%	31.44%	—
Proportion of static / dynamic webpages		1.14:1	2.18:1	—
Page length (total number of bytes)	KB	1,922,538,540,426	3,313,529,625,009	72.4%
Average number of pages per site	Piece	31,414	37,717	20.1%
Average number of bytes per page	KB	32	38	18.8%

Table 5. Number of webpages in China[⑥]

The proportion of static and dynamic webpage in China climbed from 1.14:1 at the

⑥ Data support: Netease Youdao Information Technology (Beijing) Co., Ltd and Tencent Search Technology R & D Center.

end of December 2010 to 2.18:1, because lots of websites staticize dynamic content to show affiliation to search engine, and a large number of dynamic webpages in dark network is hard for search engine to include these pages completely.

VI. Network international export bandwidth

International export bandwidth of China has seen constant development, and reached 1,389,529 Mbps by the end of December 2011, increasing by 26.4% compared with those at the same period in 2010.

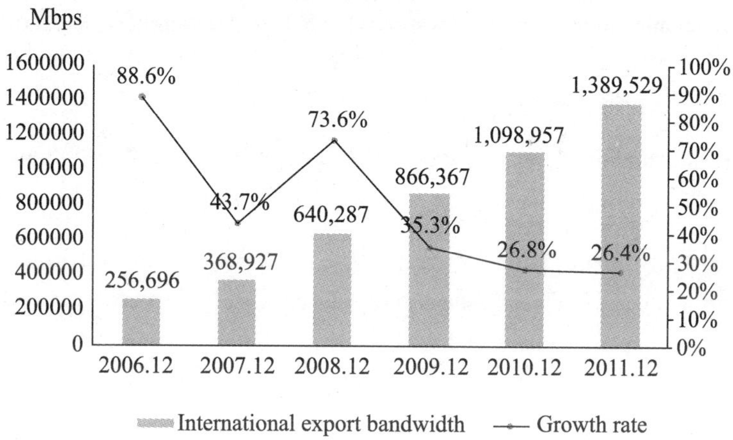

Figure 19. Variation of international export bandwidth of China

	International export bandwidth（Mbps）
China Telecom	809,881
China Unicom	466,932
China Mobile	82,559
China Science & Technology Network	18,500
China Education and Research Network	11,655
China International Economy and Trade Net (CIETnet)	2
Total	**1,389,529**

Table 6. International export bandwidth of backbone networks

IV Internet Application of Internet users

I. Overall condition of Internet applications

In 2011, Chinese Internet users have significantly changed application habits, due to rapid spread of merging Internet applications including new instant messaging and microblog etc. At the same time, utilization rate of traditional network applications declines rapidly, indicating fast innovative speed of Internet. Here follows the summary of feature change of Internet application for Chinese internet users:

Significant change of Internet communication way for internet users

In 2011, utilization ratio of Chinese Internet users rose fast, to 80.9%. Meanwhile, the size of users for many traditional communication applications shrinks: utilization ratio of e-mail down to 47.9% from 54.6% in 2010; user amount reduced by 3.92 million; Forum / BBS from 32.4% down to 28.2%, slightly reduced. After utilization ratio of social networking site declines significantly in the first half of this year, the situation has improved in the second half year. Currently, utilization ratio bottoms out, to 47.6%. The above data shows that the communication habits and ways of internet users by Internet are changed greatly.

Entertainment application is generally lower, but online video users increase significantly

The utilization ratio of most of network entertainment applications continues to decline in 2011. Online music, online game and online literature subscribers increased a lesser extent in 2011, with utilization ratio falling to 75.2%, 63.2% and 39.5% respectively. In contrast, the development momentum of online video industry is relatively good. User scale increased by 14.6% on year basis, to 325 million. Utilization ratio increased to 63.4%.

Utilization ratio of E-commerce application keeps rising

	2011		2010		
Application	Users (10,000)	Utilization ratio	Users (10,000)	Utilization ratio	Annual growth rate
Instant messaging	41510	80.9%	35258	77.1%	17.7%
Search engine	40740	79.4%	37453	81.9%	8.8%
Online music	38585	75.2%	36218	79.2%	6.5%
Online news	36687	71.5%	35304	77.2%	3.9%
Online video	32531	63.4%	28398	62.1%	14.6%
Online games	32428	63.2%	30410	66.5%	6.6%
Blog/personal space	31864	62.1%	29450	64.4%	8.2%
Microblog	24988	48.7%	6311	13.8%	296.0%
E-mail	24577	47.9%	24969	54.6%	-1.6%
Social networking website	24424	47.6%	23505	51.4%	3.9%
Online literature	20267	39.5%	19481	42.6%	4.0%
Online shopping	19395	37.8%	16051	35.1%	20.8%
Online payment	16676	32.5%	13719	30.0%	21.6%
Online bank	16624	32.4%	13948	30.5%	19.2%
Forum/BBS	14469	28.2%	14817	32.4%	-2.3%
Group buying	6465	12.6%	1875	4.1%	244.8%
Travel booking	4207	8.2%	3613	7.9%	16.5%
Online stock	4002	7.8%	7088	15.5%	-43.5%

Table 7. Utilization ratios of various network applications during 2010 and 2011

E-commerce application develops steadily. The users for online shopping, online payment, online banking and online travel booking etc grow comprehensively. Compared with 2010, online shoppers increased by 3,344 ten thousand people, a growth rate of 20.8%. Online payment and online banking utilization ratio also rise to 32.5% and 32.4%. In addition, group purchase becomes the network service of growing the fastest at second place, whose annual growth rate of users is up to 244.8%, scale to 64.65 million and utilization rate to 12.6%.

(I) Acquisition of information

1. Search engine

At the end of 2011, the scale of search engine users reached to 407 million, and penetration rate 79.4%. The use proportion remained stable. It's the second largest network application only secondary to instant messaging in 2011.

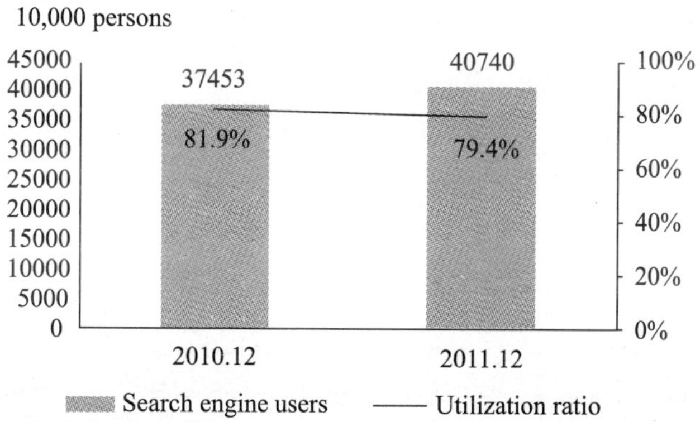

Figure 20. Number of users and utilization ratio of search engine during 2010 –2011

2. Online news

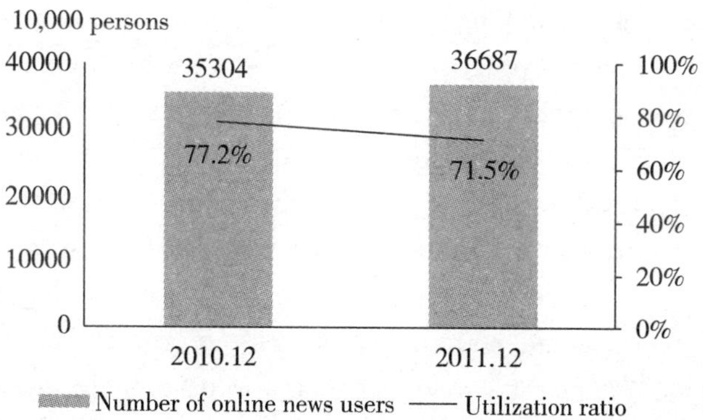

Figure 21. Number of users and utilization ratio of online news during 2010–2011

Online news utilization ratio has a downward trend year after year, down to 71.5% at the end of 2011 from 80.1% in 2009, a decrease of 8.6 percentage points in two years.

According to CNNIC 29th survey result, education is strongly relevant to network news utilization ratio. The lower education, the lower utilization ratio of network news. The utilization ratio of college degree internet users using netnews is 87.6%, and junior high school education only 62.1%. Chinese Internet has gone through the popular stage for highly educated population. The Internet users popularizing rate for junior college and above has exceeded 90 percent. Internet is penetrating towards high school and junior high school educated people. The increase of low educational population drives down the utilization ratio of overall users of network news.

(II) Business transaction

1. Online shopping

As of the end of December 2011, the online shoppers reached to 194 million. The network shopping utilization rate is up to 37.8%. Compared with those in 2010, online shoppers increase by 33.44 million, a growth rate 20.8%.

Under the context of the national stimulating domestic demand and social consumption, the deepening of network shopping service drive more Internet users to realize daily consumption by online shopping. The frequent promotion of shopping site also stimulate new purchase requirements of Internet users and urge the steady growth of online shoppers. In 2011, brand enterprise and platform mall (B2C) have become absolute main body of the market. Traditional manufacturers and distributors have obvious increased. The enterprises derivating from online shopping develop prosperously. On-line transaction goods and service types are richer, which drives frequency of online shopping and significant ascension of amount.

For full year, when online shopping market remains stable and rapid development, it also faces outstanding problems. Logistics and distribution services ability enhanced slowly, which grips speed acceleration of electronic business service. Market low price competition becomes the norm. Merchant profit ability is insufficient Capital market freezes. Subsequent development support is pessimistic. Online shopper's information is leaked, which reduces consumer trust, etc. These problems have become important factor restricting sustained and rapid development of retail market. With obvious increase of government to regulation and normalization of online retail market, issuance of payment license of the third-party, formulation of development plan of logistics service and introduciton of online shopping standardized regulation etc, in the future, online shopping market will embrace more standardized industry development environment. Engaging in scale growth, the online shopping enterprise shall explore from extensive development to intensive development, from size to depth, so as to realize overall ascension of service level of network shopping industry.

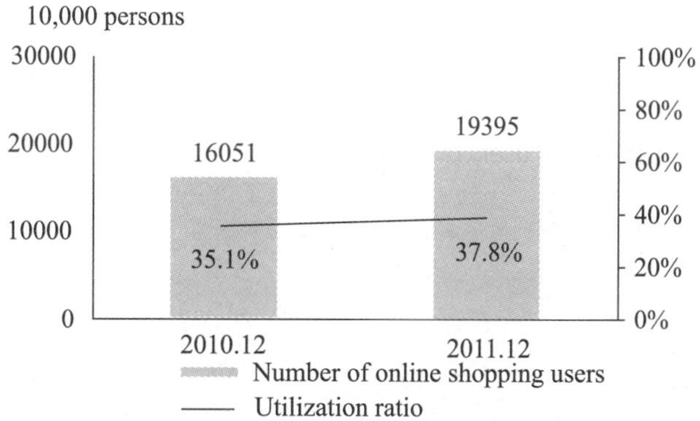

Figure 22. Number of users and utilization ratio of online shopping during 2010–2011

2. Group buying

By the end of December, 2011, the number of group buying user is up to 64.65 million, and utilization rate to 12.6%, increasing 8.5% compared with those at the end of 2010. Annual growth rate of group buyer is as high as 244.8%. It has become the network services increasing the fastest at the second place in a year.

In 2011, group buying was hot first and cold later. Since the service form of group buying meets the demand of white-collar groups for the first and second tier cities. In the first half year, number of group buying and service provider grew rapidly. The industry was in lasting high fever state. Due to low threshold and weak constraint of group buying service, in addition to great input at early period of group buying website, the overall capital market becomes cold. Market negative factors appeared in the second half of the year. The growth speed of group buying was slow, and number of group buying website declined dramatically.

The industrial "baptism" in the second half of 2011 had a certain impact on group buying development. After self-adjustment of market, it's helpful to allow overall industry to go on a healthier and sustainable development path. Part of service providers weaken market risks by positioning adjusting. The industry is turning to a new balance and stability. Due to the increase of proportion of physical group buying and deepening of service group buying. Group buying service has become "standard configuration" of shopping website and travel booking website, which weakens the competitiveness of group buying website that is positioned obscurely. Some group buying websites stand out by clear position and its own advantage, which are favored by capital market and customers.

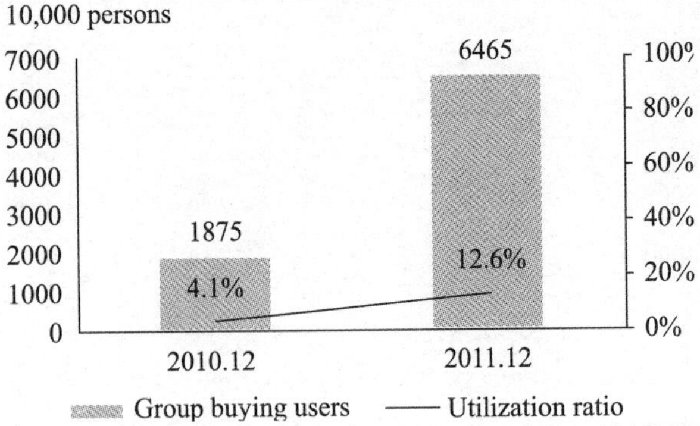

Figure 23. Number of users and utilization ratio of group buying during 2010–2011

3. Online payment

By the end of December 2011, users using online payment reached to 167 million, and utilization rate up to 32.5%. Compared with that in 2010, users increase by 29.57 million, the growth rate of 21.6%.

In 2011, People's Bank of China issued "License of Payment Transaction" to three batches of service enterprise respectively, covering main third-party service enterprise. The industry status of the third party payment is fully recognized. Payment license finishes its subsequent worry to its service qualification for payment enterprise for long term, and wins broad market space for development. By diversified cooperation forms, the enterprise continuously broad its service areas, i.e., earnestly promoting quick pay area, pushing development of innovative payment etc. The payment service covers to offline transaction of more categories, which drives more "edge crowd" to transfer towards online payment users. At the same time, the rapid development of network shopping and group buying also contributes to the sustainable growth of online payment users. In particular, the prepayment of group buying and high frequent trading characteristic greatly drive the usage of online payment.

The overall layout of payment enterprise in mobile phone payment also drives the growth of mobile phone online users. By the end of December 2011, mobile phone online payment users reached to 30.58 million, accounting for 8.6% of mobile phone internet users. In addition to the third party payment enterprise, operators and bank will push rapid development of mobile phone payment business in the future by earnestly promoting payment area and technology innovation of payment and service mode innovation etc.

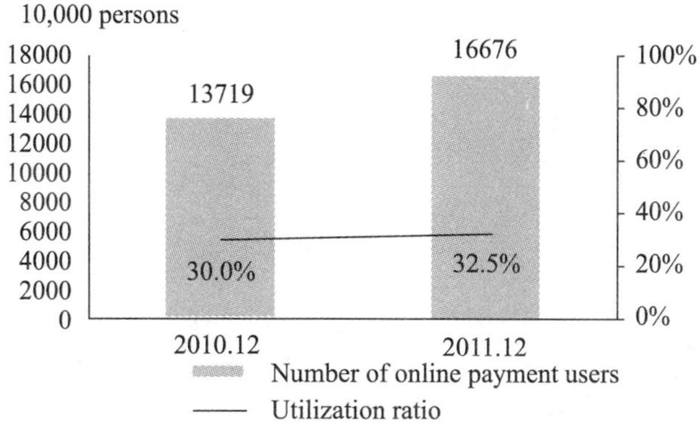

Figure 24. Number of users and utilization ratio of online payment during 2010–2011

4. Travel booking

By the end of December, 2011, our country's travel booking users are up to 42.07 million, annual growth ratio 16.5%, and user permeability enhanced to 8.2%. Internet users will use travel-booking service in a deeper way.

In 2011, the overall tourism market is supported by many positive factors: the era of high-speed rail further optimizes traffic conditions between hub cities; the state's policies on opening to individual visit to Taiwan and Hainan Islands duty-free etc., enhance the heat of travel market in local area. And by the end of 2011, the opening of online service for national train ticket booking indicates an important step for railway transportation system using informationization means to promote convenient travel for visitors. These factors urge the transition of a large amount of non-travel booking Internet users to travel booking Internet users, and cultivate the spending habit of internet users using online travel booking.

Compared with other commercial applications, Chinese users using travel booking are relatively at high-end, and penetration level of travel booking application is low. CNNIC analysis shows that currently, the demand of leisure tourism of our country has been in rapid growth track. In the coming years, the demand of leisure tourism will be released continuously. With earnest strength of major travel booking servicer on wireless booking service, direct marketing business of aviation/ hotel's official website, sustainable steady development of group buying of hotel travel, and intensive development of train ticket online booking service etc., the travel booking market in the future will embrace a new stage for rapid growth of user scale.

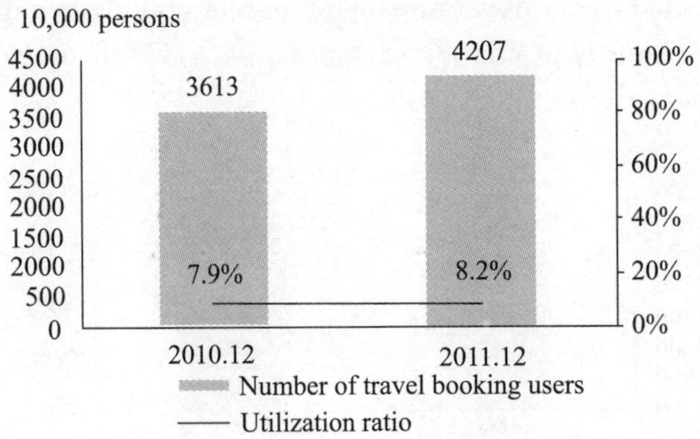

Figure 25. Number of users and utilization ratio of travel booking during 2010–2011

(III) Communication

1. Instant messaging

By the end of 2011, there were 415 million instant communication users, increasing 62.52 million compared with that by the end of 2010, annual growth rate 17.7%. The utilization rate of instant communication continues to ascend, growing to 80.9%.

Instant communication utilization rate and rising of number of users are mainly caused by the development of mobile phone instant communication. Mobile phone instant communication is the service that is used at most among Internet applications, up to 83.1%, with annual growth ratio of user amount to 44.2%. Mobile phone preassemble of instant communication software and development of smartphone application market bring convenience to the use of instant communication software, resulting in growth of utilization rate of instant communication and number of users. The instant communication products specially designed for smart phones are featured by voice content, real-time photographing, video, LBS, position making friends, and flow statistics function etc. The new instant communication mobile phone interconnecting with other Internet applications meets the new demand of users and improves number of users of instant communication mobile phone.

The great potential of instant communication field of new mobile phone induces telecom operator, mobile phone maker, Internet enterprise, software developer and new entrepreneur in the market to expect to obtain huge gains from the market, and control mobile internet entry by controlling instant communication market. In the future, there is still large room for number of instant communication subscribers to rise. But in the market, it will become an inevitable trend to seek product differentiation and develop vertical field market.

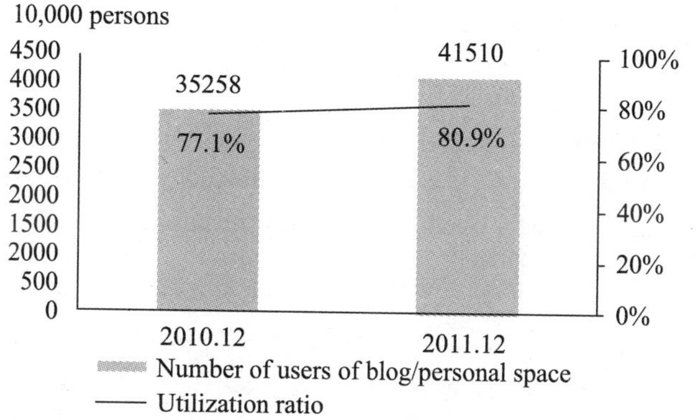

Figure 26. Number of users and utilization ratio of blog/personal space during 2010–2011

2. Blog/ personal space

By the end of December, 2011, there were 319 million blogs and personal space in China, increasing by 24.14 million compared with that at the end of 2010, the growth rate of 8.2%. The utilization rate of blogs and personal space is 62.1%, down 2.3% compared with that at the end of last year.

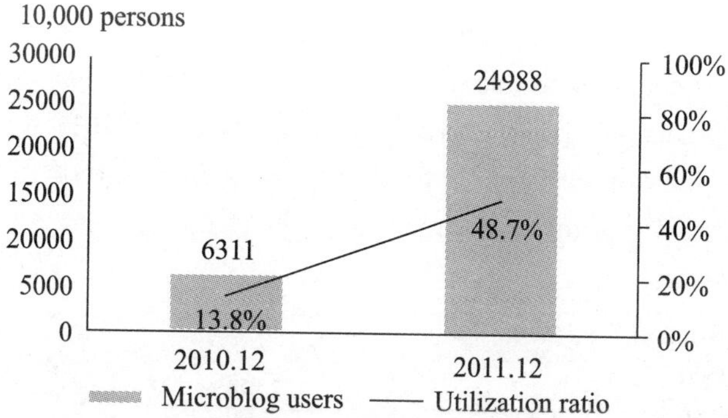

Figure 27. Number of users and utilization ratio of blog/personal space during 2010–2011

Although in recent years blogs and personal space users keep growing, its utilization rate falls in this year. As the earliest web2.0 application form, blog presents more characteristics for traditional information dissemination. Some celebrity blogs are still concerned, which are important channel for opinion leaders to transmit information. For ordinary Internet users, under the influence of micro blog, SNS and other emerging applications, users are used to rapid simple information interaction mode of strong interaction and sociability. Therefore, blogs must inject new vitality by innovating constantly. For example, light blog form appeared in 2011 is beneficial attempt. In addition, some blogs and personal space are constantly strengthening SNS attribute.

3. Microblog

By the end of December, 2011, there were 250 million micro bloggers, increasing 296.0% compared with that at the end of last year. The utilization ratio is 48.7%. Over one year, micro blog has become vital Internet application used by nearly half of Chinese internet users.

By analyzing the growth of micro blog in 2011, it's known that its users outbroke in the first half of year, and the growth speed was down to 28.2% in the second half of year. It can be seen that after micro blog utilization rate stepped into high level, the blowout growth was completed.

By analyzing, the direction of future micro blog mainly depends on three factors. First, due to large gap between different portals on strategic intention of developing micro blog platform, the development roads are diversified. All large portals provide different functions and characteristics for micro blog according to their own advantages, mainly representing on its focus on social network function and social media function. Secondly, micro blog profit model is fuzzy. Currently, the well developed websites that place great profit expectation to micro blog have begun to try multiple profit patterns. Finally, micro blog real name policy was introduced at the end of 2011. It's a concerned problem for the government for how to effectively regulate information spreading order on micro blog. Those regulatory measures will have important impact on future development of micro blog.

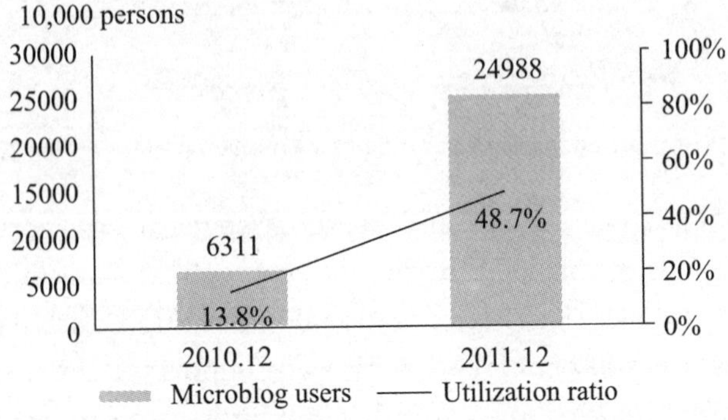

Figure 28. Number of users and utilization ratio of microblog during 2010–2011

4. Social networking website

As of the end of 2011, there are 244 million users of social networking sites in

China, slightly increasing compared with that at the end of 2010. On the aspect of utilization ratio, users of social networking site account for 47.6%, nearly four percentage points lower than the previous year.

At present, our social networking sites are undergoing various attempts to resolve site stickiness crisis. Several major SNS sites carried out strategic expansion or adjustment for long-term in 2011, such as the attempt to explore the potential of combination of social sharing and network video, seeking new growth point in video sharing; or conducting "practical" transition, including implementation of social e-commerce and mobile Internet strategy etc. However, this transition road is not ideal. Partial attempts were ended with failure, indicating the difficulties of domestic SNS breakthrough road.

The social networking sites having certain user basis are ongoing adjustment and transition, constantly accompanied by new competitors that even change competitive situation of SNS real-name system. In spite of slow growth scale of users and development in dilemma, the main competition body in SNS field is still diverse, because actually there is no successful model for our SNS though foreign mature social networking sites show great potential for development, especially in the immature construction of platform. It means there is great opportunity in SNS field, under the premise of innovation combined with psychological characteristics and communication way of Chinese internet users etc, and platform accumulation for long time and user's habit cultivation. In this respect, part of latecomers has more obvious advantages on users and resources.

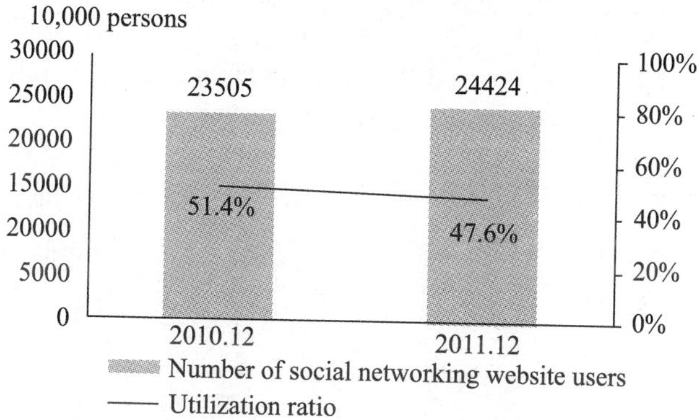

Figure 29. Number of users and utilization ratio of social networking websites during 2010–2011

(IV) Online entertainment

1. Online games

As of the end of December 2011, there were 324 million online games users, increased by only 6.6% compared with those at the end of 2010. Internet users utilization ratio is 63.2%.

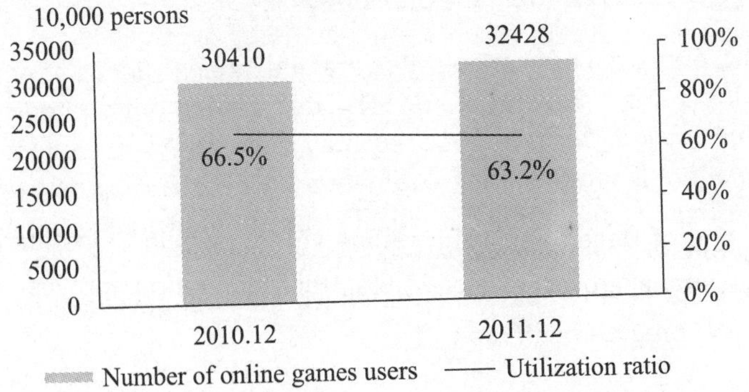

Figure 30. Number of users and utilization ratio of online games during 2010–2011

The user growth slowdown directly causes the growth slowdown of users of all game types. Although various types of games maintain growing, most of them are mutual penetration of different game types, and there are no more new users. Analyzed from sub-game type, first, user size of large-scale client game (MMOG) is generally in parallel to that in 2010. For one hand, such game type users are mainly young users, and early MMOG users begin to lose. For the other hand, MMOG game form is still subject to Daguai upgrade, racing, dancing, and FPS games etc., limited to attract non-game users. And, small-size casual games are still in mainstream position. 80% of online game users play chess casual games. Compared with other types of games, small chess games have stabler user's structure, with higher utilization rate at all ages. Finally, though mobile MMOG and webpage MMOG maintain rapid growth, they are influenced by terminal equipment and user experience respectively, and it's hard to achieve large-scale popularization similar to small size chess games and large-scale client game.

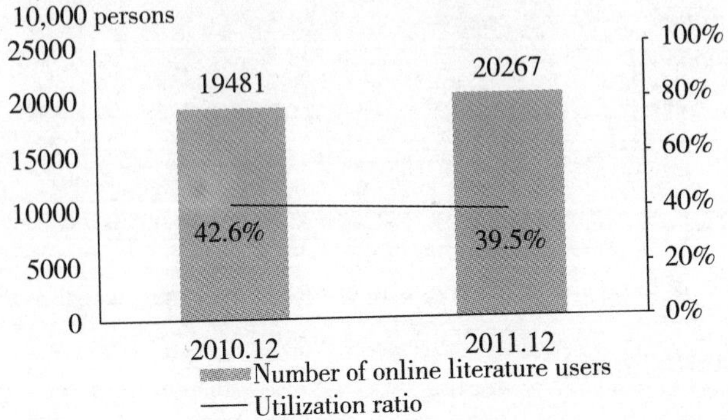

Figure 31. Number of users and utilization ratio of online literature during Dec. 2010–Jun. 2011

2. Online literature

As of the end of December 2011, network literature utilization rate is 39.5 percent, and user scale is up to 203 million. Despite of rising user scale of network literatures, the utilization rate decreased 3.1 percentage points on year basis, indicating that the development of network literature is slower than overall Internet.

3. Online video

As of the end of December 2011, online video users in China increased to 325 million, the annual growth rate of 14.6%. Utilization ratio improves to 63.4 % from 62.1% at the end of last year.

In 2011, online video utilization ratio was significantly higher, mainly due to external factors such as habit development and broadband environment construction etc and industrial reasons of video website content building and video social sharing etc. First, in 2011 in order to gain a competitive edge, major video sites constantly enrich their content by purchasing a large number of hot TV drama and programs, and actively launching homemade video. Currently, video site can not only provide most of hot TV drama and programs, but also have greater freedom on video subject content and geographical source thanks to relatively loose policy environment. Secondary, microblog and SNS have become important video distribution sites. The cultivation of video sharing expands the spreading scope of online video, which greatly broadens video distribution platform. These factors promote the scale of online video users constantly. It has become the fifth largest Internet application.

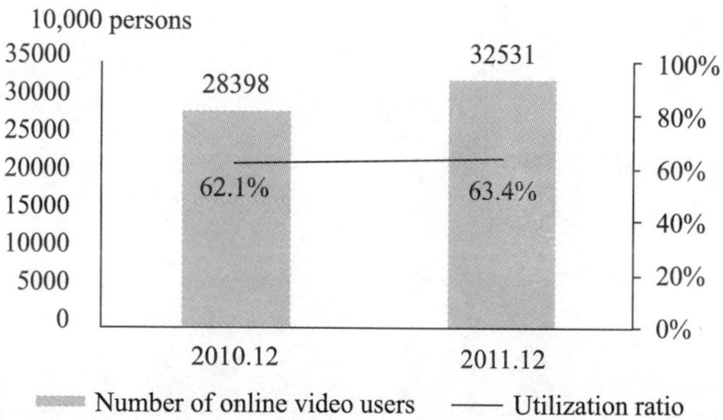

Figure 32. Number of users and utilization ratio of online video during 2010–2011

On the aspect of industry development, online video is still facing a larger test. Because video sites need to rely on more copyright content of better quality to obtain high-traffic, the copyright price of network video is improved, operating cost is in a sharp rise, while video advertising rate is lower, and other profit model can not be mature in a short time. Therefore, network video industry as a whole is at a loss, which is also difficult to change currently.

V Structure of mobile Internet users and application situation

I. Properties of mobile Internet users

(I) Gender structure

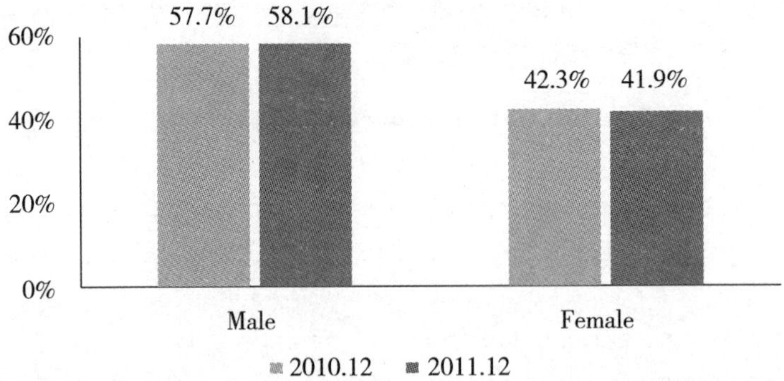

Figure 33. Structure of mobile Internet users gender during December, 2010–December, 2011

Among mobile internet users, men account for nearly 60%, to 58.1%, 16.2 percentage points higher than women, greater than the male to female proportion difference of overall internet users. It shows significant characteristics that utilization rate of male mobile internet users is higher than female. Compared with 2010, the proportion of male mobile phone users has increased slightly.

(II) Age structure

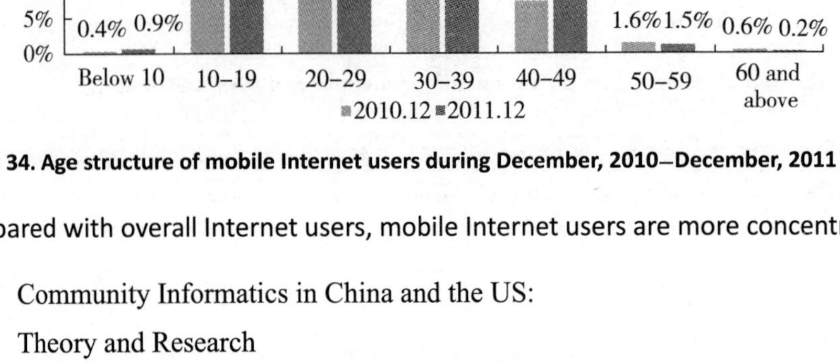

Figure 34. Age structure of mobile Internet users during December, 2010–December, 2011

Compared with overall Internet users, mobile Internet users are more concentrated in younger groups. 20–29 year-olds account for 36.0% of this age group, six percentage points higher than overall Internet users. However, 30–39 year-old Internet users increased significantly in 2011, showing maturity trend of mobile phone Internet users.

(III) Education structure

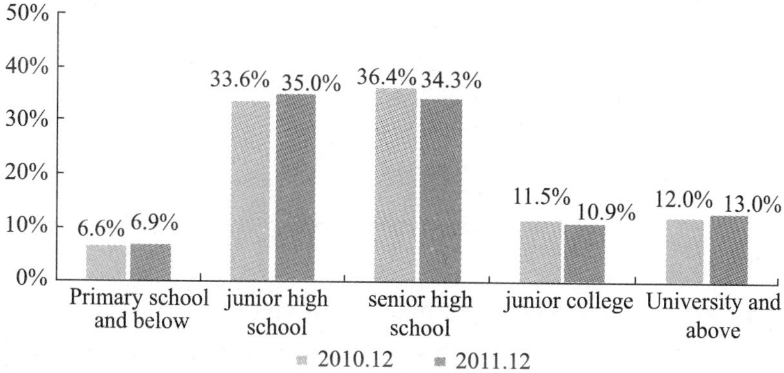

Figure 35. Education structure of mobile internet users during December, 2010–December, 2011

Education structure of mobile internet users changed little compared with 2010. The proportion of primary school and junior high school education is slightly higher, and high school population dropped to 34.3%.

(IV) Revenue structure

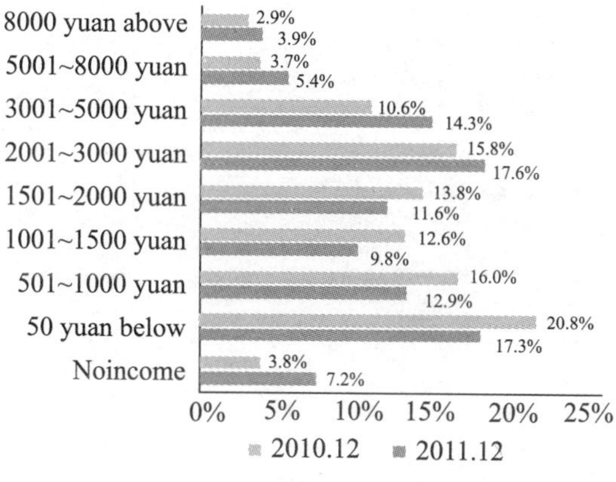

Figure 36. Monthly income structure of mobile internet users during December, 2010–December, 2011

In 2011, utilization ratio of mobile Internet users of middle/high-income groups grew fast. The group of income above 2,000 yuan increased to 41.2% from 33.0% in 2010.

(V) Urban and rural structure

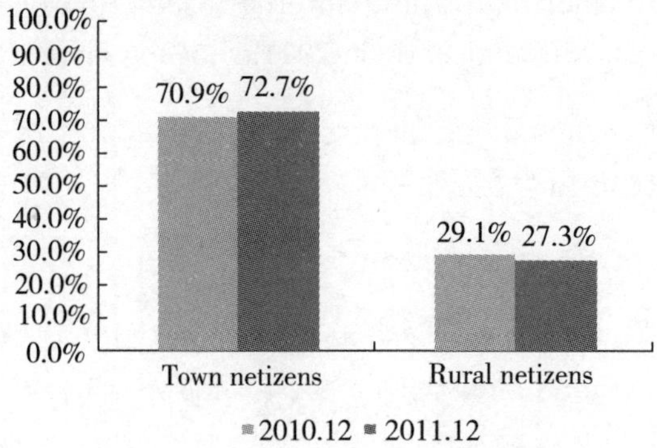

Figure 37. Urban and rural distribution of mobile Internet users during December, 2010–December, 2011

The urban and rural distribution of mobile Internet users is generally the same with overall Internet users. Mobile internet users in rural areas account for 27.3%. Its rural-urban gap has widened. Compared with 2010, rural population in mobile Internet users fell by nearly two percentage points.

II. Application status of mobile Internet users

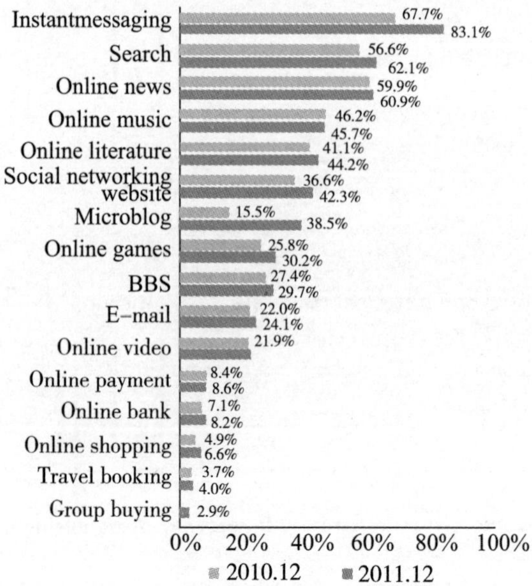

Figure 38. Network application of mobile phone Internet users in 2010–2011

In 2011, overall mobile application development is in good condition. As a whole, communication applications and information access application developed in a leading position, and entertainment and business application development was relatively slow. Among them, mobile instant messaging and mobile microblog, as a representative of the communication applications, is the mainstream at this stage to promote development of mobile Internet applications.

Utilization ratio of instant messaging stays ahead

Although mobile instant messaging is an application of the highest penetration rate, in 2011, its utilization ratio still increased substantially, an increase of 15.4% year-on-year basis, more than the ratio of instant messaging in overall Internet users (as of December 2011, use rate of overall Internet users instant messaging 80.9%). This situation is mainly caused by two reasons. On the one hand, instant communication is the only purpose for most of mobile internet users to surf the Internet with cell phone. On the other hand, the use threshold of mobile instant messaging tools is significantly reduced. Driven by instant messaging service providers, instant messaging has become standard preset product of mobile terminal. Product preset significantly reduces the threshold of mobile phone users especially non-smartphone users to use instant messaging tools, i.e., user can directly log in to by opening wireless network without downloading and installing.

Mobile microblog is an application growing the fastest

The utilization ratio of mobile microblog in 2011 increased by 23% year on year, the highest growth rate for mobile phone applications. CNNIC analysts believe that mobile microblog will be another key application attracting Internet users to use mobile Internet after instant messaging.

First, mobile microblog can better reflect the real-time characteristics of micro-blog content. Compared with computer, most of people carry their mobile phones, which make people know the latest news anywhere. Secondary, mobile microblog can better display the advantage of self media of microblog applications. The innovative "concern" mechanism of microblog allows each user to become a communication center, and greatly enhance the viscosity of users to use microblog. The featured original content is the key to attract more attention, such as improvisation pictures and video etc. Mobile phone has improvising original ability much higher than computer. The third, the context at most 70 characters in length greatly reduces the influence of screen size on microblog experience. Compared with computer, the use of mobile phone microblog doesn't bring unfriendly reading experience to user. On the contrary, with the enhancement of client development level, mobile microblog experience is even higher than computer microblog experience.

Steady development of other communication applications and information access applications

The applications of mobile search, mobile network news, mobile phones post and reply, mobile social networking sites, and mobile e-mail etc are the traditional mobile application the same with instant messaging. In 2011, its year on year utilization rate increases at less extent. The main market impetus is as follows:

On one hand, with smart phones era for WAP, Internet service providers start to deploy mobile Internet. For mainstream Internet applications, the corresponding WAP version or client is launched, which greatly enhance the use experience of mobile phone internet users. On the other hand, the fierce competition of mobile phone browser market promotes providers to increase investment in product features and services of mobile browser, which greatly improves the use experience of browser user. In particular, internet users can easily access WEB site through browser, increasing the depth of internet users using mobile Internet applications.

Slow development of entertainment and commercial application

As typical entertainment application, mobile video has little utilization rate change. In short term, the development of mobile video business faces the following difficulties: on the one hand, wireless network infrastructure cannot meet user's needs. Large amounts of wireless network traffic required for video applications, high charge of network currently and instable bandwidth become the bottleneck hindering the application development. On the other hand, there is lack of corresponding mobile video content. Feature of fragmented use makes service providers to provide short video content applicable for mobile video users. Currently, when wireless network is not mature, video service providers don't start to conduct strategic layout for mobile phone users.

E-commerce applications are generally at the early stage of development, having low penetration rate in mobile phone users by two reasons. First, the majorities of e-commerce products cannot be purchased until users compare them and consult. The mobile phone of small screen makes relatively worse purchasing experience. Second, the trust and use habit have not been established for mobile phone payment.

Special: Increasing space and restricting factor of online shopping

Introduction:

In 2008–2010, the size of online shopping users maintained rapid growth of around 50% for three consecutive years. In 2011, online shopping users reached 194 million, online shopping usage rate increased to 37.8%, but user annual growth rate was down to 20.8%, and user's absolute increment fell sharply. During the development process that online shopping gradually is stepping into mature stage, the exploration to growth space of online shopping helps us understand today's growth and clarify future direction.

Since 2009, commercial applications represented by online shopping, online payment and travel booking etc. continue to grow rapidly, leading other Internet application development, becoming the outstanding feature of development of Internet in China. In 2011, this trend still continued. Chinese online shopping application is still in rapid development channel. On one hand, group buying achieved user high growth of 244.8% as a new commerce transaction application. On the other hand, when utilization rate of more network application services declined, commerce application penetration remains steady improvement trend, and online shopping, online payments, and online banking user scale achieved faster growth. This can not be separated from the overall situation that the state increase domestic demand to stimulate social consumption. It more benefited from force marketing of shopping site, overall enhancement of online shopping services and further release of internet users consumption demand. Supply and demand booming promoted the growth of online shopping users.

However, along with the slowdown of growth rate of Internet users in China, both growth speed of Chinese online shopping users and absolute increment fall. Viewed from user growth for nearly 5 years, it can be found that since 2008, the number of online shopper in China has been in high growth. The growth rate from 2008—2010 was around 50%, and the absolute quantity of annual growth also continued to increase. In 2011, although online shopping penetration rate was still improved, growth rate of online shopper slipped to 20.8%. Absolute number of annual new users decreased significantly, for 33.44 million, decreasing 19.07 million compared with that in 2010. When the depth of online shopping was strengthened, the growth speed of online shopper has slowed down.

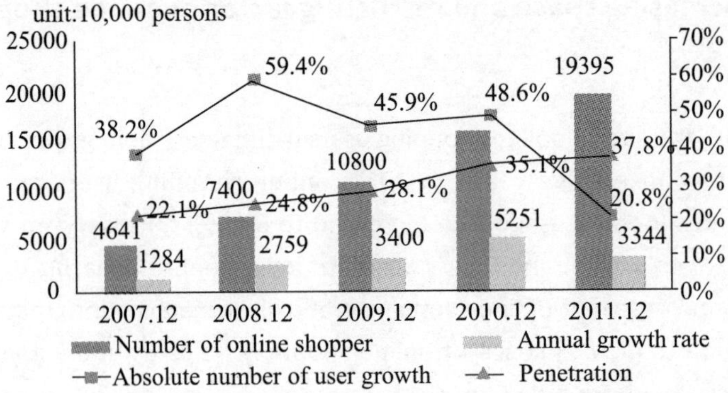

Figure 39. Number, growth rate and penetration of online shopper during Dec. 2007–Dec. 2011 in China

Decrease of total amount of new Internet users ⑦ and transmission fatigue of old Internet users are the main cause of slowdown for online shopper growth. On the one hand, new Internet users make less contribution to online shopper growth, in lasting declining (proportions of new online shopper in 2009, 2010 and 2011 are 11.4%, 10.8% and 9.3% respectively). In 2011, new Internet users scale increment decreased, further weakening the promotion of new internet users to online shopping growth. On the other hand, in 2008–2010, government's strong support and deepening operation of electrical commercial enterprises effectively promote behavior of old online shopper, and release more consumption potential. After new internet users transfer to old Internet users, certain cycle, conditions and factors are needed to become online shoppers. Due to relatively high-end commerce application, there will be longer for Internet users to use cultivation period from proceeding with it. Comparing the proportion of Internet users of different ages using online shopping, we can see that there are two key trend turning points. The first is 2–3 years. When Internet users Internet ages are 2–3 years, its proportion using online shopping is 29.7%, improving 11.8 percentage points compared with 1–2 years. The second is five years later, when penetration reached to 59.2%, enhancing 19.6% compared with 3–5 years. The users of this stage are in more rapid infiltration area of online shopping. When new internet users increase slowly and old internet users transfer in an insufficient level, the application population will experience the current situation of slowdown at less extent.

---

⑦ Statistical caliber of new Internet user is the Internet user with online age within one year (including 1 year).

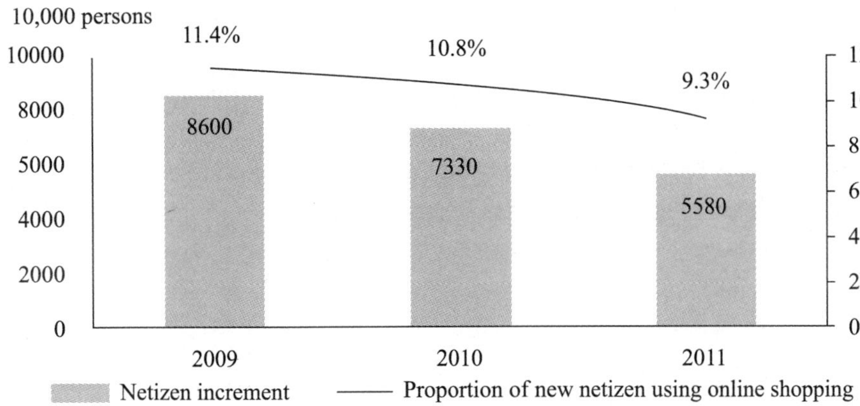

Figure 40. Internet users increment and proportion of new Internet user using online shopping

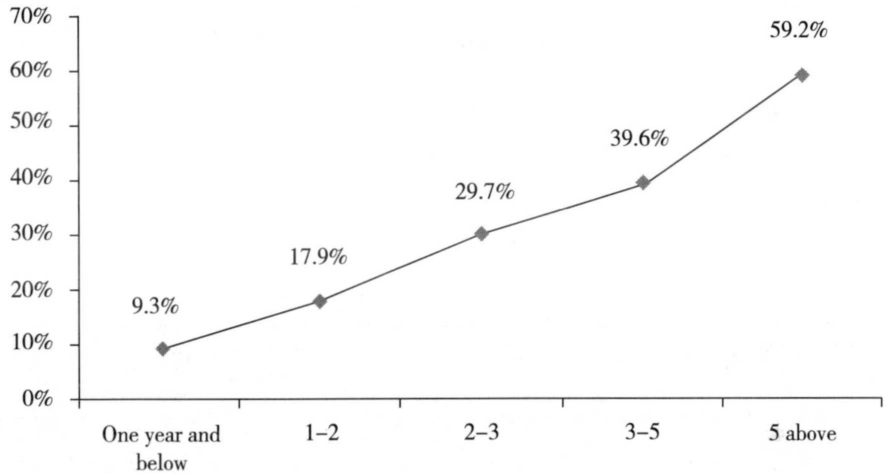

Figure 41. Proportion of Internet users of different ages using online shopping

There is huge growth space for online shopper and market in China in the future. Compared with developed countries, Chinese online shopping penetration rate is low. In 2010, the proportions of online shoppers in South Korea and the US were 64.3% [8] and 66.0% [9] respectively. As of December 2011, Chinese online shopping penetration rate was only 37.8%. Compared with penetrations of users of different ages in China and America, it's found that popularizing rate of Chinese internet users of all ages is lower than the counterpart in the United States by over 20 percentage points, especially for middle-aged groups. The penetration rates for

⑧ Source: KISA http://isis.kisa.kr/

⑨ Source: PEW http://www.pewinternet.org/

online shoppers aged 34–45, 46–55 and 56–65 are 30.1%, 32.0% and 42.6%. The growth of online shopping in China is far from peak, and there is a large penetration space especially for middle-aged groups that will become important growth groups in the future. However, Chinese social and economic development and current situation of popularity of Internet decide that the actual growth of online shopping is bound to be subject to a number of objective factors.

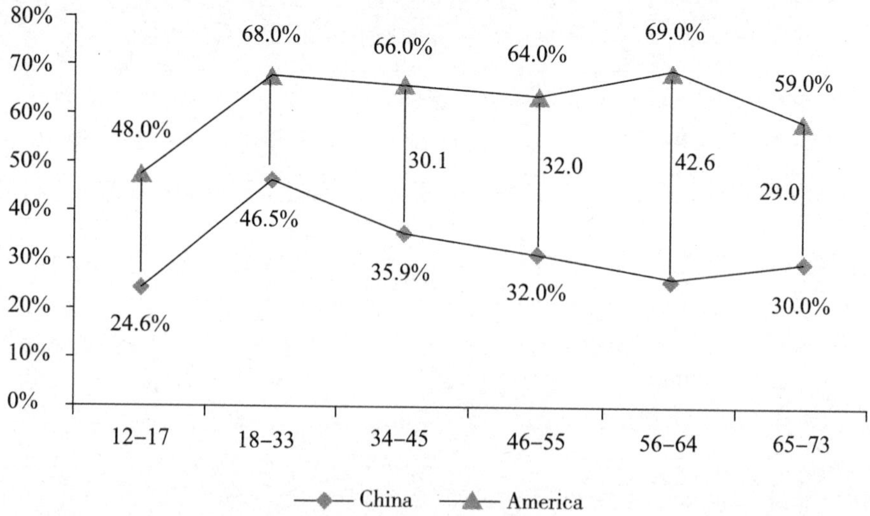

Figure 42. Proportion of online shopper of different ages in China and United States. Data for China from CNNIC, data for the US from PEW

The main factors restricting the growth of online shopper is Internet popularizing level, population consumption behavior pattern and commodity distribution service capabilities, i.e., basic condition and supply and demand. The first one is the difference of Chinese Internet penetration levels. In America, Internet penetration levels for population of all ages are relatively equal, while Chinese Internet penetration is highly different along with transmission of overall socio-economic system for Internet development. What's the most prominent is high level of Internet penetration for young groups and low level for elderly popularity, resulting in great difference for different population from bringing into contact to accepting and then to basic conditions of online shopping. The second is great difficulty for consumption pattern changing. With the development of online shopping penetration, in the future, among potential online shoppers, proportion of middle-aged and rural users will become increasingly bigger. Such group will more rely on traditional methods. Coupled with concerns about online security, there is great obstruction for consumption demand converted to practical application of online shopping, which will have impact on user growth for the next step. Third, lagged logistics development causes uneven market supply level. Although the scope of services and capacity for electrical and commercial enterprises in China have increased dramatically, there is great gap for distribution services of online shopping between city, rural areas, core cities and four-tier cities due to restriction of insufficient logistics distribution capabilities, the objective condition. It leads to the difference of online shopping supply level between different areas.

Viewed from anticipation of future development, the momentum of gradual deepened Internet penetration in China is irreversible. Supply and demand side of online shopping continues to be active, which will promote online shopping to grow steadily in the future for a long time. Though Chinese Internet penetration rate has slowed, penetration power remains strong. The popularity of low Internet level is accelerated for conversion. Along with enhancement of our residents' income and purchasing power, internet users' online consumption potential will continue to release. The momentum of development of electric commercial enterprises is strong. Online shopping supply capacity gradually grows. Service level continues to deepen. Those factors will effectively create room for further growth, and promote online shopping to grow steadily in the future for a long time.

16

中国互联网的发展历程（2012）

韩圣龙　杨学婧

The Development of the Internet in China (2012)

Han Shenglong and Yang Xuejing

1 互联网在中国的早期发展 ①

早在 20 世纪 80 年代中后期，中国的科研人员和学者就在国外同行的帮助下，开始积极地尝试利用互联网。1986 年，北京市计算机应用技术研究所实施的国际联网项目——中国学术网（Chinese Academy Network，简称 CANET）启动，其合作伙伴是德国卡尔斯鲁厄大学（University of Karlsruhe)。1987 年 9 月，CANET 在北京计算机应用技术研究所内正式建成中国第一个国际互联网电子邮件节点，并于 9 月 14 日发出了中国第一封电子邮件："Across the Great Wall, we can reach every corner in the world（越过长城，走向世界)"，揭开了中国人使用互联网的序幕。这封电子邮件是通过意大利公用分组网 ITAPAC 设在北京侧的 PAD 机，经由意大利 ITAPAC 和德国 DATEX-P 分组网，实现和德国卡尔斯鲁厄大学的链接，通信速率最初为

① CNNIC. 中国互联网发展报告 [R]2002：5–7.

300bit/s[②]。1988 年初，中国第一个 X.25 分组交换网 CNPAC 建城，当时覆盖北京、上海、广州、沈阳、西安、武汉、成都、南京、深圳等城市。

1988 年 12 月，清华大学校园网采用胡道元教授从加拿大 UBC 大学（University of British Columbia）引进的采用 X400 协议的电子邮件软件包，通过 X.25 网与加拿大 UBC 大学相连，开通了电子邮件应用。同年，中国科学院高能物理研究所（以下简称中科院高能所）采用 X.25 协议使该单位的 DECnet 成为西欧中心 DECnet 的延伸，实现了计算机国际远程联网以及与欧洲和北美地区的电子邮件通信。1991 年，中科院高能所又连入美国斯坦福线性加速中心（SLAC）的 LIVEMORE 实验室，并开通电子邮件应用。

1989 年 10 月，国家计委通过世界银行贷款重点学科项目——国内命名为中关村地区教育与科研示范网络，世界银行命名为 National Computing and Networking Facility of China（简称 NCFC ）——正式立项，11 月该项目启动。NCFC 是世界银行贷款“重点学科发展项目”中的一个高技术信息基础设施项目，由国家计委、中国科学院、国家自然科学基金会、国家教委配套投资和支持。项目由中国科学院主持，联合北京大学、清华大学共同实施。当时立项的主要目标就是通过北京大学、清华大学和中科院（中国科学院的简称）三个单位的合作，搞好 NCFC 的主干网和三个院校网的建设。

1990 年 11 月 28 日钱天白教授代表中国正式在 SRI-NIC（Stanford Research Institute’s Network Information Center）注册登记了中国的顶级域名 CN，并且从此开通了使用中国顶级域 名 CN 的国际电子邮件服务，自此中国的网络有了自己的身份标识。由于当时尚未实现与国际互联网的全功能的连接，中国 CN 顶级域名服务器建在了德国卡尔斯鲁厄大学。直到 1994 年 5 月 21 日，在钱天白教授和德国卡尔斯鲁厄大学的协助下，中国科学院计算机网络信息中心完成了中国国家顶级域名（CN）服务器的设置，由钱天白、钱华林分别担任中国互联网的行政联络员和技术联络员，才改变了中国的 CN 顶级域名服务器一直放在国外的历史。

1993 年 3 月 2 日，中国科学院的高能物理研究所租用 AT&T 公司的国际卫星信道接入美国斯坦福线性加速器中心（SLAC）的 64K 专线正式开通。专线开通后，美国政府以 Internet 上有许多科技信息和其他各种资源，不能让社会主义国家接入为由，只允许这条专线进入美国能源网而不能连接到其他

② CNNIC. 数说互联网 1997–2007 中国互联网络发展统计报告 .[R]：373.

地方。尽管如此，这条专线仍然是中国连入 Internet 的第一根专线。专线开通后，国家基金委大力配合并投资 30 万元人民币，使得各个学科的重大课题负责人能够拨号连入中科院高能所的这根专线，几百名科学家得以在国内使用电子邮件。

1994 年 4 月 20 日，NCFC 工程通过美国 Sprint 公司连入互联网的 64K 国际专线开通，实现了与互联网的全功能连接。从此中国被国际正式承认为有互联网的国家。一个月后中国科学院高能物理研究所设立了国内第一个 WEB 服务器，推出了中国的第一套网页，内容除了介绍中国高科技发展外，还有一个栏目叫“Tour in China”。此后，该栏目开始提供包括新闻、经济、文化、商贸等 更为广泛的信息，并改名为《中国之窗》。

同时为了建设与互联网发展所需的基础设施，中国开始部署筹建全国性骨干网络。

1993 年 3 月作为国民经济信息化的一项重要措施，当时的朱镕基副总理提出和部署建设国家公用经济信息通信网（简称金桥工程），同年李鹏总理拨出 300 万美元支持启动其前期工程，并于 1995 年 8 月初步建成，在 24 省市开通联网（卫星网），并与国际网络实现互联。

1994 年 8 月，由国家计委投资，国家教委主持的中国教育和科研计算机网（CERNET）正式立项。该项目的目标是利用先进实用的计算机技术和网络通信技术，实现小元件的计算机联网和信息资源共享，并与国际学术计算机网络互联，建立功能齐全的网络管理系统。

1994 年 9 月，原邮电部与美国商务部签订中美双方关于国际互联网的协议，协议中规定电信总局将通过美国 Sprint 公司开通两条 64K 专线（一条在北京，一条在上海）。中国公用计算机互联网（CHINANET）建设开始启动。其全国骨干网也于 1996 年 1 月建成并正式开通。

1995 年 4 月，中国科学院启动京外单位联网工程（简称“百所联网”工程）。其目标是在北京地区已经入网的 30 多个研究所的基础上把网络扩展到全国的 24 个城市，实现国内各学术机构的计算机互联并和互联网相连。到 1995 年年底，完成了 12 个分院到北京的连接，使京外的 80 多个研究所进入互联网。在此基础上，网络不断扩张，逐步连接了中国科学院以外的一批研究所和科技单位，成为一个面向科技用户、科技管理部门以及与科技有关的政府部门服务的全国性网络，取名“中国科技网”（CSTNET）。

随着 1995 年 12 月中科院百所联网工程完成和中国教育和科研计算机

网（CERNET）示范工程的建设完成，全国性的四大骨干网络初具规模，并相继展开全国性的服务业务，为互联网在中国的使用、发展奠定了良好的基础。在 1997 年 10 月，中国公用计算机互联网（CHINANET）实现了与中国其他三个互联网络即中国科技网（CSTNET）、中国教育和科研计算机网（CERNET）、中国金桥信息网（CHINAGBN）的互联互通，更促进了各项互联网业务的快速发展。

1996 年年初，国务院成立信息化工作领导小组及其办公室，负责组织、协调有关部门制定国际联网的安全、经营、资费、服务等规定和标准的工作，并对执行情况进行审查监督。1997 年 6 月 3 日，国务院又委托中国科学院在中国科学院计算机网络信息中心组建了中国互联网信息中心（CNNIC），行使国家互联网络信息中心的职责，提供互联网络地址、域名、网络资源目录管理和有关的信息服务。同日，国务院信息化工作领导小组办公室宣布成立中国互联网络信息中心（CNNIC）工作委员会。

同年 11 月，受国家主管部门的委托，中国互联网络信息中心（CNNIC）发布了第一份《中国互联网发展统计报告》。截止到 1997 年 10 月 31 日，中国共有上网计算机 29.9 万台，上网用户 62 万人，CN 下注册的域名 4066 个，WWW 站点 1500 个，国际出口带宽 25.408Mbit/s。

与此同时，中国电信业依靠国家一系列扶持通信发展的政策，取得了巨大发展。1994 年初，国务院发文批准组建中国联合通信有限公司，在基础电信业务领域引入有限竞争；1998 年 3 月，全国人大批准国务院机构改革方案，国家成立信息产业部，实现彻底的政企分开，启动电信业的重组；1999 年 2 月，国务院通过中国电信重组方案，此后分别批复组建中国移动通信集团公司（简称中国移动）、中国电信集团公司（简称中国电信）和中国卫星通信集团公司（简称中国卫星），三大集团公司陆续挂牌。1999 年 4 月，中国网络通信有限公司成立。2000 年 12 月，铁道通信信息有限责任公司成立。2002 年 5 月 16 日，重组后的中国电信集团公司和中国网络通信集团公司（简称中国网通）挂牌成立。经过改革重组，中国基础电信市场竞争格局初步形成。这些电信运营商分别运营带有独立国际出入口的互联网络，至 2002 年中国共有 9 家网络运营商（即九大互联网络单位），它们分别是：中国公用计算机互联网（CHINANET）、中国科技网（CSTNET）、中国教育和科研计算机网（CERNET）、中国联通互联网（UNINET）、中国网通公用互联网（CNNET）、中国移动互联网（CMNET）、中国国际经济贸易互联网（CIETNET）、中国长城互联网（CGWNET）和中国卫星集团互联网（CSNET）。这 9 家互联网络单位通过大力发展电信基础设施建设和不断提高电信服务质量，极大地推动了中国互联网的发展，中国互联网开始进入一个高速发展阶段。到 2002 年底，中国已有上网计算机 2083 万台，www 站点 37 万多个，而互联网用户达到 5910 万人，居世界第二位，成为名副其实的互联网大国。

2 中国互联网发展宏观状况

网民变化。据最新发布的 29 期互联网发展统计报告，截至 2011 年 12 月底，中国网民数量突破 5 亿，达到 5.13 亿，全年新增网民 5580 万。互联网普及率较上年底提升 4 个百分点，达到 38.3%。截至 2010 年底，网民总数达到 4.57 亿，互联网普及率达 34.3%，较 2009 年年底提高 5.4 个百分点。图 1 是从 1997 年开始统计的中国网民的数量变化图，可以看出中国互联网的网民的发展变化情况：

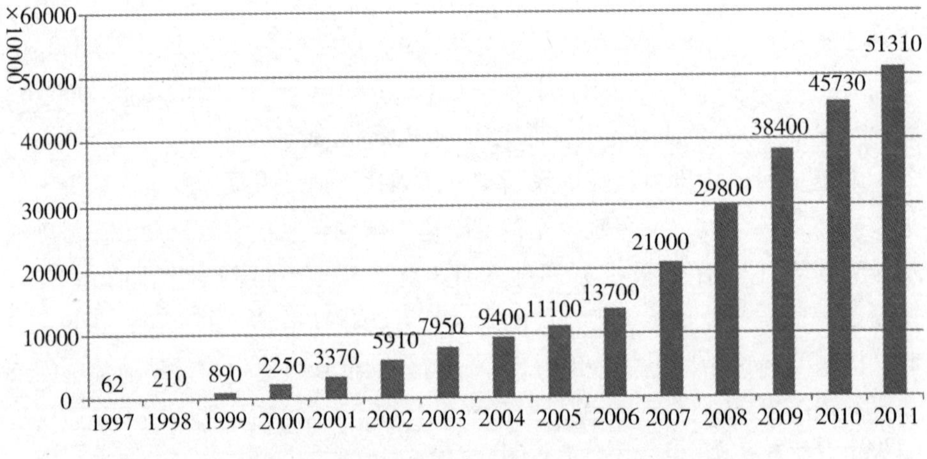

图 1　网民数量变化图（数据来源 :CNNIC 历年统计报告）

IPv4 地址数量变化。截至 2011 年 12 月底，我国 IPv4 地址数量为 3.30 亿，较 2010 年底增长 19.0%。图 2 是历年来 IPv4 的数量统计变化图。

CN 域名增长变化图。在第一部分，我们也已经交代过，早在 1990 年 11 月 28 日，我国就注册了国家顶级域名 .cn，但当时我国还没有接入互联网，由德国卡尔斯鲁厄大学运行 .cn 域名服务器。直到 1994 年 5 月 24 日，第一台中国国家域名 .cn 根服务器才终于落户中国。而 CNNIC 这个掌控中国互联网中枢神经系统的机构在 3 年之后才成立。对此，中国互联网的先驱钱华林教授回忆说："我们把域名服务器从德国拿回来的时候，.cn 域名只有几个。一直到 1997 年 6 月份，国家有关部门授权我们来做国家域名注册管理的时候，我们才有 2000 多个域名。2006 年底，国家顶级域名已经有 180 多万了。.cn 域名的增长反映了中国互联网的普及和应用发展历程。"图 3 是 CN 域名数量变化图。

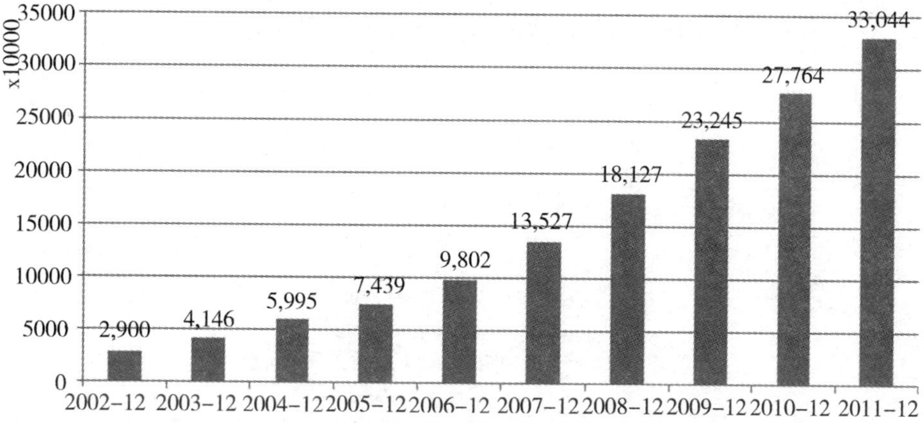

图 2 IPv4 地址数量变化图（数据来源：同上）

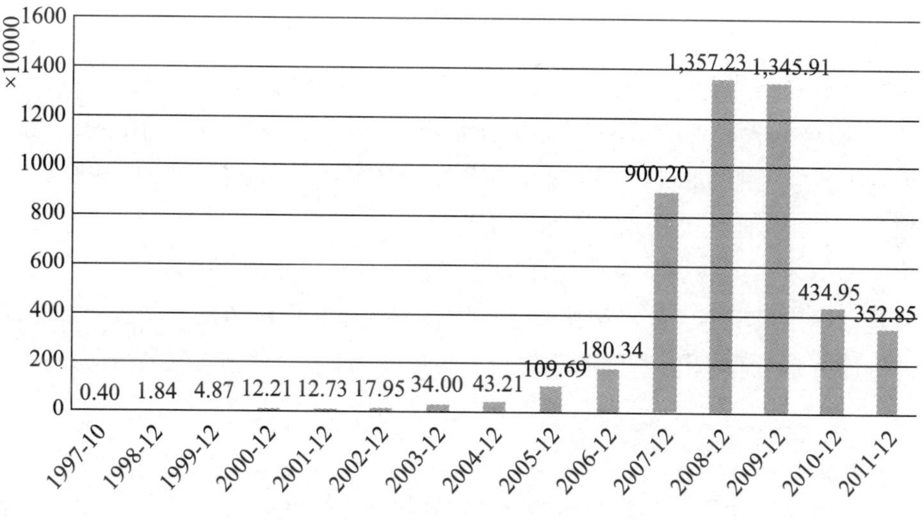

图 3 CN 域名数量变化图（数据来源：同上）

国际出口带宽。1997 年 10 月份，第一次国际出口带宽统计时只有 25.408M。而根据目前发布的第 29 次报告，截止到 2011 年 12 月份，国际出口带宽为 1 389 529M，是 1997 年的 54688 倍，其中平均年增长率为 3906 倍之多。

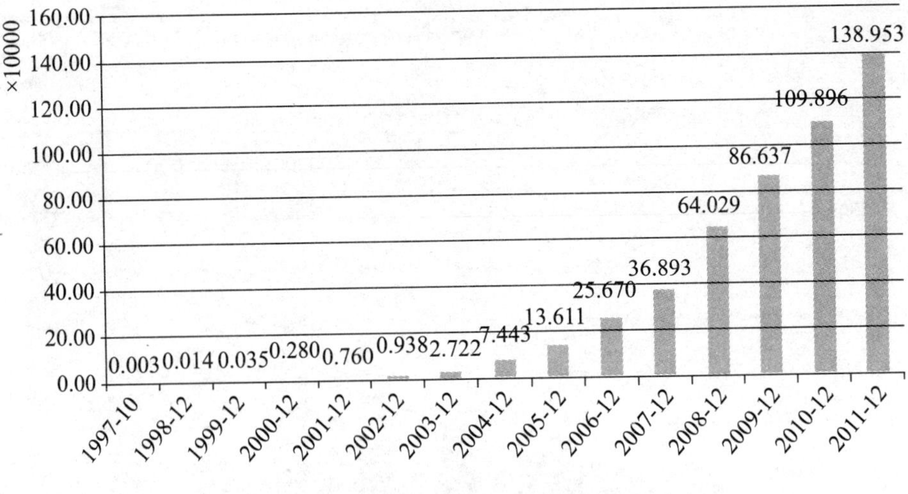

图 4　国际出口带宽变化图（数据来源：同上）

我国网民上网方式已从最初拨号上网为主，发展到以宽带和手机上网为主。我国互联网发展与普及水平居发展中国家前列。近年来，我国大力推动电信网、广播电视网和互联网三网融合，2010 年 1 月，国务院常务会议决定加快推进三网融合，明确了时间表，三网融合已经进入实质性阶段。三网融合的发展将极大提高网络资源利用率，使人们更加方便快捷地使用文字、话音、数据、图像、视频等多媒体综合业务，推动移动多媒体广播电视、手机电视、数字电视宽带上网等业务的应用，推动产业形态创新，促进文化产业、信息产业和其他现代服务业快速发展[③]。

从以上各组数据的发展变化来看，无论是网民数量、IP 地址、CN 域名还是国际出口带宽，从我国接入互联网以来其增长变化速度，令我们自己都感到惊奇。不难得出：中国的互联网事业始终处于一个快速的发展阶段。

3　移动互联网建设情况

分析历年来中国互联网发展状况统计报告，可以发现，2006 年 7 月的调查结果第一次把中国使用手机上网的网民纳入统计报告中，统计显示为中国的手机网民数量为 1300 万人。2007 年 1 月的调查显示：通过手机上网的网民人数达到了 1700 万人，占网民总数的 12.4%。同时，该统计报告还对性别特征、婚姻状况、年龄分布、网民职业等进行了详细的分析。

③　《中国互联网发展状况》白皮书 2010.

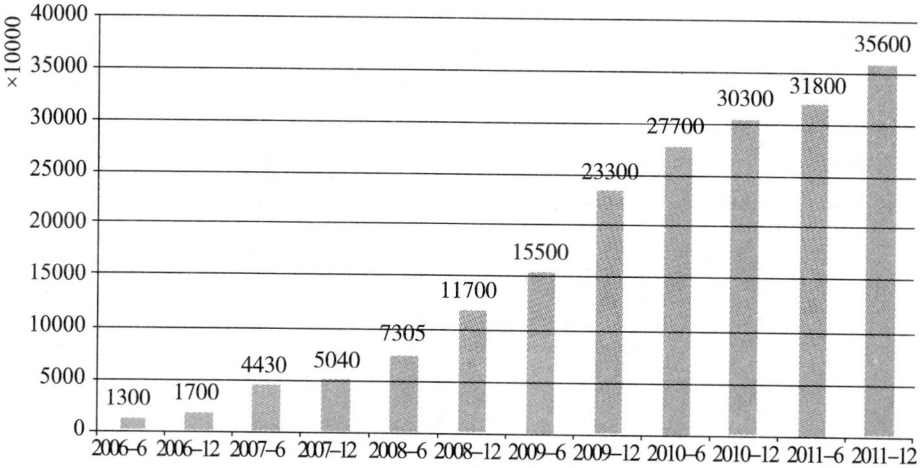

图 5　手机网民数量变化图

2009 年是电信重组和 3G 牌照发放后的关键发展年，运营商的全业务重点集中在全面推进移动能力建设上面。各运营商均稳步落实投资计划，迅猛推进 3G 网络的建设、3G 产业化 / 商业化、业务开发和市场推广的进程明显加快，呈现起步扎实、开局良好、快速推进、规范有序的发展态势[④]。

2009 年，三家基础电信企业共完成 3G 网络建设直接投资 1609 亿元人民币，完成 3G 基站建设 32.5 万个，建设规模超过十多年来累计规模的一半，开创了全球电信发展史上建设规模最大、建设速度最快的纪录。

2009 年 1 月时，中国移动在全国仅有 10 个城市建成了 TD-SCDMA 网络 TD-SCDMA 实验网，TD-SCDMA 基站约有 2 万个。2009 年年底，中国移动 TD 网络三期工程顺利完 工，全国 70% 以上地市实现了 TD-SCDMA 网络覆盖，其中东部省份 100% 地市实现覆盖，基站总数超过 10 万多个。在建设过程中，中国移动提出了“3G/2G 融合组网”的思想，最大限度地将 2G 网络优势和成熟经验延伸到 TD-SCDMA 上，有效降低了 TD-SCDMA 的建设成本，促进了 TD-SCDMA 网络的规模化。据工业和信息化部数据显示，中国移动 2009 年一年的 TD-SCDMA 建设工程量比过去十几年的工程量总和还多。

中国电信的 CDMA2000 网络具有性能稳定、便于演进和后向兼容的特点，其 3G 网络建设分为 3 个阶段：第一阶段为 2009 年 3 月完成 100 个城市的 CDMA2000EVDO 网络的覆盖；第二阶段是在 2009 年 5 月完成国内大部分

④　CNNIC. 中国互联网发展报告 [R]2010 ：144.

本地网城区 3G 网络覆盖；第三阶段是在 2009 年年底完成全国所有县以上及部分发达乡镇地区的网路覆盖。截至 2009 年 8 月，中国电信 3G 网络已覆盖全国各地，普及到全国 342 个地级城市，2055 个县及县级市，以及东部沿海省市发达乡镇在内的 6000 多个乡镇。

中国联通 3G 网络采用"统一规划，重点区域网络覆盖一步到位"的部署策略，2009 年时，投入 WCKMA 网络建设。截至 2009 年 12 月 31 日，中国联通网络覆盖全国 335 个城市，基站数量达到 10.7 万个，室内分布系统 5.6 万套，遍及全国所有城市的城区、东部地区发达乡镇和所有县城，以及中西部发达县城。

2010 年[⑤]，工业和信息化部等八部委联合印发了《关于推进第三代移动通信网络建设的意见》，要求各级政府和企业充分认识 3G 网络建设的重要性，共同推进网络建设发展；落实 3G 发展规划，促进网络协调持续发展；制定和出台 3G 网络建设的支持政策，解决网络建设困难；引导和支持 3G 网络应用发展和创新，带动 3G 网络建设升级；继续落实和完善支持 3G 发展的其他政策措施，保障 3G 网络建设；加强组织领导，确保 3G 网络各项工作落到实处。

截至2010年12月底，三家运营商共建设3G基站约43.8万个，中国电信、中国移动、中国联通分别累计建成 3G 基站 17 万、11.5 万、15.3 万个。

4　互联网网络设备和产品发展状况

4.1 网络设备

4.1.1 交换机市场

以太网交换机对于大中型企业的网络来说是必不可少的设备，它在网络建设中具有非常重要的作用，可以增加网络容量，提高网络速度。随着中国各行业、各领域的大中型企业信息化进程的展开以及以太网在技术上的成熟和在实际应用中的优势，以太网交换机的作用越来越大。

在中国，随着信息网络的进一步建设，以太网交换机市场也与其他类别的市场一样处于激烈的竞争中。金融、政府、教育等大型行业信息化工程的开展、企业上网工程的推进、宽带城域网建设力度加大等因素，促进了交换机市场快速增长。

2010 年，中国明显加快了互联网基础设施的建设，中国电信与中国联通纷纷加快了 FTTx 部署，带动中国交换机市场的发展。2010 年中国交换机市

⑤　CNNIC. 中国互联网发展报告 [R]2011 ：51.

场继续保持稳定增长态势。

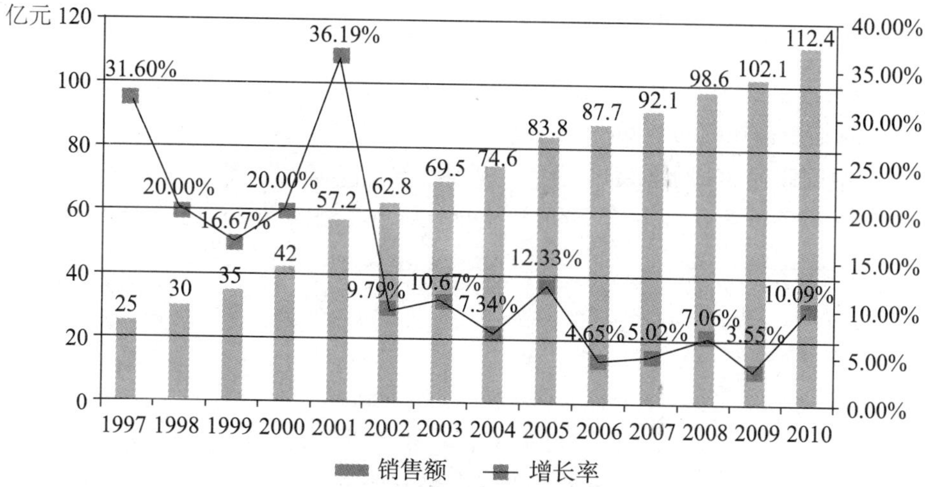

图 6　中国交换机市场规模 ⑥

上图是中国交换机市场的市场规模变化情况，可以看出：至 2010 年中国交换机市场的销售额达到了 112.4 亿元，较 2009 年的 102.1 亿元增长了 10.3 亿元，增长了 10 个百分点，是 1997 年的 4 倍之多。折线图为中国交换机市场规模的增长率变化图，随着基数的不断增长，中国的交换机市场的增长率较 2000 年前后有所下降，但是增长速度仍然很可观。

4.1.2 路由器市场

路由器在中国的使用始于 20 世纪 80 年代，最初多应用于金融行业，市场需求很小。此后随着中国信息化建设的快速发展，路由器市场规模也开始快速增长。到 2002 年，随着社会信息化、电子政务、社区信息化、企业信息化等基本网络建设的快速发展，再加上数据业务的剧增和多业务应用的增加，路由器市场更呈现出一片繁荣景象。路由器市场规模变化如图 7。

由图 7，可以看出 1997 年时，我国路由器的市场规模仅仅为 19 亿元，而截止到 2010 年我国路由器的市场规模已经达到了 118.3 亿元，增长了 5 倍。另外，较 2009 年销售额 101.3 亿元来看，一年内增长了 17 亿元，增长速度为 16.7%，是 1997 年全年销售额的 89.4%。纵观 14 年的销售率增长变化情况，其增长速度均在 5 个百分点以上，2000 年时曾经达到最高增长了 48.15%。鉴于不断增长的基数变化，我国路由器市场规模的销售增长率变化会和交换机市场相似，不会有太高的增长，但增长额度仍然会很可观。

⑥　参考：中国互联网发展报告 2002、2007、2011；数据来源 CCID.

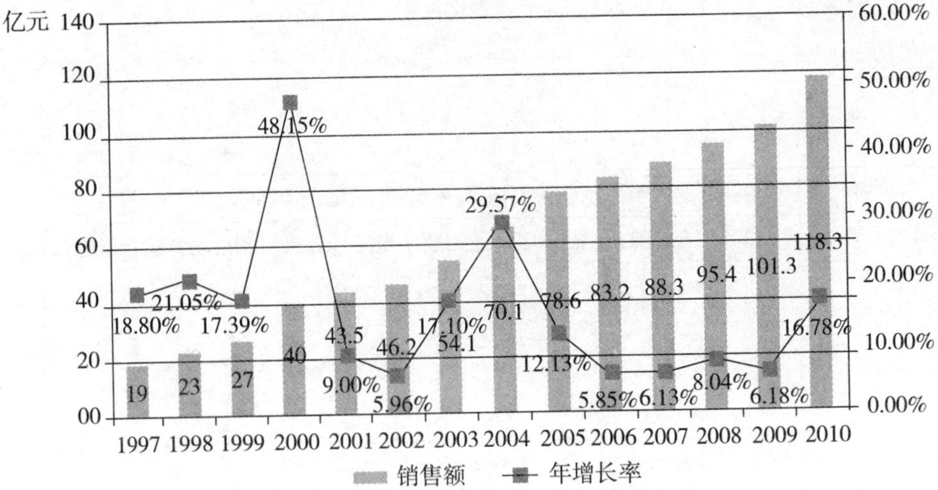

图 7　中国路由器市场规模 ⑦

4.2 终端设备

4.2.1 计算机发展

现在，计算机在中国已经有了很长足的发展，可以说，我们的衣食住行方方面面已经离不了计算机了。而要追溯计算机的源头，应该从 50 多年前说起。1956 年，在党中央“向科学进军”的号召指引下，周恩来总理亲自主持制定了我国《12 年科学技术发展规划》。8 月，成立了由华罗庚教授为主任的科学院计算所筹建委员会，组织了计算机设计、程序设计和计算机方法专业训练班，并首次派出一批科技人员赴苏联实习和考察。同年，夏培肃完成了第一台电子计算机运算器和控制器的设计工作，同时编写了我国第一本电子计算机原理讲义。1958 年 8 月 1 日，我国第一台小型电子管数字计算机 103 机诞生了，这标志着我国第一台电子计算机的诞生。至此，关于中国计算机的发展拉开了帷幕，并在 50 年来不断向前，发展迅速。表 1 是这 50 多年来中国计算机史上所发生的大事件。至此，我们可以感受到中国计算机事业的崛起。

⑦　参考：中国互联网发展报告 2002、2007、2011；数据来源 CCID.

表 1　中国计算机产业大事记[⑧]

年份	大事记
1956 年	夏培肃完成了第一台电子计算机运算器和控制器的设计工作，同时编写了中国第一本电子计算机原理讲义。
1957 年	哈尔滨工业大学研制成功中国第一台模拟式电子计算机。
1958 年	中国第一台计算机——103 型通用数字电子计算机研制成功，运行速度每秒 1500 次。
1959 年	中国研制成功 104 型电子计算机，运算速度每秒 1 万次。
1960 年	中国第一台大型通用电子计算机——107 型通用电子数字计算机研制成功。
1963 年	中国第一台大型晶体管电子计算机——109 机研制成功。
1964 年	441B 全晶体管计算机研制成功。
1965 年	中国第一台百万次集成电路计算机“DJS － Ⅱ”型操作系统编制完成。
1967 年	新型晶体管大型通用数字计算机诞生。
1969 年	北京大学承接研制百万次集成电路数字电子计算机——150 机。
1970 年	中国第一台具有多道程序分时操作系统和标准汇编语言的计算机——441B- Ⅲ型全晶体管计算机研制成功。
1972 年	每秒运算 11 万次的大型集成电路通用数字电子计算机研制成功。
1973 年	中国第一台百万次集成电路电子计算机研制成功。
1974 年	DJS － 130、131、132、135、140、152、153 等 13 个机型先后研制成功。
1976 年	DJS － 183、184、185、186、1804 机研制成功。
1977 年	中国第一台微型计算机 DJS － 050 机研制成功。
1979 年	中国研制成功每秒运算 500 万次的集成电路计算机——HDS-9，王选用中国第一台激光照排机排出样书。
1981 年	中国研制成功的 260 机平均运算速度达到每秒 100 万次。
1983 年	“银河Ⅰ号”巨型计算机研制成功，运算速度达每秒 1 亿次。
1984 年	联想集团的前身——新技术发展公司成立，中国出现第一次微机热。
1985 年	华光Ⅱ型汉字激光照排系统投入生产性使用。
1987 年	第一台国产的 286 微机——长城 286 正式推出。
1988 年	第一台国产 386 微机——长城 386 推出，中国发现首例计算机病毒。1990 年中国首台高智能计算机——EST ／ IS4260 智能工作站诞生，长城 486 计算机问世。

⑧　田野．光辉历程 中国计算机发展 50 年专栏 · 回顾 50 年新起点 [J]. 中国互联网用户，2006-12-18（49）.

续表

年份	大事记
1991 年	新华社、科技日报、经济日报正式启用汉字激光照排系统。
1992 年	中国最大的汉字字符集——6 万电脑汉字字库正式建立。
1993 年	中国第一台 10 亿次巨型银河计算机Ⅱ型通过鉴定。
1994 年	银河计算机Ⅱ型在国家气象局投入正式运行，用于天气中期预报。
1995 年	曙光 1000 大型机通过鉴定，其峰值可达每秒 25 亿次。
1996 年	国产联想电脑在国内微机市场销售量第一。
1997 年	银河－Ⅲ并行巨型计算机研制成功。
1998 年	中国微机销量达 408 万台，国产占有率高达 71.9%。
1999 年	银河四代巨型机研制成功。
2000 年	我国成为继美国、日本之后，世界上第三个具备研制高性能计算机能力的国家。
2001 年	“龙芯”计划开始，中国科学院计算技术研究所开始研制具有自主知识产权的高性能通用 CPU 芯片，他们把这一项目命名为“龙芯”。
2002 年	“龙芯”1 号研制成功，9 月 28 日正式面世。
2003 年	服务器曙光 4000L 问世。
2004 年	8 月 17 日，山东大学王小云、冯登国、来学嘉、于红波四人在美国加州圣巴巴拉举行的国际密码学会议（Crypto’2004）上公布对于 MD5、HAVAL-128、MD4 和 RIPEMD 四个著名 HASH 算法的破译结果。由中科院计算所、曙光公司和上海超级计算中心联合研制的 10 万亿次超级计算机曙光 4000A 在人民大会堂正式发布，并成功进入全球超级计算机 TOP500 排行榜前十。
2005 年	龙芯 2 号正式面世，中科院计算所国家智能计算机研究开发中心启动百万亿次超级计算机研制计划。

上述事件的发生、发展确实反映了我国计算机事业的科研进程。但是，对于我国计算机产业的发展，或许从上面的大事件上并不能全面地反映出来。行业的状况，要用我国计算机产量变化的数字来表征。

图 8 是微机产量的变化状况，从数据中可以清楚地看出，1991 年时我国的微型电子计算机的产量仅仅有 16.25 万台，至 2001 年为 672 万台，截止到 2010 年统计，微型计算机的产量已达到 24584.46 万台，是 1991 年的 1512 倍之多。

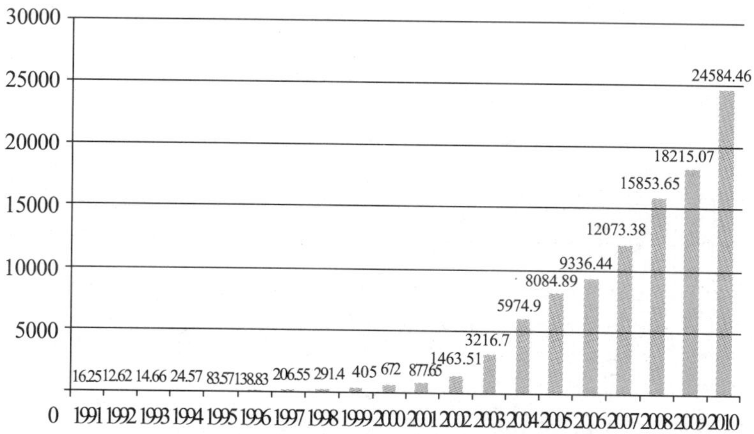

图 8 中国历年微型电子计算机产量（万台）[⑨]

尽管如此，对于计算机及硬件设备的生产企业来讲，我们仍然有很大的差距。下表是中国 2011 年 500 强与世界 500 强计算机 · 办公设备业领先企业比较统计[⑩]，数据来源有《中国 500 强企业发展报告 2011》。从表 2 中我们可以看出，与国际水平相比，我国的计算机相关企业仍有很大的差距，尤其是利润率和所有者权益，两者相比相差甚远。说明对我国的计算机及硬件生产商来讲，该产业规模虽然有了较快的发展变化，但是就其自身的发展、及利润创造上仍有很长的路要走。

表 2 中国 2011 年 500 强与世界 500 强计算机 · 办公设备业领先企业比较统计

	惠普（1）（美国）	联想集团（2）	（2）/（1）
营业收入（万元人民币）	85141593	14669743	17.23
利润（万元人民币）	5918494	323484	5.47
资产（万元人民币）	84108002	11460039	13.63
所有者权益（万元人民币）	27325322	1204643	4.41
收入利润率 (%)	6.95	2.21	31.80
资产利润率 (%)	7.04	2.82	40.06
净资产利润率 (%)	21.66	26.85	123.96
劳动生产率（万元人民币 / 人）	262.30	488.99	186.42
人均利润（万元人民币）	18.23	10.78	59.13

⑨ 数据摘自历年中国统计年鉴 .

⑩ 数据摘编自《中国 500 强企业发展报告 2011》.

4.2.2 手机

国家统计局对移动电话产量的统计是从 2000 年开始的，2000 年的统计数量为 5247.9 万台，2010 年为 99827.36 万台，增长了 18 倍，年均增长率达 90%。同时，较 2009 年的 68193.37 万台的数量来看，2010 年移动电话增长量为 3.16 亿台，年增长率为 46.38%。纵观图 9 中显示的历年移动电话产量的变化，我们可以看出：(1) 中国移动电话的数量一直在持续增长过程中，其增长变化在 2006—2008 年有一个相对缓慢的趋势，但是最近两年的增长速度有所突破。(2) 随着移动电话价格的下降，越来越多的人会成为移动电话的拥有者。(3) 由于手机更新换代的速度比较快，每年都会有相当部分手机被废弃，中国仍然有很大的移动电话市场。

移动电话产量的不断增长，反映了我国电子通讯事业的迅猛发展。中国作为一个人口大国，从一开始就有巨大的市场潜力。数据是移动电话产量的变化情况，同时也表征了中国电子通讯业的发展轨迹。

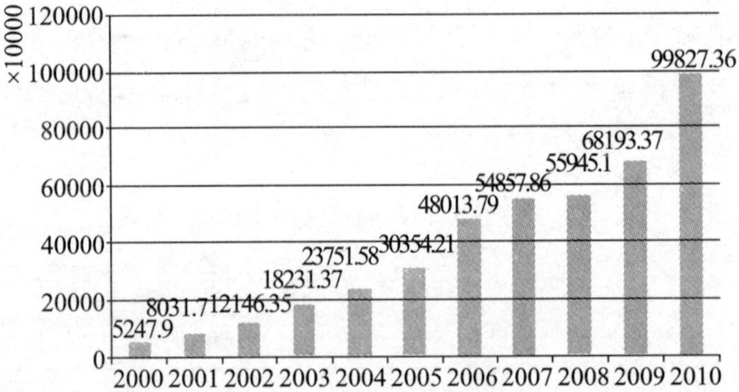

图 9 移动电话产量 [11]

当然，我国计算机和手机的产量只能反映出该产业生产实力的一个方面。我们从数据的增长变化中看到了中国 Internet 的发展，或许这些只能表示中国 Internet 的发展历程的一个方面，但是足以清晰地刻画出其变化的轮廓。

---

⑪ 数据摘自历年中国统计年鉴。

4.3 软件产业

4.3.1 软件发展30年历史回顾[12]

软件产业是知识经济的核心，信息社会的灵魂，是高科技领域的制高点。中国政府在认识到软件产业的战略意义后，启动了国家信息化战略，积极出台了多项优惠政策带动软件产业发展，例如2000年6月24日国务院下发第18号文件《鼓励软件产业和集成电路产业发展的若干政策》，2002年9月18日国务院又发布了《振兴软件产业行动纲要》等等。

而中国软件业的发展，可以追溯到改革开放时期。改革开放30年，给中国带来的巨大变化可以用“翻天覆地”来形容。30年时光变迁也是中国软件产业从最初萌芽到今日繁荣的探索历程。改革开放30年之中孕育了无数软件企业，诞生了许多软件英雄，而中国软件产业也在经历了萌芽与低谷、摸索与转型之后，开始走向世界。按照改革开放30年分期的脉络，中国软件产业也可以分成三个历史阶段进行讲述。

中国软件蹒跚起步，软件英雄厉兵秣马（1978–1988年）

1978年，中国共产党第十一届三中全会召开，正式确立对外开放、对内搞活经济的重要方针，中华民族走向繁荣之门就此打开。而在两年后，中国IT产业也开始萌发新气象。

1980年，在中关村发生了一件建国30年以来从未发生过的事情：以中国科学院物理研究所研究员陈春先为首的一批科技人员，在硅谷模式的影响下建立了“北京等离子体学会先进技术发展服务部”，这是中国历史上第一个民办科研机构，也是民营科技企业的前身。此事引发轩然大波，批判声无数，最终经中央领导批示之后才得以平息。

随着民营企业的解冻，很多程序员个人开始软件研发。1983年严援朝在PC长城机开发了CCDOS软件，其突出贡献便是解决了汉字在计算机内存储和显示的问题，具有划时代意义。同年，王永民以五年之功在河南南阳发明了“五笔字型”，也为后来中文输入奠定了基础。

1984年的9月6日，中国软件行业协会正式成立，当时的电子工业部部长江泽民同志出任名誉会长。该协会的成立，标志着软件作为一个新兴产业的历史开端：软件从硬件中分离出来，成为一个独立的产业，有了自己的一块“地盘”。在制订国家科技和行业发展规划时，软件开始被单独作为一个学科

---

⑫ 改革开放30年记录中国软件发展史．http://news.ifeng.com/special/30yearsit/200811/1119_5053_885073_2.shtml.

和行业来进行。同年，日后被媒体称为“中国第一程序员”的求伯君毕业于中国人民解放军国防科技大学，到河北徐水石油物探局仪器厂工作。

1986年3月，邓小平批示《关于跟踪研究外国战略性高技术发展的建议》：此事宜速作决断，不可拖延。863计划随后启动，开启了中国挑战尖端、以创新推动发展的新时代。今天，当我们回顾改革开放30年沧桑巨变时，会发现“863”为中国带来了翻天覆地的变化。

中国软件业真正的从启蒙到最初的繁荣，是在改革开放后的第十年。1988年，当邓小平提出“科学技术是第一生产力”的时候，正式明确了科学在当时中国发展过程中的重要位置。自此以后，中国软件业遍地开花，迎来了为之骄傲的软件英雄时代。

在改革开放前十年当中，深圳作为最具有代表性的城市，从一个无名小渔村迅速发展成为现代化都市，成为中国改革开放的“排头兵”。当求伯君在1986年只身来到深圳时，深圳的高速发展令他大为震动，求伯君毅然决定从单位辞职，去开辟自己的新天地。1988年，求伯君来到深圳，在张旋龙的帮助下开始研发中国首款字处理软件WPS，金山软件的历史就此展开。

在改革开放前十年当中，除了求伯君之外，还诞生了许多在中国软件史上有筚路蓝缕之功的软件英雄。比如严援朝在1983年推出CCDOS，走出了中文操作系统的关键一步；王永民在1983年发明“五笔字型”，专家称“其意义不亚于活字印刷术”；吴晓军41岁在1988年将CCDOS汉字系统升级到了2.13E版；“杀毒软件之父”王江民于1989年推出杀毒软件KV6；周志农在1988年设计完成《自然码汉字输入系统》；朱崇君在1988年首创中文字表编辑概念，推出CCED2.0版……

受惠于改革开放，中国软件产业在1988年前后迎来最初的繁荣期。许多软件作者成为当时的明星人物，也激励了雷军、鲍岳桥、王志东等正在大学读书的学子们成为后起之秀。而中国软件产业也即将迎来百花齐放的历史时期。

软件市场内忧外患，最初繁荣后的低谷（1988-1998年）

改革开放第二个十年中，尽管既有盗版又有国际巨头的压迫，但中国软件仍然经历了历史上第一个繁荣时期。

电脑在中国的普及首先遇到的基本问题，就是如何让英文操作系统更好地接纳中文。各种中文DOS操作系统努力打造中文操作环境，WPS等办公软件解决了中文排版的问题，而形形色色的输入法为汉字录入提供了解决方案——这些基础软件为在电脑上使用中文奠定了根基。

在中文平台方面，1991 年，离开方正的王志东开发出了中文之星；1992 年，鲍岳桥开始研发 UCDOS。据不完全统计，国内自行开发的 DOS 系统有几十种，其中 UCDOS、金山 SPDOS、CCDOS、天汇、中国龙、超想、联想、晓军系统占有一定市场。中文 Windows 平台的开发厂家也有 20 余家，其中以中文之星、中文大师、RICHWIN、UCWIN、CLEEX 中文 X 窗口为最有名，但面临着 Microsoft 的 PWIN 的挑战。

在办公软件方面，各软件厂商开发出了 WPS、巨人汉卡、王码 480、CCED、联想汉卡等 20 多种字处理软件。此外还有 500 多种编码方法，在计算机上实现的有 50 多种，在市场广为流行的有 20 多种。而在这诸多中文字处理软件当中，最为有名、市场占有率超过 90% 的是金山 WPS。1989 年，求伯君在深圳蔡屋围酒店 501 室闭关 14 个月之后，终于写就了 WPS1.0，这是中国软件史上的第一款中文字处理软件。当时，社会上各种电脑培训班的主要课程除了五笔字型输入法就是 WPS 操作，WPS 成为中国第一代电脑使用者的启蒙软件，求伯君也因此成为中国程序员的偶像。

在输入法方面，由于五笔字型强背字根、入门难的问题，1991 年由长城集团与北京大学合作推出了智能 ABC 汉字输入法。这种输入法入门轻松，只要会拼音就能上手，而且带有简单的联想和记忆功能，很快得到了初级用户的喜爱。随着 Windows 的普及，微软拼音、全拼、郑码等输入法也为不同的用户群体所使用。

在杀毒软件方面，1989 年由公安部病毒研究小组推出的、中国最早的杀毒软件 Kill 在 90 年代早期曾经一统天下。1990 年，深圳华星推出了华星防病毒卡，这也是世界上最早的一块防毒卡。到 1992 年前后，市面上开始流行的防病毒卡多达五六十种，在 90 年代初成为重要的防病毒工具。但它的致命缺陷是不能清除病毒，在安装和升级方面有诸多不便。随着江民、瑞星、金山、交大铭泰等国内杀毒软件厂商的出现，国产杀毒软件把持了大部分市场。

在各种软件百花齐放的 90 年代，不得不提的还有盗版。1994 年前后，随着 CD-ROM 和光盘的普及，盗版软件迅速成为破坏软件产业健康发展的毒瘤。而对于刚刚改革开放仅十余年口袋还很瘪的中国民众来说，动辄高达千元的软件和仅几块钱的盗版软件，大家更愿意选择后者。盗版的泛滥，更加加速了中国软件行业的洗牌。许多软件公司在无法获得合理利润的情况下，被迫倒闭或转型。在日后的采访中有记者问是微软还是盗版对金山的影响更大时，求伯君说："盗版猛于微软。在DOS时代尽管WPS几乎占据了100%的字处理软件市场，但由于盗版金山几乎赚不到多少钱，也就没有更多资金投入研发。"

在盗版之外，国外软件巨头也将触角伸向了中国。面对微软、赛门铁克、趋势等国际软件企业，刚刚萌芽的中国民族软件企业并不是对手。盗版与国际巨头的压迫，中国软件企业在经历了最初的繁荣之后黯然转身而去，像金山一样存活下来的软件企业寥寥无几。

在盗版和微软的双重冲击下，一直背负民族软件大旗的金山软件也经历了最为黑暗的时代，一度曾经濒临倒闭。而在此时，金山在不放弃WPS的前提下，制定了"以战养战"的发展策略，开始开发金山词霸、金山影霸、金山毒霸、金山单词通、金山打字通、金山游侠、剑侠情缘等软件——他们在金山历史上的意义在于让金山在绝境之中存活了下来，也才有了后来绝地 反攻的机会。而1995年金山西山居工作室的成立与《剑侠情缘》系列单机游戏的推出，为金山在随后的互联网时代进军网游埋下了伏笔。

在20世纪90年代，中国通用软件产业经历了历史上第一个繁荣时期，也为电脑在中国的普及奠定了基础。而随着盗版的日益猖獗以及国外软件巨头的入侵，国产软件失去了最初的辉煌，在黯然神伤之中唯有韬光养晦，寻求再度崛起的机会。

90年代末期，中国互联网开始萌芽。从1994年中国正式接入国际互联网，到作为网络时代标志的瀛海威时空的成立，再到中国计算机公用互联网CHINANET建成，以互联网为契机的中国软件业正在迎来新的曙光。

互联网蓬勃发展，中国软件迎来复兴（1998-2008年）

时光进入21世纪，随着改革开放浪潮的逐步推进，中国软件业迎来了新的曙光，并开始呈现复兴的迹象：2000年，中国内地第一款网络游戏运营，数字娱乐产业崛起；2001年，中国成功加入WTO，自此中国正式获得和国际市场对话的权利；2002年，全面建设小康社会成为改革的核心，同年博客进入中国，互联网春天来临；2000年左右以新浪、腾讯、网易等为代表的互联网公司先后在国际市场上市，以中国概念股的姿态夺得了资本市场的认可；同样在2000年，金山创办了电子商务网站卓越网，电子商务成为互联网主流商业模式。改革开放的第三个十年，中国经济的高速发展得到了世界的认可，而以互联网为平台的中国软件业也开始迎来历史上的第二次繁荣。以网游为代表的娱乐软件、各种工具软件、针对互联网安全的杀毒软件、以在线办公为趋势的办公软件等成为当前时代的热点应用，许多新兴公司纷纷诞生。

2001年，随着盛大、九城等游戏厂商在游戏行业中获得高额回报，也让网络游戏成为继门户网站后的另一巨大金矿，诸多具备实力的软件厂商也加入到网游行列。2003年开始，金山正式进军网络游戏行业，2003年，金山携《剑侠情缘》以中华武侠文化与自主研发为特色，强势进军网游市场。与此同时，中华网、搜狐、完美时空、腾讯、网易等都推出了各自的网游作品，网游产业成为中国软件产业中最具活力的部分。

互联网的兴起给传统软件也带来了新的发展机遇。在杀毒软件方面，金山毒霸在营销推广与产品功能上和互联网充分结合，率先实施“软件免费、服务有偿”的营销策略，并力推实时升级服务和互联网安全功能；在杀毒软件免费趋势之下，金山毒霸也正在做前沿尝试。在办公软件方面，WPS2005年把体积做到了15M，网络下载和传播快捷迅速，并以其个人版免费试用的策略，稳居国产办公软件第一的宝座；在网络在线办公探索方面，WPS也已开始实践；在词典软件方面，占92.8%市场份额的金山词霸在2005年创建了爱词霸英语学习社区，迅速聚集了数百万用户在这个平台上学习交流，为金山词霸彻底转型互联网提供了绝佳平台。

2004年以来，由于改革开放带动经济快速增长，中国迅速成为了世界第四大经济实体。中国的软件产业也迎来了高速发展的时期，进军海外市场成为中国民族软件复兴的必经之路。2006年《人民日报》发表评论“一个志在伟大复兴的民族必须坚持科学发展，一个坚持改革开放的大国理当对世界有新贡献。”

在韩国网游作品带动中国网游市场繁荣之后，国产原创网游在市场中逐步得到玩家认可，并开始走向世界。以金山、完美时空等为代表的国产网游厂商坚持中华文化根基、坚持自主研发，生产了一大批优秀的网游作品。在国际化拓展上，金山软件是典型代表。从2004年开始，金山陆续在台湾、马来西亚、日本、越南等海外市场攻城略地，积极探索中国软件国际化之路。2005年，金山网游横扫越南80%市场份额，中国武侠文化风靡东南亚。截至2007年，中国共有12家游戏企业涉足海外市场，有多款原创游戏进入北美、欧洲、韩国、日本等20多个国家和地区的市场。

在网游之外的通用软件出口方面，不仅有中软等外包企业享誉世界，中国自主研发的软件也已经得到了世界用户的认可。2005年，金山在日本成立合资公司，将金山WPS、金山毒霸输出到日本；2008年，金山又在越南成立合资公司，负责通用软件产品的分销。

与走向世界相对应，盛大、九城、完美时空、中软等中国软件企业纷纷到美国、香港等地上市，借助国际资本力量发展民族软件。2007 年，金山软件在香港主版成功上市，为金山加速国际化拓展提供了资金准备。2008 年，中国的改革开放 30 年所取得的骄人成绩让世人惊叹。而中国软件在经历了 30 年发展之后也迎来了历史上的又一次繁荣，并正在让世界看到中国“智造”的魅力。此刻，中国软件正站在一个新的历史起点上，以脚踏实地的努力展望更美好的明天。我们相信，中国软件产业必将在改革开放的下一个 10 年中诞生世界一流的软件企业。

软件业发展现状

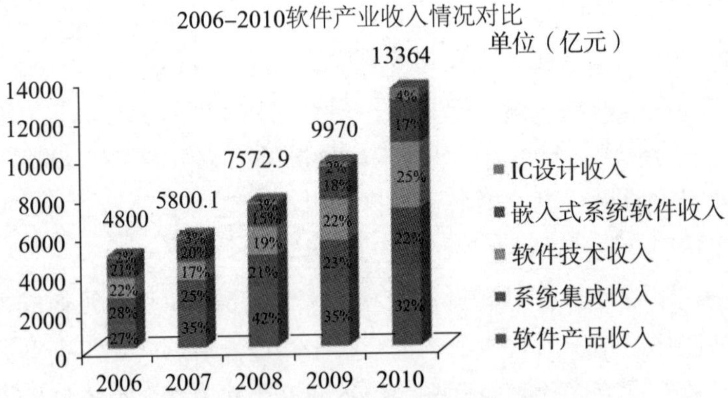

图 10 软件产业收入情况对比（数据来源：工信部）

以上数据可以看出近几年来我国软件业的持续稳步增长。收入情况对比中可以看出：份额占据最大的是软件产品收入，尤其是在 2008 年，占据了高达 42% 的份额。至 2010 年有所下降。其次依次是比例相当的系统集成收入软件技术收入、嵌入式系统软件收入。份额最小的是 IC 设计收入，仅仅占据了 4%，但是，较前几年有增长趋势。嵌入式系统收入在 2010 年占据了 17% 的份额，较前几年有下降趋势。来自工信部的报告：2010 年我国软件业实现新的突破，产业增速稳步回升，业务结构调整加快，企业发展和区域布局出现新的特点，在国民经济中的地位不断提升。目前，我国软件业呈现如下特点[13]：

收入规模突破万亿，产业地位稳步提升。2010 年，实现软件业务收

⑬ 2010 年全国软件业务收入达到 1.3 万亿元 . 中华人民共和国工信部 . http://www.miit.gov.cn/n11293472/n11293832/n11294132/n12858477/13583251.html [2012-02-12]

入 13364 亿元，同比增长 31%，产业规模比 2001 年扩大十几倍，年均增长 38%，占电子信息产业的比重由 2001 年的 6% 上升到 18%。在全球软件与信息服务业中，所占份额由不足 5%，上升到超过 15%。软件业增加值占 GDP 的比重由 2001 年不足 0.3% 上升到超过 1%，软件业从业人数由不足 30 万人提高到超过 200 万人，对社会生活和生产各个领域的渗透和带动力不断增强。

增速高位趋缓，产业步入发展新阶段。“十五”期间，我国软件产业业务收入平均增速为 47%，“十一五”平均增速为 28%，收入增速有所趋缓，软件产业开始从高速增长转入相对平稳的新阶段。但 2010 年收入增长明显快于 2009 年，增速提高 5.4 个百分点，且一至四季度软件业务收入分别为 2573、3475、3634 和 3682 亿元，增长 25.7%、31.8%、32.3% 和 34%，收入数和增速呈逐季上升态势。

业务结构调整加快，服务化趋势更加突出。服务收入增长带动软件业务调整，特别是与网络相关的信息服务发展迅速。2010 年，信息技术咨询服务和信息技术增值服务收入分别为 1233 和 2178 亿元，同比增长 37.2% 和 44.6%，高于全行业 5.9 和个 13.3 百分点，两者收入占全行业比重达 25.5%，比 2001 年提高 18.9 个百分点。软件产品收入 4208 亿元，同比增长 28.6%; 嵌入式系统软件受通信类产品增长放缓影响，完成收入 2242 亿元，同比增长 15.1%，低于全行业 16.2 个百分点。受集成电路行业复苏和软件外包市场增长带动，设计开发实现收入 593 亿元，同比增长 73.1%; 系统集成和支持服务实现收入 2910 亿元，同比增长 31.8%。

区域分布呈现分散集中格局，中心城市成为行业发展聚集点。软件产业发展聚集趋势从过去主要集中在京粤地区转向沿海地区。2010 年，东部地区完成软件业务收入 11449 亿元，同比增长 31.8%，除京粤两地外沿海多个省市均呈现快速发展势头，江苏、辽宁、福建、山东四省软件收入增长超过 35%，占全国比重比 2001 年提高了 13.4、3.8、3.1 和 1.5 个百分点，合计占比达 35%，逐步打破过去京粤两地占全国一半以上的集中局面 (两地占比下降为 35.5%)。中心城市成为软件产业发展的主要聚集地，2010 年全国 4 个直辖市和 15 个副省级城市软件收入 10643 亿元，同比增长 32%，占全国的比重为 80%，增长快于全国平均水平 1 个百分点。在中西部地区中心城市地位更为突出，成都、西安、重庆三个城市占西部地区的 90%，武汉、长春两个城市占中部地区 30% 以上。

重点企业平稳发展，行业创新进展明显。2010 年，工信部重点监测的软件前百家企业累计完成软件业务收入 2900 亿元，同比增长 21%，占全国收入的 21.7%；实现利润 553 亿元，同比增长 13%。其中软件业务收入超百亿元的企业达到 4 家，比去年又增加 1 家。企业创新成效显著，据中国版权保护中心数据显示，2010 年全国计算机软件著作权登记量突破 8 万件，“十一五”期间登记量翻了两番，平均增速达 37%，华为、中兴等企业名列前位。同时，在 2010 年度国家科技进步奖评审中，中控科技、华为、中兴、恒生电子、信雅达等多家软件企业获得科技进步二等奖。

从上面可以看出，在过去的 30 多年的历程中，中国的软件经历了一个从无到有的过程，在中国政府的各种优惠政策下，在国际上激烈的竞争环境下，中国软件业经历了一个艰难曲折的成长历程。不过，迄今为止，中国软件业已经有了较快较长足的发展，已经初具规模，并且在不断地创造出我们自己的特色。

5 电子政务

自改革开放以来，中国政府信息化建设经历了 3 个重要阶段⑭。

第一阶段是从 1984 年到 1992 年的国家经济信息主干系统初创阶段。1983 年 10 月，国务院批准组建了国家计委经济信息办公室。1986 年 2 月 20 日国务院决定由国家计委有关方面负责人组成国家经济信息管理领导小组。次年 5 月，经国务院批准正式成立国家经济信息中心。到 1990 年底初步形成了覆盖全国的四级国家经济信息系统体系。在重点建设国家经济主系统的同时，从 1984 年到 1990 年，国务院先后批准了经济、金融、铁道、电力、民航、财税、海关、气象、灾害防御等 10 多个国家级信息系统的建设。在此期间，有 43 个部门（局，总公司）先后成立了信息机构。

第二阶段是从 1993 年到 2000 年以“金”字工程和“政府上网”工程为代表的发展阶段。1993 年底，国务院正式成立了国民经济信息化联席会议，部署了“金桥”“金卡”“金关”等重大信息系统工程，并将其列入过国家中长期发展规划。1996 年 1 月，国务院成立了国务院信息化领导小组，统一领导和组织协调全国的信息化工作。

第三阶段是从 2000 年到 2006 年的网络应用快速发展阶段。2000 年 10 月，“十五”规划把推进国民经济和社会发展信息化放在优先位置。截至 2006 年

---

⑭ CNNIC. 中国互联网发展报告 .2002 ：275.

6月，使用“.gov.cn”域名的政府网站就有近1.2万个[15]。2006年信息化建设的特点表现在，积极推进政府门户网站和应急系统两大方面的建设，政府网站体系基本健全，促进信息资源共享，助力新农村建设落到实处，强化公共服务建成热潮。到2006年，政府行业已经基本告别单机应用和局部信息系统应用阶段，仅有17.1%的中国政府机构仍处于单机应用阶段，43.4%的政府机构处于局部应用阶段；更多政府机构随着深入应用而进入到整合阶段，21.1%的政府机构信息化处于信息系统整合阶段；并有13.3%的政府机构开始IT和业务整合，以及与之相对应的政府流程再造；只有5.1%的政府机构处于电子政务成熟阶段。

就目前情况来看，到2010年12月使用“.gov.cn”域名的政府网站就达5.2万个[16]。2010年政府在线服务整体水平提高，资源整合工作进一步开展。各级政府网站在公开政府信息，提供行政办事服务和便民服务，开展网上互动交流方面有一定程度的改善和提升，用户满意度上升。

据中国软件测评中心发布的“2010年中国网站绩效评估结果”显示，各部委网站普遍有所改善，但在线办事、互动水平明显存在差距。省市县政府网站呈现由高到低的“阶梯式”发展，数据显示65%省级网站在教育和社保等领域能够搭建网上服务框架，并提供一览表、政策解读、办事指南等服务资源，网上互动渠道建设和互动效果较好，信息公开水平也明显提高；而大部分区县政府网站在教育、社保、就业、医疗、住房和交通等重点民生领域服务内容很少，资源也比较分散，对公众“有帮助”的服务不全面，对公众“有用”的信息更新不够及时。

可以看出，中国电子政务，经历了比较明显的三个阶段的发展，已经具有了一定的服务水平。但是，我们也应该看到其与美国、加拿大、澳大利亚的电子政务水平仍有很大的差异，尤其表现在网站布局及服务水平上。中国电子政务的发展，喜忧参半。喜在于这么多年，其一直都在不断努力和发展过程中；忧则表现在很多地方政府网站不兼容，服务水平、效率仍然比较低。

⑮ CNNIC. 中国互联网发展报告2006：15.

⑯ CNNIC. 中国互联网发展报告2011：252.

6 电子商务

交易额持续快速增长[17]。据商务部统计，2000年我国电子商务交易总额仅有771.6亿元，到2005年（“十五”期末）已迅速增至6785亿元。“十一五”期间，我国电子商务事业迅猛发展，自2006年突破亿万元大关以来，电子商务交易总额每年以高于70%的速度持续增长，2010年我国电子商务交易总额达到4.5亿元，全社会电子商务交易额占社会总零售商品总额的3%。网购注册用户已达1.6亿，电子商务发展环境、支撑体系、技术服务和推广应用协调发展的格局基本形成，电子商务已成为重要的新兴产业，国民经济和社会发展各领域电子商务应用水平大幅提高，并取得明显成效。

各类交易模式均快速增长。2009年11月，商务部发布了《关于加快流通领域电子商务的发展意见》，明确了未来政府部门对电子商务的引导、扶持措施。据CNZZ数据中心的调查数据显示，2009年底，电子商务的总网站数达到1.56万家，同比增长了32.34%。电子商务网站的受众范围在不断扩展，2010年国内网上零售的用户规模达1.58亿人。预计未来几年，这一规模仍将迅速持续上升。

7 互联网治理的原则与实践[18]

中国坚持依法管理、科学管理和有效管理互联网，努力完善法律规范、行政监管、行业自律、技术保障、公众监督和社会教育相结合的互联网管理体系。中国管理互联网的基本目标是促进互联网的普遍、无障碍接入和持续健康发展，依法保障公民网上言论自由，规范互联网信息传播秩序，推动互联网积极有效应用，创造有利于公平竞争的市场环境，保障宪法和法律赋予的公民权益，保障网络信息安全和国家安全。

中国依法管理互联网。1994年以来，中国颁布了一系列与互联网管理相关的法律法规，主要包括《全国人民代表大会常务委员会关于维护互联网安全的决定》《中华人民共和国电子签名法》《中华人民共和国电信条例》《互联网信息服务管理办法》《中华人民共和国计算机信息系统安全保护条例》《信息网络传播权保护条例》《外商投资电信企业管理规定》《计算机信息网络国际联网安全保护管理办法》《互联网新闻信息服务管理规定》《互联网电子公

⑰ 中国信息化发展指数统计监测年度报告 [R].2011.

⑱ 国务院新闻办公室.《中国互联网状况》白皮书. 2010年6月8日.

告服务管理规定》等。《中华人民共和国刑法》《中华人民共和国民法通则》《中华人民共和国著作权法》《中华人民共和国未成年人保护法》《中华人民共和国治安管理处罚条例》等法律的相关条款适用于互联网管理。中国坚持审慎立法、科学立法，为互联网发展预留空间。相关法律法规涉及互联网基础资源管理、信息传播规范、信息安全保障等主要方面，对基础电信业务经营者、互联网接入服务提供者、互联网信息服务提供者、政府管理部门及互联网用户等行为主体的责任与义务作出了规定。法律保障公民的通信自由和通信秘密，同时规定，公民在行使自由和权利的时候，不得损害国家、社会、集体的利益和其他公民的合法的自由和权利，任何组织或个人不得利用电信网络从事危害国家安全、社会公共利益或者他人合法权益的活动。

中国政府在互联网管理中发挥主导作用。政府有关部门根据法定职责，依法维护公民权益、公共利益和国家安全。国家通信管理部门负责互联网行业管理，包括对中国境内互联网域名、IP 地址等互联网基础资源的管理。依据《互联网信息服务管理办法》，中国对经营性互联网信息服务实行许可制度，对非经营性互联网信息服务实行备案制度。国家新闻、出版、教育、卫生等部门依据《互联网信息服务管理办法》，对“从事新闻、出版、教育、医疗保健、药品和医疗器械等互联网信息服务”实行许可制度。公安机关等国家执法部门负责互联网安全监督管理，依法查处打击各类网络违法犯罪活动。

中国积极倡导行业自律和公众监督。2001 年 5 月，中国互联网协会成立，这是全国性互联网行业组织，其宗旨是服务于互联网行业发展、网民和政府的决策。该协会先后制定并发布了《中国互联网行业自律公约》《互联网站禁止传播淫秽色情等不良信息自律规范》《抵制恶意软件自律公约》《博客服务自律公约》《反网络病毒自律公约》《中国互联网行业版权自律宣言》等一系列自律规范，促进了互联网的健康发展。中国互联网协会为治理垃圾邮件作出了不懈努力，使中国的垃圾邮件占全球垃圾邮件的比例从 2002 年的 23% 下降到 2009 年的 4.1%。为加强公众对互联网服务的监督，2004 年以来，中国先后成立了互联网违法和不良信息举报中心、网络违法犯罪举报网站、12321 网络不良与垃圾信息举报受理中心、12390 扫黄打非新闻出版版权联合举报中心等公众举报受理机构，并于 2010 年 1 月发布了《举报互联网和手机媒体淫秽色情及低俗信息奖励办法》。中国政府将进一步支持互联网行业组织的工作，为行业组织发挥作用提供服务，并依法保障公众举报网上违法信息和行为的正当权利。

中国主张合理运用技术手段遏制互联网上违法信息传播。根据互联网的特性，从有效管理互联网的实际需要出发，中国政府主张依据相关法律法规，参照国际通行做法，发挥技术手段的防范作用，遏制违法信息对国家安全、社会公共利益和未成年人的危害。《全国人民代表大会常务委员会关于维护互联网安全的决定》《中华人民共和国电信条例》《互联网信息服务管理办法》《计算机信息网络国际联网安全保护管理办法》等法律法规明确规定，严禁传播含有颠覆国家政权、破坏国家统一、损害国家荣誉和利益、煽动民族仇恨、破坏民族团结、宣扬邪教以及淫秽色情、暴力、恐怖及侵害他人合法权益等内容的信息。根据这些法律法规，基础电信业务经营者、互联网信息服务提供者等应建立互联网安全管理制度，采取技术措施，阻止各类违法信息的传播。

中国主张加强互联网法制和道德教育。全社会的法制和道德素养关系互联网环境建设。中国政府支持开展互联网法制和道德教育工作，鼓励各类媒体和社会组织积极参与，积极推动把互联网法制和道德教育纳入中小学日常教学内容。中国政府十分重视青年组织、妇女组织等在提高全民网络素养中的作用，鼓励相关组织开展有利于普及互联网知识和正确使用互联网的公益活动。

中国确保未成年人上网安全。未成年人已成为中国网民的最大群体，截至 2009 年底，中国 3.84 亿网民中，未成年人约占 1/3，互联网对未成年人成长的影响越来越大。同时，网络淫秽色情等违法和有害信息严重危害青少年的身心健康，成为社会普遍关注的突出问题。中国政府高度重视依法保护未成年人上网安全，始终把保护未成年人放在维护互联网信息安全的优先地位。《中华人民共和国未成年人保护法》规定，国家采取措施，预防未成年人沉迷网络；禁止任何组织、个人制作或者向未成年人出售、出租或者以其他方式传播淫秽、暴力、凶杀、恐怖、赌博等毒害未成年人的电子出版物以及网络信息等。国家鼓励研究开发有利于保护未成年人上网安全的网络工具，鼓励提供适合未成年人的网络产品和服务。保护未成年人上网安全，家庭、学校和社会各界应共同努力，营造有利于未成年人健康成长的网络环境。中国政府将积极推进“母亲教育计划”，帮助家长引导未成年人正确使用互联网。

中国积极保护数字知识产权。2000 年以来，中国修订了《中华人民共和国著作权法》，制定了《互联网著作权行政保护办法》，以及审理涉及计算机网络著作权纠纷案件的相关司法解释，为保护数字知识产权提供了基本法律依据。国家著作权行政管理部门负责查处互联网侵权盗版行为。针对反复侵权、群体性侵权以及大规模假冒、盗版等行为，政府有关部门联合开展了一系列管理行动。中国将继续探索互联网环境下的知识产权保护工作，努力实现保障公共利益和促进创新之间的平衡。

中国依法保护公民网上隐私。保护互联网上的个人隐私关系到人们对互联网的安全感和信心。中国政府积极推动健全相关立法和互联网企业服务规范，不断完善公民网上个人隐私保护体系。《全国人民代表大会常务委员会关于维护互联网安全的决定》规定，非法截获、篡改、删除他人邮件或其他数据资料，侵犯公民通信自由和通信秘密，构成犯罪的，依照刑法有关规定追究刑事责任。依据互联网行业自律规范，互联网服务提供者有责任保护用户隐私，在提供服务时应公布相关隐私保护承诺，提供侵害隐私举报受理渠道，采取有效措施保护个人隐私。

中国政府积极探索依法管理、科学管理、有效管理互联网的途径和方法，已初步形成符合中国国情、符合国际通行做法的互联网管理模式。互联网管理是一个不断实践的过程，中国政府将在实践中进一步完善互联网管理。

8 小结

综上所言，中国互联网的发展，包括软件、硬件、科研、市场、商家、政府等各个方面都经历了一个从无到有并且飞速发展的过程。在这个过程中，其不断探索，借鉴着国外的技术优势，同时依赖自己的人才优势和人口优势，在取得突破之后快速发展。

中国互联网行业虽然一直在前进，但是其由于起步比较晚，底子比较薄，在不断发展之后，与发达国家相比仍然存在着很多的缺陷和不足。在这种情况下，我们仍然在积极地改变和完善自己。作为一个中国人，我们为中国互联网的发展速度和成绩感到由衷的骄傲。

17

中国新兴公益组织对信息社会和公益信息制度的前景预测 (2009)

——一项针对四个公益组织的民族志未来研究

闫 慧

Looking to 2035 Using Ethnographic Futures Research: The Non-Profit Information Institution in the Information Society (2009)

Yan Hui

Abstract

This chapter reports ethnographic futures research on the non-profit information institution in the information society. Leaders of four grassroots organizations look to the year 2035 and outline their optimistic, pessimistic, and most probable scenarios for Chinese society, their organizations, and themselves. The four organizations are 1KG.org, China Rural Library, Technology and Education: Connecting Cultures at Peking University, and the Senior Citizens Self-help Cooperative. They describe a more equitable, inclusive and ubiquitous information society and a larger free information space for grassroots organizations to serve the disadvantaged as the optimistic scenarios. However, they feel anxious about the widening digital gap in Chinese information society and the worsening conditions for grassroots organizations. They are considering becoming more open virtual pipelines between the digital rich and the digital poor communities, urban communities and rural communities, and a driving force for the non-profit sector itself. They also propose some feasible actions for non-profit information institution in China.

研究设计

概念界定

新兴公益组织是新时期发展起来的以公益服务为使命，不以营利为目的，帮助特定的群体解决教育、文化、健康等各类难题的第三方组织，大部分公益组织也被称作非营利组织、非政府组织等，这类组织大部分是由“民间社会自动发起的执行各类社会服务功能的社会组织，且所执行的功能与我们的官办事业单位大致相同”①。其本质特征是组织化、自治性、志愿性、非营利性、非分配约束、公益性或共益性。常见的公益组织类型包括健康保健、教育、社会与法律服务、公民组织、艺术与文化组织、研究机构、基金中介类组织如基金会等，以及民间环境保护组织等②。

公益信息制度是信息通讯技术和信息内容在市场领域和政府领域之外的“第三次”分配规则和机制③，主要由“第三方组织”，即公益组织（也称为非营利组织，NPO或非政府组，NGO）来完成信息通讯技术和信息内容的公益配置，是为了约束公益信息领域各个主体（包括政府、公益信息组织、相关企业、数字贫困社群等）行为和交互关系的一系列规则。笔者所构建的中国公益信息制度结构如图1所示。

研究对象

在中国，常见的公益组织主要有民政部门登记注册的民间组织（包括社会团体、民办非企业单位、基金会等）、工商注册的非营利组织、城市社区基层组织、单位挂靠社团、农村社区发展组织、农民经济合作组织、农村社区

① 陶传进．社会公益供给——NPO、公共部门与市场[M]. 北京：清华大学出版社，2005: 8.

② Frumkin Peter. Transparent nonprofit[J]. The public interest, 2001（142）: 83–94.

③ 赖茂生．信息制度建设——情报学的新课题．2009北京大学情报学与信息管理论坛．北京，2009年5月9-10日[C]. 北京：北京大学信息管理系，2009.

的其他公益或互益组织、海外在华资助组织、海外在华项目组织、海外在华商会、行业协会、宗教社团等[④]。本研究所涉及的新兴公益组织主要是从事教育公益事业、老年人公益事业的组织，即为笔者识别出的数字贫困社群提供公益服务的机构。

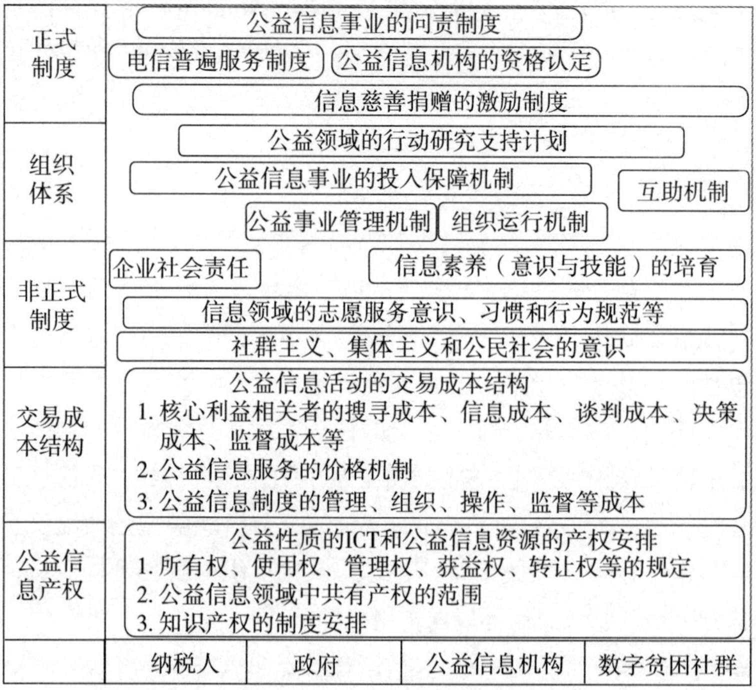

图1 中国公益信息制度架构图

笔者选取4个新兴公益组织作为未来研究的访谈目标。“多背一公斤”是为愿意从事公益旅行的个人提供网络公益社区的公益组织，“主张一种平等交流、快乐行动的价值观，它相信每一个乡村孩子都是快乐和有天赋的，公益行动是一种相互的分享和交流而非单方面的同情和给予”，“提倡自助精神，鼓励参与者的自发行动。在多背一公斤里，参与者不是某个机构下面的志愿者，而是公益的主人，自2004年4月成立以来，多背一公斤的参与者共发掘整理了超过700所乡村学校的详细信息，据不完全统计，有近万人次参与了‘多背一公斤’的活动实践，间接影响人群保守估计已超过百万”[⑤]，属于工商

④ 王名. NGO研究丛书总序 [M]/ 社会公益供给：NPO、公共部门与市场 [M]. 北京：清华大学出版社，2005: 1–21.

⑤ 爱聚（北京）咨询有限公司. 关于多背一公斤 [EB/OL]. [2009-12-07]. http://www.1kg.org/misc/about.

注册的非营利组织。

立人乡村图书馆是2007年9月由民间发起的一种乡村教育行动，旨在“以图书为载体，以教育为内容，立足乡村，连接城市，推广国民阅读，促进乡村教育革新”，到目前为止，该组织已在湖北黄冈、河南信阳、四川巴中等地开办了4个分馆，办理借书证近千个，邀请访问学者，举行各类文化和知识讲座。除此之外，该组织还为乡村提供“乡村电影院”、就业培训、养老金试点、小额贷款等服务项目，以及在征文比赛、开发乡土教材、奖助学金、国际交流、教师培训等方面推动乡村教育改革，并为学者和青年志愿者进行文化传播和交流提供机会。

“跨越太平洋的握手”（Technology & Education: Connecting Cultures，TECC）是2004年由清华大学和斯坦福大学的几名学生合作创立的国际非营利性组织，其宗旨是依靠有社会责任感的青年学生和国际合作来推动中国中西部落后地区社会科技教育和文化事业的发展，该组织的目标是举办创新性的科教活动，让科技和教育为人们创造机遇，帮助人们跨越数字化鸿沟；建立一个具备社会意识的中国人和美国人组成的跨洋网络，促进社会的创新和协作；增进中美两国人民的相互理解和文化交流；培养将来社会活动领域的领导者等。目前在国内注册为学生社会团体，由北京大学、清华大学、复旦大学、上海交通大学、香港大学、香港中文大学等学校分别进行管理。该组织曾经为多个贫困地区如四川江油和青川、江西向塘、青海大通、甘肃民勤和泾川、安徽芜湖和云南等地的高中老师提供计算机技能培训。

乐龄合作社是由志愿者发起的一个中国民间草根公益机构，旨在“集合社会各界力量，扎根草根社区，致力于提高和改善老年弱势群体和其他弱势群体的生活质量，实现社区的综合发展”；组织目标则是“实现老有所养，实践符合东方传统文化适合中国国情的社区居家养老模式”[⑥]；具体的服务项目包括：为老年人家庭提供日常服务、电器维修等上门服务；发动社区互助组，进行技能培训，支持贫困老年人开发手工艺品，帮助她们改善生活质量；建立社区乐龄会所，支持社区老年人成立唱歌、编制、聊天、保健、棋牌5个兴趣小组，实行自我管理，并为老年贫困妇女提供小额资金资助。

这4个公益组织能够比较客观地反映当前中国社会的草根公益力量，他们对中国未来信息社会和公益信息制度的观点和看法较好地代表着该领域的

---

⑥ 乐龄合作社. 关于我们 [EB/OL]. [2009-12-08]. http://www.seniorcitizen.org.cn/us.html.

声音。

研究方法

民族志未来研究方法（Ethnographic Futures Research, 简称 EFR）由美国斯坦福大学教授罗伯 特·特克斯特（Robert B. Textor）于 1976 年创造，包括该教授在内的一些人类学研究者发展起来的[⑦]，是“采用社会文化学的途径来抽取受访者对其社会及其文化可能出现的远景的感觉与偏好”[⑧]；EFR 是“文化未来研究者执行其任务的方法”，“这些研究者利用该方法从现存的社会群体中抽取出该群体对其未来文化的前景方案（scenario）以及偏好、认知与价值”[⑨]，这些远景方案包括乐观的远景（optimistic scenario）、悲观的远景（pessimistic scenario）和最有可能实现的远景（the most probable scenario）。另外，EFR 不仅关心受访者及其群体对远景方案的看法，更关心这些远景与现实之间的差距如何得到缩小甚至是消除，以及受访者对具体实现步骤的认识。从这个意义上看，EFR 不是传统的未来预测方法，而是一种旨在发现存在于社群成员头脑中文化未来景象的科学方法，以及激励社群成员主动参与到实现远景目标的全社会努力中的赋权（empowerment）过程。

EFR 的研究过程主要包括：研究者提出一个开放性的宽泛的领域，受访者根据自己的价值观和创造力描述自己想象中的最期待的乐观远景、最不期待的悲观远景，以及结合现实情况所认定的最有可能实现的远景，以及变化模型（change model），即从现在到达最有可能实现的未来的过程与路径；之后，研究者对受访者进行一些相对结构化的深度访谈，如对政策和政府的启示，以及对自身如何参与其中的启示等[⑩]。该方法采用一对一的访谈方式，样本量根据项目主题的大小而确定，其研究结果是“高度结构化、丰富且详细阐述的、基于情境的、有创造性的远景方案，甚至一些具体的行动计划”[⑪]。该

---

⑦ BELL W. Foundations of futures studies: human science for a new era[M]. New Brunswick: Transaction Publishers, 1997: 312–315.

⑧ TEXTOR R.B. The ethnographic futures research method: an application to Thailand[J]. Futures, 1995, 27(4): 461–471.

⑨ TEXTOR R.B. A handbook on ethnographic futures research (3rd edition)[M]. Standard: Cu1tural and Educational Futures Research Project, School of Education and Department of Anthropology, Stanford University, 1980: 9–14.

⑩ TEXTOR R.B. A handbook on ethnographic futures research (3rd edition)[M]. Standard: Cu1tural and Educational Futures Research Project, School of Education and Department of Anthropology, Stanford University, 1980: 44–62.

⑪ BELL W. Foundations of futures studies: human science for a new era[M]. New Brunswick: Transaction Publishers, 1997: 312–315.

研究设计的执行时间为2009年11月和12月初。

新兴公益组织对未来信息社会的预期

新兴公益组织的四位受访负责人分别预测了2035年中国信息社会的乐观前景、悲观前景以及极有可能出现的前景三种。他们所描绘的信息社会乐观前景的典型特征如下所述。

（1）信息社会全面覆盖到农村，且生活的数字化程度高

由于受访的3个公益组织都是关注农村问题的，故他们在预测中国未来发展方向时，首先是农村各个领域应用信息通讯技术的前景：包括贫困山区在内的农村将在2035年全面进入信息社会。“毫无疑问，信息化将覆盖到最偏僻的农村。（农村的数字贫困社群）完全与外界融为一体，信息的获取、沟通和传递实现了人与人之间的平等。至少每个人有一台电脑，随时可以上线，方便地搜索学习全世界的知识，与外界联系，与同龄人取得联系。而且虚拟社区会很成熟”，“农村与城市差20年，2035年的中国农村相当于2015年的城市”（受访者G语）。

农村的经济生产活动将非常依赖于信息通讯技术，“农业生产必须通过（信息通讯技术）终端，通过移动电话等（来实现有效管理）；25年后，通过移动终端做很多事情，如生计、播种、价格的查询，农产品的交易等”（G）。

农村及其他地区的生活数字化程度也非常高。“（农村地区的）每个人也能成为有知识、懂得获取信息并为之所用的社会主体”，“到时候老百姓可以利用网络开展电子商务的活动，不一定以此为主，但可以辅助日常生活”（受访者I语）。“到2035年，我们这一代人也就成了60多岁的老年人，电脑、互联网络将成为我们获取信息和与人沟通的主要方式”（受访者J语）。

（2）未来中国能够建成泛在网络社会，实现云计算

泛在网络社会理念对新兴公益组织来说也是具有强烈现实意义的，不仅改变他们对特殊人群的服务方式和途径，而且导致组织结构和运作产生剧烈的变化。“2035年，（立人乡村图书馆）分支机构的存在形式是肯定会随着社会信息化的发展发生剧烈发展；不再以纸质藏书为主，而是以电子信息的交互为主；图书馆提供的信息服务不仅仅是信息流通；服务形态会发生变化；估计到2035年电子工具三网合一的目标已经实现；一个手机不只是一个手机、只是一个接入的终端，终端可以做任何事情；（中国社会建成）无处不在的网络，（人们可以）随时随地获取信息，不仅是信息接收终端，同时也是信息制造的

主体”，“其实现在已经出现很多方面的征兆和端倪……未来立人图书馆是一个所谓的云计算和云服务的接入口，云包括所有信息的计算能力，以社会化和网络化的方式来完成。谁贡献了什么资源在宏观上看来是不清楚的，这种服务像电力和水一样可以通过标准化接口获取”（H）。

（3）直接服务乡村的公益信息组织成为自由信息空间的代表

立人乡村图书馆和 TECC 都关注农村地区的公共图书馆建设，以提高当地学生和农民的文化教育水平，他们均认为未来 2035 年中国乡村中小学教育将可能实现全面数字化，而他们参与建设的公共图书馆将成为自由信息和网络空间的一部分。“（立人乡村图书馆）首先提供一些开放性信息接口，至少像一个自由空间，可以随时接入网络，自由获取信息。同时还有我们推荐的精品信息；信息爆炸和信息海洋使得青少年不知道如何选择。我们在海量信息和对教育规律、青少年成长规律的认识基础上进行信息的整理；如果当地初中或高中有英语能力突出的学生，（提供条件）让他们直接阅读耶鲁、哈佛的信息资源；（学生可以在自由的信息空间中）自己学习；另外，我们会整理出一个基本的课程，包括历史、传播……可能我们把这些资源作为开放获取内容提供给各个社会组织和个人。总之，在对信息进行一定的组织后呈献给不太会选择的青年人”（H）。

“我希望（落后的农村地区）高中学校图书馆像美国、香港那样，建立信息共享区，目前即使在中国著名大学里也没有实现。信息素养方面，我特别希望那么大的孩子们都能获得许多网络信息，像沿海地区的孩子们一样从小接触计算机，浏览信息；知道外面世界是什么样子的；知道北京有什么；外国有什么？（这样他们才会）有学习的动力和改变命运的渴望和可能性；现在当地高中的学生们只会一味的学习，这种意识还不够，不了解世界同龄人是怎么生活，怎么思想的”，“公共图书馆提供上网电脑；在我们那里的公共图书馆，文化程度不高的人用得很少，我妈妈上学的时候特爱看书，但租书好贵，故只能放弃读书的意愿。公共图书馆门槛应该能降低一点，从而激发（读者）想阅读的欲望与查找信息的积极性”；“希望那个时候每个高中教师能有一台电脑，精通办公软件的基本操作，授课过程中灵活运用各种信息通讯技术实现教学目标”（I）。

除上述三种主要的乐观前景外，他们还提出一些对信息社会有直接影响的未来社会状态。首先，将来中国社会应该“有尊重知识产权的社会氛围，人们脑海中过于贪图‘免费的东西’的意识应该逐步摒弃掉，像美国那样保护电脑软件、图书等的知识产权”(I)。其次，城市化程度应该很高，“再过25年，农村的城市化缓慢发生，但至少往前推进（一步)，落后的农村会变成城镇，特别落后地区的农村经济发展会带来更多改变……乐观和悲观不是个人能够决定的，而且技术是中性的，但技术发展在特定利益集团（的操控下）能改变人与人之间的关系”(G)。再次，信息通讯技术的更迭换代也将为数字贫困社群带来更多的实惠，“手机（生产商）会有更多老年产品的开发活动，功能简单，显示字体大，而且电脑对老年人来说肯定成为必需品”(J)。

新兴公益组织的负责人代表所预测的中国未来2035年信息社会悲观前景主要有以下一些方面：

（1）信息社会分化现象更加严重

农村居民本来就是一个经济相对贫困、文化相对落后的群体。在新兴公益组织看来，如果社会各方采取的应对措施不得当、不及时，原有的贫困和与城镇居民的差距将进一步被拉大，而且在此基础上的信息财富分化状况将进一步恶化。受访者I根据个人从业经验认为“(极有可能城乡之间的）贫富差距进一步被拉大，那些贫困地区依然贫困；信息和网络技术需要物质条件和一定的生活水准。(这样的话可能会）拉大到一个很不能接受的地步。当地民众的最差情况是仍然很穷，(仍然为生计）奔波，更不可能查阅相关信息”。农村老年人也极易受到分化现象的负面影响，“从对老年人关注的角度来分析，可能由于政策不到位，很多老人会受到伤害和歧视。越来越多的老人在无意中受到不好的对待；大多数年轻人认为没有必要去关注老年人的生活……农村地区的老人自杀率很高，但整个社会（对他们）的关注度比较低，认可度也比较低”(J)，长此以往，数字化社会中的农村老年人只会更加落后于其他老年人，生活状态会更差。

（2）公益信息组织生存将更加困难

公共图书馆、从事公益信息事业的新兴公益组织等公益信息组织在新的经济和社会条件下将面临更多的发展瓶颈和政策障碍，尤其是新兴的公益组织对未来发展方向存在诸多疑惑和悲观情绪。如受访者H：“立人（到那个时候也许就）不存在了；即使存在，或许已经被边缘化了，不能发挥什么作用，已经偏离最初的教育探索和创新的基本定位；仅仅存在着的一个机构而已；存在方式可能是各种各样的形式，或者干脆被当地的政府部门接收或接管；原因可能就是立人（各项社会和物质）资源的匮乏以及募集能力的丧失。从今天到2035年（也许会）经历一个发展、兴盛和衰落的曲线。”

公益组织的受访者中还存在着对传统公益信息组织的不乐观情绪，比如"当地的公共图书馆也许会变得更加官僚、更加封闭，借书的门槛会变得很高；电脑都不能用。NGO 最不好的情况就是根本没法站起来，连现在都不如；人才补给不足，资金链断掉，运营无法维持。目前很多草根组织处在边缘状态。真不希望到那个时候 NGO 自身的决策行动遭到这么多障碍"（I）。

其他的悲观前景还有网络负面影响持续扩散，如"不希望贫困山区的学生继续两极分化，一些学生只去网吧打游戏，一些人只沉浸在书本中，只选择对高考志愿有用的信息"（I）；农村和少数民族地区成为另一个"非洲"，陷入极度贫困状态或者生态环境遭到破坏。

新兴公益组织的四位受访者代表在预测中国未来 2035 年最有可能出现的信息社会前景时，3 个受访者表现出了对未来诸多不确定性的担忧，以至于他们均给出了"无法预测极有可能的前景"，"（公益信息组织的）发展受限于太多现实因素，不是靠个别人来推动的，而是靠整个社会每个人来自觉推动的"（G）；"（对于 2035 年未来最有可能的信息社会前景）很难预测；其实我们都很难预测明年会发生什么。只需要脚踏实地、胸怀梦想，能够把正确事情的影响扩散出去（就是成功）。其实做一个十年规划都很难（更别提是 25 年规划）"（H）。

他们认为，在具体的数字化领域内也存在着很多积极的发展方向。信息通讯技术将赋予各类社群丰富的数字化生活机遇，"信息技术成为生存本能；从小六七岁就必须接触电脑和互联网……任何老人与亲人之间的联系都通过互联网络实现"（G）；"公共图书馆的公用电脑和互联网、聊天工具、搜索引擎等将在不同人群中得到普及"（I）。各级政府和社会力量给公益信息机构的支持力度将会越来越大，企业的社会责任感会普遍提升。

新兴公益组织对自身未来的期待

受访的四位新兴公益组织对组织自身的发展有许多丰富的、乐观的规划和期待，其中包括一些在公益信息服务方面的未来定位，这些也构成了他们组织的发展战略，是当前组织发展现状和优势的延续。

（1）数字富裕社群与数字贫困社群之间的虚拟平台和交流渠道。如"多背一公斤"组织的未来发展方向是"一个平台和渠道，我们努力建设一些联系，一个是城市志愿者与贫困乡村之间的联系，另一个是志愿者之间的联系。让有爱心的人参与进来，帮助一个乡村学校发生具体的改变。我们会做的是搭建网络平台，帮助搭建虚拟人际关系，而且将来搭建的虚拟社区会建立乡村学校网络，规模将超过 800 所；城市里有志愿者网络社区，同时还保持着城乡联系；志愿者是形象大使，向外争取资源。（这样一个网络平台将会是）高效运转的社区，比如跟一个网站合作，他们捐献 1 万只铅笔。同时（多背一公斤也是）一种交流渠道，让志愿者分发慈善物资；对志愿者来说也是一种激励，我们相当于把走访、执行和反馈工作交给志愿者"，"（我们还会去）乡村学校建立网络平台，不仅帮他们设计平台，而且还募集硬件捐赠者以及慈善资金。开放的平台才能让电脑硬件和互联网络的使用发挥最大价值"。

（2）城乡间的信息桥梁。"多背一公斤"组织也在策划一个手机服务平台。考虑到偏远农村地区的手机普及率远远高于电脑普及率，该组织将致力于在城市和乡村（尤其是贫困山区）之间搭建一种移动网络的交互机制，建设一个"WAP 网站，乡村老师只要能上网就可以登录网站，对应的乡村学校也就便成了活的信息（终端）。（这样可以）彻底改变传统的交流。我们明年就会做，费用也不高，手机上网一个月 5 块钱。（我们将要推出的）激励措施是为老师们捐赠手机和一年两万的上网费用。这样可以彻底激活学校，他们可以提供动态的需求和汇报"。

（3）公益消费的推动者。公益信息组织可以与各类网络服务提供商、电子商务服务方开展合作，倡导网民进行公益消费，如与淘宝网、携程网的合作可以促使网民将各类积分兑换成慈善学习物资，捐赠给边远山区的中小学校。

（4）民间公益教育力量的独立与壮大。立人乡村图书馆的发起者旨在未来几十年内建成一所新型的"立人大学"，可能是未来所设想的一种开放式分布的大学；"立人乡村图书馆的分支机构至少覆盖个 20 以上的（贫困）县，在此基础上立人成为成熟的教育品牌。从整体上看，我们希望是综合性的、同时也是具有持续创新能力的教育集团，产品线很丰富，从图书馆到在县域设立的立人教育服务中心……可能会提供教育管理和教育产品等咨询服务，还有直接的教育服务等"；"组织在乡村社会发挥三个层次的作用：第一：学习中心和教育基地，供当地农村百姓进行自主学习，构成他们终身教育的基地；其次是文化中心和精神家园；第三个层次是交流中心和公共平台"。

（5）公益组织对高级人才的吸引力更大。TECC 的受访者认为中国近些年来社会公益力量的发展迅速，尤其是 2008 年汶川大地震以来出现井喷式发展。但"国内草根组织、教育基金会等招聘进来的工作人员学历低、文化素质比较低、人员流动性强，这样对 NGO 的（长期）发展是很不利的”；“将来留学生、名牌大学的毕业生也愿意去公益组织就业（比如美国哈佛大学毕业的高材生选择 NGO），也许到时候国内公益组织能够像发达国家那样吸引优秀的年轻人选择作为终身职业”。

（6）快乐居家养老的公益模式得到推广。乐龄合作社负责人将“快乐居家养老”作为其核心价值观在不同社区的老年人社群中进行推广，对于未来，“（之所以）选择做这个事情，就是因为相信能改变一些事情；我们同龄人都进入老龄化，希望那个时候的老年人能够在人生最后的时间里能够快乐一些，同时觉得自己有用，而且非常有价值”，“不一定还有我们这个机构，但是这种理念要深入人心”。

新兴公益组织对公益信息制度的期待

中国新兴公益组织受访的负责人对公益信息制度的建议主要集中在民间公益信息机构的资格认定与管理制度、公益信息慈善捐赠的激励制度（含志愿信息服务的激励制度）、行动研究支持制度、信息素养的公益培育制度、网络普遍服务制度、政府财政专款资助制度、教育制度和老年人社会保障的制度等。

民间公益信息机构的资格认定和管理制度。新兴公益组织对该项制度的需求和诉求更加强烈，希望相关部门适度降低民间公益机构的准入门槛，将现行的成立许可批准制度逐步改变为登记备案制度，“希望能够适度放开草根组织的注册（管制），（将现行制度变成）备案制度，这样公益组织就可以进行开放筹资活动”（G）；“我们希望能够注册为一个真正的公益组织，工商注册是不太好的选择，组织形态和资源募集形态都受到比较大的影响；还比如采取备案的方式，（公益组织内部），任何一个人和组织都要承担法律责任和道德义务；而备案制度其实已经足够制约（草根公益组织）了”（H）；“很奇怪，我们对外国企业特别信任，外企形成压制民企的态势；当今中国已经开放民主了很多，应该出台政策鼓励民间公益组织的发展，（逐步）降低对真正公益组织的警惕心理，适当放松对学生社团的严格管理”（I）；“民间组织应该注册为真正的公益身份和法律承认的身份；（目前这么多草根组织）没有合法的身份，（一些甚至进行）工商注册。公益组织需要合法的手续注册和正规的资助程序。绝大部分捐赠和慈善资源都被政府 NGO 截流，这样对草根是不公平、不公开、不公正的”（J）。公益信息机构的管理制度除改革许可批准制度为登记备案制度外，中国政府可以采用媒体监督（H）的方式来实现对民间公益信息机构的动态管理。

公益信息慈善捐赠的激励制度。对于资源匮乏和捐赠来源渠道较少的民间公益信息组织，他们需要更加开放和公平的慈善制度。但凡不能或者不愿意注册为社会团体但注册为工商注册的民间公益信息组织，都是需要在组织内紧张的运作资金中拿一部分出来缴纳税费。目前制度下，“（公益信息组织）一般与慈善捐赠的法人或社会组织签订服务合同，为他们提供发票，我们来捐税”（G）；“（社会给我们的）捐赠还没有实现免税，有抵税资格的（公益组织基本）都是官办的基金会，（政府部门）应该开放对草根组织捐赠的免税（管制）。目前我们对捐赠者唯一的激励是没有浪费钱，所做的事情是透明的、有效率的。其实，捐赠是有捐赠市场的，有捐赠能力的人对捐赠对象是有选择的。立人这个组织不能提供抵税，但我们的优势在于：第一个，完全透明，我们一定要公布所有的善款（去向）；第二个，注重效率，对我们组织的捐赠投入产出比都很高，而且能让捐赠方看到善款实际发生的影响”（H）；“学生社团的主管部门应该在财政管理上放开一些，我们社团是去边远地区支教，而且长期坚持这样做，（再加上）之前的社会反响，（应该对我们有基本的信任）；每次都要审查，很繁琐，其实有这个时间可以做更多事情”（I）；“（尽快出台）慈善法，群众的慈善意识才会逐步提升，他们更加认可法律”（J）。除善款的管理制度外，还包括对志愿者的激励和长效管理制度，“我们社团招进来很多志愿者，但没有利用好这些志愿力量。缺乏对志愿者数据库的利用，数据挖掘的意识和技能都不具备……后续的工作、资源、经费、人力可以获得更多原有志愿者的支持”（I）。

信息素养的公益培训制度。受访的新兴公益组织负责人均表示，数字化时代的信息素养不仅对组织运行本身是非常必要的，而且对于他们的服务对象——农村各类数字贫困社群与老年人社群等来说都是需要的。比如，“（我们及偏远山区的居民）有信息技术的培训需求”（G）；“基本的信息素养是来立人服务之前都必须具备的；专业素养的话，一方面是有培训的，另一个方面是我们的服务体系比较简单，充分相信个人的成长性。培训与实习可以保证来立人工作的人具备专业素养”（H）；TECC 的主要慈善活动之一就是为偏远山区的中学老师提供计算机技能培训；“我们也开展公益培训，包括社区大讲堂、领导力培训、社区行政领导培训、下岗职工再就业培训、社区的老年人培训等，但持续性比较差，（财力和志愿者）资源有限。我们需要更多的交流活动，需要做得更好”（J）。对公益信息技能培训的最好保障是在宏观政策上制定制度，鼓励社会各方尤其是公益信息组织向各类型的特定贫困群体提供公益信息培训。

行动研究支持制度。在大学科研力量参与社群公益信息服务实践活动方面，受访者均认为相关部门应该出台制度或政策鼓励他们为草根公益信息组织提供智力支持和人力资源的支持，共同为数字贫困社群提供切实的、高质量的公益服务。“（多背一公斤组织）希望他们能够帮助建立一些活动内容数据库、教育课件资源库等”（G），为偏远乡村开展志愿活动提供高水平的智力资源保障。同时，“（大学科研力量）应该开展非营利组织、公民社会与信息通讯技术、信息慈善方面的研究，让大学生了解这些方面的基本知识”（I）；“我们也希望更多的大学生能够深入社区，开展志愿服务，比如帮助老年人使用数码相机（等电子家电）”（J）。

网络普遍服务制度和财政专款资助制度。网络普遍服务制度是应该专门为数字贫困社群设立的服务打折或免费的公益服务规则，从制度上强制规定网络服务提供商在为数字贫困社群服务时，应该给予较大程度的优惠，甚至是免费服务。财政专款资助制度是通过制度来明确政府应该规划专门的财政预算，拨付给有意愿而且有能力为数字贫困社群提供高质量且价格低廉甚至免费的网络信息服务提供方，包括公益信息组织。受访者 G 和 J 都赞同这样的政策，希望相关部门能够尽快出台并推广。

除上述一些典型的公益信息制度外，他们还提出了一些间接相关的公益制度，如教育开放制度，“我们非常希望中国在教育方面的法律能够造成教育领域向外国资本和民间资本的开放，形成（良性的）竞争和繁荣”（H）；还有老年人社会保障制度，“随着经济水平的提高，需要不断健全完善老年人社会保障制度，在社会保险和养老政策方面重点照顾困难老年妇女”（J）。受访者 H 还提出其他一些需要改善的制度，如财务会计制度、信息披露制度等。

18

What Role Can Commercial Sites Play as Public Computing Venues in China? A Case Study of Starbucks Coffeehouses ① (2012)

Wang Sufang (王素芳) with the assistance of He Yingfang (何颖芳),

Li Ping (李萍), and Zhang Yuanrui (张原瑞)

Introduction

With the rapid development of computer technology and the use of the Internet spreading, a new concept, the "digital divide," has been proposed. This refers to the gap between individuals, households, businesses, and geographic areas at different socio-economic levels, with regard both to their opportunities to access information and communications technologies (ICTs) and to their use of the Internet for a wide variety of activities. It includes the imbalance both in physical access to technology and the resources and skills needed to effectively participate

---

① This research was funded by the National Social Science Foundation of China (project No.11CTQ039) and carried out as coursework in the Peking University 2011 Community Informatics Summer School. The authors wish to thank the National Social Science Foundation of China for funding this research (project No.11CTQ039); Abdul Alkalimat and Kate Williams who introduced us to the field of community informatics and helped us with questionnaire design; and in particular Tommy Yeung, Associate Librarian of Lingnan University, Hong Kong, for his proofreading and comments.

as a digital citizen (Wiki, 2011; Van Dijk, 2005). Consequently, the key problem is how to bridge this gap and a great deal of research has been conducted in order to find solutions to it. Public computing is one of the solutions to this problem.

What is public computing? According to Williams and Alkalimat (2004), all the settings for using ICT, apart from home or work, could be called public computing sites. They contend that public computing is located in four kinds of sites: governmental sites (schools and libraries), community (schools and churches), commercial (schools and apartment complexes), and universities. Williams (2005) further investigates public computing sites across the United States. She estimates that there are between 85,000 and 144,000 such sites across the country, including but not limited to: public libraries, Internet cafés, telecenters (or community technology centers), copy shops, day care centers, community centers, laundromats, hospitals, apartment complexes, museums, and government offices.

Researchers with the University of Washington's iSchool have used the terms "public access" and "public access venue". "Public access" is defined as computer and internet services that are open to the general public. Both privately and publicly funded ICT venues can be considered public access venues, as long as their services are open to the general public (Araba, 2009; Gomez, 2011). A public access venue is an institutional venue with a mission of offering public access to information tools and resources, with services that are available to all and are not directed at one group in the community to the exclusion of others. Scholars have identified three main types of public access venues of importance in most countries, and grouped them under the generic headings "public library", "telecentre", and "cybercafé" (Gomez, 2009).

In China, according to the *27th Statistics Report on Internet Development in China*, there is a large digital divide between different communities, such as low/high income and young/old, just as in other countries (China Internet Network Information Center, 2011). There are some kinds of community organizations offering ICT and relevant services that could possibly help solve this problem. Such organizations include public libraries[②]; thousands of public electronic reading rooms

② There were about 72,150 computer terminals in electronic reading rooms and upper-level libraries in China as of 2009. (Editorial Committee of Chinese Librarianship Yearbook, 2011)

in the countryside③; community service centers④; and commercial sites such as cyber cafés and Internet bars.

Nowadays, with the development of an ubiquitous information society or ubiquitous computing, there are other commercial sites with wireless Internet service where people can use computers or access the Internet, such as Starbucks Coffee, KFC, other coffee shops, airport waiting rooms, and so on (Hampton, 2008, 2012). However, we know very little about their computing services in China. Who are their users? What computer or Internet services do they supply? How do they operate? Can they help Chinese people with ICT access and use and help to shrink the digital divide? All of these questions need to be answered.

An extensive literature has addressed traditional public access venues such as public libraries, Internet cafés, and telecenters, the profile of their users, and their impact (Gomez, 2011; Qiu, 2009). But computer and Internet access and use of wireless Internet service in coffee shops and their interaction with traditional public access venues has remained relatively unexplored, however. For the current study, we have chosen Starbucks. Starbucks is a commercial site, that is, an urban public space for consumption. The main reason for choosing Starbucks is that compared to other coffeehouses or commercial sites with wireless Internet service, Starbucks seems more visible and popular among people in big cities in China. It is a kind of a public space for people who want to relax, chat, be by themselves, or use a computer. We are asking whether it could be a special computing site compared to traditional sites, such as public libraries and community information centers.

Starbucks Coffee's history and current development in China

History and current development in China

Starbucks Coffee Company was founded in 1971. It is the world's leading coffee retailer, roaster, and coffee brand. The company has more than 13,000 coffee houses with more than 145,000 employees in 39 countries in North America, Latin America, Europe, the Middle East, and around the Pacific Rim. China is the most important, and potentially

③ Public electronic reading rooms were set up by the National Cultural Resources Sharing Program and funded by the Ministry of Culture of China beginning in 2010. (The General Office of Ministry of Culture, 2010)

④ Included among these are the 400 Shanghai Oriental Community Information Centers set up by the Shanghai municipal government in local communities, which provide computers, Internet access, digital resources, and special computer training classes for senior citizens, rural migrant workers, and others. (E-shanghai Oriental community information centers, 2011) the largest, market for Starbucks outside North America. Since the opening of the first Starbucks store in Taiwan in March 1998, and the first one in Beijing in January 1999, approximately 500 stores have opened in China, in Mainland China, Taiwan, Hong Kong, and Macau. There are now over 230 stores in Mainland China, among them 74 in Beijing, spreading over 9 districts, as shown in table 1.

Starbucks integrates its experience with local customs as part of being a responsible Chinese corporate citizen. In September 2005, Starbucks established the $5 Million USD China Education Project to help improve education in the comparatively underdeveloped regions of central and western China.

District	Number of Starbucks
Chaoyang	35
Dongcheng	11
Haidian	9
Xicheng	8
Shunyi	6
Chongwen	2
Changping	1
Fengtai	1
Xuanwu	1
Total	74

Table 1. Starbucks locations in Beijing. Almost all Starbucks are located in or near high-traffic areas such as shopping malls, department stores, hotels, office buildings, and luxury residential buildings. Source:http://www.starbucks.cn/store/store-list.html

Mission

The Starbucks Company in China makes it clear that they want to be the finest coffee house in the world by adhering to the following guiding principles (Starbucks Coffee, 2011):

a) Provide a great work environment and treat each other with respect and dignity;
b) Embrace diversity as an essential component in the way we do business;
c) Apply the highest standards of excellence to the purchasing, roasting, and fresh delivery of our coffee;
d) Develop enthusiastically satisfied customers all of the time;
e) Contribute positively to our communities and our environment;
f) Recognize that profitability is essential to future success.

The company claims they will not only provide customers with the finest coffee and service, but will also create a unique "Starbucks experience", which makes Starbucks coffee houses the warm and comfortable "third life space" for people all over the world outside their workplaces and homes.

Internet services development

Starbucks installed access to wireless networks in its 1,200 chain stores in North America and Europe in 2001. In the beginning, Starbucks offered conditionally free network service: it was free for the first two hours, $3.99 USD each hour after that. This service was competitive in the first several years, but as time went by, wireless network service became popular in other cafés. In order to get more customers, Starbucks began to offer free wireless network service in 2008.

Starbucks began to offer network service in the Chinese market in 2003. In the early years, network service was limited to a few stores in major cities, such as Beijing, Tianjin, and Shanghai. In 2008, Starbucks partnered with AT&T and began to make free network service available in more stores. In 2010, Starbucks and China Mobile jointly launched a free wireless Internet access service. Customers with laptops can search for the wireless signal CMCC-STARBUCKS. When connecting to the Internet, a log-in page will pop up. When the customer inputs a name, and clicks the button for the password, the user name and password will be sent to his mobile phone as a text message. When he logs in with the user name and password successfully, he will come to the Starbucks home page.

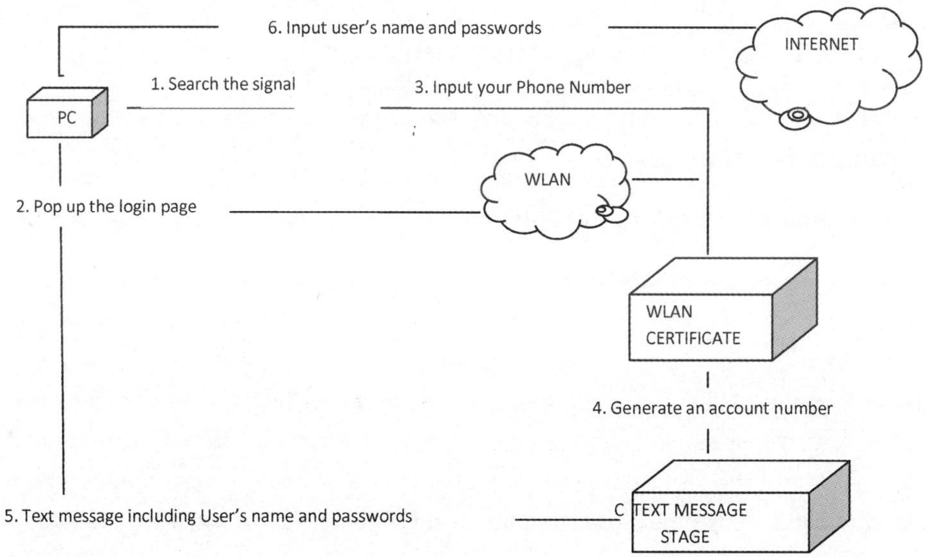

Figure 1. WLAN service process of Starbucks Coffee

Research questions and assumptions

Based on the geographic information given above, we find that almost all Starbucks coffee houses are located in busy urban areas, near shopping malls, supermarkets such as Carrefour China, and department stores such as Juntai Department Store in Xidan District and New World Department Store in Chongwen District. There are coffee houses in hotels, office buildings, luxury residences, and subway stations where usually they are crowded with people. It seems that Starbucks is market driven and its brand appeals to people with more disposable income.

As for using a computer in a Starbucks location, people need to bring in their own laptops. They usually buy a cup of coffee, which costs from 10 to 40 Yuan. Coffee is not cheap for ordinary people in China and is not a traditional beverage in Chinese society and culture. But with the increasing contact with the Western world, consuming coffee is considered fashionable in China today.

In contrast, people with a lower income generally live in less-affluent areas. They may not be able to afford a computer and other expenditures that are for the purpose of being fashionable. For this segment of the Chinese population, we want to address the following questions in depth:

a) Can Starbucks be a 'public' computing site? To which social group does Starbucks Coffee offer computing service? As a public space and commercial organization, what roles does it play in public computing? And what are the reasons?

b) If it were to be a public computing site, could Starbucks Coffee help shrink or widen the digital divide in China? What are the reasons?

Research methodology

5W conceptual or analysis framework

Public computing is the dependent variable in this research. The 5W theoretical framework will be used to structure the data collection and analysis to understand the case of Starbucks as public computing. From our perspective, any public computing site can be analyzed through this framework. The 5W refers to Who (who is involved, who is coming into the site, who gives help at this site with computing), Where (where the site is located: in a low-income or high-income community?), What (what the customers use computers and the Internet for, what the staff do to help them use computers and the Internet), How (how the customers and staff or employees use computers and the Internet), and Why (why the customers and staff behave in particular ways, why customers come to the site to use computers and the Internet, why the site does or does not charge a fee for computer or internet use.

Data collection

Three data collection techniques were used: observation, informal interviews, and questionnaire surveys. The author used these three methods to gather data and form a triangulation approach of study (as figure 2 below indicates). Background and historical data on Starbucks Coffee and its Internet services were obtained through published documents (research articles, mass media reports, information on its website, and annual reports), as well as through informal interviews with employees.

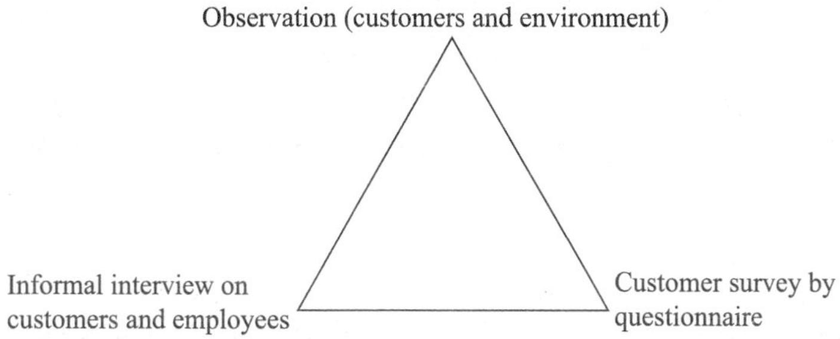

Figure 2. Triangulation of three methods

As mentioned above, nearly all of the Starbuck Coffee locations in Beijing are in or near shopping malls, supermarkets, office towers, and luxury residences. The choice of a particular sample site for this case study was therefore considered unnecessary. So we randomly chose three sites, one in Chongwenmen District and two in Haidian District, and paid visits to all of them. We observed the activities of customers and employees both inside and outside these locations and took notes. We visited the Chongwenmen Starbucks twice. The first visit was made July 11, 2011, as a pilot study. The second was made July 19, 2011, mainly to survey customers through questionnaires. Detailed information and stories about these three case studies are given in table 2.

Case Study	Name and Address	Time period of our survey	Research Methods
Site 1	Chongwenmen Starbucks	1:30-5 p.m. July 11, 2011 7-9:30 p.m., July 19, 2011	Observation; informal interview of customers and employees; survey of customers by questionnaire
Site 2	Dinghao Starbucks	6-7 p.m., July18, 2011	Observation; survey of customers ; informal interview of customers
Site 3	Carrefour China Starbucks	7:30-9:30 p.m., July 18, 2011	Observation; customer survey

Table 2. Three case studies of Starbucks Coffee in China

The most direct data collection method in our case study was the surveying of customers in Starbucks Coffee locations. We designed two questionnaires on customers' computer and Internet use in Starbucks Coffee. One of the questionnaires was in Chinese for local people; the other was in English for foreigners living, working or traveling in China. We surveyed foreign customers because we believe that in a diverse society, there should be some places or facilities where minority people can have their public computing needs met. The demographic information included in the questionnaire was mainly borrowed from the 2011 CNNIC survey on Chinese Netizens (CNNIC, 2011). We delivered 58 questionnaires altogether at these three case study sites and all were returned. The response rate was 100 percent. Based on validity and reliability analysis, all of them represent valid replies.

Case study one: Chongwenmen Starbucks Coffee—first visit

We paid our first visit to Chongwenmen Starbucks Coffee on July 11, 2011. We carried out observation from 1:30 to 5:00 p.m. We made notes on the general environment and on the number of customers and their activities. We also conducted some informal interviews with some employees there.

Chongwenmen Starbucks is located on the first floor of New World Department Store, not far from the entrance to the Chongwenmen subway station, in a relatively prosperous neighborhood. It is next to the Haagen Dazs and RBT, the beverage store favored by young people.

There are two floors in this store. Customers can find newspapers and fashion magazines in the corner of the stairway and read in a casual atmosphere while listening to classical music. The interior is a comfortable and enjoyable place for socializing.

We found that a considerably large number of people (more than one-third of the customers) came to the Chongwenmen Starbucks for computer use or Internet access. They used their own computers. On the wall of the store, there was an Internet access guide. During the observation, a customer asked a store employee how to use her laptop to access the Starbucks network. The employee patiently showed her how and left after making sure the customer could connect successfully.

According to our observations, people using computers or the Internet would usually spend more time (at least one hour) in the store. Of those who dropped in to chat with friends or relax with a cup of coffee, most left the store in less than an hour. Other than for the purpose of computer use, most customers (about 70 percent) came to Starbucks to relax or meet friends.

Customers behavior	Number	Length of stay
Using computer	36	More than half hour
Relaxing (like reading newspapers)	9	Half hour or less
Chatting	59	Half hour or less
Total	104	
Male	33	
Female	62	
Missing	9	

Table 3. What people do in Starbuck Coffee locations.
Note: Observation data in Chongwenmen Starbucks from 1:30 to 5:00 pm., July 11, 2011.

Most of the employees refused our requests for interviews because it was not an appropriate time or they did not have time to answer our questions. The only one who agreed to be interviewed was a newly employed cleaner who had begun working there less than two weeks prior and thus knew little about the store. He told us that most of the customers looked to be about 30 years of age or older, and apparently had an above-average standard of living. He also said that there were approximately the same number of Chinese people and foreigners among the customers, and that there were more foreigners in the morning and evening. He also confirmed that people came there mainly to chat, access the Internet, and drink coffee. There were more customers on the weekends. The rush hours on weekdays were 1:00–2:00 p.m. and 4:00–5:00 p.m. in the afternoon. The store typically sells 300–500 cups of coffee a day.

Case study one: Chongwenmen Starbucks Coffee–second visit

We paid our second visit to the Chongwenmen Starbucks in the evening of July 19, 2011. We stayed in the store from 7:00 to 9:30 p.m. and distributed questionnaire surveys to 30 customers. The details of the customers' responses will be shown below. What we want to address here are the observation results from this visit.

We observed a lower number of customers during the second visit, compared to the first visit. This is probably the result of visiting the store at different times. The international customers were not as numerous as what the employee mentioned above had indicated would be the case. But there were still some customers from Germany, Canada, and Hong Kong.

By chance, we met a businessman who was interested in our research data and even wanted to offer us money to share it with him. We did not expect this. He told us he had been consuming Starbucks coffee since 1999. According to his observations and opinion, Starbucks welcomed everyone into its stores, but in reality, customers generally had a higher income. The market strategy of Starbucks seemed to be focused on those middle-aged or younger groups with more spending power. He also told us the reason why two Starbucks stores located near Renmin University of China in Haidian District had closed. Starbucks was very popular among college students. However, these students did not have much money, and though many came in, they ordered very little and stayed a long time. This had an adverse effect on business. When asked why there were 35 stores in Chaoyang District, but only 9 in Haidian District, where there was a good concentration of higher-income IT professionals and well-educated researchers, he said it was because Chaoyang District was more the commercial center. There are many businessmen in Chaoyang.

Last but not least, we also found that all the power outlets that had been available for public use had been taken out. Without a power supply, people could not use computers for a long time. It appeared to us that Starbucks was not as supportive as it had claimed, in terms of providing Internet access as a public computing site.

Case study two: Dinghao Starbucks Coffee, Haidian District

We visited another Starbucks Coffee, this one in Haidian District, on July 18, 2011. We stayed there from 6:00 to 7:00 p.m. The Haidian Dinghao Starbucks is located in the southwest corner of the first floor in the Dinghao Electronics Mall. However, its logo is not very visible. The store does not see many customers in spite of the relatively large storefront and the short distance to the cafés and fast food restaurants opposite it.

The manager, a young woman in her mid-twenties, refused to be interviewed for the reason that she was very busy. She did not allow us to give the survey to other employees and customers in the store. She told us that the headquarters of Starbucks was monitoring what they were doing all the time via closed-circuit camera. So we decided to wait outside and give the survey there. We were fortunate to have four customers kindly agree to fill out the questionnaires. One was a former student at Peking University, and two were tourists from Hong Kong.

We first interviewed the two customers from Hong Kong. They said they knew little about computing service in Mainland China and they were surprised to see that free access to the Internet was available. They told us people could only use the Internet for 20 minutes a day free of charge in Starbucks stores in Hong Kong. In fact, they seldom accessed the Internet in Starbucks.

Our second interviewee, a former PKU student, never used the Internet in Starbucks though she frequently went there and knew she could use it. The reason she did not use it was that she was not sure whether she needed a specific account or a paid password. Obviously, Starbucks needs to give more instructions concerning its Internet access to customers if it wants to promote usage.

Case study three: Starbucks Coffee nearby Carrefour China, Haidian District

After leaving the Haidian Dinghao Starbucks, we directly went to the third case study site, which was nearby. We stayed there from approximately 7:30 to 9:30 p.m. The Starbucks Coffee location in the Carrefour Supermarket is quite large. Unlike the store in Chongwenmen, it provides seating, which offers a good degree of privacy. Outside the store, there are several other cafés, restaurants, and clothing stores. This Starbucks is close to the subway line 5.

There were few customers when we visited. The store was very spacious and very quiet. After a while, some foreigners came in, but all of them purchased items to go and did not stay.

Because of our experience with the Dinghao store, we did not ask the employees for permission to conduct a survey. We did survey 17 persons using our questionnaires. The details are shown below. While doing the survey, we informally interviewed two Japanese customers, who told us that they had to pay for Internet service at Starbucks locations in Japan, so they assumed that Starbucks locations in China would also charge customers for Internet access, as a global corporate policy.

Survey data analysis and findings

Demographic information of people who make use of the Internet service at Starbucks Coffee

Who the users are of computing is one of the most important aspects to consider, when examining a public computing site and its role in helping overcome the digital divide among different communities. According to our survey, as figure 3 shows, most customers (approximately 86.2 percent) came from Mainland China. Only 13.8 percent are from Taiwan, Hong Kong, and abroad, e.g., Japan, the US, and Germany. Based on this and the observation portion of study, it could be concluded that Starbucks partly meets the needs of some foreigners.

There is not much difference in gender among customers of Starbucks Coffee, as figure 3 indicates. However, observation at Chongwenmen Starbucks showed that there were slightly more female customers than male ones.

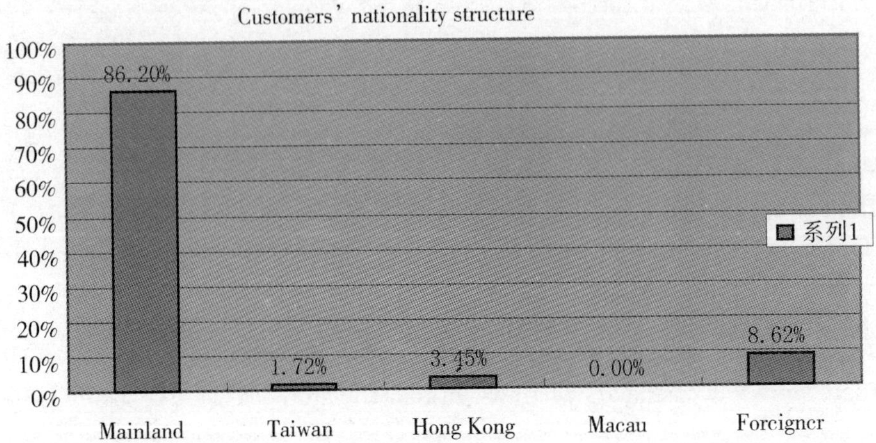

Figure 3. Nationality profile of customers at Starbucks Coffee

As figure 5 shows, most of the customers (86.44 percent) are younger people, ranging in age from 20 to 39. Teenagers make up 6.78 percent of the total. Less than 6 percent are older than 40. When this data is considered in comparison to that of the CNNIC 2011 report, we note that these age groups also make up the majority of Chinese netizens. These people have better information technology skills and more IT awareness.

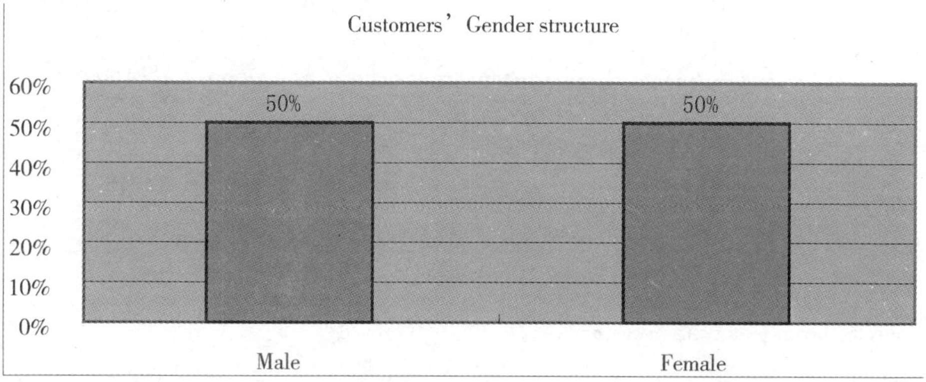

Figure 4. Gender profile of customers at Starbucks Coffee

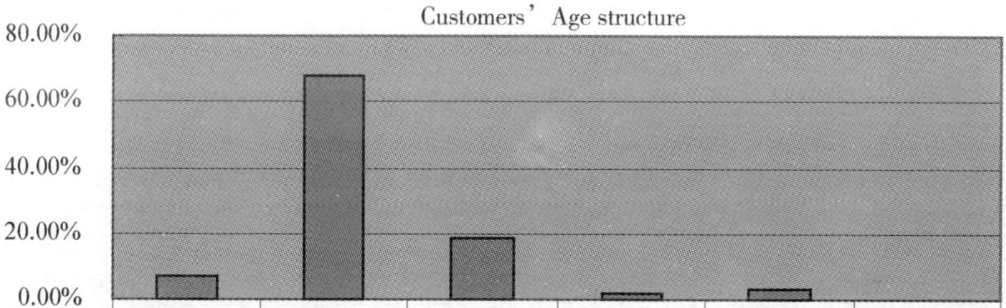

	Below 19	20-29	30-39	40-49	50-59	60 and over
■ Serial	6.78%	67.80%	18.64%	1.69%	3.39%	0.00%

Figure 5. Age profile of customers at Starbucks Coffee

The most important finding about public computing users is probably the social classes these people belong to. Social classes are groups in society categorized based on income, occupation, family background, educational attainment, geographical areas of residence, and life history (Kvasny, 2006).

As figure 6 shows, more than 27 percent of Starbucks customers have a monthly income over 8000 Yuan, nearly 40 percent have an income over 5000 Yuan, and close to 19 percent have an income of 3000-5000 Yuan. Considered in relation to the average annual income of people in Beijing (as shown in table 5), almost 59 percent of Starbucks customers belong to the middle-income and higher-income group. The 30 percent with no income are students at universities or high schools. Only about 5 percent of customers are middle-low or low income.

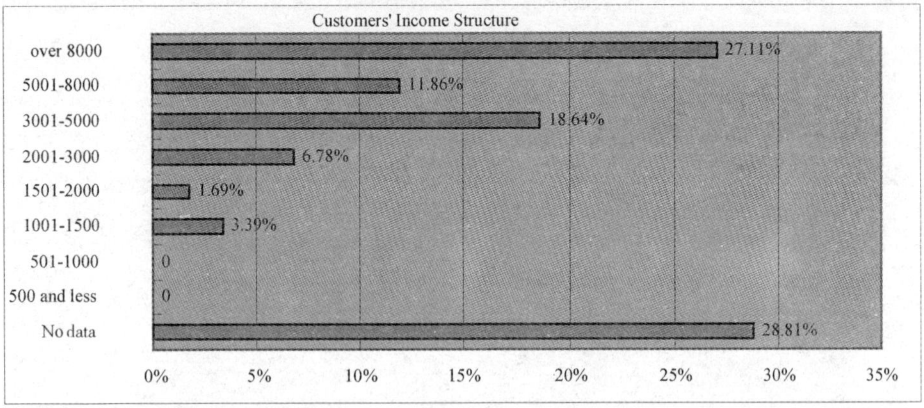

Figure 6. Income structure of customers at Starbucks Coffee

Item	Total	Low Income 20%	Medium-Low Income 20 %	Medium Income 20%	Medium-High Income 20%	High Income 20%
Family Gross Income	30674	14111	**21931**	**27375**	**34809**	57456
Annual Disposable Income Per Capita	26738	11729	**18501**	**23475**	**30476**	50816
Emolument	20537	10006	**16094**	**18797**	**24020**	38015

Table 5. Annual cash income per capita of 5000 sample urban households in Beijing (2009). Unit: Yuan. Source: Beijing Municipal Bureau of Statistics. NBS Survey Office in Beijing. Beijing Statistical Yearbook 2010, pp. 203–205

As Figure 7 shows, more than 91 percent of Starbucks customers have higher levels of educational attainment that enable them to find decent white-collar jobs, as indicated in Figure 8.

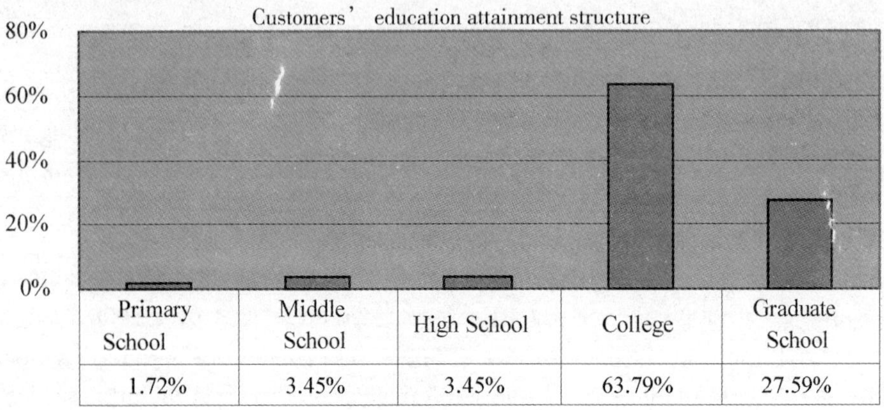

Figure 7. Education profile of customers at Starbucks Coffee

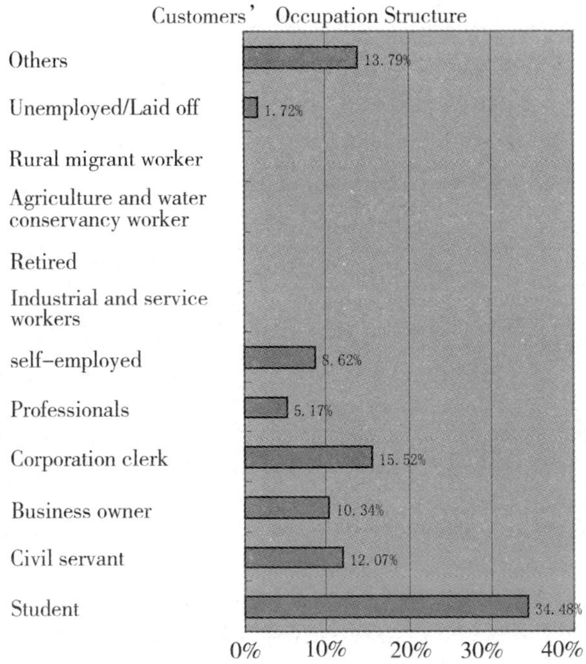

Figure 8. Occupation profile of customers at Starbucks Coffee

As Figure 8 shows, university students are obviously the main customers for internet use (about 34 percent of the total sample), followed by people in business, e.g., business employees, business owners, the self-employed, and government employees. Some unemployed people are customers, but only a few.

Based on the above information, we can say typical Chinese Starbucks customer is young, educated, and with a middle-to-high income level. This group forms the bulk of the emerging middle and upper class in Chinese society, according to the social stratification research of Li (2010). Furthermore, Starbucks Coffee also partly meets the needs of foreigners. The survey results are in line with our observations and partly prove our assumption.

What do people come to Starbucks for?

As Figure 9 shows, people go to Starbucks primarily to drink coffee, chat with friends, and discuss business. Only six people said they came mainly to use the computer in Starbucks. This result is much different from our observation at the Chongwenmen Starbucks. In that particular case study, more than 30 percent of customers were using a computer there. The difference may lie in the fact that observation and survey were done during a different time period (observation was done from 1:30 to 5:00 p.m. in the afternoon; survey was given in the evening, from 7:00 to 9:30 p.m.) at the Chongwenmen Starbucks. Of course, we cannot rule out other possibilities, e.g., some people had other computing sites to use, or others did not have any intention or need to use the computer. Therefore, Starbucks was not their first choice as a place to use the computer.

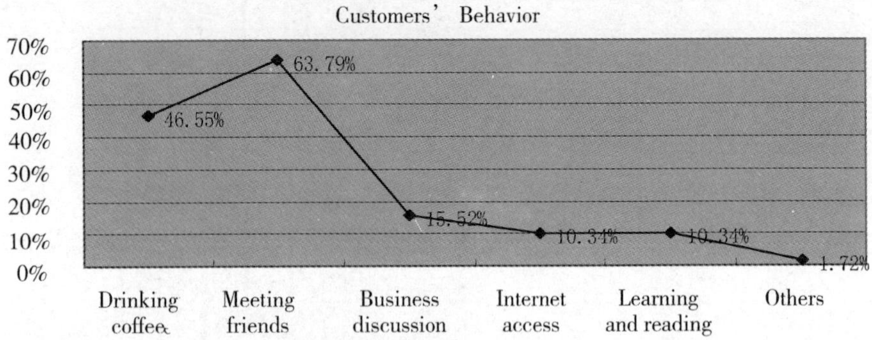

Figure 9. Behavior of customers at Starbucks Coffee

What other computer and Internet access points do customers have?

Customers who come to Starbucks for computing usually have other computer or Internet access choices. The questionnaires show that 77.59 percent of people can use computers and access the Internet at home; 39.66 percent can use computers in the office; 24.14 percent prefer to do so at their school or university; 15.52 percent prefer to do so at the library; 8.62 percent can use other Internet access points, such as KFC or the airport; and 6.9 percent have gone to a cyber café (or Internet bar), which is another common option. It should be noted that 1.72 percent access the Internet at Starbucks exclusively, according to the questionnaires.

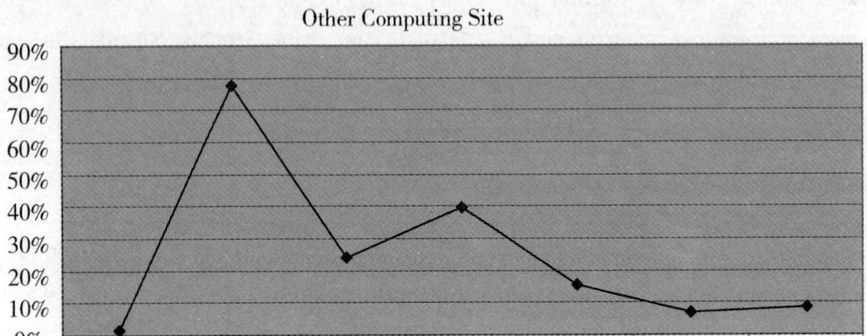

No other choices	Home	School or university	Office	Library	Cyber café	Others
1.72%	77.59%	24.14%	39.66%	15.52%	6.90%	8.62%

Figure 10. Other computing sites used by customers besides Starbucks Coffee

What do customers use computers and the Internet in Starbucks Coffee for?

As indicated by Figure 11, browsing the news and websites, dealing with e-mail, and social networking are the top three computing activities of customers going to Starbucks Coffee. Studying and doing research, enjoying music and movies, and dealing with work are the next three major computing activities, which account for 20.69, 15.52, and 13.79 percent, respectively. A few people do online shopping and play computer games.

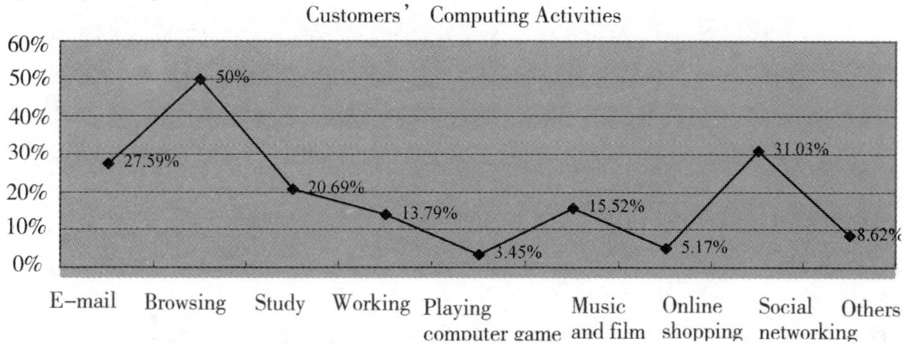

Figure 11 Computing activities of computers in Starbucks Coffee

How do the customers connect to the Internet?

Most Internet users in Starbucks use various digital devices to access the Internet, such as smartphones (56.90 percent), laptops (44.83 percent), and tablet PCs such as an iPad (22.41 percent). People who come to Starbucks seem to have a higher level of computer literacy and can afford new digital devices.

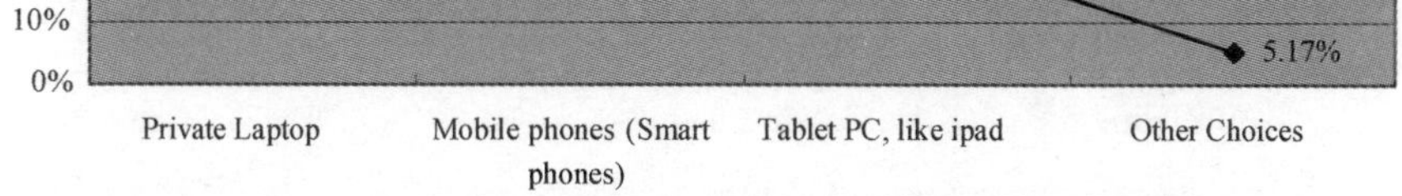

Figure 12. Devices used by customers at Starbucks Coffee to connect to the Internet

How often do customers come to Starbucks Coffee and use its Internet service?

Some additional important characteristics of public computing users are matters of frequency and intensity of use. More than 38 percent of the customers go to Starbucks once every six months or less, and 25.86 percent come to Starbucks once a week. More than one-third of the customers come to Starbucks less than four times a month. Only 1.72 percent come once a day to user computers. In general, their use is sporadic rather than consistent.

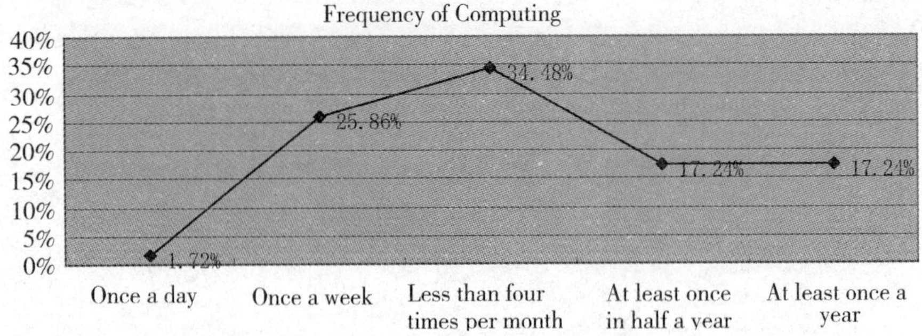

Figure 13. Frequency of computing visits by customers to Starbucks Coffee

Why do customers come to Starbucks Coffee to use its Internet services?

Why do people come to Starbucks, a commercial coffee establishment, for computing? Figure 14 shows that more people (37.93 percent) usually drop in when they are en route to work or home, or traveling on business; 27.59 percent come because of the nice environment; and only 18.97 percent come to Starbucks because of geographical proximity.

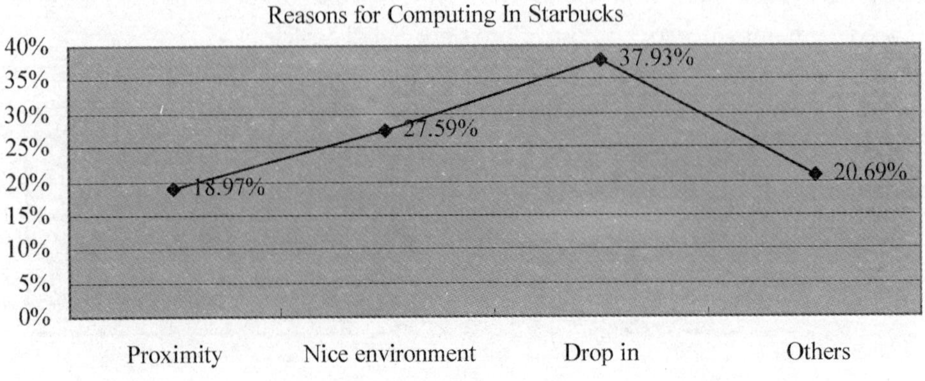

Figure 14. Reasons for computing at Starbucks

In what ways are customers unsatisfied with the Internet service of Starbucks Coffee?

With regard to dissatisfaction and complaints, 31.03 percent of users do not like the noisy environment in Starbucks; 29.31 percent complain about the slow network speed, causing dropped lines and other undesirable situations; 22.41 percent want a strengthened smoking ban in the stores, and 10.34 percent are concerned about Internet security. Unexpectedly, only 1.72 percent mentioned that there are not enough power outlets in the stores.

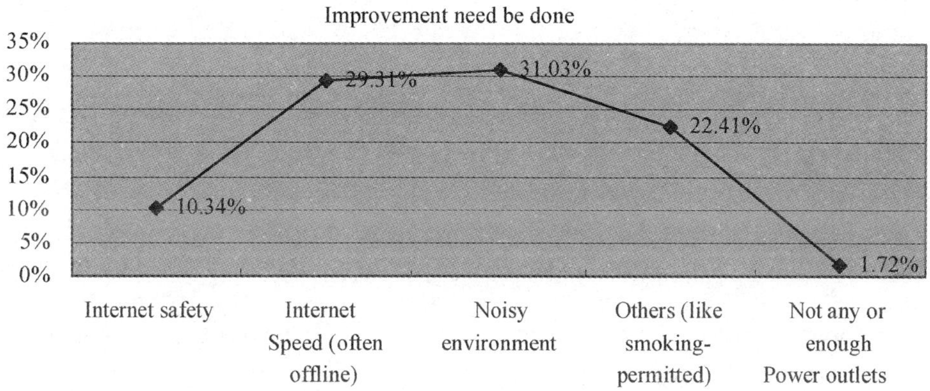

Figure 15. Improvements wanted by customers at Starbucks Coffee

It can be seen from the data in Figure 10 that 98.28 percent of Starbucks customers have other sites where they can access the Internet. Starbucks is thus not their only option. The statistics of Figure 11 showed that although people come to Starbucks for various purposes, most of them are able to meet their needs by Internet needs at Starbucks. For instance, people come to Starbucks to deal with work e-mails or other job tasks, and students come to Starbucks to study or do research by means of the Internet. Figure 12 points out that Starbucks locations do not provide network access equipment, and customers have to bring their own Internet devices, so more than half of people in Starbucks stores use smartphones, iPads or other devices, rather than computers. Based on these portions of the statistical analysis, it can be said that the group of people who come to Starbucks to use the network have a high level of computer literacy relative to the population of China as a whole.

Discussion

Commercial sites as public computing venues

There are usually two kinds of public computing spaces in urban areas: spaces free and open to the public and commercial ones, which charge fees (Hu, 2011). Obviously, Starbucks Coffee locations belong to the latter category. As privately operated but public accessed commercial sites, could they serve the public function of providing ICTs access and to what extent? Why does it still matter? According to our research, we know that the target customers, i.e., middle-class people, come to Starbucks even though they have other computer and Internet access sites. According to the survey results, these include the home, office, school or university library, etc. Based on the high percentage of drop-in customers, people coming in to check or send e-mails, and students coming to finish their homework or research, we could draw the conclusion that Starbucks mainly meets the ad hoc needs of these groups. The importance of Starbucks to middle-class Chinese society as a computing site should not be overlooked.

As a commercial site, Starbucks Coffee locations do indeed meet some people's needs in terms of providing a place for study, information seeking, entertainment, and social interaction because of its convenience and environment. However, its limitations as a public computing site are very evident.

Limitations of commercial sites as public computing venue

From the above analysis of Starbucks customers' characteristics (see Figures 4–7), we know that in comparison with the general population, the customers are not a diverse group: they are young, relatively well educated, of relatively higher socio-economic status, have a higher level of computer literacy, and have usually had prior access to the Internet at some other location. Even among the middle-class group, fewer people go to this site primarily to use computers. Based on the observation, interview, and survey information, the profit motive for offering Internet access services, on the part of Starbucks, has probably led to the current situation. After all, offering computing service is not their main business. We know that it is only an extra service meant to attract customers and increase profits:

> When talking to us about why Starbucks would supply wireless Internet service, Vice president of Meida Coffe Company, Li Fuqiang told us, "LAN construction in our store is for advancing services. Nowadays, with more and

younger people and businessmen wanting to connect to the Internet, we hope we can give them a comfortable, bright, and pleasant environment with music and Internet access. We hope more people will come to our store, and that everyone coming here will feel as comfortable as in his own home—that is what we called 'Starbucks Experience'". (From mass media interview)

Thus, once the Wi-Fi service began to impact its coffee sales, café management would employ strategies, such as removing power outlets in customer areas, to discourage people from using computers. As a commercial organization, Starbucks is not really concerned with the public welfare. Four customers we interviewed informally—two from Hong Kong, one from Japan, one from Mainland China—said they did not know Starbucks Coffee offered a free Internet connection. When we observed in the Chongwenmen store, we found that power outlets had been removed—this despite the fact that some customers we surveyed mentioned they hoped Starbucks would add outlets. One customer, who said he was very familiar with the Starbucks operation, told us this action might be to prevent customers, especially students, from using computers in the location for a long time. Seats should be made available for people consuming coffee and food. This was found to be a common practice in cafés offering free Wi-Fi service in America as well (Hampton, 2008).

All this information seems to tell us that for a business, it is difficult to meet business needs and social development goals simultaneously. Starbucks does not have the motivation to be a public computing site and it does not carry out sufficient marketing and promotion of this service. The incompatibility between being profit driven and having a concern for public welfare inevitably weakens its public computing aspect.

Last but not at least, there is also a lack of social and policy support for this kind of commercial site, which might limit its ability to serve as a public computing site. Just before we finished this research, we learned that some locations in Beijing planned to end their free Wi-Fi service because the police were requiring them to install expensive security systems that they could not afford.

Further reflection on commercial public computing sites as a solution to the digital divide

As we know, the digital divide is the gap in computer and internet use between different communities, regions, and countries. Clement and Shade (2001) clarify that networks, devices, software, service/access provision, content/services, literacy/social facilitation, and governance are the measurements of the digital divide. Dimaggio and Hargittai (2001), on the other hand, look at the issue from the viewpoints of patrons (not equipment), and emphasize access, skills, purpose of use, autonomy of use, and social support as being important aspects of the digital divide. Van Dijk (2005) builds upon the research of Dimaggio and Hargittai, and frames the issue according to different types of access: motivational access, material access, skills access, and usage access. Usage access is the last stage and the ultimate goal of the process of technological appropriation in the shape of a particular application.

Public computing was proposed to solve the problem of the digital divide. It should give the digital or information poor a place to access and use computers, access the Internet, and get help to advance their computer skills. Starbucks as a commercial site does not have any computers for anybody, including the poor, to use. Officially, they do not offer any help or training concerning use of the computer or Internet access. Though the company claims it does not exclude anyone from entering the store, people who do not have enough money for a cup of coffee are still marginalized. So even though it cannot be said that Starbucks widens the digital divide, we can conclude that Starbucks does not help shrink the divide between the rich and the poor in Mainland China, based on its customer base, services, and policies. The information poor still need proper public computing sites with policy support, such as the public library, community information centers, and so on.

Based on the discussion above, if commercial public computing sites want to be a solution to the digital divide, we think they need to fulfill three conditions. First, they should focus on the poor or underserved people in the community; second, they should be equipped with computers and Internet access for public use; and third, they should offer computer training free of charge or for a very small fee. Most important is that they have the potential to become learning centers with resources to help people with computer access and literacy.

Conclusions and Suggestions

Customers using Starbucks Coffee for Internet access are generally young people of middle-to-high income levels and a higher level of education. Most are businessmen and students. These people have good computer skills and clear needs with regard to computer and Internet use. They usually have other venues in which to access the Internet, such as the home, office, library, and other public spaces. Starbucks Coffee may not be their first choice for Internet access, but it still offers them some convenience when they cannot find another place to check their work e-mail accounts or finish their homework and study.

Williams and Alkalimat (2004) associate the four different public computing sites with three different social groups. Community sites are located close to the opposite ends of the social spectrum, i.e., the rich and the poor. Commercial and university sites are located according to market demand. In other words, they are closer to the higher-income and student groups. It appears that people in the middle of the social spectrum in Mainland China do not have ready access to public computing. Our research shows that commercial sites, in this case Starbucks locations, are indeed usually closer to people with higher income levels and to students. However, our research also indicates that commercial public computing sites in China are located close to the middle section of the social spectrum and meet their needs to a certain extent.

Starbucks is providing a service that makes it look like a public computing site, especially in foreign countries, where ordinary people go to Starbucks to use computers. But our research shows that in reality, it does not serve the purpose as a true public computing site in China. As a commercial enterprise, its profit-driven nature limits Starbucks' "public" capability as a computing site. It may meet some urgent needs for Internet access for a small but wealthy group. Without computers for loan, on-site assistance, and training, Starbucks as a commercial computing venue cannot assume an active role in terms of reaching out to disadvantaged people and providing them with the required resources in order to shrink the digital divide.

If we want to make use of public computing sites as an important solution to the digital divide, we should redefine public computing. In other words, any community organization which wants to take up the responsibility of shrinking the digital divide should become a learning center, because a learning center can increase the opportunities and literacy of the less advantaged, with regard to the use of computers and the Internet, so as to make an impact in their daily lives.

As to Starbucks, we think they could make a real effort to improve their Internet services and enhance public awareness. For example, the company could make more people, especially its employees, aware of the free Internet service and encourage them to make use of it. Furthermore, it could increase the speed of its Internet connectivity and install enough power outlets.

Limitations and future study

This is the first attempt to study a commercial site as a public computing venue and its role in shrinking the digital divide in China. In the process, we have come to see that more effort should be made in the following two directions. Because data could not be collected via interviews with managers and employees, due to the uncooperative attitude of store managers, the study lacks the viewpoint of the company administration. More in-depth interviews with Starbucks customers and management side should be conducted in our follow-up study and the survey with a revised questionnaire needs to be given to a larger sample.

19

The Divided Views of the Information and Digital Divides: A Call for Integrative Theories of Information Inequality[①] (2011)

Yu Liangzhi

Abstract

This article defines information inequality as multifaceted disparity between individuals, communities or nations in mobilizing society's information resources for the benefit of their lives and development. It then examines related research from a wide range of disciplines that focuses either on information inequality in general or on its specific forms, e.g. information poverty, information divide, knowledge gap and digital divide. It shows that it is possible to identify a number of clusters of information inequality research according to their theoretical perspectives, and that these perspectives have inherited to a great extent the traditional divisions of social sciences between structure vs agency, society vs individuals and objectivism vs subjectivism. Following earlier calls for greater dialogue between divisions of related research, this article goes further to call for integrative theorizing of information inequality in the way exemplified by Bourdieu's research on social

① This article is part of research funded by the National Science Foundation of China (project no. 70673040). It is a synthesis and expansion of two related articles published in Chinese: Yu L and Liu Y. Structure and agency: a call for integrative research approach to information inequality. *Journal of Library Science in China* 2010(36): 4–19; Yu L. Integrative social theories and their relevance for information inequality research. *The Library and Information Science Journal of Shanghai Academic Libraries* 2011(1): 1–9.

inequality.

1 Introduction

Within various disciplines of social sciences, there are some longstanding approaches that divide researchers even today. These include divisions between the individual vs society, action (agency) vs structure, and subjectivism vs objectivism. The society vs individual dichotomy concerns primarily the difference between research traditions in their choices of research object, where some focus on society as a whole, contending that society assumes independent existence as manifested in, for instance, Durkheim's social facts, while others focus on individuals, contending that society is nothing other than social relationships manifested in individual interactions. The structure vs agency dichotomy concerns primarily the difference between research traditions in the primacy they afford to structure and agency when it comes to deciding which one conditions or determines the other and which one assumes priority in social science research. Some hold that social structure, which exists and operates independently of individual players, ultimately conditions individual actions; others contend that it is players' perceptions and conceptualization of the world that guide their actions, which in turn construct social structure. The objectivism vs subjectivism dichotomy concerns the difference between research traditions in the way they see and study the reality of the social world. Some see social reality as existing independently of players' conceptualization of it, which can and should be studied objectively by observing social facts; others see it as reducible to individuals' representations which can only be interpreted by researchers. Through different conceptual and methodological tools and interpretive frameworks, these divisions have produced varied explanations of the social world, whose inconsistency with each other and competition for authority have in many ways hindered our comprehensive understanding of this world (Bourdieu 1989; Knorr-Cetina 1981).

One of the most notable trends in contemporary social theorizing is the efforts taken to bridge the above divides, exemplified most notably by the research of social theorists Bourdieu, Giddens and a few others (Ritzer 2003). Bourdieu, for example, contends that neither social structure nor individual actions alone adequately explain the social world; the two need to be studied simultaneously and dialectically. Central to Bourdieu's integrative social theory are two instrumental concepts, habitus and field (1989). To Bourdieu, habitus is socially produced dispositions which govern internally the individual's preferences and actions; it is formed through the experiences of the agent in a certain position of the social space, based on the conditions and resources available to that position (1984). Fields are those social arenas where individuals play their social roles and where struggles for various capitals—economic, social, cultural and symbolic—take place; they are also social spaces where external conditions constantly generate inward influence on individuals, leading to the inculcation of their habitus (1984, 1985, 1983). Through the conceptualization of habitus and fields, Bourdieu has demonstrated a possible approach to bridging the traditional intellectual divisions. During the past three decades, an increasing number of scholars have begun to follow this and other integrative approaches for theory building. These include some LIS scholars, primarily in the area of information behavior studies (Savolainen 1995; Rosenbaum 1993; Burnett and Jaeger 2008; Jaeger and Burnett 2010; Buschman 2006).

However, within the cross-disciplinary area of information inequality—defined here as multifaceted disparity between individuals, communities, or nations in mobilizing society's information resources for the benefit of their lives and development, which may take the form of information divide, digital divide, knowledge gap, etc.—integrative theorizing in the sense of Bourdieu is rare and patchy. Apart from some direct applications of Bourdieu's concepts to explaining the observed passivity of some people in utilizing information and communication technologies (ICTs) (Kvasny 2002; Kvasny and Keil 2002), innovative adoption of the integrative approach hardly exists. This is so despite the fact that information inequality is widely recognized as a highly complex issue involving both material and non-material, societal and individual, objective and subjective, and structural and agentic domains (Dijk 2005; Kim and Kim 2001; Lievrouw 2003), and the fact that the area of information inequality research has spanned a great variety of disciplines where sensitivity to innovative theoretical approaches is supposed to be most possible and profitable.

This article aims to promote the integrative approach in information inequality research. It does so by critically reviewing related studies and addressing the following specific questions: (1) how do related studies connect to each other theoretically? (2) To what extent have dichotomous perspectives in social sciences influenced and divided information inequality research? (3) How can the integrative approach improve understanding of information inequality? As a result of this examination, this article hopes to substantially further the call of earlier articles (Lievrouw 2003; Yu 2006) for greater dialogue between different research approaches. It can be argued that this call is particularly relevant to library and information science (LIS) which, owing to its great interest and knowledge base in human information practices, occupies a unique position in leading the integrative theorizing via the approach espoused by Bourdieu, i.e. the approach to ground theoretical constructs in a relational examination of human practices.

2 The clustering and clusters of related research on information inequality

Research about different forms of information inequality has been an area of rapid growth since the 1960s, fostered first by the popularization of the concept of an information society and the notion of information as a strategic resource, and then by the advent of new ICTs; it is also an area of constant expansion in terms of both the forms of information inequality researched and the variety of disciplines involved in the research. From the 1970s to early 1990s, related research addressed mainly such forms of information inequality as knowledge gap (Tichenor, et al 1970), information poverty (Chatman 1991; 1996) and the disparity in information access between rich and poor people (Childers and Post 1975; Dervin and Greenberg 1972; Dervin 1973; Greenberg and Dervin 1970). The 1990s saw the area expand to cover the issue of unequal access to newly emerged ICTs, which became widely publicized after 1995 by the publication of the 'Falling through the Net' reports of the National Telecommunication and Information Administration (NTIA) in the United States. This new form of information inequality, subsequently referred to as the 'digital divide', not only attracted research interest from a great variety of disciplines, but also generated a very large body of related literature. Within less than two decades since the coinage of the term 'digital divide', related discourse has already produced thousands of publications in the scholarly communication system alone. A search in the title and subject fields of Thomson Reuters's Science Citation Index (SCI) and Social Science Citation index (SSCI) using the term 'digital divide' in the summer 2011 returned 1118 items, and a search in the title field of Google Scholar using the same term returned over 5,000 entries.

Although it can be argued that all forms of information-and ICT-related divides contribute to the overall information inequality and all related research contributes to its understanding, not all research has approached the issue with the same agenda—much of the knowledge gap research in communication studies, for instance, aimed to unveil why the rate of mass media information acquisition varies so widely between different sections of population, whereas much of the information divide research in LIS is concerned with how the disadvantaged sections of society are deprived of information access. Nor have related studies approached the issue from the same points of view: a cursory browsing of a portion of the related literature reveals that they are in fact underpinned by a perplexing range of theoretical and philosophical perspectives.

Mapping the theoretical connections between studies in such a field is not easy; it is certainly infeasible for formalized research procedures like co-citation analysis. This is because: (1) for a large proportion of related studies, the theoretical foundation is not explicitly stated; and (2) studies from the same theoretical perspective often fail to note shared interests across disciplinary boundaries. To put it in another way, the pattern of co-citation may not necessarily reflect the convergence and divergence of theoretical perspectives because of the great variety of disciplines involved and the implicit adoption of theoretical perspectives. For this reason, this author has chosen to focus on identifying the theoretical groupings of related studies based on an extensive reading of the field. Related literature was searched by using terms describing various forms of information inequality (as aforementioned) in the title and subject or abstract fields of major databases (Thomson Reuters's Web of Science databases, JSTOR, EBSCO and major publishers' databases). This was supplemented by a search of the web using Google Scholar. Over 500 full texts of the returned publications were obtained through institutional subscriptions, interlibrary loans and open access repositories. Those which explicitly stated their theoretical perspectives were read first; their key concepts, focus of analysis, interpretive framework, major findings and policy prescriptions were compared and summarized (to be presented below). The remaining texts were then mapped to the identified perspectives where possible according to their resemblance with features of these perspectives. A random sample of publications from the larger clusters (containing more than 20 full texts), all publications from the smaller clusters, and all publications from the ambiguous set were re-read with a view to confirming and adjusting the initial grouping and characterization. A new cluster (community informatics) was added at this stage and a number of publications were re-classified. As a result of this reading, this article identifies the following theoretical perspectives within information inequality research: the political economy of information, the social exclusion theory, the small world theory, the diffusion of innovation theory, the knowledge gap thesis, social network analysis, the sensemaking theory, and community informatics.

Before detailing the major features of these perspectives, this article must acknowledge first that it does not claim an exhaustive treatment of all the theoretical approaches associated with the information inequality discourse. Some exclusions, including those of a number of highly influential theoretical perspectives, are made for defendable reasons, whereas others may be entirely due to the author's analytical limitations. Of those excluded for a reason, Habermas's theories of the public sphere, deliberative democracy and communicative action and Castells's theory of the network society are the most notable. Although these theories have provided very important insights into the information inequality issue—they have, for instance, helped researchers to heed the unequal distribution of digital contents in cyberspace (Couldry 2003) and the emergence of the information have-less class (Cartier, et al 2005)—their major applications so far have been directed to issues where information inequality was treated as a context or as partially exogenous (e.g. digital democracy, social structure in network society) rather than to investigating the issue itself.

With the above delimitation and caveat in mind, the identified perspectives and related research are reviewed as follows. They are roughly grouped according to the forms of inequality they examine: those concerned with information divide more than they are with digital divide are discussed first, followed by those concerned mainly with the digital divide.

2.1 Political economy of information

Political economy of information (PEI), also known as 'political economy of communication' in the field of communication studies, originated in the 1940s against the backdrop of a rising culture industry on the one hand and the growth of transnational business on the other. The former heralded a process of economic transformation of the cultural and information sector, while the latter instigated great corporate needs for information and information technologies, and hence corporate influence on the information sector. These changes significantly raised the political and economic stakes of information and led a group of scholars in communication studies to a political economy analysis of information. The field grew markedly in the 1960s and 1970s against the background of two new concomitant trends: (1) the emerging information society in which information was recognized as a strategic resource; and (2) the transfer of the third world's anti-colonization battle field from the political and military arena to the cultural and information arena. By drawing on political economy's traditions of explaining social change in light of political and economic interests, analyzing society in its totality, and adhering to moral philosophy and social intervention (Mosco 1996), the field offers a distinct counter-perspective to that which sees information production and distribution purely in economic terms.

The central concern of PEI is to examine how the established economic, political and social order shapes the structure of information production, distribution, access and utilization, as well as how information and communication resources are deployed to reproduce the existing order. It focuses particularly on such issues as: (1) capitalist control of information through the concentration of media ownership, the commercialization of the information sector, the commoditization of information products, and the maneuvering of information policy-making; (2) the advancement of transnational corporate interests in the global and domestic information markets and their prioritization of economic returns over social development; (3) the role of the state and other political powers in information production and dissemination, and their control of information for the purpose of political and social control; and (4) the impact of all these on democracy and social justice.

From the PEI perspective, the capitalist's interests in the information sector, the institutional mechanism to shield his interests and the market means to realize his interests are almost always intertwined; increased information inequality is seen as an inevitable consequence of these joined forces. Not surprisingly, therefore, a great many PEI-based studies are devoted to examining the impact of these factors on information inequality (Mansell 2002; D. Schiller 1995, 2001; H. Schiller 1996, 2007; H. Schiller and A. Schiller 1988; Murdock 1999; Golding and Murdock 2001; Mosco 1988; Stevenson 2009; Zhao 2007; Golding 1993; Murdock and Golding 1989, 2004). Schiller and Schiller (1988), for example, analyzed how corporate pursuit of profit turned information into a commodity and how this trend eroded public information services (particularly libraries) and the 'equal access for all' principle in the United States. Schiller, in a book entitled Information inequality: the deepening social crisis in America, further examined the marketization of public institutions such as schools and libraries and its impact on information equity, democracy and social justice. He contended that 'the information crisis—denial of access and debased messages and images—deepens social inequality and intensifies the general social crisis' (H. Schiller 1996, p. xvi). His concern about the effect of marketization on information inequality is also summarized in another of his books on the information society:

> The elevation of private, corporate over public, social interest is especially transparent in the dynamic communication-information sector. Here the institutional processes are being arranged to enable the already powerful to seize control and direct the new technologies to corporate ends, while the few public structures with potential countervailing influence are progressively weakened. At the same time, the practice of treating information as a commodity—an outgrowth of applying market criteria to information—promises to exacerbate old inequities in new ways (H. Schiller 2007, pp. 60–61).

In Europe, Golding and Murdock (Murdock and Golding 1989, 1999, 2004; Golding 1993) also examined the impact on information inequality of the expanding information market on the one hand and the increasing income disparity on the other. They noted that 'as communications and information goods and services transfer to the market, their accessibility among significant sections of the population is reduced, and their contribution to social cohesion becomes negative' (Murdock and Golding 1999, p. 129). In their 2001 article, Golding and Murdock further examined how corporate interests shaped UK government's policies for equitable access to ICTs. They showed that these policies not only left information inequality between the advantaged and disadvantaged sections of society intact, but also in effect created another type of information divide between the information rich consumer and the information poor citizen, i.e., between the accessibility of consumer information and that of citizen information (Golding and Murdock 1999).

In a similar vein and against the backdrop of economic reform in China, Zhao (2007) reviewed the domination of corporate interests in the process of defining and pursuing universal access in China, and revealed how the end results widened rather than diminished the rural and urban divide of access to information technologies.

From the perspective of PEI, information and culture domination can be seen as one of the most profound forms of information inequality. This is because, firstly, domination of this kind involves not just 'too little information for the disadvantaged' but also 'imposing on the disadvantaged too much information beneficial for the advantaged'; secondly, it penetrates not just information access but also information production, codification (or discourses) and utilization. It is therefore of little surprise that global information inequality in the form of information and cultural domination emerged as a central concern for many PEI scholars in the post-colonist era, whose research laid the theoretical foundation for the New World Information Order (NWIO) movement in the 1970s, which in turn served as a new battle field of anticolonization (Masmoudi 1979; H. Schiller 1976, 1978; Smith 1980). This critical analysis of global information inequality is continued in the post NWIO era by a great many studies (Mansell 2002; D. Schiller 2001; Bhuiyan 2008; Haywood 1995; Buchanan 1999; Main 2001). Together, these studies suggest that the capitalist logic which determined the unequal distribution of wealth in the industrial era is also determining information inequality in the information society; and in both cases the skewed distribution of resources tallies with the skewed distribution of power.

2.2 *The small world theory of information poverty*

Although elements of the small world approach to information inequality, e.g. emphasis on contexts, values, beliefs and attitudes, were visible in some early studies (Cochrane and Atherton 1980), the small world perspective in the context of information poverty is attributable primarily to Chatman's research during the 1980s and 1990s. Drawing on sociological studies, particularly Luckmann's (1970), Chatman defined a small world as a society where shared opinions and concerns, language and customs, social norms and world views exist to produce a strong sense of membership among its members. It is a world where a collective awareness exists about 'who is important and who is not; which ideas are relevant and which are trivial; whom to trust and whom to avoid' (Chatman 1999, p. 213). In its simplest and most observable form, a small world is a small scale community of like-minded people living in clearly defined geographic boundaries.

Chatman's small world theory was first conceived as an information behavior theory in the 1980s, based on a series of studies on the information behavior of poor people. Her earlier studies were characterized by applying existing sociological theories, such as gratification theory, social network analysis, and opinion leadership theory, to information behavior of poor people in everyday life, particularly in small world settings (Chatman 1991, 1986, 1987a, 1987b, 1990, 1992). For example, in one of her 1987 studies (1987b), Chatman tested the theory of opinion leadership by investigating the role of opinion leaders in information dissemination in a low-income environment. In her 1990 and 1991 studies, she applied alienation theory and gratification theory, respectively, to examining the information behavior of janitors at a large university in the American South: the former showed that the information behavior of these low-income workers was characterized by the lack of an informal information network and the distrust of their neighbors as information sources; the latter showed that their information need was essentially rooted in a lifestyle focusing on present day reality which was thought to be unrelated to information originating outside this life circle. Therefore although members of this low-income group often felt the need for information to cope with everyday life, they did not actively seek information from external sources outside of their social milieu.

Major contributions of these earlier studies were, of course, primarily to information behavior research: by adopting a sociological approach, these studies had greatly broadened the view of information behavior research which had been largely dominated by the cognitive perspective. However, as Chatman progressed with her small world information behavior research, it became increasingly apparent to her that these small world lives and information poverty were connected. For example, in her 1991 study of the information behavior of custodial workers, she noted that the information world of the poor is a 'first order' knowledge world, which she defined as a world which relies for information either on personal experiences or on informal communication with someone who shares the same small world and who is supposed to have related knowledge. To Chatman, a 'first order' knowledge world is also an information impoverished world because when people seek information only from people like themselves or are skeptical of claims not personally experienced, their world has an inevitably limited range of possibilities.

This led to the development of her small world theory of information poverty. In a 1996 study, Chatman revisited the evidence of her earlier studies, including those of retired women, single mothers and university janitors, and thereby developed a number of propositions regarding the information poverty of small world members based on the concepts of deception, risk-taking, secrecy and situational relevance. This theory identifies the socio-psychological schema and the resulting behavior of small world members as the major determinants of their information poverty. It asserts that the information behavior of these people is driven to a great extent by their inclination for self-protection; that they use both secrecy and deception as self-protection mechanisms; that they weigh cautiously the consequence of exposing their real problems to others, which often leads to a decision not to take the risk; and that they tend to assess the relevance of information based on immediate everyday situations and problems, which likely results in limited introduction of new knowledge. These behavioral characteristics are seen to be responsible for disconnecting small world people from the mainstream society and reinforcing their information poverty.

Having explained the phenomenon of information poverty in particular, Chatman went back to theorizing about the small world information behavior in general. Towards the end of the 1990s, she developed a new theory of information behavior based on the concepts of social norms, worldview and social types (Chatman 1999; Pendleton and Chatman 1998). According to this theory, social norms are socially constructed codes of behavior that provide a shared sense of normalcy, rightness and acceptability of things; a worldview is a collective set of beliefs and shared representation of the world held by members of a small world, which allows interpretation of things and meanings; social types are 'persons who exhibit traits or characteristics that distinguish them from other members of their world' (Chatman 1999, p. 214), which enable the construction of social roles that members of a small world assign to each other. Although this new theory aims to explain small world information behavior in general rather than information poverty in particular, it has notable explanatory power for information poverty, as Chatman's own study had already demonstrated. In examining a small word of female prisoners using this framework (1999), Chatman noted that it is through the operation of social norms, worldview and social types that the functioning of the small world is sustained; and because life functions well enough most of the time, members seldom have to seek information from the outside world in relation to day-to-day existence. 'Individuals will cross information boundaries only to the extent that the following conditions are met: (1) the information is perceived as critical, (2) there is a collective expectation that the information is relevant, and (3) a perception exists that the life lived in the round is no longer functioning' (Chatman 1999, p. 214).

While Chatman refined her small world theory, characteristics of this approach, such as focus on a small world setting, emphasis on subjects' representation of everyday life reality, and interest in insider-outsider relationships, were also visible in a number of other studies (Agada 1999; Hersberger 2002; Spink and Cole 2001; Sligo and Jameson 2000). Although conclusions of these studies do not always agree with each other or with Chatman, they have all revealed at least some connections between information poverty and the lived experience of the small world. Spink and Cole's study (2001), for example, showed that, except for employment information, community members seldom seek information from outside the community or from formal communication channels.

2.3 *The knowledge gap thesis*

The term 'knowledge gap' refers to the disparity among the general population in terms of the extent to which they acquire publicly disseminated information. The knowledge gap thesis was initially formulated by Tichenor, et al (1970, p. 159), which states that 'as the infusion of mass media information into a social system increases, segments of the population with higher socioeconomic status tend to acquire this information at a faster rate than the lower status segments, so that the gap in knowledge between these segments tends to increase rather than decrease'.

The publication of this thesis stimulated a large number of related studies on the knowledge gap issue. Gaziano followed the progress of related research and provided comprehensive reviews of the field at different stages (1983, 1995), which the current study draws on heavily. As Gaziano's reviews show, the majority of studies after Tichenor, et al confirmed the existence of some sort of gap, but they have taken distinctively different approaches in defining and explaining the gap. Some of the studies extended Tichenor, et al's study by replicating it with other media (Tichenor, et al focused particularly on printed mass media), or by examining factors or conditions which mediate the gap (Gaziano 1983; Gaziano and O'Leary 1998). Gaziano and O'Leary's study (1998), for example, tested the knowledge gap hypothesis with the communication process of childbirth and infant development knowledge; they also tested the mediating effect of other variables such as the intervention of Brazelton demonstrations of infants' abilities, experience with babies, and social networks. Studies of this type are largely supportive of the original knowledge gap thesis: in addition to confirming the existence of a knowledge gap, they have also developed the original thesis by explaining the effect of socioeconomic factors in the context of other variables. There are, however, studies that have dramatically modified or even refuted the original thesis, as exemplified by Ettema and Kline (1977), Gaziano and Gaziano (1998), and Dervin (2003). Ettema and Kline's study deviated from the original knowledge gap thesis in that it prioritized situation-specific personal factors over cross-situational social status. As a result of their refocused study, Ettema and Kline proposed the following reformulation of the original thesis:

> [A]s the infusion of mass media information into a social system increases, segments of the population motivated to acquire that information and/or

> for which that information is functional tend to acquire the information at a faster rate than those not motivated or for which it is not functional, so that the gap in knowledge between these segments tends to increase rather than decrease. (Ettema and Kline 1977, p. 188)

Dervin, whose critiques will be reviewed in greater detail in the next section, rejected the original knowledge gap thesis altogether, contending that it was led astray by a group of untenable assumptions about information and communications (Dervin 2003). Gaziano and Gaziano (1998) suggest that differences in knowledge acquisition and retention be measured at the group level and be examined in relation to the group culture. They argue that cultural properties, particularly the way in which a group defines a topic, the way it constructs the meaning of related knowledge, and the way it assigns value to the knowledge, play a greater role in knowledge acquisition than individuals' socioeconomic status. On the basis of this argument, Gaziano and Gaziano reformulated the original knowledge gap thesis into the following:

> As the infusion of mass media information into society increases, certain groups will tend to acquire this information at a faster rate than other groups, so that the gap in knowledge between these groups tends to increase because of differences in their social construction of knowledge—that is, their cultures. (1998, p. 130)

2.4 The sense-making theory

The sense-making theory was developed by Dervin at the end of 1970s as a result of her constructivist research on human communications (Dervin 1983, 1999, 2003; Savolainen 1993). It refers to a set of assumptions and propositions about the nature of information, communication and information use, which are in accordance with the constructivist assumptions about the nature of reality, the process of knowing and the nature of knowledge. Sense-making theory assumes that reality is characterized simultaneously by order and change, continuity and discontinuity, and that the same is true of the process of knowing reality. It further assumes that these ontological and epistemological features create gaps everywhere in every attempt by human beings to make sense of reality, which makes it necessary for human beings to constantly engage in gap-bridging activities, such as observing, talking, comparing, contrasting, information seeking and use. It also emphasizes that communication is not a process in which the information seeker receives information by decoding or unpacking the incoming message, but a process in which the receiver constructs information by bringing meaning to the received message.

To Dervin (2003), these assumptions contrast strikingly with the traditional view of communication which underpins the original knowledge gap thesis. The traditional view of communication, according to Dervin, assumes that information is an objective description of reality, that it has definite and fixed meaning which, if everything goes right, can be accessed in the same way by both the sender and the receiver, and that there are objective criteria to measure whether the actual communication process has achieved this effect. These assumptions lead to the belief that it is possible to assign people to either side of the knowledge gap by comparing their acquisition of information. This, Dervin argues, runs counter not only to our intuitive understanding of the actual communication practices, but also to the trend in communication studies of recognizing the creative role of the information receiver in communication.

Indeed, not only does the knowledge gap discourse appear ill-fitting for the sense-making theoretical perspective, but many other information inequality discourses do as well. These discourses imply that individuals occupy comparable locations in the social space where information production, dissemination, access and use serve as frames of reference, and also that for these frames of reference to generate universal meaning for everyone using them, information has to possess at least certain objective, stable and measurable features. The constructivist propositions of sense-making theory—that information, information needs and information use are all subjective in nature—imply, however, that any shared frame of reference based on information itself is impossible. How do we measure and compare individuals by the information they access and use when they do not even share each other's definition of information?

Criticizing information systems and service providers for ignoring the sense-making process of the poor is one way for sense-making theory to approach the information inequality issue while avoiding the 'traps' of either seeing information as objective or blaming the victims for their own predicament. This is what Dervin did in one of her very few studies on information inequality (1989). In that study, Dervin showed how existing research categorized information users into types according to their economic, psychological and geographical characteristics, how these categories were employed as predicting variables for system adoption among different groups of people, how these predictions were used by system developers to define their markets, and how advantaged users became better served and the disadvantaged became worse off as a result of this model of system development. Dervin argues that this model intensifies the existing disparity because it deploys new communication technologies to do what old technologies did at greater speed, with greater search capacity, and at greater distances (1989, p. 217).

Another way for sense-making theory to address the information inequality issue is to examine information-seeking and use in the process of sense-making and to compare the perceived outcomes of information use (Freedman and Henderson 2008; McIver and Prokosch 2002). Freedman and Henderson (2008), for example, investigated how people differ in terms of their ability to use digital information to cope with everyday life situations and what factors best explain this type of digital divide. The study showed that such a digital divide is primarily a function of sense-making activities; it is significantly related to neither education nor income.

2.5 Social network analysis

Social network analysis is a theoretical and methodological approach that originated during the first half of the 20th century in sociology, which grounds its understanding of the social world in the investigation of patterns of relations between social entities (individuals, groups, organizations or any other social units) (Haythornthwaite 1996). It maintains that social networks embed in them valuable resources for production and social mobility, hence generating one of the most important capitals of modern society: social capital.

Information is arguably one of the most significant resources embedded in and exchanged through social networks; it is also the most extensively studied. Related studies have shown that the properties of social networks affect information exchange and acquisition. In a classical social network study, Granovetter (1973) found that people who have a large number of weak ties in their social networks have an advantage in obtaining job information because strong ties tend to possess highly homogeneous information. A number of other studies also confirmed the value of weak ties in providing non-redundant information in different contexts (Granovetter 1983). It can be inferred from these studies that, for those who rely primarily on interpersonal relations for information, the properties of their social networks can have decisive effects on their information access and hence their position in information inequality.

Within LIS and communication studies, a number of studies have examined these implications (Dervin and Greenberg 1972; Chatman 1992; Pettigrew 1997; Hersberger 2003; Johnson 2006; Bishop, et al 1999). Hersberger (2003) studied social networks of homeless parents and found that the respondents' social networks were sparse, unconnected and small in number of ties, comprising primarily shelter workers, Department of Social Services staff, physicians, church support staff, other shelter residents and bail bondsmen. This suggests that, for these people, information access through interpersonal relations is likely to be constrained by the physical proximity and the small number of ties. Johnson (2006) investigated the effect of social networks on information access within and outside social networks among Mongolians and showed that the respondents' socioeconomic status, social networks and choice of information sources were significantly related. Respondents with higher socioeconomic status tended to have social networks with greater reach and diversity, were more likely to know people in prestigious occupations and more likely to choose organizations as sources of information in everyday information-seeking. In contrast, respondents with lower socioeconomic status tended to have social networks with smaller reach and diversity, were less likely to know people in prestigious occupations and more likely to choose media as sources of information.

Seen from the perspective of information inequality, the most salient common threads in the findings of these studies include:

1. As social networks differ in properties, they also tend to differ in the type and quality of information they embed and exchange.

2. There exists a connection between people's socioeconomic status and the property of their social networks, with networks of the disadvantaged being characterized by small size, strong ties and physical proximity.

3. People of the disadvantaged social group generally utilize very few other information channels, particularly formal information channels.

Together, these findings imply that, just as individuals can be categorized into the information-rich and -poor, so can social networks; and that those in information-impoverished social networks have few alternatives to remedy their network-based information poverty. It is therefore reasonable to infer that for this group of people the impoverished information exchange through their social networks is the impoverishment of their information worlds altogether, and that the differences in people's social networks contributes, to a great degree, to their overall information inequality.

2.6 The social exclusion theory

The social exclusion theory is actually a cluster of theories which attempt to explain the phenomenon that some individuals and groups are excluded from the mainstream activities of society. While the phenomenon has always existed, the concept of social exclusion did not emerge until the 1970s, when French politicians began to use the term to describe the marginalization of 'the handicapped, substance abusers, juvenile delinquents, and deviant groups whose conditions excluded them from the then-incomplete social insurance coverage' (Silver 2010, p. 185). From the late 1970s to 1990s, the concept and related discourse began to be taken up by politicians of other countries as well as scholars both within and outside French academia. As the social and ideological context in which the term is used has changed from time to time and from country to country, the concept has also been used to refer to new forms of inequality and discrimination as they come to the fore; the connotation of the term has consequently become rather elusive.

Although earlier connotations of 'social exclusion' emphasized individual deficiency and its threat to social solidarity, the majority of later social exclusion theorists seem to agree that social exclusion is a state and process of deprivation, imposed on its victims by those who have the power to exclude (Barry 2002; Quark 2008). In so far as the theory critiques the oppression of the powerful over the powerless of society, it aligns at least to a certain extent with Marxist critical theories. What differentiates social exclusion theories most notably from Marxist critical theories is that, while the latter see society as a hierarchy of social classes with some at the top (the dominating class), some in the middle, and some at the bottom (the dominated class), social exclusion theories tend to see society as an evolving social plane, with some at the centre and some at the margin. Social exclusion theories also differ from Marxist critical theories in a number of other ways. Firstly, while Marxist critical theories examine society primarily at the macro level, social exclusion research seems to engage in both macro and micro research depending on context, with some studies opting to focus on macro level phenomena like income disparity, labour market, welfare institutions and social policies, and some choosing to focus on the living conditions of individuals. Secondly, while Marxist critical theories examine social exclusion and oppression in relation to class, social exclusion theories see social exclusion as a multidimensional process based on a wide range of factors including income, education, race, housing, health and family structure, etc. As the following discussion will show, these are also the major differences between PEI-based and social-exclusion-based information inequality analysis.

From the perspective of social exclusion, inadequate access to information is undoubtedly a critical form of exclusion in the information society. To many researchers (Caidi and Allard 2005; Selwyn 2009; Lloyd, et al 2010), this form can be seen as both fostering and fostered by other forms of social exclusion, for lack of information access inevitably hinders people's social and democratic participation, while deprivation of materials, education, social services, etc. inevitably hampers people's access to information. Since the 1990s, this understanding has underpinned an increasing number of studies on various forms of information inequality (Quark 2008; Caidi and Allard 2005; Selwyn 2009; Lloyd, et al 2010; Pateman 1999; Wong, et al 2009; Warschauer 2003; Valentine, et al 2002; Vicente 2010; Mossberger, et al 2006; Japzon and Gong 2005; Caidi, et al 2007; Haddon 2000; Karabanow and Naylor 2007).

At least three sub-clusters of literature can be identified as having certain affinity with the social exclusion theoretical perspective. The first group consists of studies which examine the impact of social exclusion on information access (Wong, et al 2009; Warchauer 2003; Valentine, et al 2002; Vicente 2010; Mossberger, et al 2006; Japzon and Gong 2005; Caidi, et al 2007). Mossberger, et al (2006), for example, examined the impact of racial segregation and the concentration of poverty on the digital divide. This study shows that, for the African-Americans, it is not their ethnicity itself but racial discrimination against it that has caused this group to lag behind the digital revolution; in fact, individuals of this group are found to be more motivated to use the internet than other low-income groups. Japzon and Gong (2005) examined the relationship between community characteristics and public library use and found that social connections and racial integration stimulate public library use, while social segregation impedes it.

The second group consists of studies which pinpoint a certain excluded group of people, e.g. immigrants (Caidi and Allard 2005; Lloyd, et al 2010), single parents (Haddon 2000), street youth (Karabanow and Naylor 2007) and people in geographically marginalized areas (David 2003), and examine their lived experience of information or digital exclusion. Karabanow and Naylor (2007), for example, interviewed 20 street youth in a Canadian coastal city in relation to their interpretation and experience of ICT access. The study found that these people saw the relevance of ICT to their present and future lives and tried to maintain regular and even daily access to ICTs; however, their homeless status seemed to have greatly aggravated their difficulties in getting access to ICTs, not only because they could not afford personal computers but also because they lacked permanent addresses and therefore library cards to log on to public library computers.

The third group consists of studies which examine the role of libraries, community ICT centers and other community programs in combating social exclusion through ameliorating information inequality (Pateman 1999; Hull 2003; Dutch and Muddiman 2001). For scholars of this perspective, strategies to alleviate information inequality are meaningful only in so far as they really foster social inclusion. For this reason, they tend to go beyond services and technology provisions to examine actual use and are critical of those policies and programs focusing on physical access only. The 'Open to All? The Public Library and Social Exclusion' project in the UK, for example, has challenged the deep-rooted conviction that public libraries are a great contributor to social inclusion in and of themselves. As part of this project, Dutch and Muddiman (2001) critically reviewed UK government initiatives to upgrade public libraries with ICTs. The study shows that these initiatives have preoccupied themselves with technological access rather than real service transformation and have therefore fallen short of their stated objectives of closing the digital divide.

2.7 Diffusion of innovation theory

Research of the diffusion of new ideas, knowledge, practice and objects can be traced a long way back (Chatman 1986; Rogers 1962). In 1962, American scholar Everett Rogers conducted an extensive review of over 500 related studies, which greatly promoted research interest in the diffusion of innovation. In general, this research sees diffusion of innovation as an important driver for social change and attempts to model the process and factors through which innovations are spread. Rogers (1962), for example, confirmed that diffusion of an innovation follows an s-shaped curve, which means that for a successfully diffused innovation there tends to be a period of relatively slow take-up by a small proportion of the population (early adopters), which is followed by a period of relatively rapid adoption by the majority of members of a social system and then by a period of a gradual saturation of diffusion. This type of research, while providing insights into innovation-induced social change, can also help innovation producers and disseminators to ascertain what facilitates or prohibits diffusion; it is therefore engaged by researchers from varied disciplines, such as economics, sociology, management, and the fields where innovations are produced or utilized.

ICT is perhaps one of the most influential and transforming technologies of the 20th century; its diffusion process has consequently attracted great interest from a very wide range of disciplines. Joining the traditional diffusion discourse with the emerging digital divide discourse and assuming that the force of diffusion is dispersed among various factors whose effect can be quantitatively measured and modeled, this research has investigated a great variety of factors that supposedly affect the rate of ICT adoption. Some of the related studies are concerned primarily with the diffusion of ICT in the global market (the digital divide between countries); others are concerned with the process within a certain social system (the digital divide within a country). In reviewing the digital divide literature prior to 2005, Yu (2006) notes that the following factors were often identified as influencing ICT adoption in different countries: economic development, information infrastructure, information policies, regulatory framework and cultural characteristics. A different set of factors was often identified as influencing the rate of adoption by different sections of society: income level, education, race, gender, age, residential locations, family structure, interest and attitudes.

Examination of recent literature shows that the diffusion of innovation theory remains one of the most influential perspectives (if not the most influential) for digital divide studies. Investigation of ICT diffusion among countries (the global digital divide) continues in the studies of Billon, et al (2010), Pick and Azari (2008), Robinson and Crenshaw (2010) and many others. Investigation of ICT diffusion within a certain social system continues in the studies of Goldfarb and Prince (2008), Martin and Robinson (2007), and many more. With the emergence of new studies, there have been more complex ways of measuring the digital divide and more sophisticated models for explaining the variance; however, few studies have come up with dramatically different pictures of the digital divide or different sets of explanatory variables. In general they show that significant digital divide still persists between countries and within societies and that socioeconomic conditions continue to explain a large proportion of variance in ICT access.

2.8 Community informatics

Community informatics (CI) is an emerging discipline focusing on ICT-enabled community development. The discipline is rooted primarily in the research and development activities of the community networking movement of the 1990s, which aimed to wire up and empower communities using new information technologies. As the movement grew into continuing and widespread community-based ICT development, in around 2000–2001, a number of scholars began to address related research and development CI (Gurstein 2008). They defined CI as a discipline that brings together community development and the opportunities afforded by ICT initiatives (Gurstein 2007), which does for communities what a management information system (MIS) does for organizations, but in fundamentally different ways (Gurstein 2008; McIver 2003).

Today CI is still at an early stage of forming coherent theories. However, by drawing on theories of community development, social capital and user-centered system design, CI scholars seem to have synthesized a range of shared views about ICT and communities in relation to each other and with contemporary society (Gurstein 2007, 2008; McIver 2003; Bishop and Bruce 2005; Williams and Durrance 2008). With respect to ICT in relation to communities and society, they reject the discourses that present ICT as a neutral tool for development, and ICT-engendered empowerment as contingent upon physical access to technologies. Instead, CI scholars see ICT as a power-distributing tool subject to the influence of both technological and non-technological factors, and ICT-engendered empowerment as contingent on effective use. With respect to communities in relation to ICT and network society, they reject the notion of network society based only on individual players and their links, and argue instead for the pivotal role of communities (Gurstein 2007).

These shared views about ICT and communities have laid the theoretical foundations for CI's commitment to ensuring universal access, and provided CI scholars with a distinct community-based perspective for examining the digital divide. CI defines the digital divide as the disparity in the capacity and opportunity to use ICTs effectively to achieve identified goals between and within communities (Gurstein 2003), and endeavors to bridge this divide using community-based ICT initiatives. Therefore, CI-inspired digital divide research (Kvasny 2002; Kvasny and Keil 2002; Williams, et al 2005; Durrance and Fisher 2003) is usually, if not always, conducted in the concrete context of ICT projects for certain communities. Typical issues to be investigated include how the digital divide manifests in the specific context of community-based ICT projects, who benefits and who does not from these projects and why, and what factors affect their effectiveness and long-term sustainability in bridging the digital divide. Kvasny, Keil and colleagues (Kvasny 2002; Kvasny and Keil 2002), for instance, traced the development of two community ICT projects with a view to identifying factors that prevented them from becoming as successful as expected. Both projects aimed to address the digital divide between disadvantaged communities and the rest of society: one through operating community telecenters and the other through providing free internet access from homes; both spurred far lower interest among community members than expected. The studies found that the digital divide is rooted in the historical, institutional, economic, social, cultural and situational contexts of communities, and is determined by the economic, social and cultural capital available to community members, which suggests that the issue is of such a degree of complexity that it is beyond the solutions of a quick technology fix.

3 Reflection on the divided views of information inequality research

This brief review of information inequality research shows that, while recognizing the central position of the information inequality issue in an information society, scholars have approached the issue from very different perspectives and in very different ways. Major differences of these perspectives are summarized in Table 1.

ectives	Forms of information inequality examined	Focus of analysis	Unit of analysis	Data used in analysis	Major determining fact identified
	Disparity between social classes or countries in information production, dissemination, access and use	Relationship between the established social order and the distribution of information	Society as a whole	Facts regarding social and information inequalities	Capitalist pursuit of profits in domestic and international informati market
world theory	Information segregation between insiders and outsiders of a small world	How conceptualization and practices in a small world induce information poverty	Individual	Perceptions and lived experience in a small world	Conceptualizations and actions of small world members
ledge gap (original)	Disparity between social strata in acquiring mass media information	Relationship between social stratification and knowledge gap	Individual and/or aggregate	Measurement of social strata and knowledge gap	One's position in socia strata
ledge gap thesis	Disparity between individuals in acquiring mass media information	Relationship between context-specific personal factors and knowledge gap	Individual	Measurement of personal factors and knowledge gap	Individual motivations, attitudes, experience,
-making theory	Disparity between individuals in the perceived outcome (gap-bridging) of information use	Information-seeking and use in relation to the sense-making process	Individual	Sense-making activities and perceived outcome	Sense making activities and information systen service design
network analysis	Disparity between individuals in information exchange via social networks	Relationship between properties of social networks and information exchange	Individual relationships	Measurement of network properties	Interpersonal relations nodes and links constituting these relations
ion of innovation	Disparity between individuals in ICT adoption	The process through which ICTs are spread within a social system	Individual and/or aggregate	Measurement of demographic factors and access to ICTs	Income, education, rac location, age, family structure, etc.
exclusion theory	Disparity between mainstream society and the excluded in using information & ICT for participation	The relationship between social exclusion and information or digital exclusion	Individual and/or aggregate	Measurement or lived experience of exclusion	Multifaceted process o social exclusion
	Disparity between and within communities in using ICTs to achieve identified goals	Digital divide in the concrete contexts of ICT-enabled community development projects	Individual	Lived experience of community members	Community characteristics; various capitals available to community members

Table 1. Differences between major theoretical perspectives for information inequality research

Related perspectives differ first of all in the forms of information inequality they tend to examine (column 2 in Table 1). Although there are concerns about information inequality in general, many studies choose to focus on particular forms of information inequalities, and there seems to be a tendency to choose certain forms depending on the perspectives at work. While PEI and the social exclusion theory have been applied to both the information and digital divides, the small world theory has been applied almost exclusively to information poverty, and the diffusion of innovation theory and CI almost exclusively to the digital divide (although the two perspectives define the digital divide in notably different ways).

These perspectives differ secondly in their focus of analysis. PEI focuses on the relationship between the established social order and the distribution of media for information production and access, and therefore foregrounds class relations in its analysis. The social exclusion theory focuses on the relationship between social exclusion and information or digital exclusion, where social exclusion is understood as a process of multifaceted exclusion based on socioeconomic factors as well as other factors such as gender, location of residence, family structure, housing and health conditions. The original knowledge gap thesis focuses on the rate of mass media information acquisition among different social strata; the diffusion of innovation theory focuses on the diffusion of ICTs among various categories of people. The small world theory examines how information poverty happens in the specific contexts of a small world, while CI examines how the digital divide occurs in the specific contexts of a community and an ICT-enabled development project.

The above perspectives also differ in other ways which are not shown in Table 1 for lack of space. They differ, for example, in the way they define the nature of the divide they observe. In observing the digital divide, for instance, PEI, the social exclusion theory and CI explicitly regard the divide as a form of deep-rooted social inequality; the diffusion of innovation theory, on the other hand, tends to see it as a naturally occurring phenomenon and an inevitable stage during the diffusion of ICTs from earlier adopters to laggards. Correspondingly, while the former three perspectives maintain a highly critical stance towards the digital divide, the diffusion of innovation theory seems to have taken a fairly neutral position: research from this perspective tends to avoid value-laden terms such as 'inequality', 'deprivation', 'social justice', etc., and when it argues for narrowing the divide, it does so mainly out of economic and development concerns.

Columns four to six in Table 1 show that the differences between existing perspectives of information inequality research also embody the traditional division of social sciences in general, i.e. the division between society vs individual, structure vs agency, and objectivism vs subjectivism. In relation to the society vs individual (or macro vs micro) dichotomy, the contrast is most notable between PEI and other perspectives. While the PEI perspective focuses on the features and institutions of society as a whole, other perspectives focus mainly on individuals and their aggregates: the small world theory on individuals' impoverished lifestyle, knowledge gap thesis on their socioeconomic status or motivations, the social exclusion theory on their living conditions, and the diffusion of innovation theory on their demographic and other attributes. This difference reflects the differentiation made by Smythe, a pioneer PEI scholar, between political economy of communication and various micro approaches to communication:

> Our point of view is distinguishable from that of 'micro-analysis' in that there the focus of attention remains the individual and his group behavior is only significant in relation to him. . The central purpose of the study of the political economy of communications is to evaluate the effects of communication agencies in terms of the policies by which they are organized and operated. Our concern will therefore be with the structure and policies of these communication agencies in their social settings. (Smythe 1960, pp. 563–564)

On the 'structure vs agency' front, the contrast is most notable between PEI and the original knowledge gap thesis on the one hand, and the small world theory, the sense-making theory and the revisionist knowledge gap thesis on the other. To PEI scholars, it is a combination of structural forces (e.g. media ownership pattern, capitalist pursuit of economic interest, and information policies) that marginalize the disadvantaged in the information field and render them information-poor; to proponents of the original knowledge gap thesis, it is the position of individuals in the overall structure of society that conditions their acquisition of media messages. However, for followers of the revisionist knowledge gap thesis, the small world theory and the sense-making theory, such structural analysis misses too much of the active role of the agent, and will likely misconstrue the causal relationships. They argue instead for the centrality of individual motivations, conceptualizations and actions in explaining knowledge gap, information poverty and inequalities.

> Structure is energized by, maintained, reified, changed, and created by individual acts of communicating. Because we have sought only across time-space understanding, we have missed so much of the whole range of human existence that involves struggling with, breaking with, coming to terms with and changing whatever structure the human finds himself in. (Dervin 2003, p. 276)

The dichotomy between objectivism and subjectivism is most evident between PEI, the original knowledge gap thesis and the diffusion of innovation theory on the one hand, and the small world theory, the sense-making theory and the revised knowledge gap thesis on the other. The former strives to observe, measure and model the divide and its antecedents objectively, and the latter tries to perceive and interpret the divide and its formation from the subject's point of view. The division is particularly telling in Dervin's critiques of the philosophical assumptions of the original knowledge gap thesis. As reviewed in the previous section, Dervin sees the notions of knowledge gap and information inequities as resting on the flawed assumptions 'that the informational content of messages exists independent of either sources or receivers and can have impacts on receivers independent of any intervention by receivers' (Dervin 2003, p. 35). To Dervin, these assumptions are flawed because they ignore the essence of information as sense-made and the active role of receiver in its creation.

These divisions of perspectives in information inequality research are summarized in Table 2. As this summary and the foregoing review show, despite the fact that information inequality has been recognized as a highly complex issue straddling both sides of nearly all the above dichotomies, there has been little attempt to bridge the divided views and formulate integrative theories for the issue.

rspectives	Forms of information inequality examined	Focus of analysis	Unit of analysis	Data used in analysis	Major determining f identified
I	Disparity between social classes or countries in information production, dissemination, access and use	Relationship between the established social order and the distribution of information	Society as a whole	Facts regarding social and information inequalities	Capitalist pursuit of profits in domestic international inforr market
ıall world theory	Information segregation between insiders and outsiders of a small world	How conceptualization and practices in a small world induce information poverty	Individual	Perceptions and lived experience in a small world	Conceptualizations actions of small wo members
ıowledge gap esis (original)	Disparity between social strata in acquiring mass media information	Relationship between social stratification and knowledge gap	Individual and/or aggregate	Measurement of social strata and knowledge gap	One's position in sc strata
ıowledge gap thesis ɛv.)	Disparity between individuals in acquiring mass media information	Relationship between context-specific personal factors and knowledge gap	Individual	Measurement of personal factors and knowledge gap	Individual motivatio attitudes, experienc
nse-making theory	Disparity between individuals in the perceived outcome (gap-bridging) of information use	Information-seeking and use in relation to the sense-making process	Individual	Sense-making activities and perceived outcome	Sense making activi and information sys service design
cial network analysis	Disparity between individuals in information exchange via social networks	Relationship between properties of social networks and information exchange	Individual relationships	Measurement of network properties	Interpersonal relati nodes and links constituting these relations
ffusion of innovation	Disparity between individuals in ICT adoption	The process through which ICTs are spread within a social system	Individual and/or aggregate	Measurement of demographic factors and access to ICTs	Income, education, location, age, family structure, etc.
cial exclusion theory	Disparity between mainstream society and the excluded in using information & ICT for participation	The relationship between social exclusion and information or digital exclusion	Individual and/or aggregate	Measurement or lived experience of exclusion	Multifaceted proces social exclusion
	Disparity between and within communities in using ICTs to achieve identified goals	Digital divide in the concrete contexts of ICT-enabled community development projects	Individual	Lived experience of community members	Community characteristics; vari capitals available to community membe

Table 2. Divisions of perspectives in information inequality research

It needs to be recognized at this stage that during the past decade there has been a notable trend towards developing multidimensional/multivariate frameworks for information inequality, particularly for the digital divide. It has been increasingly recognized, for example, that the digital divide concerns not just the disparity in physical access to technologies, but disparities in multiple categories of access; and it is determined by many complex factors and processes (Dijk 2005; Kim and Kim 2001; Warschauer 2003; Norris 2001; Selwyn 2004). Dijk (2005), for example, has identified four successive and accumulative categories of access (motivational, material, skills and usage) and has sought explanations for the access-based digital divide in the relations between personal and positional categorical pairs such as old and young, and employed and unemployed. Kim and Kim (2001) similarly see the digital divide as comprising multidimensional divides (in terms of media accessibility, information mobilization, information consciousness) along different stages (opportunity, utilization and reception), with the first dimension and stage being closely linked to economic conditions, the second dimension and stage to social environment, and the third dimension and stage to individuals' ability.

These frameworks have demonstrated that it is possible to encompass different forms and levels of information inequality in one concept, and to incorporate different factors—demographic, socioeconomic and even psychological—in one model. However, studies of this type should not be mistaken for the integrative approach to theorizing espoused by Bourdieu. While the latter aims specifically at improving our understanding of the social world by bridging the deep-rooted divisions between intellectual traditions, the majority of these studies aim at improving the explanatory power of existing theories via multivariate modeling. As such, they represent a different order of theorizing from the integrative approach and differ from the latter in at least two aspects. Firstly, in the attempt to render the frameworks empirically testable, these studies tend to assume individuals as the unit of analysis, and individuals' demographic, socioeconomic and psychological factors as covariates of information and digital divides. They also assume that both information inequality and its covariates can be measured objectively and their relationships modeled objectively. In this way, they tend to embody rather than bridge the traditional divisions of social sciences. Secondly, in line with the underlying assumption of multivariate modeling, these studies tend to assume that different factors account for information inequality in a dispersed manner (that is, each accounting for a certain percentage of variance) In this way, they tend to segregate rather than integrate the effect of factors at different levels (macro and micro) or factors of different natures (the structural and agentic) on information inequality.

4 Conclusion and call for integrative research

As mentioned in the Introduction (Section 1), during the past three decades or so, there has been a notable trend toward integrative theorizing about the social world in the wider area of social sciences, which aims to reconcile the longstanding divisions between different research traditions, including the macro vs micro, the structure vs agency and the objectivism vs subjectivism divisions. Bourdieu's theory of habitus and field and Giddens' theory of the duality of structure are the most notable examples of this trend.

The interdisciplinary area of information inequality research, however, is still largely divided along traditional dichotomies. Macro research examines information inequality by focusing on skewed production and distribution society's information resources, and on societal factors responsible for the inequality. By contrast, micro research examines it by focusing on disparate individual access to information and information technologies, and on individuals' attributes and actions associated with the inequality. Structure-oriented research relates information inequality to the structural forces of society, paying particular attention to the effect of social stratification, whereas agency-oriented research relates it to the active role of individuals, paying particular attention to their motivations, interest, perceptions and actions. Objectivist research takes information inequality as an objective state of human differences and attempts to express and explain it through objectively measured variables. Subjectivist research sees it as people's lived experience (empowerment or helplessness) with information and tries to interpret it in the context of their everyday life and immediate environment. These divisions are not only evident in the clustering of related research as reviewed in this article, but also in their explicit criticism of each other.

LIS is a discipline with the responsibility to ensure maximum discoverability and accessibility of information for individuals. As such, it sees information inequality as problematic for some members of society in terms of both information discoverability and accessibility, and therefore sees it as an issue of great disciplinary concern. This stance has led the field to focus mainly on individuals when participating in information inequality research. However, with the ascendance of information as society's strategic resource, LIS has also begun to draw on concepts and theories from those studies focusing on society as a whole, particularly the PEI perspective in communication studies (Buchanan 1999; Doctor 1991, 1994; Birdsall 1997, 2000; Harris, et al 1998). The growth of this interest may well cause LIS-produced information inequality research to be divided between macro vs micro perspectives, adding to the already yawning gap between objectivist and subjectivist points of view (Budd 2001; Hjørland 2005).

There are a number of reasons why research on information inequality should heed the development of integrative theories in the wider social sciences. Firstly, intuitively and intellectually, we know that information inequality cannot be explained by societal or individual factors alone and cannot be understood from either the objective or subjective stance. Intuitively, we would easily agree with the argument that people occupying different places in the social space also occupy very different places along the information inequality spectrum; we would also easily agree that people with different mental schemes of the world will likely approach information and information services in different ways, hence assuming different positions in information inequality. Intellectually, studies reviewed in this article have provided ample evidence for both the objective and subjective origin of information inequality and revealed the effect of both structure and agency; studies from other areas of LIS, particularly information behavior research, have provided further supportive evidence. In light of this evidence, it is natural to ask where in the process of producing and reproducing information inequalities forces from both sides connect with each other and how.

Secondly, constrained by various intellectual divisions, existing theories of information inequality are inevitably limited in their explanatory power. The political economy of information perspective and the original knowledge gap thesis, for example, have provided extensive accounts of the determining role of social structure in information inequality, but they have said very little about the way in which this structure can be and is being resisted. This has afforded them a rather pessimistic view about information inequality. As Dervin (2003) once commented, these theories have in fact constructed for information inequality a trap-like quality, unbreakable by individual efforts. By contrast, the small world theory and the sense-making theory have put the active role of individuals at the centre of their study, to the extent that societal and structural features are seldom intentionally investigated. Consequently, although they have not explicitly denied the impact of structural forces, they have rarely gone as far as to explain what this impact is and how it is connected to individual choices. In fact, they have constantly maintained that personal, group and situational factors provide better explanations for information poverty. In so doing, they have actually fallen back into the 'blame the victim' trap which they wanted very much to avoid. The explanatory inadequacy of existing theories becomes particularly apparent when we are faced with some of the most intriguing questions about information inequality:

1. How does information as sense made and as society's strategic resource account for the information inequality together?
2. How is such inequality produced and reproduced in an information society?
3. Why is it produced and reproduced without resistance from the disadvantaged?
4. Why cannot and do not those left behind catch up even when seemingly equalizing measures are designed and implemented by governments and various institutions?

Thirdly, effective policies and initiatives to combat information inequality also need to be informed by integrative explanation of the issue. During the past decade, with a series of the world summits, international and national conferences being recurrently devoted to finding solutions to information inequality, the issue has become a central concern of policy debates. However, as Yu (2006) noted, if policy-makers and the general public look to the research community for intellectual support during these debates, they will probably become even more baffled, for different clusters of research have prescribed notably different and sometimes contradictory policy recommendations. Those clusters that focus primarily on social structure tend to call for radical changes to institutional arrangement; those that focus primarily on individual agency tend to urge service improvement and individual empowerment. Political and ideological interference aside, effective solutions to information inequality depend on a comprehensive understanding of the issue.

Integrative theorizing offers a possible means to address the above questions and need. To illustrate this possibility, Bourdieu's research on social inequality is worth recapturing. By analyzing people's social and cultural practices in relation to their positions in the social space, and by drawing on evidence from a huge body of both qualitative and quantitative data, Bourdieu found that individuals, having been placed in a particular social position long enough and having been constantly shaped by conditions and opportunities available to that position, will develop a certain disposition (habitus) that generates preferences and actions intrinsically compatible to those conditions and opportunities. In this way, habitus tends to lead individuals to perceive constrained possibilities as preferences and structural inequalities as differences, and to act in a way that reproduces existing inequality. Through this theorizing, Bourdieu managed to connect 'relations of domination both to identifiable social agents and to the institutions of the modern state' (Cronin 1996, p. 55). In so doing, he also proved that, firstly, it is feasible to develop theoretical constructs that bridge the deep-rooted divisions between structure and agency, society and individual, objectivism and subjectivism; secondly, it is possible for these theoretical constructs to offer a relatively universal explanation for social inequality in different contexts (that is, to retain high external validity while taking agentic and subjective factors into account); and, thirdly, it is methodologically possible to develop such theoretical constructs through empirical investigation of human practices following a relational mode of thinking (Bordieu 1989).

It can be further argued that Bourdieu's integrative approach holds particular relevance for information inequality research in LIS. On the one hand, key concepts of Bourdieu's theory (habitus, capital and field) originated primarily from empirical research in the areas of education and culture, both overlapping with the information arena, and have been applied by LIS scholars on a number of occasions (Savolainen 1995; Kvasny 2002; Kvasny and Keil 2002). This suggests that theoretical constructs modeled on Bourdieu's are likely to have great explanatory power for information issues. On the other hand, central methodologies of Bourdieu's approach utilize human practices as empirical evidence and relational modes of thinking as way of analysis. It can be argued that LIS, with its easy access to rich empirical evidence of human information practices, is uniquely positioned to take advantage of this approach.

But why do we not just apply Bourdieu's concepts directly to explaining information inequality as many scholars have already attempted? While there is no doubt that habitus and other concepts of Bourdieu may explain certain phenomena in information inequality, it is advisable to remain skeptical about direct application in lieu of innovative theory development (Jaeger 2010). In addition to the general criticism of Bourdieu from scholars of various disciplines (Cronin 1996; Adams 2006), the main reason for our skepticism here is that key concepts of Bourdieu's are rooted primarily in cultural practices and reflect that origin in both their connotations and explanatory power. Consider, for example, the habits of attending or evading concerts and public libraries. While the case of concerts may be explained by the intricate relation between material conditions, cultural capital and habitus, the case of public libraries just does not fit the framework as well: public libraries in Western countries are free, open to all and universally distributed and are therefore much less selective on the basis of material conditions and cultural capital. Consider, for another instance, a person who prefers pop music knowing that many others go for symphonies, and a second person who chooses to remain ignorant about issues pertaining to his interests knowing that others are much better informed. Compliance of the former can perhaps be attributed to the mediation of habitus which neutralizes inequality between high-brow and low-brow cultures as mere differences, but compliance of the latter can hardly be explained in the same way: the contrast between ignorance and knowledge is simply too great to be neutralized as differences.

In short, the divided views of information inequality that embody the dichotomous intellectual traditions of social sciences have left many intriguing questions regarding information inequality unanswered. Bourdieu's integrative theory of social inequality exemplifies a promising approach towards addressing these questions but it is unlikely to offer ready-made answers. An innovative adoption of Bourdieu's or other integrative approaches is called for. The end result may be a more nuanced LIS version of 'habitus' or 'duality of structure' or other constructs of even greater novelty. Whatever it is, it promises to bring together individual and society, agency and structure, subjectivism and objectivism in explaining and resolving information inequality, and in so doing, it may also open opportunities for LIS to exploit its knowledge and evidence about human information practices and lead the cross-disciplinary theory development for information inequality.

Bibliography

CNNIC. 中国互联网络状况发展报告 [R]. 2002-2011.

爱聚（北京）咨询有限公司 . 关于多背一公斤 [EB/OL]. [2009-12-07]. http://www.1kg.org/misc/about.

改革开放 30 年记录中国软件发展史 [EB/OL]. [2012-2-12] http://news.ifeng.com/special/30yearsit/200811/1119_5053_885073_shtml.

国务院新闻办公室 .《中国互联网状况》白皮书 [EB/OL]. [2012-2-12] http://politics.people.com.cn/GB/1026/11813615.html .

赖茂生 . 信息制度建设——情报学的新课题 : 2009 北京大学情报学与信息管理论坛 , 北京 , 2009 年 5 月 9-10 日 [C]. 北京 : 北京大学信息管理系 ,2009.

秦海 , 杨京英 . 中国信息化发展指数统计监测年度报告 [R]. 2011.

陶传进 . 社会公益供给——NPO、公共部门与市场 [M]. 北京 : 清华大学出版社 , 2005: 8.

田野 . 光辉历程 中国计算机发展 50 年专栏 · 回顾 50 年新起点 .[J]. 中国互联网用户 . 2006(49).

王名 . NGO 研究丛书总序 [M]/ 社会公益供给 : NPO、公共部门与市场 [M]. 北京 : 清华大学出版社 , 2005: 1-21.

中国企业联合会 . 2011 中国 500 强企业发展报告 [R]. 企业管理出版社 , 2011.

中华人民共和国国家统计局 . 中国统计年鉴 [M]. 中国统计出版社 , 1991-2010.

中华人民共和国工信部 . 2010 年全国软件业务收入达到 1.3 万亿元 [EB/OL]. [2012-2-12] http://www.miit.gov.cn/n11293472/n11293832/n11294132/n12858477/13583251.html.

乐龄合作社 . 关于我们 [EB/OL]. [2009-12-08]. http://www.seniorcitizen.org.cn/us.html.

"A New Kind of Service of Wireless Internet Access Supplied by Starbucks Coffee." Lingshou.com, 2005. http://www.lingshou.com/www/Starbucks/Starbucks_marketing/05271845855.htm.

Adams, Matthew. "Hybridizing Habitus and Reflexivity: Towards an Understanding of Contemporary Identity?" Sociology 40, no. 3 (June 1, 2006): 511–528.

"Africana Studies 4900, 'Cyberspace and the Black Experience,' at U of Toledo." The Chronicle of Higher Education, May 19, 2000.

Agada, J. "Inner-city Gatekeepers: An Exploratory Survey of Their Information Use Environment." Journal of the American Society for Information Science 50, no. 1 (1999): 74–85.

Agre, Philip E., and Douglas Schuler, eds. Reinventing Technology, Rediscovering Community: Critical Explorations of Computing as a Social Practice. Greenwich, Connecticut: Ablex, 1997.

Alkalimat, Abdul. Introduction to Afro-American Studies: A Peoples College Primer. Twenty First Century Books & Publications, 1986. http://eblackstudies.org/intro.

Alkalimat, Abdul, Doug Gills, and Kate Williams, eds. Job?Tech: The Technological Revolution and Its Impact on Society. Chicago: Twenty First Century Books & Publications, 1995.

Alkalimat, Abdul, and Kate Williams. "Social Capital and Cyberpower in the African American Community: A Case Study of a Community Technology Center in the Dual City." In Community Informatics : Shaping Computer-mediated Social Relations, edited by Leigh Keeble and Brian Loader, 177–204. London: Routledge, 2001.

American Library Association. "Code of Ethics of the American Library Association", Adopted at the 1939 Midwinter Meeting by the ALA Council; amended June 30, 1981; June 28, 1995; and January 22, 2008. http://www.ala.org/advocacy/proethics/codeofethics/codeethics.

Angelusz, Robert, and Robert Tardos. "The Strength and Weakness of 'Weak Ties'." In Values, Networks and Cultural Reproduction in Hungary, edited by P. Somlai.

Budapest: The Coordinating Council of Programs, 1991.

Associated Press. "China Closes 3,300 Cybercafes", December 27, 2002.

Banfield, Edward C. The Moral Basis of a Backward Society. New York: Free Press, 1958.

——. The Unheavenly City. Boston: Little, Brown, 1968.

Barabasi, A. Linked: The New Science of Networks. Cambridge, Massachusetts: Perseus Publising, 2002.

Barnes, J. A. Social Networks. Reading, Massachusetts: Addison-Wesley Pub. Co., 1972.

Barry, B. "Social Exclusion, Social Isolation and the Distribution of Income." In Understanding Social Exclusion, edited by J Hills, J Le Grand, and D Piachaud, 13–29. Oxford: Oxford University Press, 2002.

Becker, Gary. Human Capital. Chicago: University of Chicago Press, 1964.

Becker, S., M. Crandall, K. Fisher, B. Kinney, C. Landry, and A. Rocha. Opportunity for All: How the American Public Benefits from Internet Access at U.S. Libraries. Washington, D.C.: Institute of Museum and Library Services, 2010.

Beijing Municipal Bureau of Statistics. Beijing Statistical Yearbook 2010. Beijing: China Statistics Press, 2010.

Bell, C., and H. Newby. "Community, Communion, Class and Community Action." In Social Areas in Cities II: Spatial Perspectives on Problems and Policies, edited by David T. Herbert and R.J. Johnson, 189–207. London: John Wiley, 1976.

Bell, Wendell. Foundations of Futures Studies: Human Science for a New Era: History, Purposes, and Knowledge. New Brunswick, New Jersey: Transaction Publishers, 1997.

Belshaw, C. Traditional Exchange and Modern Markets. Englewood Cliffs, New Jersey: Prentice Hall, 1965.

Bender, Thomas. Community and Social Change in America. New Brunswick, New Jersey: Rutgers University Press, 1978.

Benjamin, P. "Telecentres and Universal Capability: A Study of the Telecentre

Programmes of the Universal Service Agency, South Africa 1996–2000". Aalborg University, 2001.

Bertot, J., and C. McClure. Public Libraries and the Internet 2000: Summary Findings and Data Tables. Washington, D.C.: U.S. National Commission on Libraries and Information Science, 2000. http://plinternetsurvey.org/sites/default/files/publications/2000_plinternet.pdf.

Bertot, John. "Public Access Technologies in Public Libraries: Effects and Implications." Information Technology and Libraries 28, no. 2 (2009): 81–92.

Bhuiyan, AJMSA. "Peripheral View: Conceptualizing the Information Society as a Postcolonial Subject." International Communication Gazette 70, no. 2 (April 1, 2008): 99–116.

Billon, M, F Lera-Lopez, and R Marco. "Differences in Digitalization Levels: a Multivariate Analysis Studying the Global Digital Divide." Review of the World Economy 146 (2010): 39–73.

Birdsall, W. F. "'New Deal' for Libraries in the Digital Age?" Library Trends 46, no. 1 (1997): 52–67.

Birdsall, William F. "The Digital Divide in the Liberal State: a Canadian Perspective." First Monday 5, no. 12 (April 13, 2007). http://frodo.lib.uic.edu/ojsjournals/index.php/fm/article/view/820.

Bishop, Ann Peterson. "Communities for the New Century." Journal of Adolescent and Adult Literacy 43 (2000). http://www.readingonline.org/electronic/jaal/2-00_Column.html.

——, ed. Emerging Communities: Integrating Networking Information into Library Services. Champaign, IL: Graduate School of Library and Information Science, University of Illinois at Urbana-Champaign, 1993.

Bishop, Ann Peterson, Imani Bazzell, Bharat Mehra, and Cynthia Smith. "Afya: Social and Digital Technologies That Reach Across the Digital Divide." First Monday 6, no. 4 (April 2, 2001). http://firstmonday.org/htbin/cgiwrap/bin/ojs/index.php/fm/article/view/847/756.

Bishop, Ann Peterson, and Bertram (Chip) Bruce. "Community Informatics: Integrating Action, Research and Learning." Bulletin of the American Society for

Information Science and Technology 31, no. 6 (2005): 6–10.

Bishop, Ann Peterson, Susan Shoemaker, Tonyia J. Tidline, and Pamela Salela. "Information Exchange Networks in Low-Income Neighborhoods: Implications for Community Networking." Proceedings of the ASIS Annual Meeting 36 (1999): 443–49.

Blakely, Edward, Stefanus Hadi, and Paul Johnson. "Information City and the Ghetto: The L.A. Experience. Working Paper LCRI-95-10P". Los Angeles: Lusk Center Research Institute, University of Southern California, 1995.

Bluming, Avrum. "History of the Los Angeles Free-Net". Los Angeles Free-Net, no date. http://www.lafn.org/webconnect/avhist.htm.

Boissevain, Jeremy. Friends of Friends: Networks, Manipulators and Coalitions. Oxford: Basil Blackwell, 1974.

Bollen, Kenneth A., Barbara Entwisle, and Arthur S. Alderson. "Macrocomparative Research Methods." Annual Review of Sociology 19 (January 1, 1993): 321–351.

Borgatti, Stephen, Candace Jones, and Martin Everett. "Network Measures of Social Capital." Connections 21, no. 2 (1998): 27–36.

Borja, Jordi, and Manuel Castells. Local and Global: The Management of Cities in the Information Age. London: Earthscan Publications, 1997.

Bourdieu, Pierre. Distinction: a Social Critique of the Judgement of Taste. Cambridge, Massachusetts: Harvard University Press, 1984.

——. "Le Capital Social: Notes Provisoires." Actes De La Recherche En Sciences Sociales 3 (1980): 2–3.

Bourdieu, Pierre, and Jean-Claude Passeron. Reproduction in Education, Society, Culture. Beverly Hills: Sage, 1977.

Bourdieu, Pierre. "Social Space and Symbolic Power." Sociological Theory 7, no. 1 (1989): 14–25.

——. "The Field of Cultural Production, or: The Economic World Reversed." Poetics 12, no. 4–5 (November 1983): 311–356.

——. "The Forms of Capital." In Handbook of Theory and Research for the Sociology of Education, edited by John G. Richardson. Westport, Connecticut: Greenwood Press, 1983.

——. The Logic of Practice. Cambridge, Massachusetts: Polity, 1990.

——. "The Social Space and the Genesis of Groups." Theory and Society 14, no. 6 (November 1, 1985): 723–744.

Bowles, Samuel, and Herbert Gintis. "Social Capital and Community Governance". University of Massachusetts, 2000.

Boxman, Ed A.W., Paul M. De Graaf, and Hendrik D. Flap. "The Impact of Social and Human Capital on the Income Attainment of Dutch Managers." Social Networks 13, no. 1 (March 1991): 51–73.

Brand, S. The Media Lab: Inventing the Future at MIT. New York: Viking, 1987.

Bray, H. "A Nice Little Cafe with a Window." Boston Globe, July 22, 2002.

Brecher, Jeremy, and Tim Costello. Global Village or Global Pillage : Economic Reconstruction from the Bottom up. Cambridge, Massachusetts: South End Press, 1998.

Breeden, Laura, Neighborhood Transformation and Family Development Initiative, and Education Development Center. Computer and Communications Use in Low-income Communities: Models for the Neighborhood Transformation and Family Development Initiative. Education Development Center, 1998.

Breton, Raymond. "Institutional Completeness of Ethnic Communities and the Personal Relations of Immigrants." American Journal of Sociology 70, no. 2 (1964): 193–205.

Brewer, Anthony. A Guide to Marx's Capital. Cambridge, England: Cambridge University Press, 1984.

Brieger, Ronald L. "Career Attributes and Network Structure: A Blockmodel Study of a Biomedical Research Specialty." American Sociological Review 41, no. 1 (February 1, 1976): 117–135.

Brooks, R. Flesh and Machines: How Robots Will Change Us. New York: Pantheon Books, 2002.

Browne, Ray, and Marshall Fishwick, eds. The Global Village : Dead or Alive? Bowling Green, Ohio: Bowling Green State University Popular Press, 1999.

Bruce, Bertram, and Ann Peterson Bishop. "New Literacies and Community Inquiry." In The Handbook of Research in New Literacies, edited by Julie Coiro, Michele Knobel, Colin Lankshear, and Donald J. Leu, 703–746. Hillsdale, N.J.: Erlbaum, 2007.

Buchanan, E. A. "An Overview of Information Ethics Issues in a World-wide Context." Ethics and Information Technology 1, no. 3 (1999): 193–201.

Budd, J. M. Knowledge and Knowing in Library and Information Science: a Philosophical Framework. Lanham: Scarecrow Press, 2001.

Buente, Wayne. "Influence of Cognitive, Social, and Psychological Factors for Digital Citizenship". Milwaukee, WI, 2009. http://ocs.sfu.ca/aoir/index.php/ir/10/paper/view/395.

Burawoy, Michael. Ethnography Unbound: Power and Resistance in the Modern Metropolis. Berkley: University of California Press, 1991.

——. The Extended Case Method: Four Countries, Four Decades, Four Great Transformations, and One Theoretical Tradition. Berk: University of California Press, 2009.

Burnett, Gary, and Paul T. Jaeger. "Small Worlds, Lifeworlds, and Information: The Ramifications of the Information Behaviours of Social Groups in Public Policy and the Public Sphere." Information Research 13, no. 2 (2008). http://informationr.net/ir/13-2/paper346.html.

Burt, Ronald S. "Autonomy in a Social Topology." American Journal of Sociology 85, no. 4 (1976): 892–925.

——. "Network Items and the General Social Survey." Social Networks 6, no. 4 (December 1984): 293–339.

——. Structural Holes: The Social Structure of Competition. Cambridge, Massachusetts: Harvard University Press, 1992.

——. "The Contingent Value of Social Capital." Administrative Science Quarterly 42, no. 2 (June 1, 1997): 339–365.

——. "The Gender of Social Capital." Rationality and Society 10, no. 1 (February 1,

1998): 5–46.

Buschman, John. "'The Integrity and Obstinacy of Intellectual Creations': Jürgen Habermas and Librarianship's Theoretical Literature." The Library Quarterly 76, no. 3 (July 1, 2006): 270–299.

Caidi, Nadia, and Danielle Allard. "Social Inclusion of Newcomers to Canada: An Information Problem?" Library & Information Science Research 27, no. 3 (2005): 302–324.

Caidi, Nadia, Danielle Allard, and C. Luk. "Locating Public Libraries in a Multicultural City: a Spatial Mismatch?" Proceedings of the American Society for Information Science and Technology 44 (2007): 1–5.

Calhoun, Craig. Habermas and the Public Sphere. Cam: MIT, 1992.

Campbell, Karen E., Peter V. Marsden, and Jeanne S. Hurlbert. "Social Resources and Socioeconomic Status." Social Networks 8, no. 1 (1986): 97–117.

Caplan, Gerald, and Marie Killilea. Support Systems and Mutual Help: Multidisciplinary Explorations. New York: Grune & Stratton, 1976.

Carnoy, Martin, Manuel Castells, and Chris Benner. Flexible Work and Labor Markets in Information Age America. New York: Russell Sage Foundation, 1996.

Carnoy, Martin, and Manuel Castells. Sustainable Flexibility: Work, Family and Community in the Information Age. Paris: OECD Education Division, 1996.

Cartier, Carolyn, Manuel Castells, and Jack Linchuan Qiu. "The Information Have-less: Inequality, Mobility, and Translocal Networks in Chinese Cities." Studies in Comparative International Development 40, no. 2 (2005): 9–34.

Castells, Manuel. The Information Age: Economy, Society and Culture. Volume 1: The Rise of the Network Society. Oxford: Blackwell, 1996.

——. The Information Age: Economy, Society and Culture. Volume 2: The Power of Identity. Oxford: Blackwell, 1997.

——. The Information Age: Economy, Society and Culture. Volume 3: End of Millenium. Oxford: Blackwell, 1998.

——. "The Informational City Is a Dual City: Can It Be Reversed?" In High

Technology in Low-Income Communities: Prospects for the Positive Use of Advanced Information Technology, edited by Donald Schön, Bishwapriya Sanyal, and William Mitchell, 25–42. Cambridge, Massachusetts: MIT Press, 1999.

——. The Informational City: Information Technology, Economic Restructuring, and the Urban-regional Process. Oxford: Blackwell, 1989.

——. The Urban Question. London: Edward Arnold, 1976.

Castells, Manuel, and Peter Hall. Technopoles of the World: The Making of 21st Century Industrial Complexes. London: Routledge, 1994.

Chapman, Gary. "Shaping Technology for the 'Good Life': The Technological Imperative Versus the Social Imperative." In Shaping the Network Society: The New Role of Civil Society in Cyberspace, edited by Douglas Schuler and Peter Day, 43–65. Cambridge, Massachusetts: MIT Press, 2004.

Chatman, Elfreda A. "Alienation Theory: Application of a Conceptual Framework to a Study of Information Among Janitors." RQ 29, no. 3 (1990): 355–68.

——. "A Theory of Life in the Round." Journal of the American Society for Information Science 50, no. 3 (January 1, 1999): 207–217.

——. "Diffusion Theory: A Review and Test of a Conceptual Model in Information Diffusion." Journal of the American Society for Information Science 37, no. 6 (November 1, 1986): 377–386.

——. "Life in a Small World: Applicability of Gratification Theory to Information-seeking Behavior." Journal of the American Society for Information Science 42, no. 6 (July 1, 1991): 438–449.

——. "Opinion Leadership, Poverty, and Information Sharing." RQ 26, no. 3 (1987): 341–53.

——. "The Impoverished Life-world of Outsiders." Journal of the American Society for Information Science 47, no. 3 (March 1, 1996): 193–206.

——. "The Information World of Low-skilled Workers." Library & Information Science Research 9, no. 4 (1987): 265–283.

——. The Information World of Retired Women. New York: Greenwood Publishing Group, 1992.

Childers, T. Information and Referral: Public Libraries. New York: Ablex, 1984.

Childers, T., and J Post. The Information Poor in America. Metuchen, N.J.: Scare, 1975.

China Internet Network Information Center. 27th Statistics Report on Internet Development in China, 2011. http://www1.cnnic.cn/uploadfiles/pdf/2011/2/28/153752.pdf.

Chow, C., J. Ellis, J. Mark, and B. Wise. Impact of CTCNet Affiliates: Findings from a National Survey of Users of Community Technology Centers. Newton, Massachusetts: CTCNET, 1998.

Chow, C., J. Ellis, G. Walker, and B. Wise. Who Goes There? Longitudinal Case Studies of Twelve Users of Community Technology Centers. Newton, Massachusetts: CTCNET, 2000.

Cisler, Steve. "Ties That Bind: Community Networking (conference Announcement)", March 2, 1995. http://scout.wisc.edu/Projects/PastProjects/NH/95-03/95-03-14/0014.html.

Civille, Richard. "The Internet and the Poor." In Public Access to the Internet, edited by Brian Kahin and James Keller. Cambridge, Massachusetts: MIT Press, 1995.

Clairmont, D., and D. Magill. Africville. Toronto: McClelland & Stewart, 1974.

Clark, Kenneth. Dark Ghetto: Dilemmas of Social Power. New York: Harper & Row, 1965.

Cleaver, Harry M. "Computer-linked Social Movements and the Global Threat to Capitalism", January 1999. https://webspace.utexas.edu/hcleaver/www/polnet.html.

——. "The Zapatista Effect: The Internet and the Rise of an Alternative Political Fabric." Journal of International Affairs 51, no. 2 (1998): 621–622.

Clement, Andrew, and Leslie Shade. "The Access Rainbow: Conceptualizing Universal Access to the Information/Communications Infrastructure". Working Paper no. 10, Faculty of Information Studies, University of Toronto, 1998.

CNNIC (China Internet Network Information Center). Semi-Annual Survey Report on the Development of Internet in China, January 2008. http://www.cnnic.net.cn.

Cochrane, Glynn, and Pauline Atherton. "The Cultural Appraisal of Efforts to Alleviate Information Inequity." Journal of the American Society for Information Science 31, no. 4 (1980): 283–292.

Cohen, Abner. Custom and Politics in Urban Africa. Berkley: University of California Press, 1969.

Cohill, A. M., and A. L. Kavanaugh, eds. Community Networks: Lessons from Blacksburg, Virginia. Norwood, Massachusetts: Artech House, 1999.

Coleman, James S. Foundations of Social Theory. Cambridge, Massachusetts: Harvard University Press, 1990.

——. "Social Capital in the Creation of Human Capital." American Journal of Sociology 94 (January 1, 1988): S95–S120.

Cope, Bill, and Mary Kalantzis, eds. Multiliteracies: Literacy Learning and the Design of Social Futures. London: Routledge, 2000.

Couldry, Nick. "Digital Divide or Discursive Design? On the Emerging Ethics of Information Space." Ethics and Information Technology 5 (2003): 89–97.

Cox, H. The Secular City. New York: Macmillan, 1966.

Craven, Paul, and Barry Wellman. "The Network City." Sociological Inquiry 43, no. 3–4 (July 1973): 57–88.

Croneberger, R., and C. Luck. "Analyzing Community Human Information Needs: A Case Study." Library Trends 24, no. 3 (1976): 515–525.

Cronin, C. "Bourdieu and Foucault on Power and Modernity." Philosophy & Social Criticism 22 (1996): 55–85.

Cronus, Carol, and Linda Crowe, eds. Libraries and Neighborhood Information Centers. Champaign, IL: Allerton Park Institute Proceedings, 17. University of Illinois at Urbana-Champaign Graduate School of Library & Information Science, 1971. http://www.ideals.illinois.edu/handle/2142/1552.

Crump, Barry. "The Portability of Urban Ties". Chicago, 1977.

Daniels, P. W. Service Industries in the World Economy. Oxford: Blackwell, 1993.

Davis, Denise M., John C. Bertot, and Larra Clark. "Libraries Connect Communities:

Public Library Funding & Technology Access Study 2009-2010. Digital Supplement." American Libraries, June 2010. http://americanlibrariesmagazine.org/archives/digital-supplement/summer-2010-digital-supplement.

Dawson, Michael. "A Black Counterpublic? Economic Earthquakes, Racial Agenda(s), and Black Politics." Public Culture 7, no. 1 (1994): 195–223.

Day, Peter, and Douglas Schuler, eds. Community Practice in the Network Society: Local Action/Global Interaction. London: Routledge, 2003.

Death Wish, 1974.

Dertouzos, M. The Unfinished Revolution: Human-Centered Computers and What They Can Do for Us. New York: HarperCollins, 2001.

——. What Will Be: How the New World of Information Will Change Our Lives. San Francisco: HarperEdge, 1997.

Dervin, Brenda. "An Overview of Sense-making Research: Concepts, Methods, and Results to Date", Paper presented at the International Communications Association Annual Meeting, Dallas, May, 1983.

——. "Communication Gaps and Inequalities: Moving Toward a Reconceptualization." In Sense-making Methodology Reader: Selected Writings of Brenda Dervin, edited by B Dervin, L Foreman-Wernet, and E Lauterbach, 17–46. Cresskill, N.J.: Hampton Press, 2003.

——. "From the Mind's Eye of the User: The Sense-making Qualitative-quantitative Methodology." In Sense-making Methodology Reader: Selected Writings of Brenda Dervin, edited by B Dervin, L Foreman-Wernet, and E Lauterbach, 269–292. Cresskill, N.J.: Hampton Press, 2003.

——. "On Studying Information Seeking Methodologically: The Implications of Connecting Metatheory to Method." Information Processing & Management 35, no. 6 (1999): 727–750.

——. "The U.S. Low-Income Urban Village: An Information Vacuum?" Literacy Discussion 4, no. 3 (1973): 237–250.

——. "Users as Research Inventions: How Research Categories Perpetuate Inequities." Journal of Communication 39, no. 3 (1989): 216–232.

Dervin, Brenda, and B. S. Greenberg. "The Communication Environment of the Urban Poor." In Current Perspectives in Mass Communication Research, edited by F. G. Kline and P. Tichenor, 195–235. Beverly Hills: Sage, 1972.

Dewey, Patrick R. "Public Access to Microcomputers: Thoughts from the North-Pulaski Experience." Reference Services Review 11, no. 3 (1983): 21–24.

"Digital Divide", no date. http://en.wikipedia.org/wiki/Digital_divide.

van Dijk, Jan A. G. M. The Deepening Divide: Inequality in the Information Society. Thousand Oaks, California: Sage, 2005.

DiMaggio, Paul, and Eszter Hargittai. "From the 'Digital Divide' to 'Digital Inequality': Studying Internet Use as Penetration Increases". Working Paper no. 15, Center for Arts and Culture Policy Studies, Princeton University, 2001. http://www.princeton.edu/~artspol/workpap/WP15%20-%20DiMaggio%2BHargittai.pdf.

Doctor, Ronald D. "Information Technologies and Social Equity: Confronting the Revolution." Journal of the American Society for Information Science 42, no. 3 (1991): 216–228.

——. "Seeking Equity in the National Information Infrastructure." Internet Research 4, no. 3 (1994): 9–22.

Drumm, J., and J. Groom. "The Cybermobile Rolls onto Capitol Hill." Computers in Libraries 18, no. 10 (1998): 18–19.

Durkheim, Émile. The Division of Labor in Society. New York: Macmillan, 1933.

Durrance, Joan C. "Community Connector". University of Michigan School of Information Community Networking Initiative, 1994. http://www.si.umich.edu/Community.

——. "Community Information Services: An Innovation at the Beginning of Its Second Decade." Advanced Librarianship 13 (1984): 100–128.

——. "Factors That Influence Reference Success: What Makes Questioners Willing to Return?" Reference Librarian 23, no. 49–50 (1995): 243–265.

Durrance, Joan C. "The Generic Librarian: Anonymity Vs. Accountability." Reference Quarterly 22, no. 3 (1983): 278–283.

Durrance, Joan C., and Karen E. Fisher. "Determining How Libraries and Librarians Help." Library Trends 51, no. 4 (2003): 305–334.

Durrance, Joan C., and Karen E. Pettigrew. "Community Information: The Technological Touch." Library Journal 125, no. 2 (2000): 44–46.

——. Online Community Information: Creating a Nexus at Your Library. Chicago, IL: American Library Association, 2002.

Dutch, Martin, and Dave Muddiman. "The Public Library, Social Exclusion and the Information Society in the United Kingdom." Libri 51, no. 4 (2001): 183–194.

Dyer-Witheford, Nick. Cyber-Marx: Cycles and Circuits of Struggle in High Technology Capitalism. Urbana, Illinois: University of Illinois Press, 1999.

Eberle, Anne, and Sandra Robinson. The Adult Illiterate Speaks Out: Personal Perspectives on Learning to Read and Write. Washington, D.C.: National Institute for Community Development, Department of Health, Education and Welfare, and the Office of the Assistant Secretary for Planning and Evaluation, National Institute of Education, 1980. http://www.eric.ed.gov/ERICWebPortal/search/detailmini.jsp?_nfpb=true&_&ERICExtSearch_SearchValue_0=ED195771&ERICExtSearch_SearchType_0=no&accno=ED195771.

Editorial Committee of Chinese Librarianship Yearbook. Chinese Librarianship Yearbook. Natinoal Library Publishing House, 2011.

Emling, S. "Internet Coming to a Corner Near You?" Toledo Blade. Toledo, OH, February 16, 2002.

Engels, Friedrich. The Condition of the Working-Class in England. St. Albans, Hertfordshire: Panther Books, 1969.

Erickson, Bonnie H. "Culture, Class, and Connections." American Journal of Sociology 102, no. 1 (July 1, 1996): 217–251.

——. "Networks, Success, and Class Structure: A Total View", 1995.

Ettema, James S., and F. Gerald Kline. "Deficits, Differences, and Ceilings: Contingent Conditions for Understanding the Knowledge Gap." Communication Research 4, no. 2 (April 1, 1977): 179–202.

Fan, H. "Nine Billion Yuan Appeared Overnight, Chen Tianqiao Becomes China's

Richest Man." Beijing Youth Daily, 2004.

Farrington, Carl, and Evelyn Pine. "Community Memory: A Case Study in Community Communication." In Reinventing Technology, Rediscovering Community: Critical Explorations of Computing as a Social Practice, edited by Philip E. Agre and Douglas Schuler, 219–227. Greenwich, Connecticut: Ablex, 1997.

Feagin, Joe R. "Community Disorganization: Some Critical Notes." Sociological Inquiry 43, no. 3-4 (July 1, 1973): 123–146.

Feagin, Joe R., and Harlan Hahn. Ghetto Revolts: The Politics of Violence in American Cities. New York: Macmillan, 1973.

Feldman, Tine Rossing, and Susan Assaf. Social Capital: Conceptual Frameworks and Empirical Evidence. The World Bank, January 1999.

Felsenstein, Lee, and Bernard Aboba. "How Community Memory Came to Be, Part 1: The Origins of Community Memory." Internaut, 1994. http://aboba.drizzlehosting.com/internaut/comm.html.

Fernandez, Roberto M., and Nancy Weinberg. "Sifting and Sorting: Personal Contacts and Hiring in a Retail Bank." American Sociological Review 62, no. 6 (December 1, 1997): 883–902.

Finn, Patrick. Literacy with an Attitude: Educating Working-Class Children in Their Own Self-Interest. Albany, New York: State University of New York Press, 1999.

Fischer, Claude S. The Urban Experience. New York: Harcourt Brace Jovanovich, 1976.

Flap, Hendrik D. "No Man Is an Island: The Research Program of a Social Capital Theory". Bielefeld, Germany, 1994.

Flap, Henk D., and Nan Dirk De Graaf. "Social Capital and Attained Occupational Status." Netherlands Journal of Sociology 22, no. 2 (1986): 145–161.

Flap, Henk. "Social Capital in the Reproduction of Inequality." Comparative Sociology of Family Health and Education 20 (1991): 6179–6202.

Freedman, J. B, and J. C. Henderson. "Digital Usage Behavior: A Sense Making Perspective", 2008.

Freeman, Linton C. A Bibliography of Social Networks. Monticello, IL: Council of Planning Librarians, Exchange Bibliographies Nos 1170-1171, 1976.

Frumkin, Peter. "Are Nonprofit CEOs Overpaid?" The Public Interest 142 (2001): 83–94.

Gans, Herbert J. "Gans on Granovetter's 'Strength of Weak Ties'." American Journal of Sociology 80, no. 2 (1974): 524–527.

——. "Gans' Response to Granovetter." American Journal of Sociology 80, no. 2 (1974): 529–531.

——. The Levittowners. New York: Pantheon, 1967.

——. The Urban Villagers. New York: Free Press, 1962.

Gates, A. S., H. Stevens, and B. Wellman. "What Makes a Good Neighbour?" New York, 1973.

Gaziano, Cecilie. "A Twenty-Five-Year Review of Knowledge Gap Research", 1995. http://www.eric.ed.gov/ERICWebPortal/contentdelivery/servlet/ERICServlet?accno=ED383009.

——. "Social Stratification and the Knowledge Gap: Some Influences on Knowledge Disparities", 1983. http://www.eric.ed.gov/ERICWebPortal/contentdelivery/servlet/ERICServlet?accno=ED237990.

——. "The Knowledge Gap: An Analytical Review of Media Effects." Communication Research 10, no. 4 (October 1, 1983): 447–486.

Gaziano, Cecilie, and J O'Leary. "Childbirth and Infant Development Knowledge Gaps in Interpersonal Settings." Journal of Health Communication 3, no. 1 (1998): 29–51.

Gaziano, E, and Cecilie Gaziano. "Social Control, Social Change and the Knowledge Gap Hypothesis." In Mass Media, Social Control, and Social Change: a Macrosocial Perspective, edited by D Demers and K Viswanath, 117–136. Ames, IA: Iowa State University Press, 1998.

Gershenfeld, N. When Things Start to Think. New York: Henry Holt, 1999.

Gilder, George. Telecosm: How Infinite Broadband Will Revolutionize Our World.

New York: Free Press, 2000.

——. "City Vs. Country: Tom Peters and George Gilder Debate the Impact of Technology on Location." Forbes ASAP, February 27, 1995.

Goldfarb, Avi, and Jeff Prince. "Internet Adoption and Usage Patterns Are Different: Implications for the Digital Divide." Information Economics and Policy 20, no. 1 (2008): 2–15.

Golding, Peter. "The Communication Paradox: Inequality at National and International Level and the Communications Media". University Sains Malaysia, Penang, 1993.

Golding, Peter, and Graham Murdock. "Digital Divides: Communications Policy and Its Contradictions." New Economy 8, no. 2 (June 1, 2001): 110–115.

Gomez, Ricardo. Libraries, Telecentres, Cybercafes and Public Access to ICT: International Comparisons. Hershey, PA: IGI Global, 2011.

——. Measuring Global Public Access to ICT: Landscape Study Summary Reports from 25 Countries Around the World. CIS Working Paper No. 7. Seattle: University of Washington Center for Information & Society, 2009.

Gordon, A., M. Gordon, E. Moore, and A. Boyd. Support for Public Access Computing Widespread and Strong. Seattle: Bill and Melinda Gates Foundation, 2002.

De Graaf, Nan Dirk, and Hendrik Derk Flap. "'With a Little Help from My Friends': Social Resources as an Explanation of Occupational Status and Income in West Germany, The Netherlands, and the United States." Social Forces 67, no. 2 (December 1, 1988): 452–472.

Graham, Stephen. "From Urban Competition to Urban Collaboration? The Development of Interurban Telematics Networks." Environment and Planning C: Government and Policy 13, no. 4 (1995): 503–524.

Graham, Stephen, and Simon Marvin. Telecommunications and the City: Electronic Spaces, Urban Places. London: Routledge, 1996.

Granovetter, Mark. "Economic Action and Social Structure: The Problem of Embeddedness." American Journal of Sociology 91, no. 3 (November 1, 1985):

481–510.

——. Getting a Job (Revised Edition). Chicago: University of Chicago Press, 1995.

——. Getting a Job: a Study of Contacts and Careers. Cambridge, Massachusetts: Harvard University Press, 1974.

——. "Granovetter Replies to Gans." American Journal of Sociology 80, no. 2 (1974): 527–529.

——. "The Strength of Weak Ties." American Journal of Sociology 78, no. 6 (May 1, 1973): 1360–1380.

——. "The Strength of Weak Ties: A Network Theory Revisited." Sociological Theory 1 (1983): 201–233.

Grant, George. "In Defence of North America." In Technology and Empire: Perspectives on North America, 15–40. Toronto: House of Anansi, 1969.

Greenberg, Bradley, and Brenda Dervin. "Mass Communication Among the Urban Poor." Public Opinion Quarterly 34, no. 2 (June 20, 1970): 224–235.

Greer, Scott A. The Emerging City: Myth and Reality. New York: Free Press, 1962.

Gurstein, Michael. Community Informatics: Enabling Communities With Information and Communications Technologies. Hershey, PA: Idea Group, 2000.

——. "Community Informatics: What's in a Name." The Journal of Community Informatics 4, no. 3 (2009). http://www.ci-journal.net/index.php/ciej/article/viewArticle/521/433.

——. "Effective Use: A Community Informatics Strategy Beyond the Digital Divide." First Monday 8, no. 12 (April 16, 2007). http://frodo.lib.uic.edu/ojsjournals/index.php/fm/article/view/1107.

——. What Is Community Informatics (and Why Does It Matter)? Milan: Polimetrica, 2007.

Gusfield, Joseph. Community: A Critical Response. New York: Harper and Row, 1975.

Guthrie, K. Kendall, and William H. Dutton. "The Politics of Citizen Access Technology: The Development of Public Information Utilities in Four Cities." Policy

Studies Journal 20, no. 4 (December 1, 1992): 574–597.

Habermas, J. Structural Transformation of the Public Sphere: An Inquiry into a Category of Bourgeois Society. Cambridge, Massachusetts: MIT Press, 1991.

Haddon, Leslie. "Social Exclusion and Information and Communication Technologies." New Media & Society 2, no. 4 (2000): 387–406.

Hallman, J. "Community Networking [hyperlinked Timeline]", 2006. http://ibiblio.org/rtpnet/community-net.html.

Hamilton, Deborah. "Sustainability of a Community Technology Center: Action Research at the Murchison Community Center, Toledo, Ohio". Master's thesis, University of Toledo, 2002.

Hampton, Keith N., and Neeti Gupta. "Community and Social Interaction in the Wireless City: Wi-fi Use in Public and Semi-public Spaces." New Media and Society 10, no. 6 (2008): 831–850.

Hampton, Keith N., Oren Livio, and Lauren Sessions Goulet. "The Social Life of Wireless Urban Spaces: Internet Use, Social Networks, and the Public Realm." Journal of Communication 60, No. 4 (December 2010): 701-722.

Harper, Douglas. Working Knowledge: Skill and Community in a Small Shop. Chicago: University of Chicago Press, 1987.

Harris, M. H., S. A. Hannah, and P. C. Harris. Into the Future: The Foundations of Library and Information Services in the Post-industrial Era. Greenwich, Connecticut: Ablex, 1998.

Haythornthwaite, Caroline. "Social Network Analysis: An Approach and Technique for the Study of Information Exchange." Library & Information Science Research 18, no. 4 (Autumn 1996): 323–342.

Haywood, T. Info-rich–info-poor: Access and Exchange in the Global Information Society. London: Bowker Saur, 1995.

Heath, Shirley Brice. "The Functions and Uses of Literacy." In Literacy: Language and Power, edited by Dianne Vipond and Ronald J. Strahl. Long Beach, California: California State University Press, 1994.

Henderson, E., K. Miller, T. Craig, S. Dorinski, M. Freeman, N. Isaac, J. Keng, P. O'Shea, and P. Schilling. Public Libraries Survey: Fiscal Year 2008. Washington, D.C.: Institute of Museum and Library Services, 2010.

Hersberger, J. "A Qualitative Approach to Examining Information Transfer via Social Networks Among Homeless Populations." The New Review of Information Behaviour Research 4 (2003): 95–108.

——. "Are the Economically Poor Information Poor? Does the Digital Divide Affect the Homeless and Access to Information?" The Canadian Journal of Information and Library Science 27, no. 3 (2003): 45–63.

Hillery, George A. "Definitions of Community: Areas of Agreement." Rural Sociology 20, no. 2 (June 1955): 111–123.

Hiltz, Starr Roxanne, and Murray Turoff. The Network Nation: Human Communication via Computer. Reading, Massachusetts: Addison-Wesley Pub. Co., 1978.

Himanen, Pekka. The Hacker Ethic and the Spirit of the Information Age. New York: Random House, 2001.

Hirsch, B. "The Social Network as a Natural Support System". San Francisco, 1977.

Hjørland, Birger, and Hanne Albrechtsen. "Toward a New Horizon in Information Science: Domain-analysis." Journal of the American Society for Information Science 46, no. 6 (July 1, 1995): 400–425.

Hjørland, Birger. "Empiricism, Rationalism and Positivism in Library and Information Science." Journal of Documentation 61 (2005): 130–155.

Hodges, D. Class Politics in the Information Age. Urbana, Illlinois: University of Illinois Press, 2000.

Holsendolph, E. "Cyberbus Brings Computing to Neighborhoods." Atlanta Journal Constitution. Atlanta, GA, December 12, 2001.

Horrigan, John. Online Communities: Networks That Nurture Long-Distance Relationships and Local Ties. Washington, D.C.: Pew Internet and American Life Project, 2001.

Howard, L. "Industrialization and Community in Chotanagpur". Harvard University, 1974.

Hudson, Heather. "Designing Research for Telecentre Evaluation". International Development Research Centre, Canada, 2000.

Hull, B. "ICT and Social Exclusion: The Role of Libraries." Telematics and Informatics 20, no. 2 (2003): 131–142.

Hunter, A., and G. Suttles. "The Expanding Community of Limited Liability." In The Social Construction of Communities, edited by G. Suttles, 44–81. Chicago: University of Chicago Press, 1972.

Hunter, Albert. "The Loss of Community: An Empirical Test Through Replication." American Sociological Review 40, no. 5 (October 1, 1975): 537–552.

IDG and WCGCP (Working Committee on Gaming of China Publishers Association). 2006-2010 Market Analyses and Predictions for the Gaming Industry in China. Beijing, 2006.

"Information Technology Indicators Residential Survey". Conducted for City of Seattle Department of Information Technology by Northwest Research Group, Inc., 2000. http://cityofseattle.net/tech/indicators/Residential_Survey_Report.pdf.

International Telecommunication Union (ITU). Definitions of World telecommunication/ICT Indicators Final Version, 2007. http://www.itu.int/ITU-D/ict/material/IndDef_e_v2007.doc.

Jacobs, Jane. The Death and Life of Great American Cities. New York: Random House, 1961.

Jacobson, David. "Fair-Weather Friend: Label and Context in Middle-Class Friendships." Journal of Anthropological Research 31, no. 3 (October 1, 1975): 225–234.

——. Itinerant Townsmen: Friendship and Social Order in Urban Uganda. Menlo Park, California: Cummings Publishing, 1973.

Jaeger, Paul T, and Gary Burnett. Information Worlds: Social Context, Technology, and Information Behavior in the Age of the Internet. New York: Routledge, 2010.

Jaeger, Paul T. "Education, Adoption, and Development: Building a Culture of Social Theory in LIS." The Library Quarterly 80, no. 3 (2010): 203–209.

James, Jeffrey. "Measuring the Global Digital Divide at the Level of Individuals."

Current Science 96, no. 2 (2009): 194–197.

Janowitz, Morris. The Community Press in an Urban Setting. Glencoe, IL: Free Press, 1952.

Japzon, Andrea Copeland, and Hongmian Gong. "A Neighborhood Analysis of Public Library Use in New York City." Library Quarterly 75, no. 4 (2005): 446–463.

Johnson, Catherine A. "Social Capital and the Search for Information: Examining the Role of Social Capital in Information Seeking Behavior in Mongolia." Journal of the American Society for Information Science and Technology 58, no. 6 (2007): 883–894.

Johnson, Harry G. "The Political Economy of Opulence." The Canadian Journal of Economics and Political Science / Revue Canadienne d'Economique Et De Science Politique 26, no. 4 (November 1, 1960): 552–564.

Jones, C. S. "The Urban Library: Proving Utility." Library Journal 101 (1976): 81–86.

Jones, Steve. Doing Internet Research: Critical Issues and Methods for Examining the Net. Thousand Oaks, California: Sage, 1999.

Jordan, Tim. Cyberpower: The Culture and Politics of Cyberspace and the Internet. London: Routledge, 1999.

Kadushin, Charles. "The Friends and Supporters of Psychotherapy: On Social Circles in Urban Life." American Sociological Review 31, no. 6 (December 1, 1966): 786–802.

Karabanow, J, and T Naylor. "Street Youth and Information Technology: An Exploration of Social Inclusion and Exclusion." International Journal of Humanities 5 (2007): 253–259.

Kasarda, John D., and Morris Janowitz. "Community Attachment in Mass Society." American Sociological Review 39, no. 3 (June 1, 1974): 328–339.

Keeble, Leigh, and Brian Loader, eds. Community Informatics : Shaping Computer-mediated Social Relations. London: Routledge, 2001.

Keller, Suzanne Infeld. The Urban Neighborhood: a Sociological Perspective. New York,: Random House, 1968.

Kelly, K. New Rules for the New Economy: 10 Radical Strategies for a Connected World. New York: Viking, 1998.

Kim, Mun Cho, and Jong Kil Kim. "Digital Divide: Conceptual Discussions and Prospect." In The Human Society and the Internet Internet-Related Socio-Economic Issues, edited by Won Kim, Tok-Wang Ling, Yoon-Joon Lee, and Seung-Soo Park, 2105:78–91. Berlin, Heidelberg: Springer Berlin Heidelberg, 2001. http://www.springerlink.com/content/yb3hwft857uc3efw/.

Kling, Rob. "What Is Social Informatics and Why Does It Matter?" D-Lib Magazine 5, no. 1 (January 1999). http://www.dlib.org/dlib/january99/kling/01kling.html.

Klovdahl, A. S. Social Networks: Selected References for Course Design and Research Planning. Monticello, IL: Vance Bibliographies, 1978.

Knorr-Cetina, K. "Introduction." In Advances in Social Theory and Methodology: Toward an Integration of Micro- and Macro-sociologies, edited by K Knorr-Cetina and AV Cicourel, 1–47. London: Routledge & Kegan Paul, 1981.

Kochen, M., and J. Donohue. Information and the Community. Chicago, IL: American Library Association, 1976.

Kominski, R., and E. Newburger. "Access Denied: Changes in Computer Ownership and Use, 1984-1997". Chicago, 1999.

Kornhauser, William. The Politics of Mass Society. Glencoe, IL: Free Press, 1959.

Kranich, Nancy. "Libraries Create Social Capital." Library Journal 126, no. 19 (2001): 40–41.

Kretzman, John P., and John L. McKnight. Building Communities from the Inside Out: A Path Toward Finding and Mobilizing a Community's Assets. Chicago: Institute for Policy Research, Northwestern University, 1993.

Kvasny, Lynette. "A Conceptual Framework for Examining Digital Inequality", 2002. http://ist.psu.edu/faculty_pages/lkvasny/AMCIS2002.pdf.

——. "Cultural (Re)production of Digital Inequality in a U.S. Community Technology Initiative." Information, Communication & Society 9, no. 2 (April 2006): 160–181.

Kvasny, Lynette, and Mark Keil. "The Challenges of Redressing the Digital Divide: A Tale of Two Cities." ICIS 2002 Proceedings (December 31, 2002). http://aisel.aisnet.

org/icis2002/84.

L.K. “Chicago PL Takes Heat over Literacy Cuts.” American Libraries 27, no. 9 (1996): 15–17.

Landry, Burt. The New Black Middle Class. Berkeley: University of California Press, 1987.

Lankshear, Colin, James Gee, Michele Knobel, and Chris Searle. Changing Literacies. Buckingham: Open University Press, 1997.

Larsen, Ronald L. “iSchools.” In Encyclopedia of Library and Information Sciences, Third Edition, edited by Marcia Bates and Mary Niles Maack, 3018. Boca Raton, FL: Taylor & Francis/CRC, 2010.

Lasch, Christopher. Haven in a Heartless World: The Family Besieged. New York: Basic Books, 1977.

Laslett, Peter. The World We Have Lost. London: Methuen, 1971.

Laumann, Edward O. Prestige and Association in an Urban Community: An Analysis of an Urban Stratification System. Indianapolis: Bobbs-Merrill, 1966.

——. Bonds of Pluralism: The Form and Substance of Urban Social Networks. New York: John Wiley, 1973.

Laumann, Edward O., Joseph Galaskiewicz, and Peter V. Marsden. “Community Structure as Interorganizational Linkages.” Annual Review of Sociology 4 (January 1, 1978): 455–484.

Lave, Jean, and Etienne Wenger. Situated Learning: Legitimate Peripheral Participation. Cambridge, Cambridgeshire: Cambridge University Press, 1991.

Lee, E. “The Labour Movement and the Internet: The New Internationalism.” In Labour and Society International, edited by A. Lipow. London: Pluto Press, 1997.

Lee, Nancy Howell. The Search for an Abortionist. Chicago: University of Chicago Press, 1969.

Lentz, Becky, Joseph Straubhaar, Antonio LaPastina, Stan Main, and Julie Taylor. “Structuring Access: The Role of Public Access Centers in the ‘Digital Divide’”. University of Texas, 2000. http://www.utexas.edu/research/tipi/reports/joe_ICA.

pdf.

Lévy, Pierre. Becoming Virtual: Reality in the Digital Age. New York: Plenum Trade, 1998.

——. Collective Intelligence: Mankind's Emerging World in Cyberspace. New York: Plenum Trade, 1997.

——. Cyberculture. Minneapolis: University of Minnesota Press, 2001.

Levy, S. "The Hottest New Tech Cities." Newsweek, November 9, 1998.

Li, Qiang. Social Stratification in Today's China: Measurement and Analysis. Beijing: Beijing Normal University Publishing Group, 2010.

Liebow, Elliott. Tally's Corner; a Study of Negro Streetcorner Men. Boston: Little, Brown, 1967.

Lievrouw, Leah A. "Reconciling Structure and Process in the Study of Scholarly Communication." In Scholarly Communication and Bibliometrics, edited by Christine Borgman, 59–69. Newbury Park, California: Sage, 1990.

Lievrouw, Leah A, and Sharon E. Farb. "Information and Equity." Annual Review of Information Science and Technology 37, no. 1 (January 1, 2003): 499–540.

Lin, Nan. "Action, Social Resources, and the Emergence of Social Structure: A Rational Choice Theory." Advances in Group Processes 11 (1994): 67–85.

——. "Conceptualizing Social Support." In Social Support, Life Events, and Depression, edited by Nan Lin, Alfred Dean, and Walter Ensel, 17–30. Orlando, FL: Academic Press, 1986.

——. "Les Ressources Sociales: Une Theorie Du Capital Social." Revue Francaise De Sociologie 36, no. 4 (1995): 685–704.

——. Social Capital: A Theory of Social Structure and Action. London: Cambridge University Press, 2002.

——. "Social Networks and Status Attainment". Montreal, 1998.

——. "Social Networks and Status Attainment." Annual Review of Sociology 25, no. 1 (1999): 467–487.

——. "Social Resources and Instrumental Action." In Social Structure and Network Analysis, edited by Peter V Marsden, 131–145. Beverly Hills: Sage, 1982.

——. "Social Resources and Social Mobility: A Structural Theory of Status Attainment." In Social Mobility and Social Structure, edited by Ronald L. Breiger, 147–171. New York: Cambridge University Press, 1990.

——. "Social Resources Theory." In Encyclopedia of Sociology, edited by Edgar F. Borgatta and Marie L. Borgatta, 4:1936–1942. New York: Macmillan, 1992.

Lin, Nan, and Yanjie Bian. "Getting Ahead in Urban China." American Journal of Sociology 97, no. 3 (November 1, 1991): 657–688.

Lin, Nan, Karen Cook, and Ronald S. Burt. Social Capital: Theory and Research. New York: de Gruyter, 2001.

Lin, Nan, and Mary Dumin. "Access to Occupations Through Social Ties." Social Networks 8, no. 4 (December 1986): 365–385.

Lin, Nan, Walter M. Ensel, and John C. Vaughn. "Social Resources and Strength of Ties: Structural Factors in Occupational Status Attainment." American Sociological Review 46, no. 4 (1981): 393–405.

Lin, Nan, Yang-chih Fu, and Ray-may Hsung. "Position Generator: A Measurement for Social Capital". Duke University, 1998.

Lloyd, A, S. Lipu, and M. A. Kennan. "On Becoming Citizens: Examining Social Inclusion from an Information Perspective." Australian Academic and Research Libraries 41 (2010): 42–53.

Loader, Brian. Cyberspace Divide: Equality, Agency, and Policy in the Information Society. London: Routledge, 1998.

Loader, Brian, W. van de Donk, P. Nixon, and D. Rucht. Cyberprotest: New Media, Citizens and Social Movements. London: Routledge, 2003.

Loader, Brian, and W. H. Dutton. Digital Academe: The New Media and Institutions of Higher Education and Learning. London: Routledge, 2002.

Loader, Brian, and B. Hague. Digital Democracy: Discourse and Decision-Making in the Information Age. London: Routledge, 1999.

Loader, Brian, and Leigh Keeble. Challenging the Digital Divide?: A Literature Review of Community Informatics Initiatives. York, England: Joseph Rowntree Foundation, 2004.

Loader, Brian. The Governance of Cyberspace: Politics, Technology and Global Restructuring. London: Routledge, 1997.

Loader, Brian, and D. Thomas. Cybercrime: Law Enforcement, Security & Surveillance in the Information Age. London: Routledge, 2000.

Long, N. Information & Referral Services: Research Findings. Volume One of the Interstudy Information and Referral Center Study. Washington, D.C.: U.S. Administration on Aging, Department of Health, Education, and Welfare, 1975.

Luckmann, Benita. "The Small Life-worlds of Modern Man." Social Research 37, no. 4 (December 1, 1970): 580–596.

Main, Linda. "The Global Information Infrastructure: Empowerment or Imperialism?" Third World Quarterly 22, no. 1 (2001): 83–97.

Mansell, Robin. "From Digital Divides to Digital Entitlements in Knowledge Societies." Current Sociology 50, no. 3 (May 1, 2002): 407–426.

Mark, J., J. Cornebise, and E. Wahl. Community Technology Centers: Impact on Individual Participants and Their Communities. Newton, Massachusetts: Education Development Center, 1997.

Marsden, Peter V. "Core Discussion Networks of Americans." American Sociological Review 52, no. 1 (February 1, 1987): 122–131.

Marsden, Peter V., and Jeanne S. Hurlbert. "Social Resources and Mobility Outcomes: A Replication and Extension." Social Forces 66, no. 4 (June 1, 1988): 1038–1059.

Martin, Steven P., and John P. Robinson. "The Income Digital Divide: Trends and Predictions for Levels of Internet Use." Social Problems 54, no. 1 (2007): 1–22.

Marx, Karl. Capital: A New Abridgement. Edited by David McLellan. Oxford: Oxford University Press, 1995.

——. Wage Labor and Capital. New York: International Publishers, 1933.

Marx, Leo. The Machine in the Garden: Technology and the Pastoral Ideal in America. New York: Oxford University Press, 1964.

Masmoudi, Mustapha. "The New World Information Order." Journal of Communication 29, no. 2 (June 1, 1979): 172–179.

Matthew, David. "The Politics of Communication: Information Technology, Local Knowledge and Social Exclusion." Telematics and Informatics 20, no. 3 (2003): 235–253.

Mayer, Philip, and Iona Mayer. Townsmen or Tribesmen: Conservatism and the Process of Urbanization in a South African City. Cape Town: Oxford University Press, 1974.

McAdam, Doug. Political Process and the Development of Black Insurgency 1930-1970. Chicago: University of Chicago Press, 1999.

McCallister, Lynne, and Claude S. Fischer. "A Procedure for Surveying Personal Networks." Sociological Methods & Research 7, no. 2 (November 1, 1978): 131–148.

McChesney, Robert. Rich Media, Poor Democracy: Communication Politics in Dubious Times. Urbana, IL: University of Illinois Press, 1999.

McGreevy, Michelene. "First Saturday: Mobilizing a Community for Achievement and Empowerment". Master's thesis. University of Toledo, 2002.

McIver, W. J. "A Community Informatics for the Information Society." In Communicating in the Information Society, edited by B. Girard and S. O'Siochrú, 33–64. Geneva: United Nations Research Institute for Social Development, 2003.

McIver, W. J., and A. P. Prokosch. "Towards a Critical Approach to Examining the Digital Divide", 2002.

McKeown, Kevin. "Social Norms and Implications of Santa Monica's PEN (Public Electronic Network)". San Francisco, 1991. http://mckeown.net/PENaddress.html.

Mele, Christopher. "Cyberspace and Disadvantaged Communities: The Internet as a Tool for Collective Action." In Communities in Cyberspace, edited by Marc A. Smith and Peter Kollock, 290–310. London: Routledge, 1999.

Mellor, Julia Rosemary. Urban Sociology in an Urbanized Society. London: Routledge

& Kegan Paul, 1977.

Merton, Robert King. "Patterns of Influence: Local and Cosmopolitan Influentials." In Social Theory and Social Structure, 387–420. New York: Free Press, 1957.

Miller, Daniel, and Don Slater. The Internet: An Ethnographic Approach. Berg, 2000.

Miller, S. Civilizing Cyberspace: Policy, Power, and the Information Superhighway. New York: ACM Press, 1996.

Mitchell, J. Clyde. "Social Networks." Annual Review of Anthropology 3 (January 1, 1974): 279–299.

——. "The Concept and Use of Social Networks." In Social Networks in Urban Situations: Analyses of Personal Relationships in Central African Towns. Manchester: University of Manchester Press, 1969.

Mitchell, William. E-topia: "Urban Life, Jim-But Not as We Know It". Cambridge, Massachusetts: MIT Press, 1999.

Mollenkopf, John, and Manuel Castells, eds. Dual City: Restructuring New York. New York: Russell Sage Foundation, 1991.

Morris, Aldon D. The Origins of the Civil Rights Movement: Black Communities Organizing for Change. New York: Free Press, 1984.

Mosco, V. "Introduction: Information in the Pay-per Society." In The Political Economy of Information, edited by V Mosco and J Wasko, 3–26. Madison, Wisconsin: University of Wisconsin Press, 1988.

——. The Political Economy of Communication: Rethinking and Renewal. London: Sage, 1996.

Moss, Mitchell. "Telecommunications, World Cities, and Urban Policy." Urban Studies 24, no. 6 (December 1, 1987): 534–546.

Mossberger, Karen, David Kaplan, and M. A. Gilbert. "How Concentrated Poverty Matters for the 'digital Divide': Motivation, Social Networks, and Resources", 2006.

Mossberger, Karen, Caroline J. Tolbert, and Ramona S. McNeal. Digital Citizenship: The Internet, Society, and Participation. Cambridge, Massachusetts: MIT Press, 2007.

Murdock, Graham, and Peter Golding. "Common Markets: Corporate Ambitions and Communication Trends in the UK and Europe." Journal of Media Economics 12, no. 2 (1999): 117–132.

——. "Dismantling the Digital Divide: Rethinking the Dynamics of Participation and Exclusion." In Toward a Political Economy of Culture: Capitalism and Communication in the Twenty-first Century, edited by A Calabrese and C Sparks, 244–260. Lanham: Rowman & Littlefield, 2004.

——. "Information Poverty and Political Inequality: Citizenship in the Age of Privatized Communications." Journal of Communication 39, no. 3 (1989): 180–195.

Nagle, Jane P. "Histories of Success and Failure: Working Class Students' Literacy Experiences." Journal of Adolescent & Adult Literacy 43, no. 2 (October 1, 1999): 172–185.

National Research Council (NRC). Being Fluent with Information Technology. Washington, D.C.: National Academy Press, 1999.

National Telecommunications and Information Administration (NTIA). A Nation Online: How Americans Are Expanding Their Use of the Internet. Washington, D.C.: U.S. Department of Commerce, 2002. http://www.ntia.doc.gov/legacy/ntiahome/dn/nationonline_020502.htm.

——. Falling Through the Net: Defining the Digital Divide: A Report on the Telecommunications and Information Technology Gap in America. Washington, D.C.: U.S. Department of Commerce, 1999. http://www.ntia.doc.gov/legacy/ntiahome/fttn99/FTTN.pdf.

——. Falling Through the Net: Toward Digital Inclusion: A Report on America's Access to Technology Tools. Washington, D.C.: U.S. Department of Commerce, 2000. http://search.ntia.doc.gov/pdf/fttn00.pdf.

——. "Technology Opportunities Program (TOP): Research and Evaluation", no date http://www.ntia.doc.gov/legacy/otiahome/top/research/research.htm.

Negroponte, Nicholas. Being Digital. New York: Knopf, 1995.

Negt, Oskar, and Alexander Kluge. Public Sphere and Experience: Toward An Analysis of the Bourgeois and Proletarian Public Sphere. Minneapolis, Minnesota: University of Minnesota Press, 1993.

Newman, Oscar. Defensible Space: Crime Prevention Through Urban Design. New York: Macmillan, 1972.

Nisbet, Robert. Community and Power. New York: Oxford University Press, 1962.

Norris, P. Digital Divide: Civic Engagement, Information Poverty and the Internet Worldwide. Cambridge, Cambridgeshire: Cambridge University Press, 2001.

——. Digital Divide: Civic Engagement, Information Poverty and the Internet Worldwide. Cambridge, Cambridgeshire: Cambridge University Press, 2001.

"Notice of the General Office of the Ministry of Culture About Working Scheme on Pilot Construction of Public Electronic Reading Rooms". General Office of the Ministry of Culture, no date. http://huodong.ndcnc.gov.cn/yuelanshi/file/6587531690e8529e516c538551734e8e537053d1300a516c517175355b50960589c85ba45efa8bbe8bd570b95de54f5c65b96848300b7684901a77e5.doc.

Numminen, Piritta, and Pertti Vakkari. "Question Types in Public Libraries' Digital Reference Service in Finland: Comparing 1999 and 2006." Journal of the American Society for Information Science and Technology 60, no. 6 (June 1, 2009): 1249–1257.

O'Neil, Dara. "Assessing Community Informatics: A Review of Methodological Approaches for Evaluating Community Networks and Community Technology Centers." Internet Research 12, no. 1 (2002): 76–102.

Organization for Economic Cooperation and Development (OECD). Information Technology Outlook, 2009. http://browse.oecdbookshop.org/oecd/pdfs/browseit/9308041E.PDF.

——. OECD Model Survey of ICT Access and Use by Households and Individuals, 2009. http://www.oecd.org/dataoecd/49/42/35930682.pdf.

Organization for Economic Cooperation and Development (OECD) Working Party on Indicators for the Information Society. ICT Access and Use by Households and Individuals: Revised OECD Model Survey, 2009. http://www.oecd.org/dataoecd/58/27/35937246.pdf.

"Oriental Community Information Centers Content Services Network." E-Shanghai, 2009. http://www.eshanghai.cn/news/2011-06-29/1309314306d122394.html.

Orr, Julian. Talking About Machines: An Ethnography of a Modern Job. Ithaca, New York: ILR Press, 1996.

Orr, Marion. Black Social Capital: The Politics of School Reform in Baltimore, 1986-1998. Lawrence, Kansas: University Press of Kansas, 1999.

Park, Robert Ezra. "Human Ecology." American Journal of Sociology 42, no. 1 (1936): 1–15.

——. "The City: Suggestions for the Investigation of Human Behavior in the Urban Environment." In The City, edited by Robert Ezra Park, E. W. Burgess, and R. D. McKenzie, 1–46. Chicago: University of Chicago Press, 1925.

——. "The Urban Community as a Spatial Pattern and a Moral Order." In Robert E Park on Social Control and Collective Behavior, edited by Ralph H. Turner, 55–68. Chicago: University of Chicago Press, 1967.

Pateman, John. "Social Exclusion: An International Perspective on the Role of the State, Communities and Public Libraries in Tackling Social Exclusion." Journal of Information Science 25, no. 6 (1999): 445–463.

Pendleton, Victoria E.M., and Elfreda A. Chatman. "Small World Lives: Implications for the Public Library." Library Trends 46, no. 4 (1998): 732–51.

Perelman, M. Class Warfare in the Information Age. New York: St. Martin's Press, 1998.

Pettigrew, Karen E. "The Role of Community Health Nurses in Providing Information and Referral to the Elderly: a Study Based on Social Network Theory". University of Western Ontario, 1997.

Pick, James B., and Rasool Azari. "Global Digital Divide: Influence of Socioeconomic, Governmental, and Accessibility Factors on Information Technology." Information Technology for Development 14, no. 2 (2008): 91–115.

Piven, Frances, and Richard Cloward. Poor People's Movements. New York: Vintage Books, 1979.

Podolny, Joel M., and James N. Baron. "Resources and Relationships: Social Networks and Mobility in the Workplace." American Sociological Review 62, no. 5 (October 1, 1997): 673–693.

"Police Life", February 22, 2004.

Policy Action Team 15 (PAT 15). Closing the Digital Divide: Information and Communications Technologies in Deprived Areas: An Executive Summary of the Report by Policy Action Team 15. London: Department of Trade and Industry, March 2000.

Popenoe, David. The Suburban Environment: Sweden and the United States. Chicago: University of Chicago Press, 1977.

Portes, Alejandro. "Social Capital: Its Origins and Applications in Modern Sociology." Annual Review of Sociology 24 (January 1, 1998): 1–24.

Portes, Alejandro, and Julia Sensenbrenner. "Embeddedness and Immigration: Notes on the Social Determinants of Economic Action." American Journal of Sociology 98, no. 6 (May 1, 1993): 1320–1350.

Powell, Alan, ed. The City: Attacking Modern Myths. Toronto: McClelland and Stewart, 1972.

"PrairieNet Community Network", 2005. http://www.cii.uiuc.edu/prairienet.

Price, Derek J. de Solla. Little Science, Big Science. New York: Columbia University Press, 1963.

——. Little Science, Big Science - and Beyond. New York: Columbia University Press, 1986.

Putnam, Robert D. Better Together: Restoring the American Community. New York: Simon, 2003.

——. Bowling Alone: The Collapse and Revival of American Community. New York: Simon and Schuster, 2000.

——. "Bowling Alone, Revisited." The Responsive Community, no. Spring (1995): 18–33.

——. Making Democracy Work: Civic Traditions in Modern Italy. Princeton, N.J.: Princeton University Press, 1993.

——. "Tuning In, Tuning Out: The Strange Disappearance of Social Capital in America". American Political Science Association, 1995.

Qiu, Jack Linchuan. Working-class Network Society: Communication Technology and Information Have-less in Urban China. Cambridge, Massachusetts: MIT, 2009.

Quark, Amy A. "Social Exclusion in the New Economy: Beyond the Digital Divide." Currents: Scholarship in the Human Services 7, no. 2 (2009): 1–20.

Ratcliffe, William D. "Social Networks and Health: An Initial Report." Connections 1, no. 3 (1978): 25–37.

Resnick, Paul. "Beyond Bowling Together: SocioTechnical Capital". University of Michigan School of Information, 2000. http://presnick.people.si.umich.edu/papers/stk/index.html.

Rheingold, Howard. Smart Mobs: The Next Social Revolution. Cambridge, Massachusetts: Perseus Publising, 2002.

——. The Virtual Community: Homesteading on the Electronic Frontier. Reading, MA: Addison-Wesley Pub. Co, 1993.

Rifkin, Jeremy. The Age of Access: The New Culture of Hypercapitalism, Where All of Life Is a Paid-For Experience. New York: Penguin Putnam, 2000.

Ritzer, G. Contemporary Sociological Theory and Its Classical Roots: The Basics. Beijing: Peking University Press, 2003.

Robison, Kristopher K, and Edward M Crenshaw. "Reevaluating the Global Digital Divide: Socio-Demographic and Conflict Barriers to the Internet Revolution." Sociological Inquiry 80, no. 1 (2010): 34–62.

Rogers, E. Diffusion of Innovations. New York: Free Press, 1962.

Rogers, Everett M., Lori Collins-Jarvis, and Joseph Schmitz. "The PEN Project in Santa Monica: Interactive Communication, Equality, and Political Action." Journal of the American Society for Information Science 45, no. 6 (July 1, 1994): 401–410.

Ronfeldt, David, and Armando Martinez. "A Comment on the Zapatista 'Netwar'." In In Athena's Camp: Preparing for Conflict in the Information Age, edited by John Arquilla and David Ronfeldt. Santa Monica, California: RAND, 1997.

Rose, Mike. The Mind at Work: Valuing the Intelligence of the American Worker. New York: Viking, 2004.

Rosenbaum, Howard. "Information Use Environments and Structuration: Towards an Integration of Taylor and Giddens." Proceedings of the ASIS Annual Meeting 30 (1993): 235–45.

Ross, Marc Howard, and Thomas S. Weisner. "The Rural-Urban Migrant Network in Kenya: Some General Implications." American Ethnologist 4, no. 2 (May 1, 1977): 359–375.

Roy, Loriene, Trina Bolfing, and Bonnie Brzozowski. "Computer Classes for Job Seekers: LIS Students Team with Public Librarians to Extend Public Services." Public Library Quarterly 29, no. 3 (2010): 193–209.

Sassen, Sassen, ed. Global Networks, Linked Cities. New York: Routledge, 2002.

——. The Global City. Princeton, N.J.: Princeton University Press, 1991.

Sassen, Saskia, and Kwame Anthony Appiah. Globalization and Its Discontents. New York: New Press, 1998.

Savolainen, Reijo. "Everyday Life Information Seeking: Approaching Information Seeking in the Context of 'way of Life'." Library & Information Science Research 17, no. 3 (Summer 1995): 259–294.

——. "The Sense-making Theory: Reviewing the Interests of a User-centered Approach to Information Seeking and Use." Information Processing & Management 29, no. 1 (1993): 13–28.

Schiller, Dan. "Ambush on the I-way: Information Commoditization on the Electronic Frontier", 1995. www.vcn.bc.ca/bcla-ip/committee/dschill2.html.

——. Digital Capitalism: Networking the Global Market System. Cambridge, Massachusetts: MIT Press, 1999.

——. "World Communications in Today's Age of Capital." Emergences: Journal for the Study of Media & Composite Cultures 11, no. 1 (2001): 51–68.

Schiller, Herbert. Communication and Cultural Domination. New York: International Arts and Sciences Press, 1976.

——. "Decolonization of Information: Efforts Toward a New International Order." Latin American Perspectives 5, no. 1 (January 1, 1978): 35–48.

——. Information Inequality: The Deepening Social Crisis in America. New York: Rou, 1996.

——. "Introduction to Who Knows: Information in the Age of Fortune 500." In The Political Economy of Communication: a Reader, edited by J Cao and Y Zhao, 59–64. Shanghai: Fudan University Press, 2007.

Schiller, Herbert, and Anita Schiller. "Libraries, Public Access to Information and Commerce". In The Political Economy of Information, edited by V Mosco and J Wasko, 146–166. Madison, Wisconsin: University of Wisconsin Press, 1988.

Schön, Donald, Bishwapriya Sanyal, and William Mitchell, eds. High Technology and Low-Income Communities: Prospects for the Positive Use of Advanced Information Technology. Cambridge, Massachusetts: MIT Press, 1999.

Schuler, Douglas. "Creating Public Space in Cyberspace: The Rise of the New Community Networks." Internet World, December 1995.

——. New Community Networks: Wired for Change. New York: ACM Press, 1996.

——. Shaping the Network Society: The New Role of Civil Society in Cyberspace. Cambridge, Massachusetts: MIT Press, 2004.

Schultz, Theodore W. "Investment in Human Capital." The American Economic Review 51, no. 1 (March 1, 1961): 1–17.

Sciadas, G., H. Lyons, C .Rothschild, and Araba Sey. Public Access to ICTs: Sculpting the Profile of Users. Seattle: Technology & Social Change Group, University of Washington Information School, 2012.

Scott, J., and L. Tilly. "Women's Work and the Family in Nineteenth Century Europe." Comparative Studies in Society and History 17, no. 1 (1975): 36–64.

Scribner, Sylvia. "Literacy in Three Metaphors." In Literacy: Language and Power, edited by Dianne Vipond and Ronald J. Strahl. Long Beach, California: California State University Press, 1994.

Selwyn, Neil, K. Facer, E. Ferro, Y. K. Dwivedi, J. R. Gil-Garcia, and M. D. Williams. "Beyond Digital Divide: Towards an Agenda for Change." In Handbook of Research on Overcoming Digital Divides: Constructing an Equitable and Competitive Information Society, 1–20. Hershey, PA: IGI Global, 2009.

Selwyn, Neil. "Reconsidering Political and Popular Understandings of the Digital Divide." New Media & Society 6, no. 3 (2004): 341–362.

Sennett, Richard. Families Against the City: Middle Class Homes of Industrial Chicago, 1872-1890. Cambridge, Massachusetts: Harvard University Press, 1970.

Servon, Lisa, and John Horrigan. "Urban Poverty and Access to Information Technology: A Role for Local Government". Toronto, 1996.

Sey, Araba, and Michelle Fellows. Literature Review on the Impact of Public Access to Information and Communication Technologies. CIS Working Paper No. 6. Seattle: University of Washington Center for Information & Society, April 2009.

Shorter, Edward. "Female Emancipation, Birth Control, and Fertility in European History." The American Historical Review 78, no. 3 (June 1, 1973): 605–640.

——. The Making of the Modern Family. New York: Basic Books, 1975.

Shulman, Norman. "Network Analysis: A New Addition to an Old Bag of Tricks." Acta Sociologica 19, no. 4 (January 1, 1976): 307–323.

——. "Urban Social Networks: An Investigation of Personal Networks in an Urban Setting". University of Toronto, 1972.

Silver, H. "Understanding Social Inclusion and Its Meaning for Australia." Australian Journal of Social Issues 45 (2010): 184–211.

Simmel, Georg. "Group Expansion and the Development of Individuality." In Georg Simmel on Individuality and Social Forms: Selected Writings, edited by Donald Levine, 251–293. Chicago: University of Chicago Press, 1971.

——. "The Metropolis and Mental Life." In The Sociology of Georg Simmel, edited by Kurt Wolff, 409–424. Glencoe, IL: Free Press, 1950.

Simpson, H. M. Makers of History. Evansville, Indiana: Warren Publishers, 1981.

Slater, Philip Elliot. The Pursuit of Loneliness: American Culture at the Breaking Point. Boston: Beacon Press, 1970.

Sligo, F. X, and Anna M. Jameson. "The Knowledge-behavior Gap in Use of Health Information." Journal of the American Society for Information Science 51, no. 9 (January 1, 2000): 858–869.

Smith, A. The Geopolitics of Information: How Western Culture Dominates the World. New York: Oxford University Press, 1980.

Smythe, Dallas W. "On the Political Economy of Communications." Journalism & Mass Communication Quarterly 37, no. 4 (1960): 563–572.

Speck, Ross V, and Carolyn Attneave. Family Networks. New York: Pantheon Books, 1973.

Spink, Amanda, and Charles Cole. "Information and Poverty: Information-seeking Channels Used by African American Low-income Households." Library & Information Science Research 23, no. 1 (Spring 2001): 45–65.

Sprengers, Maarten, and Fritz Tazelaar. "Social Resources, Situational Constraints, and Reemployment." Netherlands Journal of Sociology 24 (1988).

Starbucks Coffee. "Mission Statement", no date. http://starbucks.com.cn/en/about/mission-statement.html.

——. "Starbucks History", no date. http://starbucks.com.cn/en/about/history.html.

Stein, Maurice Robert. The Eclipse of Community. Princeton, N.J.: Princeton University Press, 1960.

Stevenson, Siobhan. "Digital Divide: A Discursive Move Away from the Real Inequities." The Information Society 25, no. 1 (2009): 1–22.

Stoecker, Randy R. "Is Community Informatics Good for Communities? Questions Confronting an Emerging Field." The Journal of Community Informatics 1, no. 3 (June 6, 2005): 13–26.

Stoecker, Randy, and Angela Stuber. "Building an Information Superhighway of One's Own: A Comparison of Two Approaches." Research in Politics and Society 7 (1999).

——. "Limited Access: The Information Superhighway and Ohio's Neighborhood-based Organizations." Computers in Human Services 14, no. 1 (1997): 39–57.

Stone, Antonia. CTCNET: History, Organization and Future. Newton, Massachusetts: CTCNET, 1996.

Stuber, Angela. The Development of CATNeT – the Coalition to Access Technology and Networking in Toledo. Toledo, Ohio: Urban Affairs Center, University of Toledo, June 1, 1997. http://uac.utoledo.edu/Publications/1997/CatNet%20Intern%20Report.pdf.

Susser, Ida. "The Construction of Poverty and Homelessness in US Cities." Annual Review of Anthropology 25 (1996): 411–435.

Suttles, Gerald D. The Social Construction of Communities. Chicago: University of Chicago Press, 1972.

Tabb, William K. "After Seattle: Understanding the Politics of Globalization." Monthly Review 51, no. 10 (2000).

Tardos, Robert. "Some Remarks on the Interpretation and Possible Uses of the 'Social Capital' Concept with Special Regard to the Hungarian Case." Bulletin De Methodologie Sociologique 53, no. 1 (December 1996): 52–62.

Taylor, R. "China Wrestles with Online Gamers." BBC News, April 9, 2006. http://news.bbc.co.uk/1/hi/programmes/click_online/4887236.stm.

Textor, Robert. A Handbook on Ethnographic Futures Research. Cultural and Futures Research Project, School of Education and Dept. of Anthropology, Stanford University, 1980.

——. "The Ethnographic Futures Research Method: An Application to Thailand." Futures 27, no. 4 (1995): 461–471.

TFN (Tallahassee FreeNet). "About Us", no date. http://www.tfn.net/TFN.

Tichenor, P. J., G. A. Donohue, and C. N. Olien. "Mass Media Flow and Differential Growth in Knowledge." Public Opinion Quarterly 34, no. 2 (June 20, 1970): 159–170.

Tilly, Charles. "Do Communities Act?" Sociological Inquiry 43, no. 3-4 (July 1, 1973): 209–240.

——. "Food Supply and Public Order in Modern Europe." In The Formation of National States in Western Europe, edited by Charles Tilly, 380–455. Princeton, N.J.: Princeton University Press, 1975.

——. From Mobilization to Revolution. Reading, Massachusetts: Addison-Wesley Pub. Co., 1978.

——. "Introduction." In An Urban World, edited by Charles Tilly, 1–35. Boston: Little, Brown, 1974.

Toffler, Alvin, and Heidi. Toffler. Creating a New Civilization: The Politics of the Third Wave. Atlanta: Turner, 1995.

"Toledo Public Schools: NetApp Scores an A+ for Improving Content Delivery". Network Appliance, Inc., 2000.

Tönnies, Ferdinand. Community and Association. London: Routledge & Kegan Paul, 1955.

Turkel, T. "Where Tech Meets Design." Portland Press Herald, July 19, 2002.

U.S. Census. "Census 2000 Demographic Profile Highlights (Chicago, Illinois)", no date. http://www.factfinder.census.gov.

Valentine, Gill, Sarah Holloway, and Nick Bingham. "The Digital Generation?: Children, ICT and the Everyday Nature of Social Exclusion." Antipode 34, no. 2 (2002): 296–315.

Vårheim, Andreas. "Social Capital and Public Libraries: The Need for Research." Library & Information Science Research 29, no. 3 (2007): 416–428.

Vari, Diane. "How Activists Used the Internet to Organize Protests Against the Spring Meetings of the International Monetary Fund, World Bank, and the World Trade Organization Scheduled for April 16-17 in Washington, D.C." Student research paper written to fulfill the Virtual Community Research Project for Sociology and the Internet taught by Professor Robert E. Wood. Rutgers University, 2000.

Vicente, María Rosalía, and Ana Jesús López. "A Multidimensional Analysis of the Disability Digital Divide: Some Evidence for Internet Use." The Information Society 26, no. 1 (2010): 48–64.

Vidich, Arthur J, and Joseph Bensman. Small Town in Mass Society: Class, Power, and Religion in a Rural Community. Princeton, N.J.: Princeton University Press, 1958.

Volker, Beate, and Henk D. Flap. "Getting Ahead in the GDR: Human Capital and Social Capital in the Status Attainment Process Under Communism". Universiteit Utrecht, The Netherlands, 1996.

Walch, J. In the Net: An Internet Guide for Activists. London: Zed Books, 1999.

Walker, G. "Social Networks and Territory in a Commuter Village, Bond Head, Ontario." Canadian Geographer 21, no. 4 (1977): 329–350.

Walker, Juliet. Free Frank: A Black Pioneer on the Antebellum Frontier. Lexington, KY: University Press of Kentucky, 1983.

Warren, Donald, and Rachelle Warren. "The Helping Role of Neighbors: Some Empirical Findings". Unpublished paper, Department of Sociology, Oakland University, 1976.

Warren, Roland Leslie. The Community in America. Chicago: Rand McNally, 1971.

Warschauer, Mark. Technology and Social Inclusion: Rethinking the Digital Divide. Cambridge, Massachusetts: MIT Press, 2003.

Wayne, J. "Networks of Informal Participation in a Suburban Context". University of Toronto, 1971.

Webber, Melvin. "Order in Diversity: Community Without Propinquity." In Cities and Space: The Future Use of Urban Land; Essays from the Fourth RFF Forum, edited by Lowdon Wingo, 23–54. Baltimore: Johns Hopkins Press, 1963.

——. "The Urban Place and the Nonplace Urban Realm." In Explorations into Urban Structure, edited by Melvin Webber. Philadelphia: University of Pennsylvania Press, 1964.

Webster, Frank. Theories of the Information Society. London: Routledge, 1995.

Wellman, Barry. Networks in the Global Village. Boulder, CO: Westview, 1998.

——. "Physical Place and Cyberplace: The Rise of Networked Individualism." In Community Informatics : Shaping Computer-mediated Social Relations, edited by Leigh Keeble and Brian Loader. London: Routledge, 2001.

——. "The Community Question: The Intimate Networks of East Yorkers." American Journal of Sociology 84, no. 5 (March 1, 1979): 1201–1231.

——. "The Rise (and Possible Fall) of Networked Individualism." Connections 24, no. 3 (2002): 30–32.

Wellman, Barry, and Barry Leighton. "Networks, Neighborhoods, and Communities:

Approaches to the Study of Community Question." Urban Affairs Review 14, no. 3 (March 1, 1979): 363–390.

Wellman, Barry, and Marilyn Whitaker. Community-Network-Communication: An Annotated Bibliography. Toronto: Centre for Urban and Community Studies: University of Toronto, 1974.

White, Harrison C., Scott A. Boorman, and Ronald L. Breiger. "Social Structure from Multiple Networks I: Blockmodels of Roles and Positions." American Journal of Sociology 81, no. 4 (January 1, 1976): 730–780.

White, Harrison. "Notes on the Constituents of Social Structure". Cambridge, Massachusetts: Department of Social Relations, Harvard University, 1965.

White, Morton Gabriel, and Lucia White. The Intellectual Versus the City: From Thomas Jefferson to Frank Lloyd Wright. Cambridge, Massachusetts: Harvard University Press, 1962.

Whyte, William Foote. Street Corner Society: The Social Structure of an Italian Slum. Chicago: University of Chicago Press, 1955.

Williams, Jocelyn E, PhD Wallace, and Frank Sligo. "Free Internet as Agent of Community Transformation." The Journal of Community Informatics 2, no. 1 (November 12, 2005). http://www.ci-journal.net/index.php/ciej/article/viewArticle/234.

Williams, Kate. "Libraries as ISPs." Ohio Libraries (Spring/Summer 2000).

——. "Library Computers Bridging the Digital Divide: An Illustration of the Usefulness of Geographic Information System". Unpublished manuscript. Available from the author. 2000.

——. "Literacy and Computer Literacy: Analyzing the NRC's 'Being Fluent with Information Technology'." Journal of Literacy and Technology 3, no. 1 (2003). http://www.literacyandtechnology.org/volume3/literacy.katewilliams.pdf.

——. "Research Note: Across the United States, 85,000 to 144,000 Public Computing Sites." First Monday, 2003. http://firstmonday.org/htbin/cgiwrap/bin/ojs/index.php/fm/rt/printerFriendly/1046/967.

——. "Social Networks, Social Capital, and the Use of Information and

Communications Technology in Socially Excluded Communities: A Study of Community Groups in Manchester, England". University of Michigan, 2005.

——. "What Is the Digital Divide?" In D3: Proceedings of the Digital Divide Doctoral Students Workshop. Ann Arbor, MI: University of Michigan School of Information, 2001.

Williams, Kate, and Abdul Alkalimat. "A Census of Public Computing in Toledo, Ohio." In Shaping the Network Society: The New Role of Civil Society in Cyberspace, edited by Douglas Schuler and Peter Day, 85–110. Cambridge, Massachusetts: MIT Press, 2004.

Williams, Kate, and Joan C. Durrance. "Social Networks and Social Capital: Rethinking Theory in Community Informatics." The Journal of Community Informatics 4, no. 3 (2008). http://ci-journal.net/index.php/ciej/article/view/465/430.

Wilson, William Julius. The Truly Disadvantaged: The Inner City, the Underclass, and Public Policy. Chicago: University of Chicago Press, 1987.

Wireman, P. "Intimate Secondary Relations". Uppsala, Sweden, 1978.

Wirth, Louis. "Urbanism as a Way of Life." American Journal of Sociology 44, no. 1 (July 1, 1938): 1–24.

Wolf, E. R. "Kinship, Friendship, and Patron-client Relations in Complex Societies." In The Social Anthropology of Complex Societies, edited by Michael Bangton, 1–22. London: Tavistock, 1966.

Wong, Yu Cheung, Chi Kwong Law, John Yat Chu Fung, and Jolie Chi Yee Lam. "Perpetuating Old Exclusions and Producing New Ones: Digital Exclusion in an Information Society." Journal of Technology in Human Services 27, no. 1 (2009): 57–78.

Woodsworth, J. S. My Neighbour. Toronto: University of Toronto Press, 1972.

Woolley, David R. PLATO: The Emergence of Online Community. Urbana, IL: University of Illinois at Urbana-Champaign Computer-Based Education Research Laboratory, 1994.

Yang, Guobin. "The Co-evolution of the Internet and Civil Society in China." Asian

Survey 43, no. 3 (June 1, 2003): 405–422.

Young, Michael Dunlop, and Peter Willmott. Family and Kinship in East London. London: Routledge & Kegan Paul, 1957.

Youtie, Jan, Philip Shapira, and Greg Laudeman. Transitioning to the Knowledge Economy: The LaGrange Internet Access Initiative; Impacts of Public Infrastructure Access Working Paper 3. Atlanta, GA: Georgia Institute of Technology, 2002.

Yu, Liangzhi. "Understanding Information Inequality: Making Sense of the Literature of the Information and Digital Divides." Journal of Librarianship and Information Science 38, no. 4 (December 1, 2006): 229–252.

Zelip, Brian. "Black People's Hair: The Digitization of Popular Culture". Master's thesis. University of Toledo, 2002.

Zhao, Yuezhi. "'Universal Service' and China's Telecommunications Miracle: Discourses, Practices, and post-WTO Accession Challenges." Info 9, no. 2–3 (March 20, 2007): 108–121.

About the contributors

Abdul Alkalimat is Professor of African American Studies and Library and Information Science at the University of Illinois and co-director of the Community Informatics Research Lab at Urbana-Champaign, USA.

Manuel Castells is Professor of Sociology and Director of the Internet Interdisciplinary Institute at the Open University of Catalonia in Barcelona, Spain. He is also University Professor and the Wallis Annenberg Chair Professor of Communication Technology and Society at the Annenberg School of Communication at the University of Southern California, USA.

Chen Jianlong（陈建龙） is Professor in the Department of Information Management, and director of the Institute of Informatization and Human Information Behavior at Peking University, in Beijing, and the Vice President of Tibet University, in Lhasa, PR China.

China Internet Network Information Center (CNNIC) is the state network information center of China, founded as a non-profit organization in 1997, reporting to the Ministry of Information Industry and operated by the Computer Network Information Center of the Chinese Academy of Sciences.

Joan C. Durrance is Margaret Mann Collegiate Professor (Emerita) at the School of Information of the University of Michigan, USA.

Han Shenglong（韩圣龙）is Associate Professor in the Department of Information Management at Peking University, PR China, on leave as of 2012 to serve as the Chinese director of the Confucius Institute at Chulalongkorn University, Thailand.

He Yingfang（何颖芳）is a PhD student in the Department of Information Resources Management in the Business School at Nankai University, in Tianjin, PR China.

Lai Maosheng（赖茂生） is Professor in the Department of Information Management and director of National Institute for Information Resource Management (Beijing), Peking University, in Beijing.

Barry Leighton is Adjunct Professor in the Law Department, Carleton University in Ottawa, Canada.

Pierre Lévy is Professor in the Department of Communication at the University of Ottawa in Canada.

Li Ping (李萍) is a graduate student at the College of Computing and Information at the State University of New York at Albany, USA.

Nan Lin (林南) is the Oscar L. Tang Family Professor of Sociology of Trinity College at Duke University in North Carolina, USA.

Wang Sufang (王素芳) is Assistant Professor in the Department of Information Resources Management, School of Public Administration at Zhejiang University in PR China.

Barry Wellman is the S.D. Clark Professor of Sociology and Director of the NetLab at the University of Toronto, Canada.

Kate Williams is Assistant Professor at the Graduate School of Library and Information Science and co-director of the Community Informatics Research Lab at the University of Illinois at Urbana-Champaign, USA.

Yan Hui (闫 慧) is Assistant Professor in the Department of Information Resources Management in the Business School at Nankai University, in Tianjin, PR China.

Yu Liangzhi (于良芝) is Professor in the Department of Information Resources Management in the Business School at Nankai University, in Tianjin, PR China.

Yang Xuejing (杨学婧) is a master's student in the Department of Information Management at Peking University.

Zhang Yuanrui (张原瑞) is a master's student at Northwest University in Xi'an, PR China.